PROFITABLE MENU PLANNING

John A. Drysdale

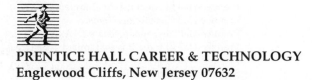

PRENTICE HALL CAREER & TECHNOLOGY
Englewood Cliffs, New Jersey 07632

Library of Congress Cataloging-in-Publication Data

Drysdale, John A.
    Profitable menu planning / John A. Drysdale.
        p.   cm.
    Includes index.
    ISBN 0–13–587833–0
    1. Menus.   I. Title.
TX911.3.M45D79   1994
642'.5—dc20   93-35542
                                          CIP

Acquisition Editor: Robin Baliszewski
Editorial/production supervision and
    interior design: Inkwell Publishing Services
Cover design: Marianne Frasco
Buyer: Edward O'Dougherty

©1994 by Prentice Hall Career & Technology
Prentice-Hall, Inc.
A Simon & Schuster Company
Englewood Cliffs, New Jersey 07632

Printed in the United States of America
10 9 8 7 6 5 4 3 2

ISBN 0-13-587833-0

Prentice-Hall International (UK) Limited, *London*
Prentice-Hall of Australia Pty. Limited, *Sydney*
Prentice-Hall Canada Inc., *Toronto*
Prentice-Hall Hispanoamericana, S.A., *Mexico*
Prentice-Hall of India Private Limited, *New Delhi*
Prentice-Hall of Japan, Inc., *Tokyo*
Simon & Schuster Asia Pte. Ltd., *Singapore*
Editora Prentice-Hall do Brasil, Ltda., *Rio de Janeiro*

In memory of my father,
F. Clark Drysdale

Contents

6
Truth in Menu   *133*

10
Theme-Ethnic Menus   *229*

11
Banquet/Show Menus   *243*

15
Menu Analysis *327*

16
Profitability and the Menu   *339*

Preface

The old adage that everything starts with the menu is as true today as it was a hundred years ago. In today's complex makeup of food service management, the menu is involved in nearly every facet of the operation. Add to this the diversity of restaurants from fast food to fine dining, as well as the nonprofit food service segment, and the subject of menu planning suddenly becomes very intricate. It is for this reason that *Profitable Menu Planning* was written. While some excellent textbooks deal with the various aspects of menus, few, if any, cover all of the points necessary for a complete dialog on the subject.

This book is divided into four sections, beginning with planning the menu. In this section, market segmentation, demographics, and food preferences of the customer are discussed along with the capabilities of the staff and equipment to produce the menu. Costing the menu is also included, along with markups to assure a profitable operation. The second section deals with writing the menu and covers menu content, descriptive terminology, and "truth in menu," concluding with menu layout and printing. The third section delves into the many types of menus from fast food to fine dining—and everything in between. The fourth section wraps everything up by evaluating what we have written using several systems of menu analysis including both objective and subjective methods.

Proper menu planning and writing are vital in today's society, with consumer advocate groups demanding fresh and healthy listings, corporate boardrooms demanding more sales and profits, and government bureaucrats demanding accurate menu terminology. This text attempts to help the student, manager, or owner answer these demands with clear, easy-to-read solutions to the problems.

ACKNOWLEDGMENTS

While the author's name appears on the cover, producing a textbook is definitely a team effort. Walt Klarner, an English Instructor at Johnson County Community College, as well as an author and editor in his own right, was the first to convince me that I could write a book and encouraged and advised me throughout the entire process. Without his help, this project never would have happened.

I am also indebted to the following people who took time out from their busy schedules to review and critique the manuscript page by page, making valuable comments that vastly improved the quality of the book.

James Bardi, Penn State University—Berks Campus

Brother Herman Zaccarelli, California Culinary Academy

Paul S. Cook, Essex Community College

Michael Piccinino, Shasta College

Maureen P. Cooper, Alfred State College

Terence McDonough, Erie Community College

To my colleagues and students at Johnson County Community College, a special thank-you. First, the head of the department Jerry Vincent CEC, AAC for his patience for the many times I requested, "Can I give you the report later, I've got a deadline." To Judy Boley who dropped everything to get letters and permission slips out for illustrations that were needed yesterday. To Patrick Sweeney CEC, AAC for his review and help with the manuscript. To Lindy Robinson who not only reviewed the rough draft, but taught several classes from it and gave me very valuable, thought-provoking, feedback. And finally to the students who endured taking their menu planning class with an incomplete text and who put up with my office door being closed because I was "on a roll" writing.

To the industry professionals who gave of their time to read and critique various chapters, I thank you. To those who supplied me with menus, illustrations, and charts and guided my requests through their legal departments, I am indebted to you. To those who tried and couldn't get it done, I thank you also for trying.

To the people at Prentice Hall who advised me and helped make sense of all of the in's and out's of publishing, particularly Fred Dahl and Rose Mary Florio. A very special indebtedness to Rose Kernan who edited the text and magically made sense out of a few chaotic chapters. To Robin Baliszewski, Executive Editor, who encouraged, counselled, and guided, but never pushed.

And finally to my family, Judy, Jeanne, and Jackie and my mother who put up with my stress attacks when things were not going right or deadlines were creeping near. Your patience and understanding were very much appreciated.

John A. Drysdale

Introduction

Ask a group of food service professionals what a menu is and don't be surprised if you get a different answer from each of them. No other area of study in our industry covers such a broad spectrum as does menu planning. The reason for this is that the menu affects virtually every aspect of the management and operation of a food service facility.

The most obvious and, coincidentally, the most important thing that a menu does is that it lists the products offered for sale to our customers. It is a vital communication link between management and guest. The type and variety of products listed are crucial to the success or failure of the enterprise. Beyond the obvious, however, are a number of other management functions that the menu performs.

Start with recipe development. When the decision has been made to offer a new item on the menu, the person responsible for product quality and development can then formulate it into a standardized recipe. In independent restaurants, this duty could be performed by the owner, manager, or chef. In large chains, however, this function is performed by the research and development department.

Once the recipes are known, product specifications can be written for purchasing. This ties back into the menu in that the menu listing will quite often give the quality level or unique characteristic of a specific product. Examples of this would include freshly squeezed orange juice, Grade A eggs, or USDA prime steak.

The quantity of products to be purchased is also determined by the menu. By tracking the number of items sold, the person responsible for purchasing can then parlay these numbers into the item amount to be purchased.

After the products are purchased, the kitchen staff uses the standardized recipes along with the menu to properly prepare each item. Terminology on the menu is often a key as to exactly how a particular listing should be prepared. Examples of this are *broiled* strip steak, *sauteed* scallops, *fried* chicken, or *chilled* shrimp. Quantity menu listings also dictate to the kitchen the amount of product to be served. A *12 oz.* broiled strip steak, *10* sauteed scallops, *one-half* fried chicken, or a *half dozen* chilled shrimp.

The menu plays a major role in the qualifications and number of employees to be hired and scheduled. Some menus require a high skill level to achieve the desired results while others require virtually no skills at all. There is a vast difference in education, experience, and training between executing a fast food menu and a fine dining menu. By using the number of covers sold, management can determine exactly how many employees need to be scheduled at each position.

The entire accounting function of a food service operation, in reality, starts with the menu. The relationship between the selling price of an item and its cost will determine the food cost percent of that item and hence the profit potential of that operation. Properly selecting what listings should be on the menu, carefully and accurately costing out those listings, and marking them up to the correct selling price will determine to a large part the success or failure of that restaurant. Product mix will subsequently point out accepted and rejected, as well as profitable and non-profitable, menu offerings.

By now it should be readily apparent that a menu is not merely an artistic piece of cardboard that is handed to a customer, but rather the vortex around which the entire operation revolves. These concepts along with other rules, principles, and ideas will be explored in detail throughout the text so that the reader will understand the importance of properly planning and writing a menu.

It should be pointed out that there is a difference between planning a menu and writing one. Menu planning involves the goals of the organization and the strategies to obtain those goals. The final output (the menu) must be compatible with those goals and strategies. It is also imperative that the menu planner never lose sight of the most important objective of any food service operation—pleasing the customer.

Once the plan is conceived, the writing process begins. Proper execution of product terminology, accuracy in menu listings, layout, artwork, merchandising, and printing are all of paramount importance to the success of the plan.

The terms "menu planner" and "menu writer" are used interchangeably throughout the text because while they involve two distinct areas, they are usually performed by the same person. The important thing is that whoever does the menu must do it correctly. The two most often cited reasons for restaurant failure are a lack of capital and a lack of knowledge. While this text cannot correct the former, it is hoped that it will go a long way to correct the latter.

CHAPTER ONE

Know Your Customer

OBJECTIVES
- To understand the difference between demographic surveys and feasibility studies.
- To appreciate how competition can influence a restaurant's menu listings.
- To differentiate between the popularity of certain foods among age groups, ethnic origins, education, occupation, and income.
- To know the difference between fads and trends and how to use them to your advantage.

IMPORTANT TERMS

Demographics	Trends
Fads	Market Saturation
Competition	Disposable income
Feasiblity studies	

INTRODUCTION

One of the most important aspects of menu planning is determining and defining your customer. The location of a restaurant, more than anything else, will determine who will patronize it. In order to be successful, the menu must cater to this person. Therefore, a restaurant is not necessarily successful because of its location per se, but rather the menu is the prime force in bringing customers to that particular restaurant's location. Therefore, prior to writing a menu, we will explore location, the customers and their desires, and the relationship between them.

Statler, the hotel magnate, once stated that there were three criteria necessary for success: location, location, and location. Of course, Mr. Statler was referring to the hotel business. In the case of the restaurant business, I'm not too sure I could agree with this statement. There are relatively few areas in this vast country where a restaurant could not be successful, if (and that's a big if) the restaurant caters to its customers.

All too often, people confuse good locations with a busy intersection, downtown, or shopping malls. Locations with traffic obviously are important to certain types of restaurants such as fast food operations. But, take a look around your own community and you can find exceptions to this location rule. What about that hard to find steak house or that little country inn in the middle of nowhere that you drive for an hour to get to?

An extreme exception comes to mind. Vacationing in the backwoods of northern Minnesota's Voyager Country, a relative suggested having lunch at the Kettle Falls Hotel. We rode in a boat for 35 miles viewing beautiful scenery along the way, docked the boat, hiked two miles, and finally arrived at the hotel. Imagine my surprise when we had to wait for a table because the place was packed! There were no roads. The only access to this hotel was by boat and by hiking in the last two miles. Why was this place successful? Two reasons. One, it has been in business since the 1800s (word gets around after a while) and two, the menu was basic, simple, and catered to the clientele. No frills or surprises. The menu was right, the preparation was right, and the service was right. (The thought crossed my mind that the purchasing would also have to be exact as the trek to the nearest supermarket was some 50 miles and the nearest wholesale market some 75 miles—part by boat, the rest by truck.)

The point is that while location is important to some facets of the restaurant industry, it is by no means the crucial factor. Indeed, the menu must cater to the customer no matter the location.

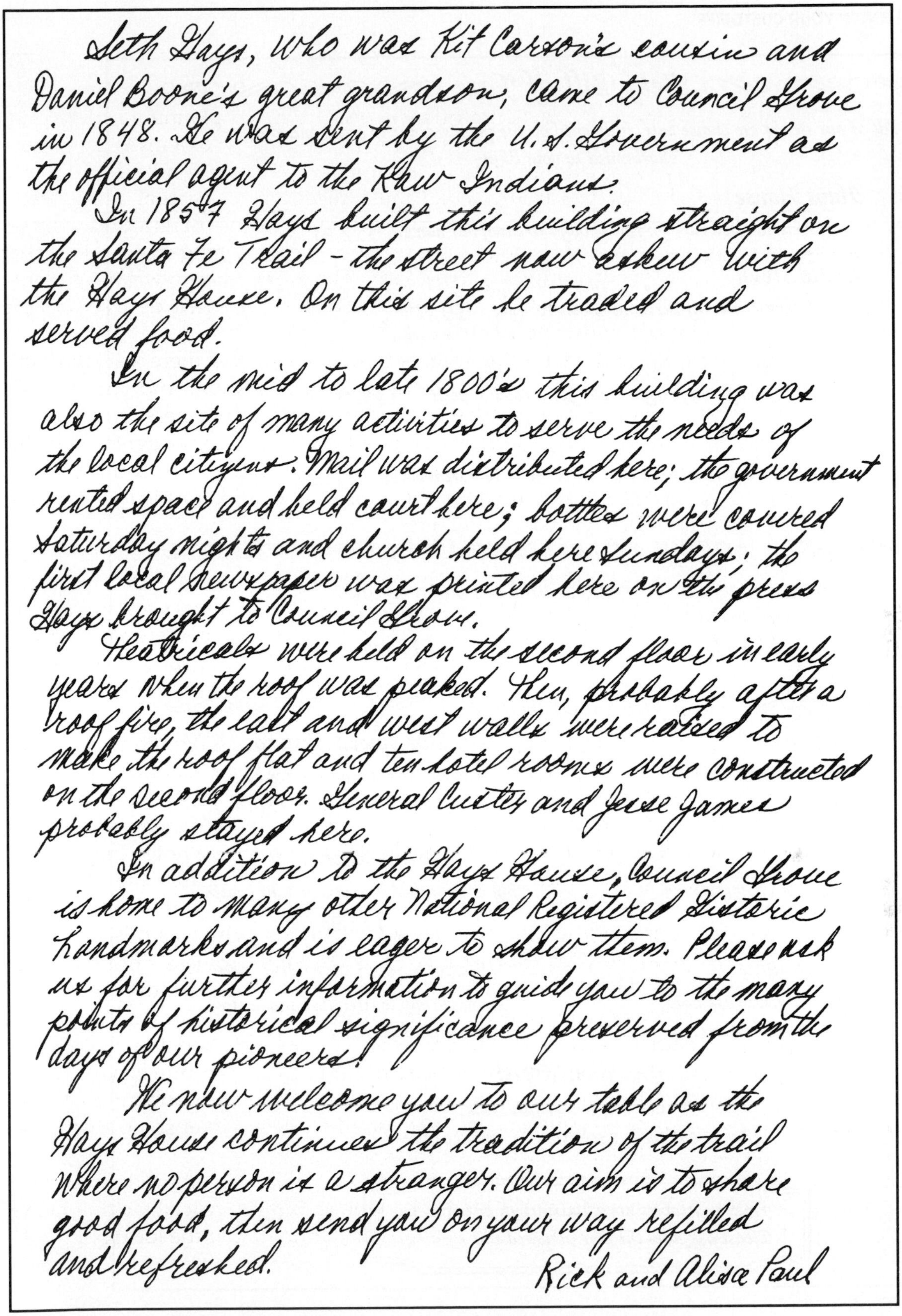

Seth Hays, who was Kit Carson's cousin and Daniel Boone's great grandson, came to Council Grove in 1848. He was sent by the U.S. Government as the official agent to the Kaw Indians.

In 1857 Hays built this building straight on the Santa Fe Trail - the street now askew with the Hays House. On this site he traded and served food.

In the mid to late 1800's this building was also the site of many activities to serve the needs of the local citizens. Mail was distributed here; the government rented space and held court here; bottles were covered Saturday nights and church held here Sundays; the first local newspaper was printed here on the press Hays brought to Council Grove.

Theatricals were held on the second floor in early years when the roof was peaked. Then, probably after a roof fire, the east and west walls were raised to make the roof flat and ten hotel rooms were constructed on the second floor. General Custer and Jesse James probably stayed here.

In addition to the Hays House, Council Grove is home to many other National Registered Historic Landmarks and is eager to show them. Please ask us for further information to guide you to the many points of historical significance preserved from the days of our pioneers.

We now welcome you to our table as the Hays House continues the tradition of the trail where no person is a stranger. Our aim is to share good food, then send you on your way refilled and refreshed.

Rick and Alisa Paul

FIGURE 1-1. This restaurant is located 100 miles from the nearest metropolitan area, yet draws much of its business from that area. (*Menu courtesy of the Hays House, Council Grove, Kansas*)

Beef Bill of Fare

All of our steaks are choice beef, fully aged on the premises, cut to order and then charbroiled to your liking.

Hays House
Well marbled rib-eye; fine enough to carry our name. $12.95

Little Steak
A smaller cut off the same choice rib-eye. $9.75

K.C. Strip
Thick and flavorful; good size for a good appetite. $13.75

Filet
Lean, thick tenderloin that we wrap in bluestem bacon. $12.95

Fridays & Saturdays Only

We roast whole Prime Ribs and cut them to order.

Regular Cut	Extra Thick
$13.75	$17.95

Fish & Seafood

Catfish
Meaty, tasty, fried whole fish so big they take 30 minutes. $9.25

Hot Spiced Shrimp
A crock of steaming jumbos boiled in tasty spices & ready to peel. $12.95

Scallops
Large morsels in a light & crispy coating. $11.95

Breaded Shrimp
Big & beautiful in a crispy light coating. $11.95

Orange Roughy
A premium white filet. Please ask how it is being prepared this evening.

Shrimp Stuffed with Crab
Large shrimp, butterflied and stuffed, then lightly breaded. $12.50

Charbroiled Fish
A thick and tender fish steak. Ask about today's selection. market price

---

Fresh vegetables are a hallmark of our dinners. Please ask how they are prepared this evening.

FIGURE 1-1. *(Continued)*

Hays House Specialties

Beulah's Ham

We take whole bone-in hams, cut thick slices, and bake them in fruit juices, wine & spices for a delightful flavor.

$9.50

Fried Chicken

Fresh chicken dipped in egg & milk, then in our crunchy mix and fried in old cast iron skillets. (Allow 30 minutes)

$8.75

All white meat $9.50

Brisket

Beef marinated overnight with seven seasonings, then slowly baked until very tender & flavorful.

$8.95

Mid-Western Favorites

Chicken Fried Steak

Fresh beef we bread to order & grill in real chicken fat 'til golden brown.

$7.95

Pork Chops

Two center cut chops charbroiled to enhance their naturally good flavor.

$9.95

Chicken Livers and/or Gizzards

Fresh, dipped by hand & sauteed in chicken fat.

$7.50

All dinners include. . .
Our garden fresh salad bar featuring special combinations and several house dressings.
Choice of the fresh vegetable of the evening, homemade curly fries, homemade hash browns, baked potato or steak fries.
Our special recipe Hays House bread, hot from the oven with real butter.

For the Lighter Appetite

Lite Beef Supper

Marinated steak pieces with a fresh vegetable and an interesting salad of crisp lettuce, fresh orange segments, a sliced ripe olive and topped with our tarragon dressing. Served with a homemade muffin. $7.95

Charbroiled Chicken Breast

A boneless, skinless breast served with a garden salad (choice of dressing), fresh vegetable of the day, and a homemade muffin. $7.50

Vegetarian Platter

Three fresh vegetables (seasonal) served with baked potato or rice. $7.50
with salad bar $9.50

Small Servings

S.S. Fried Chicken Thigh $5.50   S.S. Marinated Brisket $5.50

S.S. Fried Chicken Breast $5.95   S.S. Beulah's Ham $5.75

S.S. Pork Chop $6.25   S.S. Hot Spiced Shrimp $8.50

Each includes homemade bread and a choice of two of the following . . .
Garden fresh salad (salad bar is $2.00 extra), fresh vegetable of the evening, or choice of potato.

FIGURE 1-1. (Continued)

Extra Special Desserts

Cranberry-Strawberry Pie

Our famous sweet-tart creation piled high into a graham cracker crust.

$2.95

Kahlua Pie

Creamy smooth & coffee flavored; this sinful delicacy is set in a chocolate cookie crust.

$2.95

Grasshopper Pie

A rich, minty filling is heaped into a dark chocolate crumb crust.

$2.95

Homemade Ice Cream

We use fresh cream and whip it into an array of delightful flavors. Please ask because flavors change daily.

$2.00

Other Sherberts & Ice Creams $1.50

Fresh Fruit Platter *Available upon request.*

Drinks

Coffee, *rich & flavorful.* $.75

Tea, *fresh brewed, hot or iced.* $.75

Homemade Lemonade, *hand squeezed & delicious.* $1.60

Cider, *steaming hot or in a frosty cold mug.* $1.00

Milk, *white or chocolate.* $1.00

Soft Drinks $1.00

Oldest Restaurant West of the Mississippi

Hours

Open daily from 6 A.M. until 8:30 P.M. in winter, 9 P.M. in summer. (Closed Christmas Day and New Year's Day)

···—◦●◦—···

Our club upstairs opens at 5 P.M. nightly.

On the Santa Fe Trail in historic Council Grove, Kansas

FIGURE 1-1. *(Continued)*

DEMOGRAPHICS

The study of location and the potential customer is known as *demographics*. More specifically, according to *Webster's New Collegiate Dictionary*, demographics is "the statistical study of populations with reference to size, density, distribution, and vital statistics and the ability (of the market) to expand or decline."

In order to use demographics properly in menu planning, two factors must be evaluated.

1. The demographic study itself. In other words, who exactly is the customer in our market?
2. The matching of these customers along with their needs and preferences to the proper menu.

First, let's look at the demographic study itself. How does it develop? There are basically three sources for this information.

1. Feasibility Studies
2. Demographic Surveys
3. Personal Knowledge

FEASIBILITY STUDIES

A feasibility study is a creative, objective, and rational process whereby marketing and financial data are collected and analyzed. It is an in-depth study that attempts to predict with reasonable accuracy whether or not a potential business will succeed or fail. Feasibility studies are quite large, sometimes running several hundred pages in length. Needless to say they are very complete documents which explore every variable that would indicate whether or not a business has the potential to make a profit. Normally, these studies are performed by accounting firms or consultants who are members of the Foodservice Consultants Society International (FCSI). You could perform this task yourself, but it is very time consuming and the professionals have the knowledge of where to obtain the data. Make sure that the person or firm with which you are dealing has a good track record and is reliable. Two parts of the feasibility study that are of particular importance to the menu planner are the section dealing with demographics and the section dealing with competition.

DEMOGRAPHIC SURVEYS

For those restaurants or food service firms that do not need a complete feasibility study, there are demographic surveys available from a number of companies for a reasonable fee. The larger firms have the demographics for the entire United States on computers. These studies can be broken down to any size quadrant for any area that the customer desires. They list the general population by age group, median age, ethnic origins, household type, marital status, occupation, education, housing, income, number of vehicles and other related data. Specialized data can also be obtained which detail consumer restaurant expenditures for the area and can further refine this statistic by giving a breakdown as to category such as fast foods, coffee shop, fine dining, etc.

If you do not wish to purchase a demographic study, you could opt to do the project yourself. While it would be somewhat time consuming to do this, a demographic survey is far less extensive and, therefore, takes less time to complete than a feasibility study. Data are available from the Census Bureau, the local Chamber of Commerce, City Hall or other governmental and private sources.

PERSONAL KNOWLEDGE

The third source for demographic information is your own knowledge, even a gut feeling, for an area. While this method is certainly unscientific, it can be valid. It cannot, however, be used haphazardly. Too often persons going into the restaurant business pick what they feel is an excellent location, only to open the business and proceed to go broke. Odds are, they failed to sell what their customer wanted. They just didn't have the right menu listings or the selling price to fit their clientele. Of course, other factors could have contributed to their loss such as lack of working capital, unknowledgeable management, poor service, poor quality, or a dirty operation. The restaurant business comprises many details, each one affecting the overall performance. But it all starts with the menu. List the wrong items at the wrong price and you're done before you start.

On the other hand, your feel for the market is an important tool if used properly. Demographic studies look at an area with cold, hard facts. Knowledge of situations behind these facts is quite important. For example, if a demographic study indicated that in a certain area the average income was in the upper middle range and that a large share of the market owned their own homes, this would indicate at the outset a good restaurant location. However, if the majority of people in the target area had their homes heavily mortgaged, their disposable income would be low and their propensity to dine out would be less.

SOCIO-ECONOMIC PROFILE: 1990   URBAN DECISION SYSTEMS, INC.
CLEVELAND,OH:BROOKPARK RD & PEARL RD   07/23/93
3.0 MILE RING

INCOME:	HOUSEHOLDS	%	FAMILIES	%
Total	59697		38805	
0-4.9T	2949	4.9	1245	3.2
5-9.9T	6022	10.1	1376	3.5
10-14.9T	5938	9.9	2729	7.0
15-19.9T	6038	10.1	3173	8.2
20-24.9T	5854	9.8	3523	9.1
25-29.9T	5503	9.2	3823	9.9
30-34.9T	5856	9.8	4457	11.5
35-39.9T	4727	7.9	3743	9.6
40-49.9T	7114	11.9	6098	15.7
50-74.9T	7462	12.5	6619	17.1
75-99.9T	1610	2.7	1453	3.7
100-124.9T	365	0.6	334	0.9
125-149.9T	143	0.2	130	0.3
150T+	116	0.2	103	0.3
Median	$ 27564		$ 33825	
Average	$ 31126		$ 37497	

POPULATION 142175

POPULATION IN...		%
Households	141233	99.3
Group qtrs	942	0.7
College	0	0.0
Inst	895	0.6
Other	47	0.0

OCCUPATION		%
Prof/tech	9322	14.4
Mgr/prop	6835	10.6
Clerical	13220	20.5
Sales	7337	11.4
WH/COL	36713	56.8
Crafts	8282	12.8
Operatives	8148	12.6
Service	8380	13.0
Laborer	2782	4.3
Farm worker	281	0.4
BL/COL	27873	43.2

LABOR FORCE		%	UNEMP	PARTIC
Male	37336	54.3	6.5%	70.3%
Female	31382	45.7	5.0%	51.0%
In Armed Forces		0.2%		

SCHOOL YEARS COMPLETED	
Population age 25+	99063
Less than 9th	8.3%
Some high school	20.3%
High school diploma	38.1%
College 1-3 years	22.2%
Bachelor's degree	8.2%
Graduate/Prof degree	3.0%

WORKERS/FAMILY	%	AVG INCOME
0	18.0	$ 21199
1	28.8	$ 30783
2	40.8	$ 43194
3+	12.3	$ 58215

VEHICLES/HSHLD		%
0	7788	13.0
1	24072	40.3
2	20614	34.5
3+	7223	12.1

ANCESTRY	
Tot. rptg	135639
	%
Arab	1.1
Austria/Swiss	0.6
Belgian/Dutch	0.6
Canadian	0.3
Central Eur.	17.5
English	4.4
French	1.1
German	24.3
Greek	1.0
Irish	9.8
Italian	9.2
Polish	13.3
Portuguese	0.0
Russian	4.1
Scandinavian	0.7
Scottish	1.6
Sub. African	0.0
United States	2.8
West Indian	0.0
FOREIGN BORN	6.9

SCHOOL ENROLLMENT		% PVT
Nursery school	2278	50.8
Elmntary/High	19117	33.9
College	8031	21.1

NON-ENGLISH SPKG HH	
Spanish	2.0%
Asian/PI	0.6%
Other	14.3%

HOUSING UNITS	
	62150
Owner occ	65.0%
Renter occ	31.1%
Vacant yr-round	2.8%
Vacant seasonal	1.2%

UNITS/STRUCTURE		%
1	42763	68.8
2	6216	10.0
3-4	1052	1.7
5+	10941	17.6

	BUILT %		MOVED IN %	
	OWNER	RENTER	OWNER	RENTER
1985-90	0.7	1.0	16.6	22.5
1980-84	0.5	0.7	7.0	4.6
1970-79	3.1	6.4	14.9	3.7
1960-69	9.5	6.1	13.3	0.9
<--1959	53.9	18.1	15.9	0.6

Source: 1990 Census STF3   (CS)

Urban Decision Systems/PO Box 25953/Los Angeles, CA 90025/(800) 633-9568

FIGURE 1-2. An example of a demographic study for a three-mile radius of the intersection of Pearl and Brookpark in Cleveland, Ohio. (*Courtesy of Urban Decision Systems Inc. A Blackburn Group Company, Los Angeles, California*)

```
DEMOGRAPHIC TRENDS: 1990-93-98          URBAN DECISION SYSTEMS, INC.
CLEVELAND,OH:BROOKPARK RD & PEARL RD                      06/21/93
3.0 MILE RING
```

	1990 Census		1993 Est.		1998 Proj.	
POPULATION	142175		140295		133261	
In Group Quarters	942		1024		1064	
HOUSEHOLDS	59697	%	60554	%	60246	%
1 Person	18635	31.2	19720	32.6	20789	34.5
2 Person	19509	32.7	19696	32.5	19443	32.3
3-4 Person	16847	28.2	16807	27.8	16316	27.1
5+ Person	4706	7.9	4331	7.2	3698	6.1
Avg Hshld Size	2.37		2.30		2.19	
FAMILIES	38805		38066		36041	
		%		%		%
RACE: White	136464	96.0	133342	95.0	124602	93.5
Black	2343	1.6	3911	2.8	5505	4.1
Asian/PI	1477	1.0	1384	1.0	1694	1.3
American Ind	245	0.2	238	0.2	280	0.2
Other	1646	1.2	1420	1.0	1180	0.9
HISPANIC ORIGIN	3871	2.7	4276	3.0	4785	3.6
		%		%		%
AGE: 0 - 5	11641	8.2	11584	8.3	10995	8.3
6 - 13	13074	9.2	12997	9.3	12321	9.2
14 - 17	5891	4.1	5878	4.2	5262	3.9
18 - 20	4767	3.4	4034	2.9	3390	2.5
21 - 24	7734	5.4	6982	5.0	5861	4.4
25 - 34	26217	18.4	25691	18.3	23105	17.3
35 - 44	18450	13.0	18905	13.5	19348	14.5
45 - 54	12789	9.0	12936	9.2	13519	10.1
55 - 64	14072	9.9	12259	8.7	10383	7.8
65 - 74	16643	11.7	16049	11.4	14869	11.2
75 - 84	8870	6.2	9766	7.0	10568	7.9
85 +	2027	1.4	3213	2.3	3640	2.7
Median Age	36.0		36.6		37.9	
MALES	67168	%	66855	%	64458	%
0 - 20	18077	26.9	17596	26.3	16546	25.7
21 - 44	26265	39.1	26015	38.9	24933	38.7
45 - 64	12222	18.2	11529	17.2	10966	17.0
65 - 84	10072	15.0	10900	16.3	11113	17.2
85 +	532	0.8	815	1.2	900	1.4
FEMALES	75007	%	73440	%	68803	%
0 - 20	17295	23.1	16897	23.0	15423	22.4
21 - 44	26137	34.8	25564	34.8	23381	34.0
45 - 64	14639	19.5	13666	18.6	12936	18.8
65 - 84	15442	20.6	14916	20.3	14325	20.8
85 +	1495	2.0	2397	3.3	2739	4.0
Owner-Occupied Hshlds	40395		40626		39823	
Renter-Occupied Hshlds	19302		19929		20423	

```
Source: 1990 Census, April 1, 1993 Est., 1998 Proj.            (DTP)
------------------------------------------------------------------------
Urban Decision Systems/PO Box 25953/Los Angeles, CA 90025/(800) 633-9568
```

FIGURE 1-2. (Continued)

INCOME: 1990-93-98   URBAN DECISION SYSTEMS, INC.
CLEVELAND,OH:BROOKPARK RD & PEARL RD   06/21/93
3.0 MILE RING

	1990 Census		1993 Est.		1998 Proj.	
POPULATION	142175		140295		133261	
In Group Quarters	942		1024		1064	
PER CAPITA INCOME	$ 13113		$ 15057		$ 17644	
AGGREGATE INCOME ($Mil)	1864.3		2112.4		2351.3	
HOUSEHOLDS	59697	%	60554	%	60246	%
By Income						
Less than $ 5,000	2950	4.9	3199	5.3	2631	4.4
$ 5,000 - $ 9,999	6025	10.1	5928	9.8	5166	8.6
$ 10,000 - $ 14,999	5939	9.9	5458	9.0	4254	7.1
$ 15,000 - $ 19,999	6039	10.1	5599	9.2	4566	7.6
$ 20,000 - $ 24,999	5854	9.8	5460	9.0	4657	7.7
$ 25,000 - $ 29,999	5503	9.2	5196	8.6	4700	7.8
$ 30,000 - $ 34,999	5855	9.8	5721	9.4	5488	9.1
$ 35,000 - $ 39,999	4726	7.9	4849	8.0	5083	8.4
$ 40,000 - $ 49,999	7113	11.9	7916	13.1	9452	15.7
$ 50,000 - $ 59,999	4452	7.5	4951	8.2	5960	9.9
$ 60,000 - $ 74,999	3008	5.0	3367	5.6	3980	6.6
$ 75,000 - $ 99,999	1610	2.7	1990	3.3	2721	4.5
$100,000 - $124,999	365	0.6	494	0.8	763	1.3
$125,000 - $149,999	143	0.2	172	0.3	308	0.5
$150,000 +	116	0.2	254	0.4	519	0.9
Median Household Income	$	27564	$	29459	$	33781
Average Household Income	$	31126	$	34562	$	38604
FAMILIES	38805	%	38066	%	36041	%
By Income						
Less than $ 5,000	1245	3.2	1354	3.6	1248	3.5
$ 5,000 - $ 9,999	1376	3.5	1198	3.1	877	2.4
$ 10,000 - $ 14,999	2729	7.0	2290	6.0	1468	4.1
$ 15,000 - $ 19,999	3173	8.2	2731	7.2	1778	4.9
$ 20,000 - $ 24,999	3523	9.1	3000	7.9	1935	5.4
$ 25,000 - $ 29,999	3823	9.9	3316	8.7	2312	6.4
$ 30,000 - $ 34,999	4457	11.5	4086	10.7	3295	9.1
$ 35,000 - $ 39,999	3743	9.6	3713	9.8	3518	9.8
$ 40,000 - $ 49,999	6098	15.7	6601	17.3	7525	20.9
$ 50,000 - $ 59,999	3875	10.0	4236	11.1	4951	13.7
$ 60,000 - $ 74,999	2743	7.1	2969	7.8	3408	9.5
$ 75,000 - $ 99,999	1453	3.7	1731	4.5	2315	6.4
$100,000 - $124,999	334	0.9	449	1.2	675	1.9
$125,000 - $149,999	130	0.3	162	0.4	281	0.8
$150,000 +	103	0.3	231	0.6	457	1.3
Median Family Income	$	33825	$	36425	$	42114
Average Family Income	$	37497	$	41623	$	46909

Source: 1990 Census, April 1, 1993 Est., 1998 Proj.   (INP)

Urban Decision Systems/PO Box 25953/Los Angeles, CA 90025/(800) 633-9568

FIGURE 1-2. *(Continued)*

```
RETAIL POTENTIAL: RESTAURANTS          URBAN DECISION SYSTEMS, INC.
CLEVELAND,OH:BROOKPARK RD & PEARL RD                     06/21/93
3.0 MILE RING
```

RESTAURANTS: ANNUAL SALES POTENTIAL, 1990

	AGGREGATE ($000)	PER CAPITA	MARKET INDEX*
TOTAL FOOD IN RESTAURANTS	84693	594.52	122
Fast Food/Take Outs	32797	230.22	119
Family/Coffee Shops	28816	202.28	121
Cafeterias	2811	19.73	122
Atmosphere/Specialty	20269	142.29	129
TOTAL ALCOHOLIC BEVERAGES IN RESTAURANTS	8718	61.20	127

SUPPORTABLE:	NUMBER OF SEATS	FLOOR SPACE Gross Leasable Area
Fast Food / Take Outs	4207	146072
Family / Coffee Shops	6645	207799
Cafeterias	511	18140
Atmosphere / Specialty	7014	226451
TOTAL	18377	598463

---

*Market Index Reference Area:
 UNITED STATES

Source: Apr. 1,1990 UDS Estimates   (RP11)

Urban Decision Systems/PO Box 25953/Los Angeles, CA 90025/(800) 633-9568

FIGURE 1-2. *(Continued)*

FIGURE 1-2. *(Continued)*

CLEVELAND, OH: BROOKPARK RD & PEARL RD
3 Mile Ring

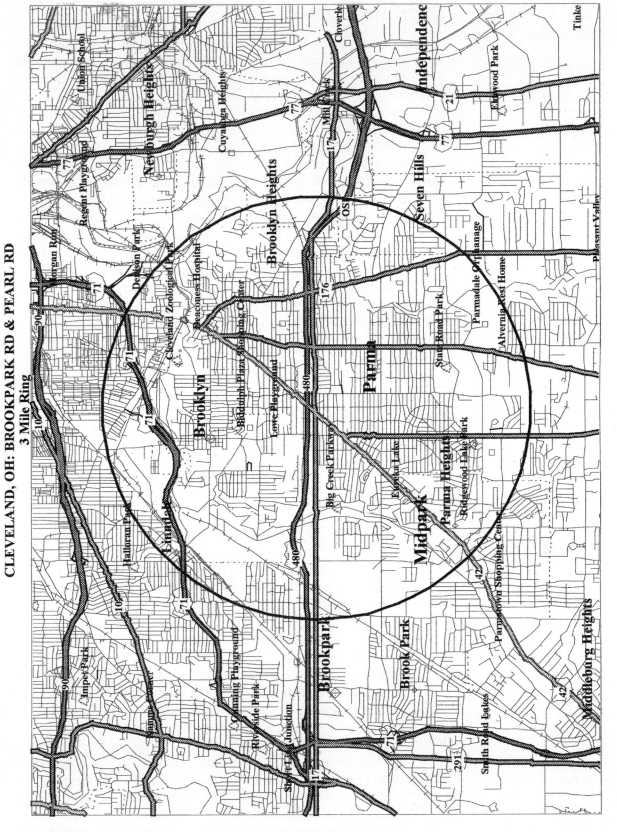

Urban Decision Systems, Inc. / 2040 Armacost Avenue / Los Angeles, CA 90025 / (800) 633-9568

July 23, 1993

COMPETITION

Another factor to consider is competition. While feasibility studies include a section on competition, demographic studies do not. Just exactly what is competition? In a broad sense of the word, it is any business that sells food. Thus, a grocery store or super-market could be considered competition for the food service in-dustry. In the strictest sense of the word, it is any food service that sells a similar product at a similar price as your operation. Care must be exercised when planning a menu since a market will support only a given number of similar operations. When this level is reached, it is known as *market saturation*. Many people and/or companies are afraid of competition, but competition is healthy. It promotes a good price value relationship, excellent service, and a quality product. In a competitive market, it forces business to excel in order to succeed. Market saturation, on the other hand, is not a healthy situation to get into as the number of available customers can only be spread so thin. Personal knowledge of this condition is important to the person responsible for writing the menu. Rather than copying the competition, attack it via menu listings and turn a problem into an opportunity. For example, an area that has an overabundance of deli style operations would probably wel-come a restaurant that features excellent soups and salads and downplays sandwiches.

Analysis of the demographic study is necessary for matching the customers with their needs. Little if any research has been con-ducted on this subject for our industry; however, generalizations can be made based on observation and experience.

AGE GROUPS

The knowledge of customer age groups is vital to proper menu selection. For purposes of this discussion, let's bracket the age groups as follows: children, teens, young adults, middle age, and older adults.

Why in the world would children be included? Children, more than anyone, influence, often times dictate, the decision as to where a family will dine out. Remember also that children are heavily in-fluenced by television, both in the advertising and programming.

In an area that is family-oriented with children (as opposed to families with teenagers) certain considerations must be made in menu selection. This is not an easy task as the menu writer is torn between two sets of criteria. One, the parents want their children to have a well-balanced meal. Two, the children, being bombarded with slick ads, will opt for junk food. Since the children are influ-encing the decision as to where to eat out, they must be satisfied. Since the parents are paying for the experience, they too must be satisfied. The most logical solution is to split the difference—nutritious junk food. Hamburgers or cheeseburgers with lettuce and tomato, gelatin with fruit, tacos, hot dogs, ice cream, and chicken are but a few examples of foods that appeal to children while at the same time provide a degree of nutrition. In addition to the menu, the restaurant can cater to the children in other ways, with special menus, prizes, and clean plate clubs. The experience must be enjoyable for both the children and the parents.

Teenagers pose special problems of their own. On the one hand they still cling to their childhood eating habits and on the other hand they are beginning to mature into adulthood and, consequently, many are refining their requirements into a more nutritionally balanced diet. (Many, but not all!) They also need to be considered as two separate markets. One, as part of the family unit that is dining out and two, as a market of their own.

When dining out with the family, teens are more nutritionally oriented, probably more as a result of parental coercion than an independent choice. They disdain children's menus and will order from the regular menu, frequently consuming more than their parents. When eating out with their peers, they often revert back to the junk food syndrome. Theirs is a large market, with more disposable income than many restaurateurs realize.

When writing menus for this group, treat it as two separate markets. With the family, they will require the same menu as the young adults. When with their peers, a fast food menu will suffice.

The young adult market needs to be further broken down into three divisions: singles, marrieds with no children, and families. Although the type and style of food for this market will be similar, menu considerations must be made for each division. Overall, this group is becoming more health conscious. They are into physical fitness and, consequently, into lighter, healthier, and more natural foods. They are beginning to avoid junk foods and fried foods. They particularly enjoy fresh fruits and vegetables. The person responsible for menus should, in this market, consider salads, fresh fruits (both as a menu offering and as a garnish), natural breads such as bran or fruit muffins, wheat and stone ground breads, more broiled entrees (chicken, fish, seafood) and fewer fried entrees. This group is also particularly trendy. It is imperative that one stay on top and ahead of trends.

As far as the market breakdown of this group is concerned, special considerations for menu planning need to be mentioned. Singles, as a whole, will have a greater disposable income and will be less inclined to take the trouble to cook for one person. Consequently, they tend to eat out more and are not as concerned with price as are others in their market. The restaurant needs to be trendy with appropriate decor and, most of all, fun. The menu should reflect these facts and offer a variety of foods that reflect the theme and decor of the establishment.

Children's Menu

STEPHENSON'S

APPLE FARM
RESTAURANT

GRACIOUS COUNTRY DINING

Hey Kids . . .

Don't forget the cider-barrel at the entrance. It is filled with sweet, pure, cold cider made here on the farm from red, ripe, juicy apples and squeezed in our press.

You may have all you like, that is, as long as your parents don't object. Sweet cider is very good for you. In fact, you can drink it in the morning for breakfast instead of orange juice. So, on the way out, get a cup, turn the wooden spigot and have another drink of health.

FIGURE 1-3. A good example of a children's menu written with children in mind. The regular menu from this restaurant can be found in Chapter 7. (*Menu courtesy of Stephenson's Old Apple Farm Restaurant, Kansas City, Missouri*)

Children's Meals

Smokey Wokey - ¼ hickory smoked chicken. Finest in the world. Smoked over hickory wood. . . . 5.25

Little Red Hen - ¼ baked chicken in butter and cream. Tender and delicious. 5.25

The Specialty of the House

Three Little Pigs - Hickory smoked ribs, really cooked over hickory wood. Pick up and eat with your fingers. 5.25

Piggy Wiggy - A hickory smoked pork chop. This is an entirely different flavor in pork chops. . . . 5.25

Porky Pig - ½ center-cut hickory smoked ham - served with honey sauce. 5.25

Fishy Wishy - Fried Jumbo Shrimp. Served with our own shrimp sauce. 7.95

Above meals include your choice of the following: Tossed, frozen or marshmallow salad, baked or french fried potatoes and hot bread.

Kid's Plates

Henny Penny - 2 pieces of hickory smoked chicken, baked potato or french fries and hot bread. . . 4.50

Chicken Little - 2 pieces of baked chicken, baked potato or french fries and hot bread. 4.50

Soda, Milk or Iced Tea 85
Cider 1.25

Mom! If you like, we will be glad to bring you an empty plate so you may share some of your meal with your child.

FIGURE 1-3. *(Continued)*

Young married couples, if they are renting, tend to follow the same menu criteria particularly if both partners are working. They have a high disposable income and tend to spend a large portion of this eating out. On the other hand, young couples who are purchasing a home have an entirely different set of standards. Mortgage payments, yard and lawn care, decorating, and furniture purchases tend to consume a large portion of their income, leaving a smaller amount for eating out. While the diet demands of this group do not change, price becomes more of a dominant criterion in selecting a restaurant.

According to the National Restaurant Association, pizza, bakery items, barbecue, and pasta are particularly popular with those in the 25 to 34 age group. Apparently, these younger customers are more willing to try new foods. Cajun cooking, mesquite grilling, and sushi are ordered with more frequency by this group than with any other. In addition, they may opt for lower cost menu items because their dining budget is restricted. When a young couple starts raising a family, two changes take place. One, price becomes more important and two, restaurants catering to children and families become very attractive.

Taking all of these factors into consideration, it becomes increasingly clear that the menu writer in a market consisting of young adults needs to investigate further the more specific factors of that market. Referring back to the demographic studies done for the restaurant will make this an easier chore.

The middle-aged market tends to be more traditional in its menu selection. Basically, they cling to the older standards. Larger portions and fried foods are more popular, as well as value for their dollar. Patrons from 35 to 49 show a preference for chicken and pasta entree items, as well as baked goods. Middle-of-the-road, family-style restaurants are the norm with an occasional experience in fine dining for special occasions with the children being tended by a babysitter. When the family dines out, price is a factor. On special occasions price becomes less of a factor.

Patrons age 18 to 49 are heavy consumers of hamburgers. After age 49, this item drops drastically in overall sales. Sandwiches are popular with those 18 to 49 who make up a large portion of the workforce and are more likely to eat out for lunch.

The older segment of the population is probably the most predictable of all the age groups. Smaller portions and balanced meals become the norm. Those 50 to 64, representing 16 percent of the population, prefer roast beef, steak, fish or seafood, and veal entrees. These menu items are also most popular with those age 65 and over and should be considered by restaurateurs wanting to attract older customers. As they retire and rely on fixed incomes, price becomes important. After the family has grown and prior to retirement, price is less of a factor as it is normally during this time span that income is at its greatest and financial responsibilities at their lowest. Cafeterias and coffee shops are predominant in this group.

ETHNIC ORIGINS

Another factor to be taken into consideration when selecting items for the menu is the ethnic makeup of the restaurant trade area. Certain ethnic groups prefer certain foods over others. Caution should be a key here as the majority of ethnic groups in this country do not partake exclusively of the basic foods of their native land. It is fascinating how people enjoy trying foods of countries other than their own native land or the land of their ancestors. As a matter of fact, even the cuisine that is known as American borrows heavily from other countries in its own "melting pot" fashion.

When discussing ethnic foods it should be pointed out that there are two areas of discussion. One is the American consumer purchasing ethnic foods of other cultures and the other is a person purchasing food from his/her own native culture. The former will be dealt with in a subsequent chapter. What we are discussing here is ethnic likes and dislikes. Since research on this subject is almost nonexistent, we must rely on basic knowledge of specific groups. Stereotyping is a dangerous thing when it comes to ethnic groups. However, it works quite well when dealing with menu planning. Remember that while the majority of an ethnic group might like certain foods, seasonings, or cooking methods, it does not hold true that everyone in the group will agree. The menu writer needs to take into account the fact that particular foods will appeal to certain ethnic groups most of the time. This is not to suggest that this will hold true all of the time.

EDUCATION, OCCUPATION, AND INCOME

These three factors are tied together as they normally tend to influence each other. For example, a person with a high school education or less would tend to have a blue-collar occupation, while a person with a postsecondary education would tend to opt for a white-collar position. Generally, a person in a white-collar position earns more than a person in a blue-collar job. There would be, however, no noticeable income difference on the upper-blue-collar scale and the lower-white-collar scale.

Education and occupation play a minor role compared to income. With income being a primary factor, the key determination for the menu writer becomes affordability for the market. Another key factor is not necessarily the income in a particular demographic area, but the disposable income in that market. Disposable income is that part of earnings and investment income that is left over after the basic needs of food, shelter, clothing, and other necessities have been met. It can generally be stated that the higher the person's income, the greater the available disposable income. When more disposable income becomes available, two things happen. People tend to eat out more often and they tend also to trade up.

FIGURE 1-4. Demographic characteristics of consumers patronizing specialty restaurants and their purchasing preferences. (*Courtesy of the National Restaurant Association, Washington, D.C.*)

	Bakery Items	Pizza Delivery	Barbe-que	Pasta	Hot Dogs	Ham-burgers	Ice Cream
	%	%	%	%	%	%	%
Total	49	47	47	46	42	34	34
Sex							
Male	50	48	51	47	48	37	35
Female	48	46	44	45	37	31	33
Race							
White	48	48	46	48	41	34	35
Non-white	51	42	54	30	51	38	30
Age							
18 to 24 years	56	73	59	57	53	45	38
25 to 34 years	52	58	52	54	48	39	38
35 to 49 years	50	49	44	48	40	34	37
50 to 64 years	43	29	41	37	36	27	31
65 years or older	41	22	43	29	34	22	25
Marital Status							
Married	47	46	46	46	41	32	36
Single	52	49	49	46	44	37	31
Education							
College graduate	55	52	44	59	39	40	44
High school graduate	50	50	49	47	43	34	35
Less than high school graduate	40	35	45	30	43	30	24
Annual Household Income							
$30,000 or more	56	52	49	55	43	39	40
$20,000 to $29,999	47	50	48	46	44	29	38
$15,000 to $19,999	47	45	50	49	43	40	33
Under $15,000	46	41	45	34	39	31	26
Women's Employment Status							
Employed full-time	52	52	49	49	39	37	38
Employed part-time	41	50	37	43	34	31	34
Not employed	46	38	42	41	36	26	29
Region							
East	54	45	33	52	42	32	36
New England	54	47	30	66	38	28	34
Middle Atlantic	53	45	34	48	43	34	36
Midwest	46	50	46	47	44	36	33
East Central	45	56	45	50	49	34	37
West Central	47	39	49	42	36	38	28
South	42	44	59	39	41	32	33
Southeast	43	45	60	40	46	33	35
Southwest	41	42	58	38	32	32	28
West	57	51	49	47	42	38	36
Rocky Mountain	46	56	41	38	28	39	35
Pacific	61	48	52	51	47	37	36

Diet/ Lite	Oriental	Fresh Cookies	Gourmet Take-Out	Chicken	Cajun	Display Cooking	Mes- quite	Sushi	Inter- views
%	%	%	%	%	%	%	%	%	
29	29	26	21	20	18	13	9	5	(2021)
26	28	24	20	22	20	14	9	6	(998)
31	30	28	21	19	16	13	9	4	(1023)
29	28	25	20	20	16	13	8	5	(1779)
28	34	31	28	19	27	16	9	9	(239)
30	38	32	25	26	26	14	9	5	(287)
30	32	30	20	26	20	17	12	8	(540)
31	29	29	20	21	18	12	9	6	(613)
26	22	20	20	14	14	11	6	5	(347)
25	22	16	20	12	9	10	5	3	(208)
29	26	26	19	20	17	13	9	5	(1319)
29	34	26	23	21	19	13	8	7	(702)
33	34	32	20	28	23	17	12	10	(537)
29	30	27	22	20	16	14	8	5	(1239)
24	19	18	18	15	17	8	6	2	(240)
32	33	29	21	27	21	15	13	8	(763)
30	27	31	20	22	18	14	7	6	(415)
32	34	26	20	19	19	11	8	4	(237)
23	21	18	22	14	16	10	5	3	(389)
38	36	35	22	21	20	15	10	7	(449)
29	30	34	18	18	15	14	9	4	(144)
26	24	20	20	17	12	10	8	3	(428)
26	32	30	19	17	17	11	6	8	(514)
29	37	29	14	16	19	10	5	8	(121)
25	31	30	20	17	16	11	7	8	(343)
34	27	23	23	17	14	14	5	2	(527)
35	28	25	25	19	18	14	5	2	(319)
32	24	20	20	14	9	13	5	2	(208)
28	23	23	21	19	22	13	9	3	(606)
29	24	24	23	15	21	14	7	4	(382)
26	22	23	18	27	23	11	13	3	(224)
27	35	29	19	30	17	15	15	10	(374)
28	29	23	15	26	19	12	11	3	(102)
27	37	32	20	32	16	16	17	12	(272)

FIGURE 1-4 How likely are you to choose spicy dishes or those with exotic ingredients when eating out?

	Total	Sex		Age				
		Male	Female	18–34	35–44	45–54	55–64	65+
Total unweighted	1001	500	501	382	224	140	110	123
Total weighted	1859	876	983	702	359	247	220	293
	100.0	100.0	100.0	100.0	100.0	100.0	100.0	100.0
Spicy dishes rather than ones that are not spicy	792	398	395	336	174	92	86	95
	42.6	45.4	40.1	47.9	48.5	37.0	39.4	32.4
Dishes with intense concentrated flavors instead of mild ones	650	313	337	273	141	72	64	91
	35.0	35.8	34.2	38.9	39.4	29.0	29.2	31.2
Unfamiliar items rather than ones you are familiar with	461	223	238	192	90	46	65	62
	24.8	25.4	24.2	27.4	25.1	18.5	29.6	21.1
Dishes with exotic ingredients	426	220	206	183	98	43	35	56
	22.9	25.1	21.0	26.0	27.4	17.4	15.8	18.9

Note: Frequencies are reported in 100,000's. 1859 = 185,900,000 which represents the U.S. Population 18 years of age or older.

Further income analysis shows that people in the poverty level would eat out very little, if at all, and that their dining out experience would probably be limited to fast food. People in the $5,000 to $10,000 income range would eat out more, but again be limited to primarily fast food and occasionally a coffee-shop-type range. People in the $10,000 to $20,000 range would increase substantially in both the number of times eating out and the spectrum of price ranges. In the $20,000 to $30,000 range a like increase would take place along with a drop in the lower price range establishments. Over $30,000 would react in similar fashion with more frequency in the higher range and less frequency in the lower range. Exceptions to the above could, of course, be found. Surprisingly, sandwiches are also more likely to be ordered by patrons from households with an income of $30,000 and a white-collar occupation. A couple in the $10,000 to $20,000 range might celebrate a special occasion in a fine dining restaurant once or twice a year. However, you cannot develop a business, much less a menu, on such sporadic sales.

POPULARITY POLLS

While little research has been conducted on the relationship between a restaurant's demographics and menu listings, several popularity polls are available to assist the menu writer. Therefore, a person responsible for a menu needs to deal in generalities demographically, while at the same time listing items which are popular with the population as a whole.

Household Income					Region				Metro Status	
Under $15K	$15K–$24.9	$25K–$39.9	$40K–$49.9	$50K+	North East	North Cntrl	South	West	Metro	Nonmt
122	174	259	109	240	221	260	330	190	755	246
273	326	494	188	388	389	443	640	387	1430	429
100.0	100.0	100.0	100.0	100.0	100.0	100.0	100.0	100.0	100.0	100.0
121	134	213	83	184	126	168	324	173	620	172
44.2	41.0	43.1	43.9	47.4	32.4	38.0	50.7	44.9	43.3	40.2
107	103	170	71	151	117	140	253	140	523	126
39.1	31.7	34.4	37.7	39.0	30.1	31.6	39.5	36.2	36.6	29.5
77	71	126	33	113	99	101	159	102	350	110
28.1	21.9	25.4	17.4	29.1	25.3	22.8	24.8	26.5	24.5	25.7
53	64	106	27	143	89	83	147	107	342	85
19.4	19.8	21.5	14.3	36.9	22.8	18.8	23.0	27.7	23.9	19.7

In as much as a generic menu, which lists only popular items, is for the most part dull, menu writers need also be concerned with trends within their demographic area. Take, for example, fish which has a good to moderate acceptance across the spectrum. In the past, deep fried cod would have been an acceptable menu listing. However, our studies have shown that there is a trend away from fried foods. This does not mean you must remove this item from the menu, but rather change it to gain customer acceptance. If we changed it to broiled cod with a lemon butter sauce, we would fit this criterion. Next, is it priced right? Does it fit the criteria for family/singles, ethnic groups, age, and so on? In a high-income area, broiled cod might be changed to broiled filet of dover sole at a higher selling price.

A word of caution should be given here. While it is important to be aware (and even on the cutting edge) of trends, do not overreact. Avoid embracing the trend completely. For example, when light, broiled, lean meats along with fresh fruits and vegetables became the trend, less than a third of the population ordered these items when dining out. The media would lead one to believe that everyone was, or should be, eating this way. Certainly one-third of our customer base is important, but don't forget the two-thirds who do not wish to participate.

Recognize also the difference between fads and trends. A *fad* is an idea that comes and goes quickly, while a *trend* stays around for a while and many times becomes the norm. If you react to fads, the ink will be barely dry on your new menu and your storeroom will be full of new ingredients and no one will be purchasing it. While fads cost money if you follow them, trends can make money. Many

FIGURE 1-5. Important menu additions, deletions, and anticipated changes in new menus from surveyed restaurants in the United States. (*Courtesy of the National Restaurant Association, Washington, D.C.*)

	Sales Volume			Number of Establishments				
	$500K	$500K–$999K	$1000K+	1	2	3+	2–4	5+
What are the one or two most important additions you made to your menu in 1992?								
TOTAL	92	142	151	326	52	67	83	36
	100%	100%	100%	100%	100%	100%	100%	100%
LIGHTER FOODS/HEALTHIER FOODS	5	14	29	35	7	14	13	8
	5%	10%	19%	11%	13%	21%	16%	22%
CHICKEN/POULTRY	9	13	14	32	5	5	7	3
	10%	9%	9%	10%	10%	7%	8%	8%
SALADS	7	16	11	28	3	5	6	2
	8%	11%	7%	9%	6%	7%	7%	6%
SEAFOOD/FISH DISHES	7	9	14	27	2	6	6	2
	8%	6%	9%	8%	4%	9%	7%	6%
VEGETARIAN	7	8	7	18	3	4	4	3
	8%	6%	5%	6%	6%	6%	5%	8%
PASTA	4	8	10	22	–	3	2	1
	4%	6%	7%	7%	–	4%	2%	3%
RED MEAT DISHES	3	6	11	17	4	3	6	1
	3%	4%	7%	5%	8%	4%	7%	3%
ETHNIC DISHES (GENERAL)	4	11	6	17	2	4	4	2
	4%	8%	4%	5%	4%	6%	5%	6%
FEATURED ITEMS/SPECIALS	3	9	8	16	2	3	4	1
	3%	6%	5%	5%	4%	4%	5%	3%
CHANGING/RE-DOING MENU (GENERAL)	2	11	3	15	1	3	1	3
	2%	8%	2%	5%	2%	4%	1%	8%
NOTHING ADDED	4	4	5	12	2	2	2	2
	4%	3%	3%	4%	4%	3%	2%	6%
DESSERTS	5	5	2	9	2	2	3	1
	5%	4%	1%	3%	4%	3%	4%	3%
SANDWICHES/HAMBURGERS	4	3	4	11	1	1	2	–
	4%	2%	3%	3%	2%	1%	2%	–
APPETIZERS	3	1	5	6	2	3	3	2
	3%	1%	3%	2%	4%	4%	4%	6%
BUFFET	2	3	3	5	2	1	3	–
	2%	2%	2%	2%	4%	1%	4%	–
LOW COST ITEMS	2	3	1	5	–	1	1	–
	2%	2%	1%	2%	–	1%	1%	–
GRILLED/BROILED/BARBEQUED	2	3	1	6	–	–	–	–
	2%	2%	1%	2%	–	–	–	–
ALCOHOLIC BEVERAGES	–	2	2	4	–	–	–	–
	–	1%	1%	1%	–	–	–	–
CHILDREN'S MEALS	2	2	–	2	1	1	2	–
	2%	1%	–	1%	2%	1%	2%	–
SEASONAL FOODS	–	1	3	2	–	2	–	2
	–	1%	2%	1%	–	3%	–	6%
COFFEES	1	1	1	2	–	1	1	–
	1%	1%	1%	1%	–	1%	1%	–
SENIOR CITIZEN PLATTERS	1	2	–	3	–	–	–	–
	1%	1%	–	1%	–	–	–	–

	Menu Theme				Check Size				Check Size			
Ameri-can	Inter-natnal	Steak/Seafood	Other	<$8	$8–$14	$15–$24	25+	<$10	$10–$19	$20+	$20–$29	$30+
129	84	72	160	84	165	82	96	139	166	122	47	75
100%	100%	100%	100%	100%	100%	100%	100%	100%	100%	100%	100%	100%
17	9	11	21	7	22	14	14	12	29	16	3	13
13%	11%	15%	13%	8%	13%	17%	15%	9%	17%	13%	6%	17%
10	3	11	17	10	19	6	6	21	14	6	2	4
8%	4%	15%	11%	12%	12%	7%	6%	15%	8%	5%	4%	5%
12	4	–	20	10	18	5	2	17	12	6	6	–
9%	5%	–	13%	12%	11%	6%	2%	12%	7%	5%	13%	–
8	4	11	12	4	14	10	7	13	12	10	4	6
6%	5%	15%	8%	5%	8%	12%	7%	9%	7%	8%	9%	8%
7	9	5	5	1	8	6	8	4	8	11	5	6
5%	11%	7%	3%	1%	5%	7%	8%	3%	5%	9%	11%	8%
4	3	10	7	1	9	8	7	3	11	11	5	6
3%	4%	14%	4%	1%	5%	10%	7%	2%	7%	9%	11%	8%
7	2	4	9	3	12	6	2	9	9	5	4	1
5%	2%	6%	6%	4%	7%	7%	2%	6%	5%	4%	9%	1%
6	5	3	9	5	10	4	4	8	10	5	2	3
5%	6%	4%	6%	6%	6%	5%	4%	6%	6%	4%	4%	4%
7	4	3	7	1	10	6	3	3	13	4	1	3
5%	5%	4%	4%	1%	6%	7%	3%	2%	8%	3%	2%	4%
5	3	3	7	1	8	3	6	3	6	9	4	5
4%	4%	4%	4%	1%	5%	4%	6%	2%	4%	7%	9%	7%
6	4	3	3	4	4	2	4	6	4	4	1	3
5%	5%	4%	2%	5%	2%	2%	4%	4%	2%	3%	2%	4%
2	1	–	9	7	3	2	1	8	3	2	1	1
2%	1%	–	6%	8%	2%	2%	1%	6%	2%	2%	2%	1%
5	–	2	6	5	6	1	1	8	4	1	1	–
4%	–	3%	4%	6%	4%	1%	1%	6%	2%	1%	2%	–
7	1	1	2	1	4	3	3	2	5	4	2	2
5%	1%	1%	1%	1%	2%	4%	3%	1%	3%	3%	4%	3%
1	1	2	4	1	3	4	–	3	5	–	–	–
1%	1%	3%	3%	1%	2%	5%	–	2%	3%	–	–	–
1	3	–	2	–	2	2	1	1	1	3	2	1
1%	4%	–	1%	–	1%	2%	1%	1%	1%	2%	4%	1%
3	1	–	2	3	2	–	–	5	–	–	–	–
2%	1%	–	1%	4%	1%	–	–	4%	–	–	–	–
2	1	1	1	–	1	1	3	1	1	3	–	3
2%	1%	1%	1%	–	1%	1%	3%	1%	1%	2%	–	4%
2	1	–	1	1	3	–	–	4	–	–	–	–
2%	1%	–	1%	1%	2%	–	–	3%	–	–	–	–
2	1	–	1	1	2	–	1	2	1	1	1	–
2%	1%	–	1%	1%	1%	–	1%	1%	1%	1%	2%	–
–	–	1	2	–	1	–	1	1	–	1	1	–
–	–	1%	1%	–	1%	–	1%	1%	–	1%	2%	–
1	–	–	2	1	2	–	–	3	–	–	–	–
1%	–	–	1%	1%	1%	–	–	2%	–	–	–	–

FIGURE 1-5. *(Continued)*

	Sales Volume			Number of Establishments				
	$500K	$500K–$999K	$1000K+	1	2	3+	2–4	5+

What are the one or two most important additions you made to your menu in 1992?

BREAKFAST ITEMS	–	1	2	1	–	2	1	1
	–	1%	1%	–	–	3%	1%	3%
STIR FRY	–	2	–	1	–	1	1	–
	–	1%	–	–	–	1%	1%	–
FRUIT DISHES	–	1	1	–	2	–	2	–
	–	1%	1%	–	4%	–	2%	–
VARIETY OF BEVERAGES/FREE REFILLS	–	–	1	2	–	–	–	–
	–	–	1%	1%	–	–	–	–
SMALLER PORTIONS	–	1	1	2	–	–	–	–
	–	1%	1%	1%	–	–	–	–
EGG DISHES	1	–	–	1	–	–	–	–
	1%	–	–	–	–	–	–	–
CATERING SERVICES	1	–	–	1	–	–	–	–
	1%	–	–	–	–	–	–	–
OTHER	2	12	6	19	3	1	3	1
	2%	8%	4%	6%	6%	1%	4%	3%
NO CHANGE	36	42	44	109	18	16	26	8
	39%	30%	29%	33%	35%	24%	31%	22%
DON'T KNOW	3	1	2	6	2	3	3	2
	3%	1%	1%	2%	4%	4%	4%	6%

What are the one or two most important deletions you made to your menu in 1992?

TOTAL	92	142	151	326	52	67	83	36
	100%	100%	100%	100%	100%	100%	100%	100%
NOTHING DELETED	39	72	75	159	19	38	35	22
	42%	51%	50%	49%	37%	57%	42%	61%
BEEF	6	7	8	15	4	4	7	1
	7%	5%	5%	5%	8%	6%	8%	3%
FISH	3	7	8	17	2	1	3	–
	3%	5%	5%	5%	4%	1%	4%	–
HIGH FAT FOODS	4	4	6	8	5	1	5	1
	4%	3%	4%	2%	10%	1%	6%	3%
HIGH PRICED ITEMS (GENERAL)	2	1	1	3	–	1	–	1
	2%	1%	1%	1%	–	1%	–	3%
APPETIZERS	3	1	–	4	–	–	–	–
	3%	1%	–	1%	–	–	–	–
CHICKEN	1	–	1	1	1	1	1	1
	1%	–	1%	–	2%	1%	1%	3%
STREAMLINING (GENERAL)	–	1	2	3	–	–	–	–
	–	1%	1%	1%	–	–	–	–
DESSERTS	1	1	1	1	1	1	2	–
	1%	1%	1%	–	2%	1%	2%	–
CUT DOWN ON SALT/SODIUM	–	1	1	–	2	–	2	–
	–	1%	1%	–	4%	–	2%	–
SANDWICHES	–	1	1	1	–	1	1	–
	–	1%	1%	–	–	1%	1%	–
SLOW MOVING ITEMS	–	2	–	2	–	–	–	–
	–	1%	–	1%	–	–	–	–

Menu Theme				Check Size				Check Size				
Ameri-can	Inter-natnal	Steak/Seafood	Other	<$8	$8–$14	$15–$24	25+	<$10	$10–$19	$20+	$20–$29	$30+
2	–	1	–	–	2	1	–	1	2	–	–	–
2%	–	1%	–	–	1%	1%	–	1%	1%	–	–	–
–	–	–	2	1	1	–	–	1	1	–	–	–
–	–	–	1%	1%	1%	–	–	1%	1%	–	–	–
2	–	–	–	–	1	1	–	–	2	–	–	–
2%	–	–	–	–	1%	1%	–	–	1%	–	–	–
1	1	–	–	1	1	–	–	2	–	–	–	–
1%	1%	–	–	1%	1%	–	–	1%	–	–	–	–
1	–	1	–	–	1	1	–	1	–	1	1	–
1%	–	1%	–	–	1%	1%	–	1%	–	1%	2%	–
1	–	–	–	–	1	–	–	1	–	–	–	–
1%	–	–	–	–	1%	–	–	1%	–	–	–	–
–	1	–	–	–	–	1	–	–	1	–	–	–
–	1%	–	–	–	–	1%	–	–	1%	–	–	–
7	9	3	5	4	4	4	11	4	6	13	3	10
5%	11%	4%	3%	5%	2%	5%	11%	3%	4%	11%	6%	13%
38	28	21	55	34	48	19	32	47	49	37	12	25
29%	33%	29%	34%	40%	29%	23%	33%	34%	30%	30%	26%	33%
5	1	2	4	2	3	1	4	2	4	4	–	4
4%	1%	3%	3%	2%	2%	1%	4%	1%	2%	3%	–	5%
129	84	72	160	84	165	82	96	139	166	122	47	75
100%	100%	100%	100%	100%	100%	100%	100%	100%	100%	100%	100%	100%
61	42	34	80	42	72	45	50	73	70	66	28	38
47%	50%	47%	50%	50%	44%	55%	52%	53%	42%	54%	60%	51%
9	4	6	4	3	9	6	4	4	14	4	–	4
7%	5%	8%	3%	4%	5%	7%	4%	3%	8%	3%	–	5%
6	2	6	5	1	9	5	3	4	9	5	3	2
5%	2%	8%	3%	1%	5%	6%	3%	3%	5%	4%	6%	3%
5	4	1	4	2	5	2	4	5	4	4	–	4
4%	5%	1%	3%	2%	3%	2%	4%	4%	2%	3%	–	5%
2	1	1	–	–	1	2	–	–	3	–	–	–
2%	1%	1%	–	–	1%	2%	–	–	2%	–	–	–
–	1	1	2	2	2	–	–	3	1	–	–	–
–	1%	1%	1%	2%	1%	–	–	2%	1%	–	–	–
–	2	1	–	–	3	–	–	–	3	–	–	–
–	2%	1%	–	–	2%	–	–	–	2%	–	–	–
1	1	–	1	–	2	1	–	1	2	–	–	–
1%	1%	–	1%	–	1%	1%	–	1%	1%	–	–	–
2	1	–	–	–	1	1	1	–	1	2	1	1
2%	1%	–	–	–	1%	1%	1%	–	1%	2%	2%	1%
2	–	–	–	–	1	–	1	–	1	1	–	1
2%	–	–	–	–	1%	–	1%	–	1%	1%	–	1%
–	–	–	2	–	2	–	–	–	2	–	–	–
–	–	–	1%	–	1%	–	–	–	1%	–	–	–
1	–	–	1	–	2	–	–	1	1	–	–	–
1%	–	–	1%	–	1%	–	–	1%	1%	–	–	–

FIGURE 1-5.   *(Continued)*

	Sales Volume			Number of Establishments				
	$500K	$500K–$999K	$1000K+	1	2	3+	2–4	5+
OTHER	–	6	6	9	2	2	3	1
	–	4%	4%	3%	4%	3%	4%	3%
DON'T KNOW	–	1	1	1	1	1	1	1
	–	1%	1%	–	2%	1%	1%	3%
Next year what additions are you planning?								
TOTAL	92	142	151	326	52	67	83	36
	100%	100%	100%	100%	100%	100%	100%	100%
NO ADDITIONS	5	12	12	23	5	7	8	4
	5%	8%	8%	7%	10%	10%	10%	11%
MENU CHANGES/ADDITIONS (GENERAL)	7	14	9	26	2	5	4	3
	8%	10%	6%	8%	4%	7%	5%	8%
LIGHT/HEALTHY FOOD	3	10	8	17	3	4	6	1
	3%	7%	5%	5%	6%	6%	7%	3%
SEAFOOD/FISH	1	6	5	9	3	2	5	–
	1%	4%	3%	3%	6%	3%	6%	–
CHICKEN	1	4	2	8	–	1	–	1
	1%	3%	1%	2%	–	1%	–	3%
VEGETARIAN	–	4	3	4	–	3	–	3
	–	3%	2%	1%	–	4%	–	8%
UPGRADE SPECIALS/VALUE MEAL DEALS	1	2	3	5	1	–	1	–
	1%	1%	2%	2%	2%	–	1%	–
GRILLED/BROILED/BARBEQUE	2	2	–	5	–	–	–	–
	2%	1%	–	2%	–	–	–	–
PASTA	1	3	1	5	–	–	–	–
	1%	2%	1%	2%	–	–	–	–
DESSERTS	1	1	2	3	–	1	–	1
	1%	1%	1%	1%	–	1%	–	3%
SALADS	–	–	3	–	1	2	2	1
	–	–	2%	–	2%	3%	2%	3%
ETHNIC FOODS	–	2	1	3	–	–	–	–
	–	1%	1%	1%	–	–	–	–
WINE LIST	–	2	–	2	–	–	–	–
	–	1%	–	1%	–	–	–	–
OTHER	5	10	5	15	2	4	3	3
	5%	7%	3%	5%	4%	6%	4%	8%
DON'T KNOW	20	21	40	62	15	14	19	10
	22%	15%	26%	19%	29%	21%	23%	28%
NO CHANGES PLANNED	49	65	72	168	22	33	40	15
	53%	46%	48%	52%	42%	49%	48%	42%
Next year what deletions are you planning?								
TOTAL	92	142	151	326	52	67	83	36
	100%	100%	100%	100%	100%	100%	100%	100%
NO DELETIONS	18	43	33	78	10	18	18	10
	20%	30%	22%	24%	19%	27%	22%	28%
BEEF ITEMS	2	6	1	9	1	1	2	–
	2%	4%	1%	3%	2%	1%	2%	–

	Menu Theme			Check Size				Check Size				
Ameri-can	Inter-natnal	Steak/Seafood	Other	<$8	$8–$14	$15–$24	25+	<$10	$10–$19	$20+	$20–$29	$30+
4	3	3	2	1	6	3	3	3	7	3	1	2
3%	4%	4%	1%	1%	4%	4%	3%	2%	4%	2%	2%	3%
1	1	–	1	–	3	–	–	1	2	–	–	–
1%	1%	–	1%	–	2%	–	–	1%	1%	–	–	–
129	84	72	160	84	165	82	96	139	166	122	47	75
100%	100%	100%	100%	100%	100%	100%	100%	100%	100%	100%	100%	100%
7	5	5	18	7	10	5	10	13	8	11	3	8
5%	6%	7%	11%	8%	6%	6%	10%	9%	5%	9%	6%	11%
9	4	7	13	4	15	6	7	8	15	9	3	6
7%	5%	10%	8%	5%	9%	7%	7%	6%	9%	7%	6%	8%
9	4	4	8	2	11	6	5	3	14	7	3	4
7%	5%	6%	5%	2%	7%	7%	5%	2%	8%	6%	6%	5%
5	1	2	6	1	7	5	–	2	11	–	–	–
4%	1%	3%	4%	1%	4%	6%	–	1%	7%	–	–	–
6	–	2	1	–	4	4	1	1	5	3	3	–
5%	–	3%	1%	–	2%	5%	1%	1%	3%	2%	6%	–
2	–	3	2	–	4	1	2	1	4	2	–	2
2%	–	4%	1%	–	2%	1%	2%	1%	2%	2%	–	3%
1	1	1	3	–	3	2	1	1	3	2	1	1
1%	1%	1%	2%	–	2%	2%	1%	1%	2%	2%	2%	1%
3	1	1	–	1	2	1	–	3	1	–	–	–
2%	1%	1%	–	1%	1%	1%	–	2%	1%	–	–	–
3	–	2	–	–	2	2	1	2	–	3	3	–
2%	–	3%	–	–	1%	2%	1%	1%	–	2%	6%	–
2	–	1	1	–	2	1	–	1	1	1	1	–
2%	–	1%	1%	–	1%	1%	–	1%	1%	1%	2%	–
2	1	–	–	1	1	–	–	2	–	–	–	–
2%	1%	–	–	1%	1%	–	–	1%	–	–	–	–
–	–	–	3	2	–	–	1	2	–	1	–	1
–	–	–	2%	2%	–	–	1%	1%	–	1%	–	1%
–	1	–	1	–	1	–	1	–	1	1	1	–
–	1%	–	1%	–	1%	–	1%	–	1%	1%	2%	–
8	5	2	6	6	7	6	–	10	7	2	2	–
6%	6%	3%	4%	7%	4%	7%	–	7%	4%	2%	4%	–
27	20	12	33	19	33	12	23	33	27	27	8	19
21%	24%	17%	21%	23%	20%	15%	24%	24%	16%	22%	17%	25%
56	47	37	81	45	75	41	53	65	84	65	24	41
43%	56%	51%	51%	54%	45%	50%	55%	47%	51%	53%	51%	55%
129	84	72	160	84	165	82	96	139	166	122	47	75
100%	100%	100%	100%	100%	100%	100%	100%	100%	100%	100%	100%	100%
34	14	18	41	18	37	24	20	38	35	26	10	16
26%	17%	25%	26%	21%	22%	29%	21%	27%	21%	21%	21%	21%
1	1	3	6	4	4	1	2	5	4	2	–	2
1%	1%	4%	4%	5%	2%	1%	2%	4%	2%	2%	–	3%

FIGURE 1-5. *(Continued)*

	Sales Volume			Number of Establishments				
	$500K	$500K–$999K	$1000K+	1	2	3+	2–4	5+
Next year what deletions are you planning?								
FRIED FOODS	1	2	1	3	1	–	1	–
	1%	1%	1%	1%	2%	–	1%	–
SLOW MOVING ITEMS	–	2	–	3	–	–	–	–
	–	1%	–	1%	–	–	–	–
STREAMLINING (GENERAL)	1	1	1	2	1	–	1	–
	1%	1%	1%	1%	2%	–	1%	–
HIGH FAT FOODS/ADDITIVES/ NON–HEALTHY FOODS	–	1	1	1	1	1	1	1
	–	1%	1%	–	2%	1%	1%	3%
MEXICAN FOODS	1	–	1	1	–	1	–	1
	1%	–	1%	–	–	1%	–	3%
FISH/SEAFOOD	–	1	1	1	–	1	–	1
	–	1%	1%	–	–	1%	–	3%
OTHER	2	3	5	7	2	1	3	–
	2%	2%	3%	2%	4%	1%	4%	–
DON'T KNOW	–	3	3	6	2	–	2	–
	–	2%	2%	2%	4%	–	2%	–

successful independent restaurateurs as well as chains have made careers developing trends. They have already started the next trend as soon as the rest of the industry is following their lead.

CONCLUSION

Know your trade area, your customers, their lifestyles, income, ethnic origins, occupations—all about them. Fit the menu selections and price specifically to your customer. Ride the trends. Successful restaurateurs do this all the time. You should, too. It's just that simple.

QUESTIONS

1. In your own words, define the term *demographics* and relate this to proper menu planning.
2. Discuss the difference between a *demographic study* and a *feasibility study*. Tell what information from each would be useful in developing a menu.
3. Using the demographic study in Figure 1-2, tell what type of restaurant would most likely be successful in that area and write a menu for that restaurant.

Menu Theme				Check Size				Check Size				
American	Inter-natnal	Steak/Seafood	Other	<$8	$8–$14	$15–$24	25+	<$10	$10–$19	$20+	$20–$29	$30+
2	–	2	–	–	4	–	–	–	4	–	–	–
2%	–	3%	–	–	2%	–	–	–	2%	–	–	–
2	–	–	1	1	2	–	–	1	2	–	–	–
2%	–	–	1%	1%	1%	–	–	1%	1%	–	–	–
–	1	–	2	1	1	–	1	1	1	1	–	1
–	1%	–	1%	1%	1%	–	1%	1%	1%	1%	–	1%
2	–	–	1	–	2	–	1	–	2	1	1	–
2%	–	–	1%	–	1%	–	1%	–	1%	1%	2%	–
1	–	1	–	–	1	1	–	–	2	–	–	–
1%	–	1%	–	–	1%	1%	–	–	1%	–	–	–
–	1	1	–	–	1	–	–	–	1	–	–	–
–	1%	1%	–	–	1%	–	–	–	1%	–	–	–
3	1	2	4	1	5	3	1	2	5	3	3	–
2%	1%	3%	3%	1%	3%	4%	1%	1%	3%	2%	6%	–
4	1	1	2	2	3	2	1	2	3	3	3	–
3%	1%	1%	1%	2%	2%	2%	1%	1%	2%	2%	6%	–

4. Research one square mile in your area. List the number and type of restaurants. Describe the type of restaurant you feel would be successful with the competition you have plotted. Determine who will be your customer and develop a menu to meet your customer's preferences.

5. Using a typical coffee shop menu in your area, create a children's menu that is nutritious and yet at the same time will appeal to children.

6. Discuss the difference between *fads* and *trends*. What new concepts, themes, or specific menu items have been developed in your area? Are they fads or trends? Defend your answer.

7. Which is more important to the menu planner, income or disposable income? Why?

Know Your Restaurant

OBJECTIVES
- To recognize what considerations need to be made when changing the menu in an existing operation.
- To understand the importance of product availability, selling price, equipment availability, station capacities, flow, skill level, and theme when making menu changes.
- To learn how the new operation interrelates with and is totally dependent on the menu.

IMPORTANT TERMS

Product availability	Equipment availability
Station capabilities	Skill level
Product flow	

INTRODUCTION

Before attempting to write a menu or add new items to the present menu, the menu writer must fully understand the capabilities and limits of the restaurant involved. The same holds true for a new operation in the planning stage. Everything starts with the menu. The layout, design, decor, theme, equipment, and staffing will all depend, in general, on the menu and, specifically, on the items selected for that menu. As previously discussed, the menu should reflect the needs of the potential customers as outlined by the demographics portion of the feasibility study. In order to further discuss restaurant capabilities, it is necessary to approach the problem from two different points of view:

1. The existing restaurant that is in need of menu change; and
2. the new restaurant which is in the planning stage.

THE EXISTING OPERATION

Several factors need to be taken into consideration when contemplating menu changes in an existing operation. They are product availability, selling price, equipment availability, physical capabilities of the station, traffic and product flow, staff skills, and the theme of the restaurant.

Product Availability

The first factor, product availability, is often overlooked by menu planners. How many times have you seen "available in season only" listed after a menu item? All of the ingredients necessary to produce the new menu item should be available on a year-round basis from a local source. If the new listing has an anticipated sales volume that could be considered extraordinary, assurances should be sought from the purveyor that they will be able to supply the demand. Nothing is more embarrassing than to "roll out" a new menu listing with much hoopla and advertising only to tell the customer, "I'm sorry we're out of it."

Selling Price

While the menu planner is checking the availability of the ingredients, the cost of these items should also be determined. As will be learned in a subsequent chapter, the food cost of a menu item is important when deciding what the selling price of that particular item should be. At this point, care must be exercised that the listing can be sold at a price which is compatible with the price range of the present menu as well as within the range of what the customer is willing to pay.

Equipment Availability

The third factor, equipment availability, requires the menu writer to ascertain that the necessary equipment is on hand to produce the proposed item. This encompasses the whole kitchen. The storage area—including refrigerator, freezer and dry storage—needs to be checked to see if there is sufficient capacity to handle the ingredients that the new menu item will require. The production area needs to be evaluated in terms of the particular piece or pieces of equipment needed to produce the new listing. If this is not carried out thoroughly and accurately, the results could be disastrous.

A Case in Point. A restaurant decided to add some Mexican entrees to its menu to capture a share of the popular Mexican food trade. This decision was made in order to stem the flow of customers to several trendy new spots. The restaurant in question was basically a saloon and short order operation, its revenue coming mostly from drinks. Two pieces of equipment were lacking to produce these items, a steam table to hold the burrito and taco fillings and a cheese melter to finish off the products. To solve the problem, items were put into a microwave. The result was a product that was inferior to the competition, resulting in lost sales and product credibility.

Too often, menus are indiscriminately changed with consideration given only to sales. Certainly sales are important, but if the product cannot be properly presented, the theory reverses itself and sales are the ultimate loser.

Physical Capabilities

The next factor to consider, physical capability, is closely related to equipment availability. However, in this case, we assume that we have the proper equipment and, consequently, now must consider the equipment's capacity to produce this product. This factor raises two points.

First, can the equipment itself handle the increased demand? Second, can the station handle the increased volume? Every piece of equipment in your kitchen has its maximum production capabilities. These are stated in the manufacturer's specification books. Most often these capabilities are stated under *optimum conditions.* (To expect more out of your equipment would be foolhardy.) To ascertain if a particular piece of equipment in your operation can handle an increase in production, take its usage at the peak hours in your operation and subtract this from the manufacturer's

MENU CHANGE FORMAT
EXISTING RESTAURANT

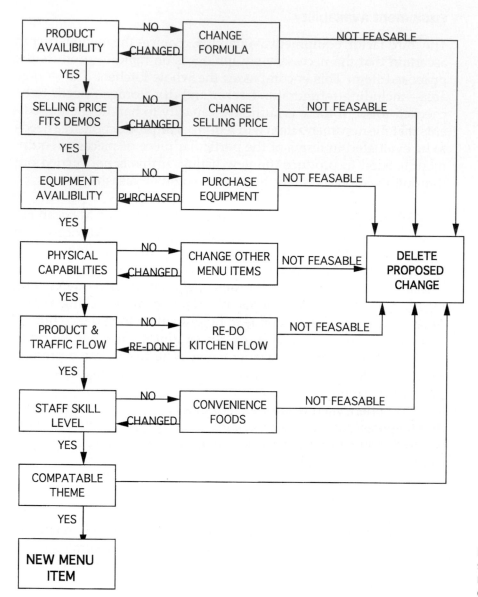

FIGURE 2-1. A model showing the steps that should be taken in determining if a new item should be placed on an existing menu.

maximum production capabilities. Compare this result with the anticipated sales of the new menu item to see if it can be adequately prepared. For example, say that the manufacturer's stated capacity for a griddle was 1,200 six-inch pancakes per hour, your peak sales at breakfast were 300, and you want to add French toast with an estimated sales of 150 pieces per hour. Do the math and you'll find that your griddle could adequately handle this additional production. Investing the time and research early in the

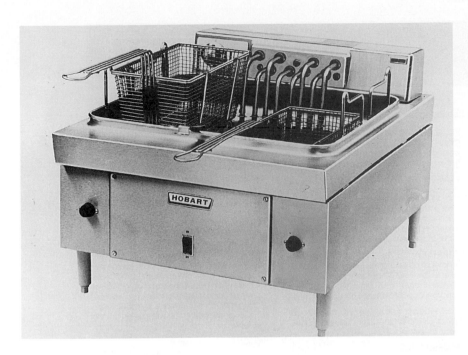

FIGURE 2-2. The capacities for this particular fryer are listed on the accompanying illustration. (*Photograph courtesy of the Hobart Corp. Troy, Ohio*)

planning process will ensure the successful introduction of a new menu item and will avoid a long wait by dissatisfied customers as the result of a new menu item added haphazardly.

The second factor to consider under physical capabilities is the station's capacity to handle a new menu item. A station in a kitchen is the same thing as a work center. It is an area where a group of closely related tasks are performed. These are normally performed by one person, but in rare instances of extremely high volume could be performed by several people. Examples of stations on a production line could include a sauté, fry, broil, or grill station. There are two things to be considered when evaluating a station to see if a new listing can be added to the menu. One is the station's capacity, which is similar to our previous discussion on equipment, only here we are talking about several pieces of equipment. The second consideration is the ability of the person working the station to keep up with the demand factor.

We are not discussing skill level here (that will be dealt with later), but rather the physical limitations of the people involved. If you have ever worked at a restaurant—either in service or production—you have probably observed a particular station being "swamped" at peak hours. This is caused by either the improper selection of employees, poor training, or an improperly written menu. More often than not it is the latter. Why this condition exists is puzzling since the solution is so simple: Change the menu to reflect the production capabilities of the physical plant.

For example, an Italian restaurant which had been in existence for over 50 years in a downtown location decided to open a second

CK20-CK201 ELECTRIC FRYER

HOBART
FOOD EQUIPMENT

SPECIFICATIONS: Listed by Underwriters Laboratories Inc and by National Sanitation Foundation.

GENERAL: Freestanding electric fryer holds up to 28 lbs. of shortening.

CONSTRUCTION: Stainless steel cabinet and support head. Mounts on 4″ plastic legs (furnished). Optional 4″ stainless steel legs are available. Accommodates accessory shortening removal and straining device; furnished with two standard fry baskets. Enclosed tubular stainless steel heating elements which swing up and burn clean in the raised position. Shortening container is equipped with easy-grip, lift-out handles; scored to indicate level of fat-fill.

CONTROLS: "Power On" switch ties in with signal light on heating unit support head. A separate signal adjacent to the "Power On" signal light, cycles with the thermostat, indicates when fryer is heating and when preset temperature is reached. Preheats to 350°F in 6-7 minutes. Temperature range: 200-400°F. QUAD-GUARD control protection features two contactors and two thermostats to provide reliable interruption of power to heating elements to prevent overheating. Extra fuses protect thermostat circuit. Temperature-limiting thermostat is reset manually by raising heating units and pressing exposed reset lever. Standard internal POWER TURNOFF (optional on CK201) connect fryer (via terminal block located behind ⁷/₈″ diameter knockout) to hood fire-extinguishing system circuit.

ELECTRICAL TIMERS: CK201 has two integral push button timers with automatic reset and adjustments from 0-15 minutes. Each timer activates one basket lowering and lifting mechanism for automatic, simultaneous frying of identical or different products requiring the same or different processing times.

CAPACITY: 28 lbs. of shortening in a removable container (one furnished). Produces up to 61 lbs. or 313 two-ounce servings of raw-to-done French fried potatoes or 600 two-ounce servings of blanched potatoes per hour.

ELECTRICAL: 12KW (3 phase models); 9.8 KW (1-phase CK20). See "Electrical Data" block for phase loading.

ACCESSORIES:

BASKETS
Full size fry basket, standard mesh **(CK20).**
Extra pair standard twin size fry baskets.
Twin fry baskets, fine mesh.
Triple fry basket, fine mesh **(CK20).**

(Left) One twin basket, standard mesh.
(Right) One twin basket, standard mesh.

LEGS
Set of four 4″ adust. stainless steel.
Set of four 4″ adjust. plastic.

OTHER
Miraclean siphon w/filter bag.
Miraclean w/extra long arm f/use w/cutting board.
Extra filter bags (set of 6).
Extra fat container.
Cover **(CK20).**

For fryers **without** TOUCHTIME® basket lifts:
Step-down transformer from a 480-volt, 240-volt or 208-volt supply source to 120-volt power for the control circuit of fryers **without** TOUCHTIME® lifts where a four-wire supply source or separate 120-volt power are not available.

WEIGHT: (Approximate)

	Shipping	Net
CK20	75 lbs.	60 lbs.
CK201	108 lbs.	88 lbs.

As continued product improvement is a policy of Hobart, specifications are subject to change without notice.

FRYING GUIDE

FOOD	TEMP. SET-TING °F	TIME (IN MIN.)	CAPACITY/LOAD 1-PHASE	CAPACITY/LOAD 3-PHASE
French-Fried Potatoes ³/₈″ strips one-temperature method	375	6-9	5.4 lbs.	6.1 lbs.
Two-temperature method blanch	325	4-6	4.62 lbs.	5.25 lbs.
brown	375	2-3	7.94 lbs.	9.02 lbs.
Potato chips, thin slices	350	3-4	1.70 lbs.	1.94 lbs.
Fish Fillets, 5″ x ½″	365	3-4	7.7 lbs.	8.8 lbs.
Shrimp	375	2-3	4.9 lbs.	5.58 lbs.
Oysters and Clams	395	2-3	3.3 lbs.	3.7 lbs.
Chicken, 2-lbs. size quartered (8-oz. serving)	325	12-13	6 portions*	7 portions*
halved (1-lb. serving)	325	12-16	6 portions*	7 portions*
Croquettes	365	3-4	7.7 lbs.	8.8 lbs.
Fritters, fruit, vegetable or meat 2½″ dia.	375	4-5	26*	30*
Doughnuts, 2½″ dia.	375	2-3	26*	30*
French Toast, 4″ x 4″ slices	325	2-3	10*	12*
Turnovers, fruit, vegetable or meat 4″ x 2½″	375	3-4	16*	18*

*Capacities given are limited by energy available to maintain continuous frying temperature, except those marked with an asterisk(*) in which case capacity is limited by surface of the item in preparation.

FIGURE 2-3. A typical equipment specification cut sheet showing the capacities of a Hobart CK 20 Fryer. (*Courtesy of the Hobart Corp. Troy, Ohio*)

operation in suburbia. The new restaurant used the same menu as the original. Due to a different demographic area, there was a substantial increase in sauté items. The sauté station, consisting of one eight-burner range and one sauté cook, could not adequately handle the orders during peak periods resulting in as much as a 45-minute delay for the customer. This further complicated the logistics of the waitresses trying to obtain orders from other stations.

This scenario is identical to adding new items in an existing restaurant where no forethought is given to overloading a station. The solution to the problem was simple: eliminate several sauté items and replace them with broiled and roasted items, thus giving the production area a smoother flow. This resulted in excellent timing and well-served, satisfied customers. The physical capability of stations is probably the most overlooked and violated principle when new listings are added to the menu. Unfortunately, when this happens the intent is reversed: Instead of increasing sales, sales are lost.

Product and Traffic Flow

The third factor to be considered, product and traffic flow, involves consideration of new menu items in relation to existing flows within the restaurant. A well-designed restaurant will have both people and products moving in such a way that there is no cross traffic and no backtracking. The menu writer needs to analyze each potentially new menu item to see if there will be a flow change resulting from such an addition.

For example, a fast food restaurant decided to add lemonade and limeade to its beverage selection in order to increase sales. It was further decided that a Jet Spray would be used to properly merchandise these drinks. The only available counter space was at the end of the line some eight feet away from the current beverage station. The result was that the beverage attendant had to cross two direct traffic lines twice to obtain these drinks, resulting in confusion to the staff and undue delays to the customer. Proper foresight on the part of the manager could have avoided this disorder. Conversely, if a restaurant were to have a poor traffic and product flow it is entirely possible that an astute person could correct this problem via one or several menu changes.

Staff Skill Level

The skill of the staff, both the kitchen and service personnel, is another factor to consider when contemplating new menu items. Most often this problem arises when the restaurant is attempting to upgrade itself. Care must be exercised. Not only must the staff skill levels be taken into account, but consideration must also be given to the demographics of the area and a determination made as to whether or not the customer will accept such upgrading. If this is the case, then analysis of the present staff in terms of ability must be carried out.

Production staff skills can be expressed in three levels, with the first level being a line cook who has the ability to cook an item to order and plate it according to the restaurant's specifications and standards. The second level is the prep cook who has the ability to follow structured and tested recipes. The third level would be an American Culinary Federation Certified Executive Chef who has the ability to create recipes as well as the expertise to carry out more complicated recipes. The menu planner must exercise care so as not to exceed the skill of the kitchen staff.

Likewise, the skill levels of the service personnel must be taken into consideration. There are four basic styles of service used in this country: self-service, American, Russian, and French. *Self-service*, predominant in fast food operations, requires the customer to place and pick up the order himself. In *American* or *table service*, an order is prepared and plated in the kitchen and delivered to the customer. This style of service is more predominant in coffee shops and theme restaurants. With *Russian service*, the order is prepared in the kitchen and plated at the table. *French service* carries the process one step further. The order is semi-prepared in the kitchen, but finished and plated at the table. The last two styles are normally reserved for fine dining establishments, however, many Oriental restaurants use a variation of Russian service. In adding new items to a menu, the safest rule to follow is to stay within the bounds of the style which you are presently using. If it is deemed necessary to upgrade an operation in terms of menu offerings, then the decision must be made as to whether or not the production and service staff can be trained to handle such upgrading.

Theme

The last factor to consider in an existing operation is the theme of the restaurant. This theme needs to be taken into consideration before a menu change should be put into effect. Care must be taken by the menu writer that the new items are compatible with the theme as well as the decor. All too often, restaurants destroy their image by veering away from their original intent by creating incompatible items. Quite often the intention is to create a new market but results in a "being all things to all people" type of mentality that destroys the originality that made the restaurant unique.

All of these factors—product availability, selling price, equipment, physical capabilities, flow, staff, and theme—need to be considered before a new item is added to the menu. For example, a seafood restaurant manager would be wise to totally explore the addition of beef to the menu. First, since it is an entirely new product, the equipment would have to be analyzed to determine if it is the right type to handle beef adequately. Could the station chosen to handle this item prepare a product of a different nature? Is the staff skilled enough or could they be trained to prepare a beef item, and could beef be fit into the decor and theme of the restaurant without destroying its ambience?

An excellent way to answer these questions would be to do a "walk through." That is, take the item, and "walk" the new item through purchasing, storage, production, and service. Will this item fit into the already established parameters of the restaurant? Finally, will the market expand because of this item or will the existing customers resent the addition, with the feeling that this is no longer a specialty restaurant? Is the quality of seafood lowered because of the addition? Even if the item satisfies all these factors, your evaluation is not complete. Cost and selling price must be figured and a determination made as to whether the potential selling price is compatible with the market. The next two chapters will explore these facets of menu development.

THE NEW RESTAURANT

To create a menu for an entirely new restaurant is quite different from revising an existing menu. In the new operation, the menu becomes a planning tool. The old adage "everything starts with the menu" for the most part holds true here. However, one important process takes place before the menu is planned—namely, the feasibility study. The demographics section of the feasibility study will dictate to a large degree the type of menu written and, consequently, the type of restaurant to be opened. We would be quite remiss if we were to open a fine French restaurant in a blue-collar factory neighborhood.

Once the style of restaurant is determined, the menu can then be planned. From the menu the theme and decor can be determined, the equipment selected, and the staff hired.

Theme

Theme, decor, and menu go hand in hand. When planning the menu, the items selected should match the chosen theme. The descriptive terminology should reinforce and elaborate on the theme and decor. For example, a restaurant that sports an Old English Tudor style of architecture with a dark, heavy wood and stucco interior would support a menu of beef, lamb, and North Atlantic fish. Descriptive terminology would contain key and familiar English phrases. The menu would probably be on a parchment style paper with an Old English style of type. All of these factors will be discussed in subsequent chapters in detail, but at this stage it is important to recognize the relationship between the menu and the restaurant's theme.

With the menu selected, based on demographics and in conjunction with the theme and decor, the next step is to select the proper equipment to produce the menu. While the entire subject of equipment

FIGURE 2-4. This menu and accompanying photographs illustrate how theme, decor, and menu go hand in hand. (*Menu and photographs courtesy of The Colonial Williamsburg Foundation, Williamsburg, Virginia*)

FIGURE 2-4. (*Continued*)

Chowning's
TAVERN

Inn keep-er

Evening Fare
Good FOOD
to Satisfy Hearty
APPETITES

APPETIZERS	Sliced Fresh MELON with *Smithfield* HAM 2.95	Crock of *Cheddar* CHEESE with SIPPETS 4.50	Potato and Leek SOUP 1.75

Josiah Chowning's Brunswick STEW DINNER

Potato and Leek SOUP, *Josiah Chowning's* Brunswick STEW (made from Young FOWL and Garden VEGETABLES, seasoned to Taste and served up Hot), Garden GREENS with Choice of DRESSING, *Chowning's* Good BREAD, BEVERAGE, and a Pecan TART with Vanilla ICE CREAM
17.25

Suggested wine: Bin No. 40 or No. 91

Hen

Chowning's Chesapeake DINNER

Potato and Leek SOUP, Garden GREENS with Chutney DRESSING, Sautéed Backfin CRAB-MEAT and HAM (a Slice of *Smithfield* HAM complemented with *Chesapeake* Backfin CRABMEAT, topped with BUTTER, and laced with SHERRY), VEGETABLE of the Day, Baked POTATO, *Chowning's* Good BREAD, BEVERAGE, and Buttered Apple PIE with *Cheddar* CHEESE
23.95

Suggested wine: Bin No. 93 or No. 71

Josiah Chowning's SPECIALTIES

PRIME RIB

Roast PRIME RIB of BEEF (cut to your Liking Rare, Medium, Well Done), HORSERADISH, Baked POTATO, and VEGETABLE of the Day
20.75

Served with *Smithfield* HAM   21.75
Suggested wine: Bin No. 84 or No. 42

Cow

Barbecued RIBS

Broiled Pork Back RIBS braised in a Barbecue SAUCE served with a Baked POTATO and Garden VEGETABLE
18.25

Suggested wine: Bin No. 197

Pig

Chowning's SPECIAL of the Day
Market Price

Mr. *Chowning's* Favorite DISH

Fillet of Chicken BREAST stuffed with Fresh CRABMEAT and CHEESE. This Delicious BIRD is topped with a White Wine SAUCE and served with a Baked POTATO and Garden VEGETABLE
19.95

Suggested wine: Bin No. 194

Duck

Roast DUCK with Orange SAUCE

Served over Blended Wild RICE with a Garden VEGETABLE
17.95

Suggested wine: Bin No. 40 or No. 88

All selections are served with *Chowning's* Garden GREENS and Good BREAD.

DESSERTS

Please ask your Server for our Complete MENU of Homemade DESSERTS.

BEVERAGES

Sparkling APPLE CIDER	1.50	Iced TEA	.95
APPLE CIDER	.95	ORANGEADE	.95
Hot COFFEE or Hot TEA	1.25	MILK	.95
MINERAL WATER	1.50	Carbonated BEVERAGES	.95
LEMONADE	.95	Root BEER	1.50

Cup and Saucer.

Please, NO SMOKING inside the Tavern.

Several popular tavern foods are available at M. DuBois Grocer's Shop on Duke of Gloucester Street and at EVERYTHING *Williamsburg* on Prince George Street. A complete selection of tavern china and other accessories can be found at Craft House adjacent to the Williamsburg Inn and at Craft House at Merchants Square. Recipes for many tavern foods can be found in *The Williamsburg Cookbook* and *Favorite Meals from Williamsburg*. These cookbooks may be purchased at M. DuBois Grocer's Shop, Craft House, EVERYTHING *Williamsburg*, and other Colonial Williamsburg stores.

FIGURE 2-4. *(Continued)*

Williamsburg, *October* 10, 1766

"I HEREBY acquaint the publick that I have opened tavern . . . where all who please to favour me with their custom may depend upon the best of entertainment for themselves, servants, and horses, and good pasturage.

JOSIAH CHOWNING"

THE "publick" that frequented Chowning's Tavern on Market Square were mostly local residents—farmers who sold produce at the market, those with business at the Courthouse, and idle bystanders with time to kill. Some were shoppers at the market or in the uptown stores, craftsmen who repaired weapons or delivered supplies to the Powder Magazine, and militiamen who mustered on Market Square green. Occasionally a traveler dropped in.

In size, clientele, and services Chowning's bore more resemblance to rural Virginia taverns located at ferries, crossroads, and courthouses or to small English alehouses than to the larger taverns nearer the Capitol. Despite Chowning's boast of the "best of entertainment," the selection of food and drink at his tavern was limited. Most customers drank rum, local beer, or cider, although Josiah also stocked a little wine and brandy and provided bowls of punch on demand. His customers were content with the plain fare that he set before them. The few travelers who patronized this establishment probably lodged together in one room upstairs.

Little is known about Josiah Chowning and his family. In many modest Virginia taverns like Chowning's the tavern keeper and his wife and children lived on the premises so they could help with the work of waiting on customers, cooking, cleaning, and laundering.

Tavern keeping was often a precarious trade for small operators like Chowning who rented a tavern; Chowning's business here lasted only two years. After his death in 1772, some land that Chowning owned and one of his slaves were sold at an auction held in front of the Courthouse—within sight of his former tavern.

Modern-day travelers and locals alike gather informally at Chowning's Tavern for hearty food and drink just as their counterparts did two hundred years ago.

Chairs, benches, and tables represent the sturdy, country-made furniture found in colonial taverns catering to the middling sort. Excavated fragments show that the yellow rooster on the dinnerware was one of several colorful bird motifs that appeared on the tablewares used by eighteenth-century Williamsburg residents. Iron candlesticks, called "hogscrapers" because some early Americans used the base to scrape hair from hogs, are listed in inventories of several colonial Virginia taverns. Other accessories—utilitarian salt and pepper shakers and sugar casters made of stoneware, plain tin sconces, simply framed maps and prints—further accentuate the informality of Josiah Chowning's Tavern.

All income from Chowning's Tavern is used for the purposes of The Colonial Williamsburg Foundation, which operates the Historic Area of Williamsburg, and to carry forward its educational programs.

Colonial Williamsburg also welcomes tax-deductible contributions. Friends interested in discussing gifts to the Foundation are asked to write the President, The Colonial Williamsburg Foundation, Williamsburg, Virginia 23187.

The print reproduced on the cover, "DOCTOR SYNTAX in the Middle of a smoking hot Political squabble, wishes to Whet his Whistle," was drawn by Thomas Rowlandson and was published in London by Thomas Tegg sometime between 1807 to 1821. Courtesy, Library of Congress.

The illustrations used inside the menu are reproduced from catchpenny prints, popular eighteenth-century English engravings.

FIGURE 2-4. *(Continued)*

FIGURE 2-4. *(Continued)*

selection and layout is not within the scope of this text, it is important that it be mentioned as an integral part of menu planning.

Equipment

What equipment to purchase involves determining the actual pieces needed. To do this, an item-by-item review of the menu is necessary as well as the development of a list of equipment needed to produce each item. For example, to produce a hamburger, you would need the following pieces of equipment:

Refrigeration—To store the hamburger patties, garnishes, and condiments.

Dry storage

Griddle or broiler—To cook the hamburger (Note: A decision must be made here as to the style of cookery)

Plate lowerator or plate shelf

Refrigerated makeup table

Pickup station with heat lamp

Wait station

Dishwasher

Each item on the menu should be gone through in this fashion until a complete list is developed for the entire menu.

The second step is to develop the size and number of pieces needed to produce the menu. There are three factors to be considered here:

1. The number of times a piece of equipment is used to produce an item. A broiler, for example, might be used to produce several items on the menu.

2. The capacity of the dining room in terms of the number of seats.

Schedule for Equipment in Use

Equipment	6:00	7:00	8:00	9:00	10:00	11:00	12:00	1:00	2:00	3:00	4:00
Deck Oven 1		XXXX	XXXX	XXXX	XXXX		XXXX	XXXX	XXXX	XXXX	
Deck Oven 2			XXXX	XXXX	XXXX	XXXX					
Range—O.B.	XXXX	XXXX	XXXX	XXXX	XXXX				XXXX	XXXX	XXXX
Flattop	XXXX	XXXX	XXXX	XXXX	XXXX	XXXX	XXXX	XXXX	XXXX		
30 Gal Steam Kettle	XXXX	XXXX	XXXX	XXXX			XXXX		XXXX	XXXX	XXXX
10 Gal Steam Kettle					XXXX	XXXX	XXXX	XXXX			
Tiltskillet		XXXX	XXXX	XXXX	XXXX				XXXX	XXXX	XXXX
Oven—Steamer		XXX			XXXX	XXXX	XXXX				XXXX
Steamer						XXXX	XXXX				XXXX

FIGURE 2-5. A chart showing the schedule of equipment in use during various parts of the day. Any additional menu items would have to fit in with this schedule.

3. The projected sales mix of the proposed menu. When this information is assembled, the capacities for the various pieces of equipment then can be determined by estimating the number of each item to be sold.

The third step would involve the layout of all of the equipment deemed necessary to produce the menu. The two most important factors of layout are product flow and traffic flow. Product flow encompasses all foodstuffs necessary to produce the menu from their raw state to finished product and the path they take through the restaurant. Traffic flow concerns itself with the people factor and their patterns of movement with the product. The key elements to product and traffic flow are no backtracking and no crossovers. To develop good flows in your restaurant, start with the receiving function of raw products and trace them through the entire operation to the point of customer service and on to the warewashing function. Next, take the employee functions and trace their movement through the restaurant. Chances are, if you have a smooth product flow, you will have a good traffic flow. However, this is not always true; so check it to make sure. Mistakes made at this point of the planning stage could last the life of the restaurant. Several hours of careful planning will help to avoid years of problems.

TYPICAL KITCHEN PRODUCT/TRAFFIC FLOW

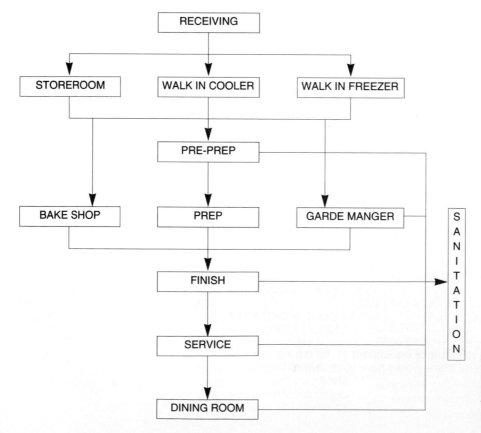

FIGURE 2-6. A chart showing the movement of product through a kitchen from receiving to service. Notice how crisscrossing and backtracking are virtually eliminated.

The type and amount of equipment as well as the proposed layout should all be done on scratch paper as numerous changes, additions, and deletions will be necessary prior to the final plan. As stated earlier, this is but a rough overview of what goes into the planning of a new restaurant. There are well-qualified consultants, many of whom are members of the Foodservice Consultants Society International (FCSI), to assist in this stage of development. One final word on equipment selection and layout: All decisions are based on the proposed menu. As the Scottish poet Robert Burns so aptly put it, "the best laid plans of mice and men oft times go astray." Check your plans to make sure that you have provided for some built-in flexibility. No matter how much research goes into planning a new restaurant, there is no assurance that the proposed menu will sell. Changes probably will have to be made on at least part of it. Allowances made on equipment selection for flexibility will offer the menu writer a wide latitude for changes. As previously discussed, any menu additions must be within the scope of equipment availability.

Staffing

The last factor to be considered is the staffing of the new operation. The menu must be an integral part in the development of job descriptions for the new operation. Review the proposed menu to determine the skill level needed to produce the items desired. These skill levels should then become a part of the job description. All too often a new restaurant hires an overqualified (and expensive) executive chef to produce a menu that a person with less skills could produce. Conversely, a worse scenario involves unqualified chefs

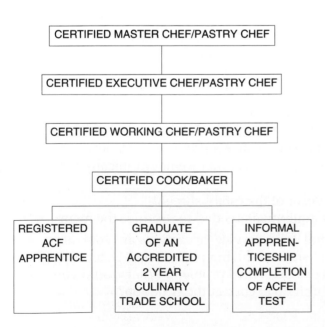

**CAREER LADDER
ACFEI CERTIFICATION**

FIGURE 2-7. A chart depicting the ACFEI certification process. (*Courtesy of the American Culinary Federation, St. Augustine, Florida.*)

hired to produce menus for which they are totally untrained. The result? Dissatisfied customers, lost sales, and bankruptcy. When the proposed skill level of a chef has been determined, use the various achievement levels of the American Culinary Federation to select an individual with the proper training to do a proficient job at the appropriate salary level.

CONCLUSION

Proper planning is an integral part of menu preparation. The more the person writing the menu knows about the operation involved, whether existing or new, the more the results of their efforts will be enhanced. Take all of these factors into consideration—equipment, physical capabilities, traffic flow, staff skills, and theme. They all play an important role in selecting a menu. By all means don't forget the discussion in chapter one—The Customer. It is for them that all of this is done. If you do all of this, the menu will reflect a smooth running, profitable operation. It's just that simple.

QUESTIONS

1. Define and explain the importance of the following terms in relation to writing a menu:
   a) product availability
   b) equipment capabilities
   c) station capabilities
   d) skill level
   e) product flow

2. Using the attached menu, list three new items you could add and:
   a) List all of the ingredients necessary to produce the items and determine if they are available in your locale.
   b) List all of the pieces of equipment necessary to produce these three items.
   c) Determine the skill level of production and service staff necessary to produce the items.
   d) Defend how those items fit into the theme of the operation.

3. Assuming the attached menu is a proposal for a new restaurant:
   a) Describe what type of customer demographically you could expect.
   b) Describe the decor of the establishment.
   c) List the major equipment needed to produce the menu.

4. Investigate several food service operations in your area. Are there "swamped" stations during peak times? Determine if it is a menu problem or a personnel problem. What would you as the manager of that unit do to correct the situation?

STARTERS

Wild Northwest Mushroom Soup
3.95

Seasonal Soup
3.25

Day Selected Oysters with a Peppered Huckleberry Mignonette
5.95

Penn Cove Mussels with Tomato & Herbs
6.95

SALADS

Dungeness Crab and Shrimp Salad with a Brie Dressing
Entrée 8.95   Starter 5.95

Warm Spinach Salad with a duo of Northwest Salmon
Entrée 9.95   Starter 6.95

Kasu Cod Club Salad
Entrée 7.95   Starter 6.95

Salad of Mixed Lettuces
Entrée 6.95   Starter 4.95

ENTREES

Seasonal Whitefish with an Aromatic Herb & Vegetable Purée
11.00

Dungeness Crabcakes with Roasted Vegetable Vinaigrette
12.50

Roasted Monkfish with a Sweet Garlic Confit of Onions & Cabbages
11.75

Grilled Breast of Chicken with a Ragoût of Black Beans
11.00

Sautéed Salmon with a Tomato Tarragon Coulis
12.50

Grilled Pork Sandwich on Sage Brioche
9.25

Grilled Beef Tenderloin with Gorgonzola Merlot Sauce
11.25

BEVERAGES

WHITE WINE

Franciscan "Cuvee Sauvage" Chardonnay, California 7.50
Gordon Brothers 1990 Chardonnay Washington 5.25
Chateau Ste. Michelle 1990 Johannisberg Riesling, Washington 4.00
Arbor Crest 1989 Sauvignon Blanc, Washington 4.50

RED WINE

Pinnacles 1989 Pinot Noir, California 6.50
Columbia Crest 1987 Cabernet Sauvignon, Washington 5.25
Franciscan 1988 Meritage, California 6.50

SPARKLING AND NON-ALCOHOLIC

Tagaris 1988 Blanc de Noir, Washington 5.00
Roederer Estate NV, Anderson Valley, California 6.50
Ariel Non-Alcoholic Blanc De Noir, California 4.00
Savoir Faite Sparkling Apple Cider 2.75

MINERAL WATER AND SELTZER

Evian or Perrier 2.50
Ty Nant 2.75
Koala Springs 2.35
Winterbrook Seltzer 2.35

NORTHWEST MICROBREWS

Pyramid Wheaten Ale, Kalama, WA 4.00
Pike Place Pale Ale, Seattle, WA 4.00

(*Menu courtesy of Fuller's Restaurant, Seattle Sheraton Hotel and Towers, Seattle, Washington.*)

CHAPTER THREE

Costs

OBJECTIVES
- To understand how to develop a cost card from a standardized recipe including conversion of invoice costs into recipe costs, extensions, totaling and portion costs.
- To differentiate between AP (as purchased) and EP (edible portion).
- To learn ingredient and cost conversions.
- To be able to cost a complete meal.
- To determine how to figure the cost of a salad bar or an "all you can eat" buffet.

IMPORTANT TERMS

Standardized recipe	Cost card
AP (as purchased)	EP (edible portion)
Conversions	Q factor.

INTRODUCTION

One of the most important functions of menu planning is charging the correct amount for items listed on the menu. Failure to do so will result in a selling price that is too high or too low. Either of these situations is bad for the restaurant. In order to determine the correct selling price, it is imperative that the exact costs are known because selling prices are figured, to a large extent, on food cost. This chapter will explore how to figure costs for standardized recipes, meats and shrinkage, beverages, sandwiches, complete meals, buffets, and salad bars. A word of caution is in order here. Ingredient costs vary from area to area and, in many cases, can change from day to day. Do not be concerned about the costs used in the examples as many of them will be obsolete by the time you read this. Rather, master the concepts. They do not change: Costs do.

STANDARDIZED RECIPES AND COST CARDS

To effect a solid control system in any restaurant, standardized recipes are a necessity. They control the quantity and quality of ingredients used to prepare a particular dish, as well as to control the portions that are to be served. They are also a necessary tool in figuring the costs. Simply having standardized recipes in an operation is not enough; it is also imperative that everyone follow them. Any deviation from the standardized recipe will result not only in poor quality but in inaccurate costs being figured for that item and, consequently, an incorrect selling price will be charged.

There are two methods used to write standardized recipes. They are *AP* which means "as purchased" and *EP* which stands for "edible portion." There is a large difference between the two methods which affects both the quality of the recipe and also the costs.

In the AP method, all ingredient quantities are listed on the standardized recipes in the form in which they are purchased. For example, if a recipe were to call for "10 pounds of onions, diced," the cook would weigh the onions with their skins on (as purchased), then peel the onions, dice them, and add them to the recipe. In costing the recipe, the invoice cost of 10 pounds of onions would be used.

In the EP method, all ingredient quantities are listed using the edible portion only of that particular ingredient. In the case of the recipe calling for 10 pounds of onions, the onions would be peeled, diced, then weighed, and added to the recipe. To obtain a cost in this instance, the original weight of the product would have to be used. Thus, if we started with 11 pounds of onions to obtain 10 pounds EP of diced, we would use the 11 pound figure to determine our costs.

In spite of the fact that the EP method is more time consuming when it comes to figuring costs, it is the preferred method. The reason for this is that it is more exact. If you gave several cooks an onion to peel, some would remove the skin only, and some would remove the skin along with one or two layers of the onion. Thus while everyone started out with the same amount, the yield in each case would be different.

To simplify matters, for those operations using the EP method, conversion charts are available to assist in determining the costs. These work well in most cases. However, if an operation uses an inordinate amount of a certain ingredient, yield tests should be conducted periodically to ascertain if the correct costs are being maintained.

FIGURE 3-1. AP-EP conversion chart. Weight of edible portion from one pound as purchased.

	lb		lb
Apples	0.78	Lettuce, head	0.76
Asparagus	0.53	Lettuce, leaf	0.66
Avocado	0.67	Lettuce, romaine	0.64
Bananas	0.65	Mangoes	0.69
Beans, green or wax	0.88	Mushrooms	0.98
Beans, lima	0.44	Nectarines	0.91
Beets	0.77	Okra	0.87
Blueberries	0.96	Onions, mature	0.88
Broccoli	0.81	Orange, sections	0.40
Brussels sprouts	0.76	Parsnips	0.83
Cabbage, green	0.87	Peaches	0.76
Cabbage, red	0.64	Pears, served pared	0.78
Cantaloupe, served		Peas, green	0.38
without rind	0.52	Peppers, green	0.80
Carrots	0.70	Pineapple	0.54
Cauliflower	0.62	Plums	0.94
Celery	0.83	Potatoes, sweet	0.80
Chard, Swiss	0.92	Potatoes, white	0.81
Cherries, pitted	0.87	Radishes, without tops	0.94
Chicory,	0.89	Rhubarb, without leaves	0.86
Collards, leaves	0.57	Rutabagas	0.85
Collards, leaves		Spinach, partly trimmed	0.88
and stems	0.74	Squash, acorn	0.87
Cranberries	0.95	Squash, butternut	0.84
Cucumber, pared	0.84	Squash, Hubbard	0.64
Eggplant	0.81	Squash, summer	0.95
Endive, escarole	0.78	Squash, zucchini	0.94
Grapefruit, sections	0.52	Strawberries	0.88
Grapes, seedless	0.97	Tomatoes	0.99
Honedew melon,		Turnips, without tops	0.79
served without rind	0.46	Watermelon	0.57
Kale	0.67		

Adapted from Food Buying, Guide for School Food Service, U.S. Dept. Agriculture, Washington, D.C., 1980.

Divide the weight of EP in the recipe by the factor given above. For example: if the recipe calls for 15 pounds EP of head lettuce, 15 pounds EP ÷ .76 = 19.7 or 20 pounds to purchase.

To figure costs based on a standardized recipe, it is advisable that a cost card be used. To make the entire cost control system effective, there should be a cost card for every multiple ingredient item listed on the menu. The object of cost cards is to get an accurate cost per portion so that the proper selling price can be determined.

To figure standardized costs, follow these steps:

1. Copy the ingredients used for a particular dish from the standardized recipe to the cost card.

FIGURE 3-2. Portion cost card.

NAME OF RECIPE_____ REFERENCE_____

DATE_____ NUMBER OF PORTIONS_____ COST PER PORTION_____

RECIPE		INGREDIENTS	INVOICE		RECIPE		EXTENSION	
			COST	UNIT	COST	UNIT		
						TOTAL		

2. List the amount and unit used for each ingredient in the appropriate column.

3. From an invoice, list the cost of that ingredient as well as the unit that that cost represents.

4. If the recipe is AP, break the invoice unit down to the unit for the recipe in the recipe column and figure the cost per recipe unit. If the recipe is written EP, use the cost after trim.

5. In the last column, figure the extended cost by multiplying the number of units needed for the recipe times the cost per unit.

6. Add together the cost of all ingredients in the extension column.

7. Divide the total cost by the number of portions the recipe will produce to get the cost per portion.

While this may seem complicated and confusing at first glance, it is, in reality, quite simple. For example, developing a cost card for Salad Del Monte would be as shown in Figures 3-3 and 3-4.

Salad Del Monte

YIELD: 50 portions	EACH PORTION: 3 oz. asparagus	
Ingredients	*Quantity*	*Method*
Asparagus, cooked, drained, chilled Lettuce, washed and trimmed Pimentoes	10 lb. 4 heads 7 oz.	1. Arrange asparagus on crisp lettuce or lettuce cups. 2. Decorate with thin strips of pimento placed diagonally across asparagus.
Hard Cooked Eggs, chopped Parsley, chopped French Dressing	14 1 oz. 1 ¼ qt.	3. Sprinkle with chopped, hard cooked eggs mixed with fresh chopped parsley. 4. Serve with French dressing.

FIGURE 3-3. Recipe for Salad del Monte from *The Professional Chef* by Folsom, Copyright 1974 by CBI, reprinted by permission of Van Nostrand Reinhold.

After listing the ingredients, amounts of ingredients, and the invoice costs and units, the next step would be to break the costs down into the base unit used in the recipe. The first ingredient, frozen asparagus, costs $86.91 for a case of 12 2-1/2 pound boxes. Therefore, we need to determine the cost of asparagus per pound. To do this, multiply the 12 boxes times 2-1/2 pounds per box to get 30 pounds per case. Next, divide the cost per case ($86.91) by the 30 pounds to get the cost per pound ($2.897). The cost per pound, $2.897, is then multiplied by the amount of asparagus called for in the recipe (10 pounds) to get the total cost of that ingredient, $28.97. This figure is then put in the extension column.

This process is then repeated for each ingredient on the cost card. For example:

FIGURE 3-4. Portion cost card.

NAME OF RECIPE Salad Del Monte   REFERENCE Pro Chef Pg. 233

DATE Jan 1, 1995   NUMBER OF PORTIONS 50   COST PER PORTION $0.671

RECIPE		INGREDIENTS	INVOICE		RECIPE		EXTENSION	
			COST	UNIT	COST	UNIT		
10	Lb.	Frozen Asparagus	$86.91	12/2.5 Lb.	$2.897	Lb.	$28	970
4	Heads	Lettuce	8.65	24 Heads	0.36	Head	1	440
7	Oz.	Pimento	32.89	24/14 oz.	0.98	Oz.		686
14	Ea.	Eggs	.84	Dozen	0.07	Egg		980
1	Oz.	Parsley	.10	Recipe				100
1.25	Qt.	French Dressing	17.31	4 Gal.	0.34	Oz.	1	360
							TOTAL	$33	536

Lettuce—24 heads to the case at a cost of $8.65 per case. Base unit—head. $8.65 divided by 24 equals $.360 per head. Four heads of lettuce are needed. $.360 times 4 equals $1.44 which represents the total cost of lettuce for this recipe. $1.44 goes in the extension column.

Pimento—24-14 oz. cans to the case. Base unit—oz. 24 cans times 14 ozs. equals 336 oz. per case. $32.89 cost per case divided by 336 oz. equals $.098 per oz. times 7 oz. called for in the recipe equals a total cost of $.686 for pimento.

Eggs—$.84 per dozen. Base unit—each. $.84 divided by 12 equals $.07 per egg times 14 eggs called for in the recipe equals $.98 total cost of eggs.

Parsley—one oz. This is a negligible cost and will be assigned a total cost of 10¢. This method is employed to avoid the time-consuming task of breaking down a price when the result of that price will not substantially affect the total cost of that recipe. This method can also be utilized when the recipe refers to such items as salt and pepper to taste.

French dressing—4 one gallon jars to the case. Base unit—quart. Four quarts to the gallon times four gallons equals $17.31 divided by 16 quarts equals $1.082 cost per quart times 1.25 (1 1/4 quarts) called for in the recipe, equals $1.353 total cost for the French dressing. Another approach to use on the French dressing would be to break the cost into ounces. To do this, first get the cost per gallon. $17.31 divided by four (four gallons to the case) which equals $4.328. Next, divide $4.328 by 128 (number of oz. in a gallon) which equals $.034 per oz. There are 32 oz. in a quart, so multiply 32 times 1.25 (1 1/4 quarts called for in the recipe) which equals 40 ozs. needed for the recipe. Then multiply 40 times $.034 (cost per oz.) to get the total cost of French dressing of $1.360.

When the costs for each ingredient are placed in the extension column, the next step is to add these costs which gives us a total cost to produce this recipe of $33.529. Finally, the total cost of $33.529 is divided by the number of portions (50) that the recipe will produce which gives us a cost of $.671 per portion. The most complicated part of figuring recipe cost cards for most students is the conversion of units from the invoice to the base recipe unit.

FIGURE 3-5. Equivalent measurement chart.

Fluid

3 teaspoons	= 1 tablespoon	= 1/2 ounce	
4 tablespoons	= 1/4 cup	= 2 ounces	
5 1/3 tablespoons	= 1/3 cup	= 2.8 ounces	
8 tablespoons	= 1/2 cup	= 4 ounces	
11 tablespoons	= 2/3 cups	= 5.4 ounces	
16 tablespoons	= 1 cup	= 8 ounces	
2 cups	= 1 pint	= 16 ounces	
2 pints	= 4 cups	= 1 quart	= 32 ounces
4 pints	= 2 quarts	= 1/2 gallon	= 64 ounces
4 quarts	= 16 cups	= 1 gallon	= 128 ounces

Dry

8 oz.	= 1/2 lb.	
16 oz.	= 1 lb.	
8 quarts	= 32 cups	= 1 peck
4 pecks	= 1 bushel	

Note: A general rule of thumb in commercial cooking is that solid ingredients are weighed where applicable while liquid ingredients are measured by volume.

Food Buying, Guide for School Foodservice, U.S. Dept. of Agriculture, Washington, D.C. 1980

This is a necessary skill in the restaurant industry, not only in costing, but in converting recipes into smaller or larger quantities. The more one works with conversion, the easier it becomes. Eventually, it will become committed to memory and second nature to the astute manager or executive chef.

COSTING SINGLE ITEMS

Some items on the menu do not require cost cards. Listings such as roasts, steaks, or chops—in other words, single items listed—are figured individually. In the case of meats, in particular, the shrinkage and trim must be taken into account. Imagine my surprise on a recent consulting job, when confronting a restaurant owner who was losing money. "You're not getting enough for your prime rib," I stated. "Oh, yes," was the reply. "It costs me $3.45 per pound, which is 22¢ per oz., with a 10 oz. portion cost of $2.20. I sell it for $6.95. That's a 31 percent food cost." What he neglected to take into account was the fact that part of the fat cover was trimmed off after roasting, and that the bones were removed, and that the ribs shrink when they are roasted. After taking these facts into consideration, I pointed out that the prime rib was costing him $4.93 a pound, 31¢ an oz., and $3.10 a portion, resulting in a food cost of 44 percent. In other words, he was costing out the prime rib on AP (as purchased) price rather than on an EP (edible portion) price. A very critical mistake!

To figure the cost to serve on a roast follow these steps:

1. Determine the total cost of the roast as purchased (price per pound times the number of pounds equals the total cost AP).
2. After roasting and trimming (bones and fat) weigh the roast. The result is the saleable weight or EP (edible portion).
3. Divide the total cost as purchased by the saleable weight. The result is the cost per pound to serve.
4. Divide the cost per pound to serve by 16 (number of ozs. in a pound). The result is the cost per oz. to serve.
5. Multiply the cost per oz. to serve times the standard portion size. The result is the cost per serving.

To illustrate this further, take an example of a BBQ restaurant which serves brisket. Assume they paid $1.80 a pound and received 75 pounds. The total cost as purchased of these briskets would be $135 (Step 1). The briskets were then smoked in the pit, removed when done, and the excess fat trimmed from them. At this point assume they weighed 38 pounds (Step 2). The cost to serve the briskets would then be $3.55 a pound (Step 3) or 22¢ an oz. (Step 4). Assuming a 4 oz. standard portion is served, the cost per serving would be

COSTING SINGLE ITEMS **59**

88¢ (Step 5). As shown in the example, this formula can work for several roasts of the same kind. It is just as effective on one.

Although there are many charts available for cooking loss and trim, each restaurant should conduct their own tests, particularly on items that have a high volume in their operation.

FIGURE 3-6. Cooked yields of meat.

Type of Meat	Net Servable Cooked Yield
Beef	
Roast sirloin (boneless)	70%
Pot roast	60%
Chopped beef	75%
Short ribs (bone in)	60%
Corned beef (brisket)	60%
Beef liver	75–90%
Stew (boneless)	75%
Swiss steak	70%
Tenderloin steak	90%
Sirloin steak (boneless strip)	75%
Sirloin steak (bone in strip)	80%
Minute steak (boneless butt)	80%
Boneless top and bottom round roast	70%
Knuckle butt roast	65%
Shoulder clod roast	70%
Oven-prepared beef rib	50%
Chef's delight beef rib	60%
Boneless round	60%
Fresh bone in beef brisket	45%
Hotel special rib steak roll	75%
Beef round, rump and shank off	50%
Lamb	
Roast leg	45%
Roast loin	40%
Lamb stew (boneless)	75%
Veal	
Veal cutlet (boneless)	80%
Calf's liver	75%
Roast leg	50%
Roast loin	50%
Veal loin chop (bone in)	75%
Veal rib chop (bone in)	75%
Pork	
Breaded tenderloin	100%
Sausage patties	55%
Breaded pork chop (boneless)	90%
Pork chops (bone in)	80%
Spareribs	65%
Roast pork loin	50%
Ham steak (bone in)	80%
Baked ham (bone in)	65%
Roast fresh ham	50%
Poultry	
Fried chicken, 2 lbs.	100%
Turkey, 18 lbs./up	40%

All yields are general averages based on many hundreds of tests. They allow for waste in trimming the meat, cooking, shrinkage, and small-end waste. Determination of exact shrinkage for each meat item cooked is advisable.

Food Buying Guide for School Foodservice, U.S. Dept. of Agriculture, Washington, D.C. 1980.

The charts are fine for "rule of thumb" planning, but oven temperature, personnel, and even the same cuts of meat will vary, giving a cost different than the charts. The results could be disastrous when the primary income is dependent on the accurate cost of an item.

The shrink and loss test would not be used on all meat items on the menu. Listings, such as steaks and chops, are all listed on the menu as precooked weight. Thus, if you were to purchase a proportioned 14 oz. strip steak, the cost would be the same as the invoiced cost. Assume that the strip steak costs $3.50 a pound, it would be $3.50 divided by 16 or 22¢ an oz. times 14 oz., for a cost of $3.08 for that steak.

On the other hand, if an operation were to cut its own steaks then the trim loss would have to be taken into account. For example, a beef tenderloin is purchased for the purpose of serving filet mignon. Assume the tenderloin weighs 7 pounds at a cost of $4.50 per pound for a total cost of $31.50. The person cutting the steaks would first trim off all of the fat and the connective tissue (silver), then weigh the tenderloin again. The result is the saleable weight. Assume the saleable weight is 5 pounds. The cost to serve would then be $6.30 a pound or $.394 an oz. (total cost divided by saleable weight). The cost per oz. would then be multiplied by the standard portion size for filet mignon. Assuming a 10 oz. portion, the cost would be $3.94.

Since filet mignon comes only from the center portion of the tenderloin, the ends (tips) would have to be used on another menu item such as a beef brochette. They would have the same cost of $6.30 per pound. Some industry people use a different method to determine the cost of tips based on percentage of value of the entire carcass. This system can get quite complicated. The point is that some dollar value needs to be assigned to the ends. Do not make the mistake that many restaurants make when they say, "The scraps do not cost anything. I'm making 100 percent profit on them." Wrong!

BEVERAGE COST

In addition to knowing how to determine the cost of recipes and meats, it is also important to know the methods of costing out beverages, as they have the highest mark up of any item on the menu. Start with coffee, which is the highest percentage of beverage sales in most restaurants.

1. Multiply the number of gallons of water (usually 2-1/2 gallons per pound of coffee) times 128 (number of oz. per gallon) to get total oz.
2. Multiply total oz. by 10% (water absorbed by the coffee grounds).

3. Subtract the loss from total oz. to get the net yield per urn of coffee.

4. Divide the net yield by the number of oz. served per cup to get the number of cups per pound. NOTE: If the brewing ratio and cup size do not change, then this number stays the same and you can start the formula with step 5.

5. Divide the cost per pound by the number of cups per pound. The result is the cost of coffee per cup.

6. Take the cost of cream and sugar per serving and divide by 2 (assuming 50 percent of the customers will use cream and sugar).

7. Add the cream and sugar cost to the cost of the coffee per cup. The result is the net cost per cup to serve.

8. Multiply the net cost per cup times the average number of refills per customer plus the original cup. (If you charge per cup with no refill, then ignore this step.)

Different sections of the country brew coffee in varying strengths. If the brewing ratio is different in your area, then substitute the correct ratio. Assuming the brewing ratio is 3 to 1, that is three gallons of water to one pound of coffee, that the coffee costs $2.25 per pound, and we serve 6 oz., the cost per cup is shown in Figure 3–7.

CARBONATED BEVERAGES

Next, let's investigate carbonated beverages. There are two types of carbonated beverages—premix and post mix. *Premix* is that type in which the syrup and carbonated water are mixed at the factory in five gallon cans or cartons, hence premix. *Post mix* is that type which is mixed as the drink is served. The syrup is in five gallon tanks or cartons and is mixed with the water, which has passed through the carbonator to give it its effervescence, in the mixing chamber at the point of service. Post mix is less expensive than premix and thus has a lower cost and a higher gross profit. However, post mix needs water, electricity, and a drain running to the unit and requires a larger investment in equipment. For these reasons some operations opt for the premix even though the profit margin is lower.

In addition to the above differences, the costs of premix and post mix are also figured differently. Premix is relatively simple to figure since the product is ready to serve as purchased. When costing cold beverages, if the operation has an ice machine, the cost of ice is normally not figured in as it is usually so negligible that it does not have an impact. If, however, an operation is purchasing ice from a vendor, then its cost would be great enough to be added to the

FIGURE 3-7. Coffee cost problem.

Brew ratio—3:1	Cream $1.80/qt. (1 oz. serving)
Coffee cost—$2.25/lb.	Sugar .35/lb. (1/2 oz. serving)
Serving size—6 oz.	Refills—one

Step 1
```
    128   (oz. in gal.)
 ×    3   (brew ratio)
    384   (total oz.)
```

Step 2
```
    384   (total oz.)
 ×  .10   (absorption loss)
   38.4   (loss)
```

Step 3
```
   384.0  (step 1)
 − 38.4   (step 2)
   345.6  (net volume)
```

Step 4
```
                      57.6    (cups per 1 lb.)
        6 (oz. serving) 345.6  (net volume)
```

Step 5
```
                         $ .039  (cost per cup)
        57.6 (cups per lb.) $2.25  (cost per lb.)
```

Step 6
```
                    .056 cream
        32 oz./qt.   $1.80/qt. cream

                       .011 sugar
        32 (½ oz./lb.) 0.35/lb. sugar
        .056 cream
        .011 sugar
        .067 total

                      .034 cost
        (50% usage) 2  .067
```

Step 7
```
        $.039 coffee
         .034 c/s
        $.073
```

Step 8
```
        original cup   1
        refill        + 1
                        2

        $.073
        ×   2
        $.146 net cost
```

beverage cost. Paper supplies, such as cups or straws, are in most operations considered a supply cost and, therefore, are not figured in food cost. Some operations, however, consider these items to be a part of the product cost and in these instances their cost would be added in. Check with your company's operations manual to ascertain whether these costs should be included. Since the majority of firms do not consider ice and paper supplies a cost of goods, we will not include them in the examples. If a garnish such as a lemon or lime slice or wedge is used, it is by all means added to the cost.

Premix Carbonated Beverages

1. Multiply 128 (number of oz. in a gallon) times 5 (number of gallons in a premix tank) to get 640 oz. (in a five gallon tank).
2. Divide the cost of the tank by 640 to get the cost per oz.

FIGURE 3-8. Premix cost example.

Cost per 5 gal. tank—$20.00
Serving size—16 oz.
Ice displacement—8 oz.
Ice cost—N/A

Step 1

$$
\begin{array}{r}
128 \\
\times\ \ 5 \\
\hline
640
\end{array}
\quad
\begin{array}{l}
\text{oz. in gal.} \\
\text{gal. tank} \\
\text{oz. in tank}
\end{array}
$$

Step 2

$$
\begin{array}{r}
.031 \quad \text{cost per oz.}
\end{array}
$$
640 oz. in tank $\overline{\smash{\big)}\ \$20.00}$ cost per tank

Step 3

$$
\begin{array}{r}
16 \\
-\ 8 \\
\hline
8
\end{array}
\quad
\begin{array}{l}
\text{oz. serving size} \\
\text{oz. ice displacement} \\
\text{oz. of product served}
\end{array}
$$

Step 4

$$
\begin{array}{r}
.031 \\
\times\ \ 8 \\
\hline
.248
\end{array}
\quad
\begin{array}{l}
\text{cost per oz.} \\
\text{oz. of product served} \\
\text{net cost}
\end{array}
$$

3. Subtract the amount of ice displacement from the total ounces of the serving glass to get net ounces of product served.

4. Multiply net ounces of product served by the cost per ounce to get net cost.

To figure the cost of post mix, utilize the following formula. This formula assumes mixing the water and syrup at a 5 to 1 ratio. That is five parts of water and one part of syrup. If a different ratio is used, then the formula should be changed accordingly.

Post Mix Carbonated Beverages

1. Multiply five gallons of water by five gallons of syrup to get 25 gallons of water (5:1 ratio).

2. Add the five gallons of syrup to the 25 gallons of water to get a 30 gallon yield per five gallon tank of syrup.

3. Multiply 30 gallons of product by 128 (number of oz. gallon) to get total oz. of product per tank (3,840). NOTE: If the ratio does not change, then this number does not change and you can start the formula with step #4.

4. Divide the cost per tank of syrup by 3,840 to get the cost per oz. of product.

5. Subtract the amount of ice displacement from the size of the serving container to get the amount of product served.

6. Multiply the amount of product served by the cost per oz. of product to get total cost.

FIGURE 3-9.   Post mix cost example.

Cost per 5 gal. tank syrup $18.75
Serving size—16 oz.
Ice displacement—8 oz.
Ice cost—N/A
Water cost—N/A
Water to syrup ratio   5:1

Step 1

$$
\begin{array}{rl}
5 & \text{gal. water} \\
\times\ 5 & \text{gal. syrup} \\
\hline
25 & \text{gal. water}
\end{array}
$$

Step 2

$$
\begin{array}{rl}
25 & \text{gal. water} \\
+\ 5 & \text{gal. syrup} \\
\hline
30 & \text{gal. product}
\end{array}
$$

Step 3

$$
\begin{array}{rl}
30 & \text{gal. product} \\
\times\ 128 & \text{oz. per gal.} \\
\hline
3{,}840 & \text{oz. of product}
\end{array}
$$

Step 4

$$
\begin{array}{r}
\$0.005 \text{ cost per oz.} \\
\hline
3{,}840 \text{ oz. of product } \big|\ 18.75 \text{ cost of 5 gal. syrup}
\end{array}
$$

Step 5

$$
\begin{array}{rl}
16 & \text{oz. serving container} \\
-\ 8 & \text{oz. ice displacement} \\
\hline
8 & \text{oz. of product served}
\end{array}
$$

Step 6

$$
\begin{array}{rl}
.005 & \text{cost per oz. of product} \\
\times\ 8 & \text{oz. of product served} \\
\hline
\$0.040 & \text{net cost}
\end{array}
$$

To figure the cost of other beverages which require the mixing of water such as frozen orange juice concentrate, lemonade, or powdered punches, simply follow the above formula for post mix carbonated beverages. Be careful in step one as these products all have varying water to syrup (or base) ratios.

Ready-to-serve beverages, such as milk or canned juices, are relatively easy to figure. Simply divide the cost per container by the number of oz. per container and multiply this figure (cost per oz.) by the number of oz. served. Don't forget to subtract ice displacement (if applicable) from the size of serving container.

SANDWICHES

The next area of costing to consider is sandwiches and other listings such as appetizers, which have multiple ingredients in their makeup. The most important consideration in this segment is remembering to include low-cost items such as condiments. For example, on a hamburger, all too often the mustard, ketchup, and pickle are overlooked when the product is costed out because of their low cost. Consider, for a moment, the consequences of this omission. Assume the condiments cost 2¢ and the restaurant is working on a 30 percent food cost. The omission of 2¢ cost would result in a selling price of 6¢ lower than what it should be. (Mark ups will be explained in the next chapter.) If this restaurant were to sell 100 hamburgers a day, the lost income would come to $6.00 and if it were open 350 days a year, lost income of $2,100 could be

FIGURE 3-10. Portion cost card.

NAME OF RECIPE Bacon, Lettuce, & Tomato   REFERENCE House File #3-72

DATE 3/13/94   NUMBER OF PORTIONS 1   COST PER PORTION $0.692

RECIPE		INGREDIENTS	INVOICE		RECIPE		EXTENSION	
			COST	UNIT	COST	UNIT		
3	Slices	Bacon (18/22)	$30.00	15 Lb.	.111	Slice		333
2	Leaves	Lettuce	6.00	12 Heads	.025	Leaf		050
3	Slices	Tomato	18.00	5×6 Lug	.030	Slice		090
2	Oz.	Mayonnaise	20.00	4/1 Gal.	.039	Oz.		078
2	Slices	Bread	.95	Loaf	.048	Slice		096
1	Spear	Pickle (85–105 Count)	23.00	6/10	.045	Spear		045
							TOTAL	692

expected. All over a lousy 2¢ omission! Is it any wonder that knowing the *exact* cost is imperative in running a successful restaurant?

To illustrate the cost of a sandwich, take the example of a bacon, lettuce, and tomato (BLT).

Bacon—The 18/22 refers to 18 to 22 slices per pound. It is advisable in situations such as this to use a "worst case scenario" to protect yourself and to give a margin for error. Therefore, figure only 18 slices per pound for cost even though you will probably get more like 20 on the average. Divide the cost per pound by 18 to get the cost per slice.

Lettuce—A wide variation in cost can be experienced in produce like lettuce. Heads can either be tight and heavy or loose and light. Price per case also varies greatly depending on the season. Again use a worst case scenario with the highest price you expect to pay at the lowest yield.

Tomato—Another highly seasonal item, tomatoes, must be costed for a period when supplies are low and prices high. Tight purchasing specs will help to determine yield. Always purchase the same size (e.g., 6 × 6 or 5 × 6). The example used, 10 slices per tomato using a 5 × 6 size. The pricing would be 5 times 6 or 30 tomatoes to the layer times 2 layers to the lug or 60 tomatoes times 10 slices per tomato or 600 slices to the lug. Divide the cost per lug by 600 to obtain the cost per slice.

Mayonnaise—Cost per gallon divided by 128 (oz. per gallon) to get cost per oz. times 2 oz. needed.

Toast—Slices per loaf vary by the weight of the loaf and the thickness of the slice. In the example, 20 slices per loaf were used.

Garnish—Pickle spear—The count for this item is usually listed on the can. Simply divide the count by the cost per can.

Speaking of garnish, recently I saw a large sign in a kitchen admonishing the wait staff, "Don't forget the garnish." While reviewing the cost structure of this particular restaurant, I questioned the owner as to how much he had allowed for garnish cost. "I don't include it," he replied. (Yes, the same one who messed up on the prime rib.) Don't forget the garnish!

COMPLETE MEALS

The next area of planning is the cost of a complete meal. There are four steps to this process. The first step is to get a total cost of accompanying items that would be the same on all meals served. Let's assume that above the entrees, the following listing occurred. "All

FIGURE 3-11. Portion cost card.

NAME OF RECIPE Dinner Salad   REFERENCE House File #8-3

DATE 6/19/96   NUMBER OF PORTIONS 50   COST PER PORTION $0.297

RECIPE		INGREDIENTS	INVOICE		RECIPE		EXTENSION	
			COST	UNIT	COST	UNIT		
5	Heads	Iceburg Lettuce	$11.75	Cs.-24 Hds.	.490	Head	2	450
6	Ea. AP	Leaf Lettuce	6.00	Cs.-12 Ea.	.500	Ea.	3	000
1	Lb. AP	Cucumbers	24.00	50 Lb.	.480	Lb.		480
1	Lb. AP	Radishes	5.00	30 Lb.	.167	Lb.		167
1	Lb. AP	Carrots	7.50	25 Lb.	.300	Lb.		300
5	Ea.	Tomatoes	18.00	5×6 Lug	.300	Ea.	1	500
		Total Salad Cost					7	897
		Cost Per Portion (50 Portions)						158
		Bleu Cheese Dressing (2 oz. Portions)						139
						TOTAL		297

entrees served with a crisp garden salad with your choice of dressing; baked, french fried, or hash browned potatoes; and warm cinnamon rolls with butter." Therefore, the first step is to get a total cost of these items. To do this, develop cost cards for all of the accompanying items.

As was previously illustrated, the worst case scenario should be used. In the case of the garden salad, bleu cheese dressing would be used. Do not list bleu cheese 25¢ extra—tacky! tacky! Rather include it in your cost. If the customer orders French dressing you are

FIGURE 3-12.   Portion cost card.

NAME OF RECIPE Baked Potato   REFERENCE House File #10-22

DATE 4/12/94   NUMBER OF PORTIONS 50   COST PER PORTION $0.495

RECIPE		INGREDIENTS	INVOICE		RECIPE		EXTENSION	
			COST	UNIT	COST	UNIT		
50	Ea.	Baking Potatoes	$15.00	90 Ct.	.167	Ea.	8	350
4	Oz.	Shortening	27.00	50 Lb.	.034	Oz.		136
6.25	Lb.	Sour Cream	12.00	20 Lb.	.600	Lb.	3	750
6.25	Lb.	Butter	2.00	Lb.	2.000	Lb.	12	500
							TOTAL	$24	736

ahead of the game. Likewise, use baked potato with butter and sour cream for cost (ditto bleu cheese example). Once the cost cards are figured, the cost of the accompanying items, using the most expensive, are totaled and this figure is used to obtain the total cost of the accompanying items.

The second step in the process is to figure the cost of the entree itself. Again cost cards are used. Any additional costs for that particular item such as an accompanying side dish or garnish should

FIGURE 3-13. Portion cost card.

NAME OF RECIPE Cinnamon Rolls   REFERENCE House File #4-43

DATE 10/21/95   NUMBER OF PORTIONS   48 (2 Rolls Ea.)   COST PER PORTION $0.153

RECIPE		INGREDIENTS	INVOICE		RECIPE		EXTENSION	
			COST	UNIT	COST	UNIT		
2	Oz.	Dry Yeast	$18.40	10 Lb.	.115	Oz.		230
1.5	Cups	Water, Warm	No	Cost	—	—		—
3	Cups	Water, Hot	No	Cost	—	—		—
3	Oz.	Dry Milk	73.00	50 Lb.	.091	Oz.		273
1	Lb.	Sugar	15.75	50 Lb.	.315	Lb.		315
1	Lb.	Shortening	27.00	50 Lb.	.540	Lb.		540
2	Oz.	Salt	Per	Recipe	—	—		100
9	Ea.	Eggs	.90	Dozen	.075	Ea.		675
5.5	Lb.	Flour	7.50	50 Lb.	.150	Lb.		825
12	Oz.	Butter	2.00	Lb.	.125	Oz.	1	500
2	Lb.	Sugar	15.75	50 Lb.	.315	Lb.		630
1	Oz.	Cinnamon	18.25	5 Lb.	.228	Oz.		228
		Total Cost Per Recipe - Yield 96 Rolls					$5	316
		Cinnamon Roll Cost Per Portion (2 Ea.)						111
		Butter (2 Ea. Pats)						042
						TOTAL		153

FIGURE 3-14. Total cost of accompanying items.

Dinner salad with Blue Cheese	$.297
Baked potato with sour cream and butter	.495
Cinnamon Rolls with butter (2 ea.)	.153
Total	$.945

be added to the cost of the entree. For example, rice pilaf with a beef brochette, spiced whole crabapple with a stuffed pork chop, or sauteed mushrooms with a strip sirloin steak.

Finally, the Q factor is added. This covers all of the incidentals that have not been accounted for in the cost cards and includes such items as the salt and pepper on the table, crackers, steak sauces, and possibly butter. The dollar amount that is assigned to the Q factor will vary from restaurant to restaurant depending on circumstances surrounding the "extras" that are provided the customer.

FIGURE 3-15. Total meal cost chart.

Entree	Cost	Garnish	Acc. Items	Q Factor	Total
Broiled chicken half	1.225	.300	.954	.150	$2.629
Poached salmon	2.965	.355	.954	.150	$4.424
Strip sirloin steak	3.080	.420	.954	.150	$4.604
Rack of lamb	3.745	.195	.954	.150	$5.044

BUFFETS AND SALAD BARS

The last cost area to be investigated is the one pertaining to all-you-can-eat buffets and salad bars. The object is to get an average cost per customer. There are several theories expressing the quickest and simplest way to achieve this. They are useless. The only way to get an accurate cost is via the inventory method.

Plus	(+)	Starting inventory (number of units)
Minus	(−)	Additions to the table (number of units)
Equals	(=)	Ending inventory (number of units)
Times	(×)	Number of units of product sold
Equals	(=)	Unit cost of product
		Total cost of product used

FIGURE 3-16. Salad bar cost analysis.

Item	Unit	Start (+)	Additions (+)	(+)	(+)	(+)	(+)	Total =	End (−)	Total =	Unit Cost (×)	Total Cost =
Tossed greens	lb.	3	3	3	2	2		13	2	11	.50	$5.50
French dressing	qt.	1	1					2	1/2	1 1/2	1.32	1.98
Italian dressing	qt.	1	1	1				3	1/2	2 1/2	1.56	3.90
Tomato wedges	lb.	1	1	1	1			4	1	3	.65	1.95
Green onions	lb.	1/2	1/2					1	1/4	3/4	.30	.23
Shred. carrots	lb.	1/2	1/2	1/2				1 1/2	1/2	1	.25	.25
Sliced cukes	lb.	1/2	1/2	1/2				1 1/2	—	1 1/2	.50	.75
Sliced radishes	lb.	1/2						1/2	1/4	1/4	.80	.20

Cost per customer

Customer count | Total cost

Total cost $14.76
Customer count 48
Cost per customer .308

The formula should be used for each product on the buffet table or salad bar and then totaled at the end of the meal period and divided by the number of customers served during that period to obtain a cost per customer.

Now that the costs for the menu have been determined, there is one more consideration to keep in mind. Keep current. Every menu item should have a cost card filed in a book and these cards should be kept up-to-date. That is not to say that every time an item in inventory increases or decreases in price, the cost card should be refigured. This would quickly develop into a full-time job. Rather, key ingredients should be monitored and when they pass a certain level, then cost cards containing these ingredients would be changed accordingly and a determination made regarding a price increase or decrease. For example, in recipes using 80/20 ground beef, if a cost of $1.50 a pound were used and it eventually crept up to $1.65 a pound, then all recipes utilizing this ingredient would be refigured.

CONCLUSIONS

The science of keeping accurate costs and figuring the proper selling price is an exacting one. However, as we will see in the next chapter, the astute chef, manager, or owner who has the knowledge and takes the time to accomplish these tasks will greatly increase the odds for survival. Exact knowledge of your costs leads to charging the correct amount for a product, which leads to profitability. It's just that simple.

QUESTIONS

1. In your own words, define and explain the importance of the following terms:
   a) standardized recipes
   b) cost cards
   c) AP vs. EP
   d) Q factor

2. Figure the cost of a 5 oz. cup of coffee using a brew ratio of 3:1. Assume the coffee costs $3.25 a lb., cream .02 per serving, sugar .02 per serving, and there are no refills given.

3. Explain to a new manager the method used to figure the cost per person of an all-you-can-eat buffet.

4. Using the following data and recipe, complete the cost card including the cost per portion.

Egg Foo Young
Yield: 50 portions

1 lb. fresh mushrooms	mushrooms $1.89 per lb.
1 No. 10 can bean sprouts	bean sprouts $15.80 - 6 No. 10 cans
2 lb. onions AP	onions $11.60 per 50 lbs.
3/4 cup cooking oil	oil $33.00 per 6 - 1 gal.
40 eggs	eggs $23.50 per 36 doz.
1 lb. cooked chicken	chicken $24.90 per 10 lb.
2 qt. sauce	sauce $3.50 per gal.

Portion cost card.

NAME OF RECIPE_____ REFERENCE_____

DATE_____ NUMBER OF PORTIONS_____ COST PER PORTION_____

RECIPE		INGREDIENTS	INVOICE		RECIPE		EXTENSION	
			COST	UNIT	COST	UNIT		
					TOTAL			

CHAPTER FOUR

Pricing the Menu

OBJECTIVES
- To understand the makeup of an income statement including the inter-relationships of controllable and non-controllable costs and their effect on sales and profits.
- To learn several of the important markup methods including the factor method, markup on cost, gross markup, ratio method, and the TRA method and the relationship each has with the other.
- To introduce the concept of psychological pricing and its importance in selecting the final menu price.
- To explore the relationships of selling price, cost, and amount sold of each menu item utilizing the menu precost method.

IMPORTANT TERMS

Income statement	Sales
Food cost	Gross profit
Controllable costs	Non-controllable costs
Profit	Factor method
Markup on cost method	Gross markup method
Ratio method	TRA method
Psychological pricing	Menu precost.

Now that the proper cost has been figured for the listings on the menu, the next determination is the selling price. Prior to the discussion of selling price, one point should be made clear. The object of any business is to make a profit. There should be no argument over this point; it is fact. Far too many managers lose sight of this and, consequently, do not develop a profit mentality. To be sure, many factors go into achieving a profit. Certainly, sales are important because sales must exceed costs before a profit can be realized. Menu items that do not cater to a customer's desires will result in lost sales and, consequently, lost profit. Controls are important for without them waste and theft will eliminate any profit potential. The menu selling price, however, is the key ingredient in making a profit, the starting point on which profit is built. Without the proper selling price, all the promotions and all the controls will not assist in producing a profit. If the selling price is too high, sales will be lost. If the selling price is too low, profit will be lost. In an earlier chapter, we said that "everything starts with the menu." I would emphasize that "profit starts with the menu."

Some food service operations such as hospitals, in-plant feeders, and schools are required not to make a profit, but only break even or make their budget. Before those readers decide to skip this chapter, they should recognize that without the proper selling price, it is fruitless to expect to break even or make budget, in spite of other management factors such as controls.

FIGURE 4-1. Cheatum & Steele Restaurant income statement year ending 19___.

SALES		$500,100	100%
LESS: COST OF FOOD SOLD			
OPENING INVENTORY	$8,250		
PLUS: PURCHASES	168,500		
EQUALS: TOTAL AVAILABLE	176,750		
LESS: CLOSING INVENTORY	7,480		
COST OF FOOD SOLD		169,270	34%
GROSS PROFIT		$330,830	66%
LABOR EXPENSE		172,380	35%
OTHER CONTROLLABLE EXPENSES		48,960	10%
NON-CONTROLLABLE EXPENSES		76,290	15%
TOTAL EXPENSES		$297,630	60%
PRE-TAX PROFIT		$33,200	06%

UNDERSTANDING THE INCOME STATEMENT

To fully understand the relationship between the menu selling price and profit, an examination of an income statement is in order. While it is not the purpose of this text to explain accounting, it is necessary to have some basic knowledge to determine how much to charge for an item.

Referring to the income statement in Figure 4-1, assume that Harry Cheatum and Sammy Steele owned a restaurant named Cheatum & Steele. The first line on this income statement is sales. Sales are nothing more than the selling price of each item times the number of units sold of that item and then totaled. If Harry and Sammy sold 30,000 hamburgers over a year's time at a selling price of $1 each, their total sales of hamburgers would be $30,000. If they sold 20,000 orders of french fries at 50¢ an order, their total sales for french fries would be $10,000. Their combined sales of these two items would be $40,000. The other $460,000 sales shown on the income statement would be made up of other items on the menu, figured in like fashion, that is, the number of units sold per item times the selling price.

Incidentally, sales are always 100 percent on an income statement because expenses are measured against sales. Look at sales as a whole and expenses and profit as parts of the whole.

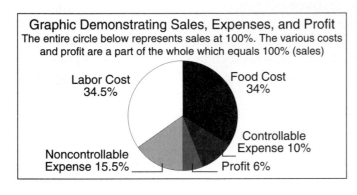

Graphic Demonstrating Sales, Expenses, and Profit
The entire circle below represents sales at 100%. The various costs and profit are a part of the whole which equals 100% (sales)

Labor Cost 34.5%
Food Cost 34%
Controllable Expense 10%
Noncontrollable Expense 15.5%
Profit 6%

FIGURE 4-1A. Sales, expense, profit chart. The entire circle represents sales at 100%. The various costs and profit are parts of the whole, equaling 100% (sales).

The next line, cost of food sold, is figured by taking opening inventory plus purchases minus closing inventory, which equals cost of food sold.

$$
\begin{array}{l}
\text{Opening Inventory} \\
+ \text{ Purchases} \\
\hline
= \text{ Food Available For Sale} \\
- \text{ Closing Inventory} \\
\hline
= \text{ Cost of Food Sold}
\end{array}
$$

To simplify matters, let's assume that Harry and Sammy sold only one item—strip steaks. If they started off with 30 steaks at a cost of $4 each, they would have an opening inventory of $120 (30 steaks × $4). During the day, they purchased 100 more, also at a cost of $4. Their purchases would be $400 (100 steaks × $4). This would then give them 130 steaks available for sale at a cost of $520 (130 steaks × $4 = $520 or $120 + $400 = $520). At the end of business they counted the steaks and found they had 10 left or $40 worth. Subtracting this from the available steaks for sale of 130 or $520 value, their cost of food sold would be 120 steaks (units) or $480. The formula would then look like this:

Opening Inventory	$120
+ Purchases	+ 400
= Food Available For Sale	$520
− Closing Inventory	− 40
= Cost of Food Sold	$480

Note. Cost of food sold could be a misnomer. If someone stole a steak and if Sammy burned a steak and had to throw it away, these two steaks would show up in cost of food sold even though in actuality they were not sold. I sometimes feel that the title "cost of food sold" should be changed to something like "cost of food used." One client whom I had consulted for called it "food gone" which is a very appropriate title. One would hope that it had gone to the cash register rather than the trash can.

To figure the food cost percent, take food cost in dollars and divide it by sales in dollars and the result is food cost percent. Costs or expenses are always expressed in percent in order to provide a means for easy comparison. In the case of the steaks, the food cost is $480. In the income statement (Figure 4-1) the food cost is $169,270. As such, these numbers are meaningless. If, however, we say that the steaks have a 34 percent food cost and the income statement has a 34 percent food cost, we can make some rationalizations regarding cost. Even though the dollar costs are drastically different, the percents are the same. By using percentages we are simply taking the ratio of dollar costs to dollar sales which gives us a more meaningful discussion of costs.

The next line, gross profit, is the amount of money that the Cheatum & Steele Restaurant made from its raw ingredients. Gross profit is determined by subtracting cost of food sold from sales.

	Sales
−	Cost of Food Sold
=	Gross Profit

To figure the gross profit percent, take gross profit in dollars and divide by sales in dollars. If you subtract the food cost percent from sales in percent, the result will be the same.

Gross Profit %	Sales %
Sales $ ⟌ Gross Profit $	− Food Cost %
	= Gross Profit %
66%	100%
$500,000 ⟌ $333,730	− 34%
	66%

The next line, labor expense, is the total payroll for the Cheatum & Steele Restaurant. In some operations, this is broken down into management salaries, hourly personnel payroll, payroll taxes, FICA, and fringe benefit expenses. Fringe benefits would include employees' hospitalization insurance, life insurance, vacation and holiday pay, company paid retirement benefits and so on. Labor expense and food cost added together are known as prime cost because these two expenses together are the largest expenses that are controlled by management. To figure labor expense percent, divide labor expense in dollars by sales in dollars.

$$\text{Sales \$} \, \overline{\left)\, \frac{\text{Labor Expenses \%}}{\text{Labor Expense \$}} \right.} \qquad\qquad \text{\$500,000} \, \overline{\left)\, \frac{34.5\%}{\text{\$172,380}} \right.}$$

The next line, other controllable expenses, includes such items as paper goods, dishmachine detergents, cleaning supplies, and are quite often broken down into separate lines on an income statement. These are all expenses which can be controlled by management.

The next line, non-controllable expenses, are all those fixed expenses which (basically) management has little if any control over. This would include such items as utilities, rent, insurance, or property taxes.

The next line, total expenses, is figured by adding together all of the expense lines except food cost, and then subtracting this figure from gross profit. The result is profit (before depreciation and taxes). To figure profit percent, divide profit in dollars by sales in dollars or add all of the expense percents and subtract from gross profit percent. To put all of this into perspective, let's review the following facts:

- FACT—All restaurants are in business to make a profit.
- FACT—All restaurants have costs.
- FACT—In order for a restaurant to make a profit, sales must exceed costs.

As we saw earlier, sales are nothing more than the selling price times the number of items sold. Therefore, the key to profit is determining the correct selling price. To do this we need to charge a price that will not only cover the cost of goods (food cost), but will also cover all of our other expenses *and* produce a profit. There is a misconception that abounds in our industry that selling price is dependent solely on the cost of ingredients or is based only on the cost of ingredients and labor. Wrong! The selling price must include not only food and labor costs, but all other expenses and profit as well. To do otherwise will put you on a collision course for disaster.

MARKUP METHODS

With an understanding of where profit comes from and the interrelation of expenses to sales, the various methods of marking up costs to determine a selling price can be explored. There are a multitude of formulas available to assist the restaurant manager in determining what should be charged for an item. Some are simple, some are complicated, and some make absolutely no sense at all. Out of this multitude of formulas only those which have passed the test of time and are worthy of assisting management in determining a fair selling price will be explored.

THE NO-METHOD METHOD

Perhaps the most popular method of determining what to charge for an item (although few managers will admit to doing it) is simply to charge what the competition charges. This method, as such, is foolhardy because no two restaurants are alike. Style, decor, location, rent, utilities, insurance, labor costs, and so on all change from location to location. To charge the same price for an item as a competitor ignores these differences and profitability becomes a hit or miss proposition. Certainly, with a large investment in a restaurant, a more scientific approach would be in order. While this method appears to violate the statement that only worthy formulas will be presented, it is mentioned for two reasons. First, it is popular, and second, it has its place when used correctly, which will be discussed later.

THE FACTOR METHOD

Perhaps the simplest formula to use is the *factor method*. In this method, it is necessary to have predetermined what the food cost should be. Therefore, it should be used only in established restaurants where past performance indicates that the gross profit is sufficient to cover all expenses and profit. To obtain the selling price, take the desired food cost percent and divide it into 100 percent. The result is the factor. Next, take the factor and multiply it by the item cost (from the cost card) of the menu item. The result is the menu selling price of that item (Figure 4-2). Once the factor has been determined, it is unnecessary to repeat step one each time a selling price is needed. Simply multiply the item cost by the factor to determine what to charge on the menu for that item. If all controls are effective and the costs remain constant, the desired food cost percent will be accurate. Should the costs of that item increase or decrease, it will be necessary to multiply the new cost by your factor to determine a new selling price which would reflect the change in cost.

FIGURE 4-2. Factor method.

1. Determine desired food cost percent.
2. Divide this number into 100. (100%)
3. The result is your factor.
4. Multiply the factor times the cost of the meal or item.
5. The result is the selling price of that meal or item.

Example: Desired food cost %—34%
    Meal cost—$2.18

$$
\begin{array}{ll}
2.94 \text{ (factor)} & \$2.18 \ \text{meal cost} \\
.34\ \overline{)\ 1.00} & \underline{\times\ \ 2.94} \ \text{factor} \\
& \$6.41 \ \text{selling price}
\end{array}
$$

THE MARKUP ON COST METHOD

Another simple method, very similar in nature, is the *markup on cost method.* Take the food cost of the item and divide it by the desired food cost percent. The result is the selling price to be charged for that item (Figure 4-3). As in the factor method, it must be a known fact to management that the desired food cost is adequate to obtain a satisfactory gross profit to cover all other expenses and achieve a profit.

FIGURE 4-3. Markup on cost method.

1. Determine your desired food cost percent.
2. Divide this percent into the cost of the meal or item.
3. The result is the selling price of that meal or item.

Example: Desired food cost %—34%
    Meal cost—$2.18

$$
\begin{array}{l}
\qquad\qquad\quad 6.41 \ \text{selling price} \\
\text{(food cost \%)}\quad .34\ \overline{)\ \$2.18 \ \text{meal cost}}
\end{array}
$$

THE GROSS MARKUP METHOD

The third system to be examined is the *gross markup method.* Unlike the previous methods which took into account only food cost, the gross markup method takes into account all expenses and profit as well as food cost to determine a selling price. In years past, marking up a menu item in relation to its food cost was an adequate way to ensure profitability. However, in the present economy where escalating fixed costs (such as insurance, rent, and utilities) are the rule, many restaurateurs believe that the total income statement must be taken into account when determining a selling price to ensure profitability.

To figure the gross markup method, first take the gross profit in dollars and divide this figure by the number of customers served. The result is the contribution rate per customer. Second, take the food cost of the item and add this to the contribution rate per customer. The result is the selling price. Several things have happened here. First, by using gross profit, we have accounted for all of our costs (except food) and profit. If this confuses you, refer back to the income statement and you will see that gross profit represents not only food cost minus sales, but also represents all other expense plus profit; thus, these are accounted for in this markup formula. The second thing that has happened here is that all of our other expenses and profit (gross profit) has been divided equally among all of our customers (gross profit in dollars divided by number of customers).

FIGURE 4-4. Gross markup method.

1. Take gross profit in dollars from your income statement.
2. Determine the number of customers served.
3. Divide the gross profit dollars by the number of customers served.
4. The result is the cost per customer.
5. Add the cost per customer to the cost of the meal or item.
6. The result is the selling price.

Example: Gross profit dollars—$330,730
Number of customers served—75,000
Meal cost—$2.18

$$\frac{4.41 \text{ cost per customer}}{75,000 \mid \$330,730 \text{ gross profit}}$$

4.41 cost per customer
+ 2.18 meal cost
6.59 selling price

Note: Cost per customer also includes profit.

In this method all of the labor expense, other controllable expense, non-controllable expense, and profit (all of these equaling gross profit) are taken into consideration and are divided equally among all customers. Consequently, I call this method the "quasi-communistic" approach to the restaurant business. Nevertheless, it is an excellent way to determine the selling price on a menu where all items are in the same price range.

As can be seen it tends to average prices more toward a median than with the factor method, charging a higher price for a low cost item and a lower price for a high cost item. Therefore, the entire menu must be in the same general item cost range. Consider some of the strange pricing on a coffee shop menu, which has a wide item cost range, using this method (Figure 4.6). In addition to using this method on operations with a tight item cost range, it is also very useful in table d'hote restaurants where one price is charged for all entrees as well as all you can eat buffets and/or salad bars.

FIGURE 4-5. Gross markup method vs. factor method.

Meal	Cost	Selling Price	
		G.M.M.	F.M.
Prime Rib	$4.15	$8.55	$12.20
Strip Rib	$3.95	$8.35	$11.60
Fried Chicken	$1.80	$6.20	$ 5.30
Broiled Fish	$2.10	$6.50	$ 6.15
Rack of Lamb	$3.55	$7.95	$10.45

Note: Figures from previous examples were used (i.e., $4.41 cost per customer in the gross markup method and 2.94 for the factor in the factor method). Notice the tighter spread between the highest and lowest selling price using the gross markup method.

FIGURE 4-6. When not to use the gross markup method!

Item	Cost	Cost per Customer	Selling Price
Coffee	$ .10	$4.41	$4.51
Apple Pie	$ .40	$4.41	$4.81
BLT	$ .60	$4.41	$5.01
Shrimp Cocktail	$1.75	$4.41	$6.16

Some strange things can happen when using the gross markup method on a menu with a wide range of costs. While the illustration may be humorous, your customers would likely take an opposite point of view.

THE RATIO METHOD

The fourth method is the *ratio method*. Like the gross markup method, it also takes into account all expenses and profit. To obtain a selling price using the ratio method, you must have a valid income statement because the numbers used to develop the ratio are total expenses. These can be either monthly or yearly figures: however, yearly figures will be more accurate in determining the proper markup. To obtain a selling price using the ratio method, first take the labor cost, other controllable costs, non-controllable costs and profit (these equal gross profit) and divide these costs by the cost of food sold in dollars. The result is your ratio. To the ratio add 1.00 (sales as a percent). Multiply this figure by the item cost (Figure 4-7). Once this multiplying factor has been developed, it can be used repeatedly to determine selling prices as long as the desired results are maintained on the income statement.

FIGURE 4-7. Ratio method.

1. Obtain cost of food sold in dollars from the income statement.
2. Add all other expenses and profit in dollars.
   (The result is the same figure as gross profit.)
3. Divide all other expense and profit by cost of food sold.
4. The result is your ratio.
5. Add 1.00 to the ratio.
6. Multiply this by the cost of the meal or item.
7. The result is the selling price.

Example: Cost of food sold in dollars—$169,270
             All other expenses and profit—$330,730
             Meal cost—$2.18

$$1.95 \text{ ratio}$$

$$169,270 \overline{)330,730}$$

$$\begin{array}{r} 1.95 \text{ ratio} \\ + 1.00 \\ \hline 2.95 \\ 2.95 \\ \times \$2.18 \text{ meal cost} \\ \hline \$6.43 \text{ selling price} \end{array}$$

THE TRA METHOD

The last method to be discussed was developed by the Texas Restaurant Association and, consequently, is known as the *TRA method*. This method, like the previous two, takes into account all expenses and profit in determining a selling price. To figure the selling price of an item, add together labor cost percent, controllable expense percent, non-controllable expense percent, and profit percent. The result is cost percent without food. Take the cost percent without food and subtract it from 1.00 (sales). The result is the food cost percent. Divide food cost percent into the cost of the item to obtain the selling price.

FIGURE 4-8. Texas Restaurant Association Method.

1. From your income statement, take labor cost in percent, operating cost in percent, (both controllable and non-controllable) and profit in percent.
2. Add the three figures together.
3. Subtract this number from 1.00.
4. The result is the divisor.
5. Divide the cost of the meal by the divisor.
6. The result is the selling price.

Example: Meal cost—$2.18
             Figures taken from the income statement (Figure 4-1).

Labor Cost %—	35% or .35
Operating Cost %—	25% or .25
Profit %—	6% or .06
	66% or .66 cost without food

$$\begin{array}{r} 1.00 \\ - .66 \\ \hline .34 \text{ divisor} \end{array}$$

$$\begin{array}{r} \$6.41 \text{ selling price} \\ .34 \overline{)\$2.18} \end{array}$$

Assume you wanted to increase your profit to 8 percent, the new selling price would be as follows:

Labor Cost	.35
Operating Cost	.25
Profit	<u>.08</u>
	.68

1.00	$6.81 new selling price necessary to
− <u>.68</u>	.32 ⌐ $2.18 increase profit by 2%
.32 divisor	

By now it should be apparent to the astute reader that with one exception the selling prices are all similar. The one exception being the gross markup method. The reasoning behind this is simple. In order to obtain a certain food cost that will achieve a profit, an appropriate amount must be charged which will cover the cost of the item and allow enough money left over to offset other costs and profit.

What is happening in the factor, markup on cost, ratio, and TRA methods is that costs (other than food) and profit are divided in direct relation to the selling price. In other words, a hamburger costing 70¢ and selling for $2.10 would contribute $1.40 toward labor, overhead, and profit, while a grilled cheese costing 40¢ and selling for $1.20 would contribute 80¢. In the gross markup method labor, overhead, and profit are divided equally among all customers with, say, 40¢ per customer making the selling price $1.60 for the hamburger and $1.30 for the grilled cheese.

Another thing that should be noticed is that in the factor method and the ratio method, the item costs are being multiplied by relatively the same number, and in the markup on cost and the TRA method, the item costs are being divided by relatively the same divisor. In all four of these cases, the selling price is pretty much the same. Interesting, isn't it? What has happened is that we have looked at the same numbers in different ways but have come up with the same answers.

SELECTING A METHOD

These are but a few of the many methods used to obtain a menu markup. I prefer the TRA method because it forces the student or manager to look at the complete picture. Once it is ascertained that a particular food cost will cover all expenses and profit, the formula is no more time consuming than the rest. Remember, management is responsible for the total profitability of the restaurant, not just achieving an arbitrary food cost.

Incidentally, what should a restaurant's food cost be? Jack Miller, in a report on menu pricing, tells the story of why a 40 percent food cost was chosen as the preferred operating figure. In the year 500 B.C., on the road to Rome, a man built a restaurant; his first customer was an accountant. The accountant happened to stop to have dinner and when he finished, he said, "Say, I think you have a pretty good thing going. It looks like this restaurant business may develop into something that will spread all over the world. How would you like it if I kept books for you?" The restaurateur had no one working on his books, so he hired the accountant/customer to keep the books for his first month of operation. At the end of the month, the accountant came back to the restaurant operator and reported. "You have a 40 percent food cost." The restaurateur asked, "Is that good?" The reply was "That is very good." So from that time forward it has been accepted that all food service operations should maintain a 40 percent food cost.[1]

Many food service managers still cling faithfully to this theory. Occasionally, I will ask restaurant owners, managers, or students: what should food cost run? I receive answers from 20 percent to 50 percent. The correct answer to this question is "it depends." It depends on many factors which are peculiar to that particular restaurant. Hence, when consulting, I always refer to the TRA to be sure all costs and profits are covered when determining the correct selling price for the menu. The method that you or your company uses is not as important as the fact that some rational method is adopted. Charging what the competition charges is not a rational method. There is a point, however, when checking the competitors becomes important: that is, after the determination has been made as to what the selling price should be after all costs and profits are covered. Then it should be ascertained whether or not this item at this selling price is competitively priced in your market area. It should also be decided if the selling price is within the existing price range of the present menu and within the demographic market range.

PSYCHOLOGICAL PRICING

Once a rational selling price has been determined, using the aforementioned steps, the job is not complete. The next consideration is psychological pricing. What has been determined so far is the restaurant's needs, in other words, how much money the restaurant needs to charge to cover expenses and profit. Psychological pricing theories take into account the customer—how the customer reacts to certain pricing structures. Psychological pricing has a long history in retailing; however, only recently has it been incorporated into food service pricing. Studies conducted at Purdue University and Cornell University have given insight into some interesting facts as they pertain to restaurant pricing.

---

[1]From Jack Miller, *Menu Pricing*, p. 58. Reprinted by permission of Van Nostrand Reinhold ", New York."

One of the primary theories behind psychological pricing is the *odd cents price.* This reduces the restaurant customers' resistance to buy because it gives the illusion of a discount. Instead of charging $1.50 for an item, charge $1.49 and the customer will perceive this as a better price value relationship. When using odd cents pricing, the two best ending figures to use are 9 and 5. This holds true for selling prices under $7. With prices in the $7 to $10 range, the best ending figure to use is 5. When dealing with prices over $10 the best ending figure is not an odd cents one but rather a 0. The reasoning behind this is that in a restaurant with prices over $10 the illusion of a discount would tarnish the establishment rather than enhance it because selling prices over $10 are primarily confined to finer restaurants.

Another factor in psychological pricing is the importance of the left-hand digit and the distance between two prices. In other words, the customer will perceive a greater distance between 69 and 71 than he will between 67 and 69 even though the distance is the same (two cents). This is of particular importance to the restaurateur when price increases are being contemplated. The decision to break a price barrier by increasing the left-hand digit should be resolved in light of possibly having a unit sales decrease of that item.

A third factor in psychological pricing is the length of the price or the number of digits in the price. As in the left-hand digit theory, the customer also perceives distance here. In other words, there is a greater distance between $9.99 and $10.25 than there is between $9.55 and $9.99 even though there is a 26¢ difference between the first set of numbers and a 44¢ difference between the second set. Again this strategy is of particular importance when increasing prices. The decision of when to break a dollar barrier is a crucial one. Many restaurant managers maintain that when this occurs, the price should be held below the dollar barrier as long as is economically possible and when an increase is taken that breaks this barrier a substantial increase should be taken to offset previous losses when an increase was not taken. This makes sense in that after a barrier is broken the customer resistance to the price is the same if it is close to or far from the barrier. In other words, if the selling price of an item should be $1, it would be wise to hold it at 99¢ for as long as possible and then increase it to $1.10.[2]

Psychological pricing can change the selling price determined by any of the formulas described in this chapter. As a matter of fact this is not at all unusual. Every item on the menu will not have the identical food cost percentage. The reason for this is the price value relationship.

[2]Kruel, Lee M. "Magic Numbers: Psychological Aspects of Menu Planning" *Cornell Quarterly*, August 1982 © Cornell University. Used by permission, all rights reserved.

FIGURE 4-9. In the past two years have you noticed a change in customer expectations regarding PORTION SIZE? How have customer expectations changed?

	Sales Volume			Number of Establishments				
	<$500K	$500K–$999K	$1000K+	1	2	3+	2–4	5+
TOTAL	11	23	30	42	14	12	21	5
	100%	100%	100%	100%	100%	100%	100%	100%
EXPECT LARGER PORTIONS	6	10	13	19	6	5	9	2
	55%	43%	43%	45%	43%	42%	43%	40%
EXPECT MORE FOOD FOR THE MONEY	3	7	7	9	4	6	7	3
	27%	30%	23%	21%	29%	50%	33%	60%
EXPECT SMALLER/ WANT SMALLER PORTIONS	2	4	10	11	4	1	5	–
	18%	17%	33%	26	29%	8%	24%	–
OTHER	–	–	–	1	–	–	–	–
	–	–	–	2%	–	–	–	–
DON'T KNOW	–	2	–	2	–	–	–	–
	–	9%	–	5%	–	–	–	–

FIGURE 4-9. (Continued) In the past two years have you noticed a change in customer expectations regarding VALUE RECEIVED FOR PRICE PAID? How have customer expectations changed?

	Sales Volume			Number of Establishments				
	<$500K	$500K–$999K	$1000K+	1	2	3+	2–4	5+
TOTAL	29	63	85	128	30	36	50	16
	100%	100%	100%	100%	100%	100%	100%	100%
EXPECT MORE VALUE/MORE FOOD FOR PRICE PAID	28	60	80	122	28	35	48	15
	97%	95%	94%	95%	93%	97%	96%	94%
EXPECT BETTER QUALITY MEALS	2	1	4	5	1	1	1	1
	7%	2%	5%	4%	3%	3%	2%	6%
OTHER	–	2	1	2	1	–	1	–
	–	3%	1%	2%	3%	–	2%	–

PRODUCT MIX

Certainly, the selling price, as determined by management, must be perceived by the customer as being a good value. Consequently, different categories on the menu will have different food costs assigned to them.

FIGURE 4-10. Food cost percent by menu categories.

Listed below are some typical ranges for food cost percent on an average menu.

Appetizers	20%—60%
Salads	30%—45%
Entrees	30%—60%
Sandwiches	25%—45%
Desserts	20%—50%
Beverages	5%—30%

Menu Theme				Check Size				Check Size				
Ameri-can	Inter-natnal	Steak/ Seafood	Other	<$8	$8–$14	$15–$24	25+	<$10	$10–$19	$20+	$20–$29	$30+
23 100%	12 100%	14 100%	19 100%	11 100%	28 100%	18 100%	12 100%	20 100%	30 100%	19 100%	8 100%	11 100%
8 35%	5 42%	7 50%	11 58%	4 36%	13 46%	8 44%	6 50%	9 45%	12 40%	10 53%	5 63%	5 45%
9 39%	4 33%	3 21%	2 11%	4 36%	8 29%	5 28%	2 17%	6 30%	9 30%	4 21%	2 25%	2 18%
5 22%	2 17%	4 29%	5 26%	3 27%	6 21%	5 28%	2 17%	5 25%	8 27%	3 16%	1 13%	2 18%
– –	– –	– –	1 5%	– –	1 4%	– –	– –	– –	1 3%	– –	– –	– –
4 4%	1 8%	– –	– –	– –	– –	– –	2 17%	– –	– –	2 11%	– –	2 18%

Menu Theme				Check Size				Check Size				
Ameri-can	Inter-natnal	Steak/ Seafood	Other	<$8	$8–$14	$15–$24	25+	<$10	$10–$19	$20+	$20–$29	$30+
69 100%	37 100%	34 100%	56 100%	28 100%	71 100%	50 100%	42 100%	51 100%	85 100%	55 100%	22 100%	33 100%
65 94%	36 97%	31 91%	55 98%	27 96%	68 96%	49 98%	38 90%	50 98%	82 96%	50 91%	20 91%	30 91%
4 6%	– –	2 6%	1 2%	1 4%	3 4%	1 2%	2 5%	2 4%	2 2%	3 5%	1 5%	2 6%
– –	1 3%	2 6%	– –	– –	1 1%	– –	2 5%	– –	1 1%	2 4%	1 5%	1 3%

Why then would one go to all the trouble of figuring a selling price using one of the formulas when, in fact, that price is probably going to change anyway?

Just because a restaurant desires, for example, a 35 percent food cost, not every item on the menu is marked up to give that specific cost. The 35 percent food cost would come from an aggregate of all items sold at their various costs. This is known as *product mix*. It is the product mix, the actual number of items sold at their various markups, that makes up cost of food sold on the income statement. Let us suppose, for example, that we opened a stand that sold nothing but tamales and we had a selling price that gave us a 35 percent food cost. As long as we purchased properly, had no waste, controlled our costs, and had no theft, we could in all probability end up with a 35 percent food cost. However, our customers got thirsty eating our tamales, so we added cola to our menu at a 12 percent cost. Selling both items reduced the 35 percent figure. As a matter of fact, the more cola we sold the lower the composite food cost would be. The number of tamales and cola sold would be our product mix.

FIGURE 4-11. Pam's tamale cart.

Item	Number Sold	Cost	Selling Price	Total Cost	Total Sales
Tamales	100	.12	.40	12.00	40.00

$$\frac{.30}{\$40\,\lceil\,\$12.00} \qquad \text{sales}\,\lceil\,\text{cost}$$

Food Cost % – 30%
With cola added to menu.

Item	Number Sold	Cost	Selling Price	Total Cost	Total Sales
Tamales	100	.12	.40	12.00	40.00
Cola	50	.06	.35	3.00	17.50
Totals				15.00	57.50

$$\frac{.26}{\$57.50\,\lceil\,\$15.00} \qquad \text{sales}\,\lceil\,\text{cost}$$

Food Cost % – 26%

MENU PRECOST

The final step in determining new menu selling prices is the menu precost. It is very similar in nature to a product mix which tells us what is happening now in our restaurant. The menu precost tells what is likely to occur to the food cost in the future. In order for either of these methods to be successful, it is obvious that careful records must be kept by management. The number of each item sold is critical if these numbers are to have any meaning. This information can be obtained by tallying the guest checks or by reading the printout if the restaurant has a data processing register. Another critical piece of information is the food cost of each item. Cost cards must be kept up to date if the product mix or the menu precost is to have any validity.

The first step in figuring a menu precost based on new selling prices is to take the product mix chart and change the selling prices of those items that are to be changed. The second step is to anticipate the number to be sold based upon the price change. If the selling price is increased substantially, the number sold could conceivably drop dramatically. If it is a slight increase, it may not change at all. If the selling price is decreased, the number sold could well increase. It is important here to predict, as accurately as possible, what is likely to occur so that the precost will be a valid management tool upon which to base decisions. The next step is to take the selling price times the projected number sold and put this figure in the total sales column. Then take the food cost times the number sold and put this figure in the total cost column. Next, total the sales column and the cost column and divide the projected sales into the projected cost, the result being the projected food cost percent. If the percentage meets the expectations or the desired standard, then all that is left to do is to implement the changes. If not, it is necessary to go back and institute further changes until the desired food cost percentage is achieved.

FIGURE 4-12. Example of product mix and menu precost.

	# Sold	Cost	Selling Price	Food Cost %	Total Cost	Total Sales	Total Forecast	Cost	Selling Price	Food Cost %	Total Cost	Total Sales
Prime Rib	110	4.15	10.95	38%	457	1.205	100	4.15	11.50	36%	415	1.150
Strip Steak	75	3.95	9.95	40%	296	746	85	3.95	Same	40%	336	846
Fried Chicken	190	1.80	4.85	37%	342	921	190	1.80	5.45	33%	342	1.035
Broiled Fish	130	2.10	6.50	32%	273	845	130	2.10	Same	32%	273	845
Rack of Lamb	60	3.55	10.50	34%	213	630	60	3.55	Same	34%	213	630
Total				36%	1.580	4.347				35%	1.579	4.506

In the above example, the current food cost is 36 percent. By increasing the selling price of Prime Rib and Fried Chicken the cost will be lowered to 35 percent. Notice the change in forecast. It is anticipated that Prime Rib will drop 10 orders because of the increase with customers shifting their selection to Strip Steak. Fried Chicken remained unchanged because it is still the lowest priced item on the menu.

CONCLUSION

Determining the correct selling prices on a menu, as you can see, is a time-consuming and exacting science. It is imperative that accurate records, such as cost cards and income statements, are kept. If they are not, the results could be disastrous. Remember, profit starts with the menu. If the correct selling price is not established, all of the work and effort that goes into managing a successful enterprise is wasted. The person who charges what competition charges will eventually have a "For Sale" sign in the window. The astute manager who runs his/her business like a professional will enjoy success. It's just that simple!

QUESTIONS

1. Explain in your own words
   a) Gross profit
   b) Psychological pricing
   c) Product mix
   d) Menu precost

2. When analyzing financial statements and discussing costs, why are percentages used rather than dollar figures?

3. Given the following data, figure the selling price of an item that costs you $1.19 using
   a) The factor method
   b) The markup on cost method
   c) The gross markup method
   d) The ratio method

Sales	$765,000
Cost of food sold	224,500
Gross profit	?
Labor expense	198,750
Other controllable expenses	74,000
Non-controllable expenses	85,500
Total expense	?
Pre-tax profits	?

   Number of customers served 200,000.
   Assume all costs are desired costs.

4. Using the product mix and menu precost chart (Figure 4-12) on page 89, give the new food cost percent, assuming the following changes on the precost side of the chart.
   Prime rib—cost drops to $3.95
   Strip steak—cost increases to $4.15
   Fried chicken—same
   Broiled fish—increase selling price to $6.75
   Rack of lamb—delete
   Rack of Lamb will be replaced with stuffed baked pork chops with a cost of $2.25, a selling price of $7, and anticipated forecast of 100 units sold.

5. As a Food and Beverage Director of a large downtown hotel, tell when and how you would use psychological pricing in the following units under your control. Defend your answer.
   a) Coffee shop—moderately priced
   b) Fast food operation—street level, outside entrance, local customers as well as guests
   c) Fine dining—roof top, high priced

CHAPTER FIVE

Menu Content

OBJECTIVES
- To learn the various categories that are used on menus and to differentiate when each is used.
- To understand the criteria that are used to determine specific menu listings.
- To appreciate the importance of utilizing descriptive terminology to explain and sell menu listings.

IMPORTANT TERMS

Menu categories	Appetizers
Entrees	Extenders
Menu listings	Balance
Plate composition	Descriptive terminology

CATEGORIES

All menus, regardless of size or complexity, are broken down into various categories. The number of categories used on a menu is determined by the needs and desires of that particular establishment. Such factors as style, decor, type of service, price range, and area demographics are all taken into consideration when determining how many categories will appear on a menu.

The traditional categories for menu writing are Appetizers, Soups, Salads, Cold Entrees, Hot Entrees, Vegetables, Sandwiches, Side Dishes, Starches, Desserts, Cheeses, Fruits, and Beverages. In a high ticket, fine dining restaurant all of these categories are likely to be used, while in other operations only several would be used. The following is an explanation of each of these categories.

APPETIZERS

To many people, appetizer is a combination of two words—appetite teaser. Indeed, that is the true intent of an appetizer—to tease the palate and awaken the digestive system to want more. Because of the nature of appetizers (stimulating the palate), the portion size is small. They are usually sharp to the taste. If the particular food used is bland, it is served with a tangy, sharp, pungent sauce. They may be served hot or cold. The type of food used varies, ranging from fruits and vegetables to meat, seafood, and poultry.

SOUPS

In many food service operations, particularly those with limited menu listings, soups and appetizers are included in the same category with one being served in lieu of the other. Like appetizers, they can be served either hot or cold, although in North America hot soups are definitely preferred. There are three different bases: clear, thick, and special. Clear soups include consommes, broths, and variations which occur when various vegetables and/or meats are added to them. Thick soups include chowders, bisques, creams, purees, and potages and have endless varieties when fruits, vegetables, meats, seafoods, or poultry are added. Special soups, sometimes referred to as national soups, include minestrone and vichyssoise among others. There is probably no other sector of modern day cookery where variations and individualism are more prevalent than in the preparation of soups. The possibilities are endless. Many a smart operator has chosen this category to utilize leftovers to create a high selling, high profit menu item.

APPETIZERS

Fullers Cured Northwest Salmon Napoleon
$7.95

Roasted Quail with Grilled & Marinated Portobello Mushrooms
$8.75

Northwest Oysters with Green Apple Mignonette
Market Price

Smoked Lamb with a Dried Berry & Grapefruit Compote
$7.25

Pecan & Cornmeal Dusted Pacific Oysters with Chipolte Aioli
$7.75

Sautéed Sea Scallops with Tempura Onion Rings & Balsamic Rosemary
Vinaigrette
$8.95

Hudson Valley Foie Gras with Carmelized Belgian Endive & Rhubarb Compote
$13.50

Grilled Shrimp & Eggplant Lasagna
$7.50

Warm Sautéed Sweetbread "Nuggets" with Chimichurri
$6.95

FIGURE 5-1. Sample appetizers menu.

SALADS

Salads basically come in two sizes, an accompanying salad or an entree salad. Reference here is made to accompanying or side salads with the large entree varieties being covered in the following section. In most food service operations, accompanying salads are served prior to the main entree. However, in fine dining restaurants with a more traditional style of service, they are served after the entree as a means of cleansing the palate. Where they are served prior to the meal, they may take the place of an appetizer and/or soup, or they may be served in addition to these. Salads in this category are usually made with fresh, crisp vegetables, but can also contain fruit. Meat, seafood, and poultry are normally not

PALM TERRACE RESTAURANT

◊ ◊ ◊ ◊ ◊

APPETIZERS

*Norwegian Smoked Salmon Roll filled with
Potato, Sevruga Caviar, and Fresh Herbs in Sour Cream*
$12.50

Casserole of California Vineyard Snails in a Merlot Wine and Garlic Sauce
$12.00

*"Salad Gourmande"
Louisiana Crayfish, Grilled Sea Scallops, Foie Gras, Asparagus, and
Wild Mushrooms on a bed of Mesclun and Herbs, Banyuls
Wine Vinegar and Truffle Oil Dressing*
$13.00

Quick Fried Quail over Frisée Salad with Roasted Garlic and Truffles
$14.00

Maine Lobster Croustillant with an Oriental Salad
$13.00

*Polenta and Farm Goat Cheese Tarte with
Glazed Onion and Fresh Tomatoes with Basil Oil*
$11.00

Sautéed Fresh Duck Foie Gras with Grapes in a Black Muscat Wine Sauce
$16.50

California Baby Field Greens with Aged Red Wine Vinaigrette
$8.50

A Sauté of Spring Wild Mushrooms in Brioche, Madeira Wine infusion
$13.00

FIGURE 5-1. *(Continued)*

SOUP

Chilled Vine Ripe Tomato Soup with Lobster Medallions and Basil Sauce
$9.50

Fresh Green Asparagus Soup with Morel and White Asparagus
$8.50

The Palm Terrace is pleased to provide Italian mineral water for our guests.
FONTE LIMPIA NON-CARBONATED MINERAL WATER *(1000 ml)* **$4.50**
SAN PELLEGRINO SPARKLING MINERAL WATER *(750 ml)* **$4.50**
TYNANT ORIGINAL NATURAL SPRING WATER *(25 fluid oz.)* **$5.50**

FIGURE 5-2. Sample soup menu.

SOUP AND SALADS

Saffron Scented Seafood Soup
$5.25

Sweet & Bitter Greens with
Roasted Beet & Shallot Vinaigrette
$5.95

Warm Spinach Leaves with
Smoked Duck & Honey Sesame Dressing
$7.25

Salad of Mixed Organic Greens
$4.95

Baby Romaine Spears with
Viejo Cheese, Calamari and Caesar Vinaigrette

FIGURE 5-3. Sample salad menu.

used in accompanying salads due to cost factors. Rarely does a restaurant or food service skip this category, this reasons being twofold. Salads are popular because of their healthy ingredients. They also have a low cost giving them a high gross profit. Most operations opt for the popular tossed salad, giving it an endless variety or names, to entice the customer. Smart restaurateurs offer a variety and, depending on the season and locale, the variety is endless. Clean, crisp, well chilled, and colorful are passwords that make this category successful in your operation.

COLD ENTREES

The predominant listing in the cold entree section in most food service operations is the ever famous chef's salad. However, the selection shouldn't stop here. In warmer climates year round and northern areas in the summer, cold entrees can be a welcome addition and change to the menu. The variety of cold plates and entree salads is limitless. Fresh fruits chilled and colorfully arranged on a platter served with a fruit sherbet or chicken salad. Cold meat and cheese platters offer an excellent means to utilize leftover roasts. A tomato stuffed with either chicken, shrimp, or tuna salad. A chilled seafood platter featuring shrimp and crab. The list goes on and on. Consult your recipe books. Use your imagination to create new and exciting cold entrees that add variety and interest to your menu.

Salads

HOUSE SALAD *seasonal greens, fresh mushrooms, croutons, roasted nuts, feta cheese and tomato. Tossed with a honey-balsamic vinaigrette* *3.95*

A SALAD OF FRESH SPINACH *crisp bacon, croutons, sweet red onion and hickory-smoked almonds with a warm bacon dressing* *5.95*

A SALAD OF SLICED TOMATOES AND RED ONION
herb vinaigrette . . . . *2.95*   *with bleu cheese* *3.95*

CAESAR SALAD *garlic, olive oil and parmesan cheese* *4.95*

GRILLED SEA SCALLOPS & SHRIMP SALAD *seasonal greens, double-smoked bacon, Fontina cheese and bell pepper with an herb vinaigrette* *7.95*

GRILLED CHINESE CHICKEN SALAD *seasonal greens, assorted bean sprouts, mushrooms, snow peas and toasted almonds with a light sesame dressing* *6.95*

FIGURE 5-4. Sample salad menu.

HOT ENTREES

The listings for hot entrees are considerable. For this reason, they are broken down into the following subcategories or groups: meat, poultry, fish and seafood, and extenders as well as non-meat.

Meat

This being the largest group within the hot entree category the possibilities for menu listings are endless. Beef, veal, pork, lamb, and variety meats offer a wide choice for the menu writer. Combine this with the various cookery methods—roasting, braising, steaming, broiling, barbecuing, grilling—and the door is wide open for many exciting menu offerings.

The most popular offering in this group is beef. In practically every survey taken on the likes and dislikes of the American population, beef always scores high. Pork runs a distant second in the meat category with lamb running third. Current trends are changing these ratings with pork increasing slightly while beef is decreasing slightly. Also on the increase are chicken, fish, and seafood.

The predominant reason behind these changes is the consumer's increasing awareness of the relationship of diet to overall health and the reduction of cholesterol. The beef industry,

---

Steaks & Combinations

*Served with vegetable and your choice of
roasted garlic mashed potatoes and gravy, wild rice pilaf, steamed new potatoes.*

To continue with our tradition of excellence, along with our seafood, we offer Certified Angus Beef. Only top of the line and choice grades are labeled and sold under the Certified Angus Beef trademark. Carefully aged and cut to our rigid standards, the C.A.B. label is your guarantee of fresh Certified Angus Beef, never frozen.

FILET MIGNON *(8 oz.)* *16.95*

KANSAS CITY STRIP *(14 oz.)* *11.95*

FILET MIGNON *(6 oz.)* **& BROILED OR STEAMED LOBSTER TAIL** *26.95*

FILET MIGNON *(6 oz.)* **& JUMBO FRIED SHRIMP** *19.95*

FILET MIGNON *(6 oz.)* **& MARYLAND-STYLE CRABCAKE** *19.95*

In consideration of all our guests, cigar and pipe smoking is permitted.

FIGURE 5-5. Sample beef menu.

however, is now producing a leaner product and the ratings are changing again.

Analyze any menu and odds are beef will be the predominant listing among the meat groups. Taste is the foremost criterion, but keep in mind that pork and lamb are taboo in some religions thus eliminating them from the diet of these people regardless of taste. Do not, however, preclude that since beef is so popular that it should be listed to the exclusion of other meats. People opt for diversion as they get bored eating the same things and will readily order tantalizing meats other than beef.

Poultry

Poultry has always been and will continue to be a popular food. Chicken is the most popular in this group ranking second behind beef in the overall listing of entrees. Very close to chicken is turkey. Other game birds such as duck, quail, and pheasant rank lower, but can add excitement to any menu. Frying chicken is by far the number one method of preparation, however, baking, broiling, barbecuing, and smoking are also well accepted and increasing in popularity because of less cholesterol and calories. Roast turkey and dressing is the traditional method of preparation for this item. Smoked turkey is an excellent alternative to this method. Game birds are normally preferred roasted or smoked.

Fish and Seafood

This group is the rising star in the hot entree category. Low in fat and cholesterol, rich in protein, and light in taste, it is increasing in popularity daily. While batter-dipped deep frying has been the accepted method of preparation, broiling and baking are coming on strong. It's no wonder. Why cover up the delicate taste and add calories and cholesterol to an item and defeat its purpose? The types and species of fish and seafood are endless and, consequently, so are the menu listings. There is hardly a section of the country where freshwater fish is not available. In the coastal regions freshwater as well as saltwater fish and seafood are readily available. Fresh fish and seafood can be flown inland, giving an endless variety to a menu.

Extenders

More commonly known as casseroles, extenders can run the gamut from low cost to high. They incorporate as their main ingredient any of the above listed groups. Sometimes they are made from fresh ingredients, and at other times they are prepared from leftovers. Extenders which use low cost ingredients are an excellent method to keeping costs down in an institutional type food service or offset-

---

MEAT AND POULTRY

Roasted Half Free Range Chicken
with a Confit of Garlic and Shallots and a Medley of Vegetables
$25.00

Sautéed Magret of Moulard Duck with
Pineapple in a Vanilla Scented Szechwan Pepper Sauce
$26.00

Medallions of Loin of Veal with Fresh Oregon Morels and Asparagus
$28.00

Medallions of Beef Tenderloin in a Light Roquefort and Aged Red Shallots
$28.00

Oven Roast Loin of Spring Lamb in Moroccan Spice Crust
with a Vegetable and Lemon Couscous
$29.50

Roasted Rib of Beef "Marchand de Vin," Vegetables Bouquet
$56.00   (2 Persons)

Any entree can be prepared plain broiled, grilled, or poached without sauce upon request.

GRATUITY IS NOT INCLUDED, 15% IS CUSTOMARY IN THE UNITED STATES FOR GOOD SERVICE.

FIGURE 5-6. Sample grill menu.

ting high cost items in a restaurant that demands a good product mix. The variety of extenders is endless. Using the many ingredients available, one can follow standardized recipes or release the imagination with personalized variations.

Non-meat

Eggs and cheese are the primary sources of non-meat hot entrees. Comparatively low in cost, they are excellent sources of protein. While eggs are predominant on the breakfast menu, they can also be a welcome addition to a lunch or dinner menu with such listings

---

FISH AND SEAFOOD

Roasted Sea Scallops with Verjus Ravigote Dressing,
Fresh Field Salad, and Root Vegetable Chips

$27.00

Sautéed Dover Sole Filets with Dungeness Crab Meat Millefeuille
in a Lobster Sauce and Tarragon Oil

$28.00

Seared Canadian Salmon Filets and Root Vegetable filled Smoked Salmon Ravioli
with Green Lentils in a Fine Herb Vinaigrette

$28.00

Northern Atlantic Black Sea Bass Filets with
Caribbean Fruits in a mild spicy sauce

$27.00

Fresh Atlantic Turbot cooked in a Potato Crust
with Porcini Mushrooms and a Merlot Wine Sauce

$28.00

Grilled Gulf Shrimp in a Roast Garlic Sauce and Red Chili Oil

$26.00

FIGURE 5-7. Sample seafood menu.

as Quiche or Omelets. Another non-meat hot entree which is quite popular is pasta with various sauces or combined with meat, poultry, or seafood.

Vegetarians are prime potential customers for this category with such offerings as vegetable plates, as well as entrees and extenders made with non-meat ingredients.

VEGETABLES

This group used to be an integral part of every menu. In the 1970s, it started disappearing from the product listing of many restaurants. While still popular with captive audience menus, its demise continued in restaurants until the present where it is virtually nonexistent. The reasoning behind this is puzzling. Vegetables, for the

Specialties

*Our Specialties are served with vegetable and your choice of
roasted garlic mashed potatoes and gravy, wild rice pilaf, steamed new potatoes or shoestring fries.*

FIRE ROAST "FLATTENED" CHICKEN *with roasted garlic mashed potatoes,
natural gravy and fresh vegetable saute* *10.95*

SAUTEED FRESH SEA SCALLOPS *with chef's seasoned butter* *15.75*

TRIO COMBO *crisp-fried shrimp, scallops and jumbo lump crabcake with a trio of sauces* *16.95*

GRILLED SHRIMP & SCALLOP PASTA *spicy tomato sauce and cream. With vegetable* . . . *13.95*

SHELLFISH CIOPPINO *fresh fish, sea scallops, Maine Mussels and Gulf Shrimp
in a red wine tomato-herb sauce. Garlic cheese toast* *14.95*

LOBSTER TAIL *broiled or steamed* *19.95*

JUMBO SHRIMP *crisp-fried. With traditional cocktail sauce* *15.95*

JUMBO LUMP MARYLAND-STYLE CRABCAKES *17.95*

MIXED GRILLE *jumbo sea scallops and shrimp over sauteed savoy spinach and grilled
Mahi Mahi with tomato-basil salsa.* *16.95*

FIGURE 5-7. *(Continued)*

most part, are low cost, nutritious, well accepted by customers, low in calories, and when properly prepared very colorful additions to any plate. With the population's food attitudes changing, the time is right to return this group to the menu.

SIDE DISHES

We now come to the miscellaneous part of the menu. If the restaurant desires to sell an item and doesn't know where to list it in the other categories, it ends up here. Normally, side dishes are nothing more than a list. Consider for a moment what they really are and what they can mean to sales. Add ons, when properly merchandised on a menu, can mean more sales. Items that a customer would normally not consider ordering, when sold via calling attention to them, mean a higher check average and, consequently, higher sales.

ENTREES

Mustard & Beer Marinated Pork Loin with Cumin and Curry
$18.25

Pan Seared Kasu Cod with Mango Chili Relish
$17.50

Garlic Stuffed Beef Tenderloin with Sweet Onion Merlot Sauce
$23.50

Northwest Halibut Roasted with
Smoked Onion & Sun-dried Tomato Vinaigrette
$18.95

Rosemary Glazed Farm Raised Chicken
with a Fig & Lentil Salad
$17.50

Tellicherry Peppered Tuna Steak Niçoise
$19.50

Sautéed Salmon with a Fennel Saffron Vinaigrette
$19.25

Venison Medallions with a Pear and Pepper Armagnac Sauce
$23.50

Grilled East Coast Scallops with Gingered Vegetables and Coconut Carrot Jus
$17.75

Rack of Ellensburg Lamb with a Currant Star Anise Sauce
$23.50

Roasted Atlantic Monkfish with Lobster Sauce
$18.50

PRIX FIXE MENU

A sampling of Fullers' most popular selections

Fullers Cured Northwest Salmon Napoleon

Saffron Scented Seafood Soup

Wild Greens with Roasted Beet & Shallot Vinaigrette

FIGURE 5-8. Sample mixed entre menu.

Pastas & Sandwiches

GRILLED CHICKEN & PASTA *spicy red pepper cream sauce*
tossed with linguine. Garlic cheese toast *11.95*

GRILLED BREAST OF CHICKEN *melted mozzarella and crisp hickory smoked bacon*
on a toasted roll with dill-mustard mayonnaise. With cole slaw and French fries *6.95*

LINGUINE & SHRIMP *tossed in a light broth with fresh basil*
and diced tomatoes. Garlic cheese toast *12.95*

CHEDDAR BURGER *grilled fresh ground chuck on a toasted roll.*
With cole slaw and French fries *5.95*
   With crisp hickory-smoked bacon strips *6.95*

FRESH FISH SANDWICH *mesquite-grilled on a toasted roll. Served with*
cole slaw and French fries. Your server will tell you today's fresh fish selection *4.95*

FIGURE 5-9. Non-meat menu.

STARCHES

Starches are one of the low-cost, high-profit categories of the menu. They include potatoes, pastas, and rice. With proper use of this category, a smart operator can increase profits. A smaller high-cost meat or entree portion served with a starch can lower costs while maintaining the same selling price. This method is not recommended in all situations, but should be analyzed to ascertain if it is feasible. While in many cases customers' moods are changing, starches are still and will continue to be popular. Proper mention of them on the menu is mandatory.

DESSERTS

This is the easiest category in which to obtain add-on sales, if (and that's a big if) they are properly merchandised. Desserts are items that require suggestive selling. They are rarely ordered as a matter of course. Not only should they be predominantly merchandised on the menu, but additional merchandising via table tents, prominent lobby displays, rolling carts, and suggestive selling will motivate the customer into ordering. A well-rounded selection is important, including pastries, baked goods, ice creams, sherbets, sorbets, puddings, mousses, gelatins, fresh fruits, and on and on. Avoid the typical listing of pie and ice cream exclusively unless, of course, you don't need the additional sales. If you don't, maybe you're in the wrong business.

PALM TERRACE RESTAURANT

◊ ◊ ◊ ◊ ◊

DESSERT
$8.00

ANIS CREME BRULEE
Star Anis Flavored Custard with a Caramelized Crust

PASSION FRUIT SOUFFLE
*A rich Custard flavored with fresh Passion Fruit Juice folded into an Italian Mousse
then baked and served with a Mango Coulis*

FRENCH APPLE TART
With Caramel Sauce and Vanilla Ice Cream

CHOCOLATE CARACAS
*Fine Chocolate Sponge Cake layered with a Chocolate Mousse and Caramelized Butter
covered with an Italian Meringue and served with a Rum Crème Anglais*

CREPES SUZETTE
*Warm Crêpe filled with Banana Ice Cream surrounded by Citrus Fruit,
a Grand Marnier Orange Sauce, and Banana Spice Infusion*

"MINESTRONE" OF FRESH TROPICAL FRUIT
*Tropical Fruits sitting on a Spiced Tomato and Vanilla Infusion Broth,
served with a Fromage Blanc Ice Cream and a Crispy Cookie*

SORBETS AND ICE CREAMS

◊ ◊ ◊ ◊ ◊

FIGURE 5-10. Sample dessert menu.

CHEESES

This category is used only in the finer restaurants. While cheese is an important ingredient in items in other categories, its listing as an exclusive item is limited. When used it should contain a well-

---

Desserts

SOUR CREAM APPLE PIE *with walnut streusel topping*.. 3.95
  With ice cream... *Add .50*

HOMEMADE NEW YORK-STYLE CHEESECAKE.. 3.75
  With fresh strawberries in sauce.. *Add .50*

CARROT CAKE.. 3.75

CHOCOLATE EXTREME CAKE *with coconut cream anglaise*............................ 3.95

DEEP DISH KEY LIME PIE.. 3.95

FRESH BERRIES .... *market*

"HAAGEN DAZS" VANILLA ICE CREAM
with chocolate chip cookie.. 2.95

FIGURE 5-10. *(Continued)*

rounded assortment. Brie, Gouda, Edam, Bleu, Camembert, Cheddar, and Swiss are a few of the many popular varieties. They can be sold either as an assortment of several varieties or as a single entity, where the customer would choose from a listing. Many times cheese is listed in conjunction with fruits. When so listed, only fresh fruits are appropriate.

FRUITS

Ever popular on institutional menus, fruits are also widely used on restaurant menus particularly for breakfast. With excellent availability either as a canned, frozen, or fresh product, they can add variation to any menu. Fresh fruit plates for luncheon or light supper menus, in conjunction with other cold entrees, listed as an alternative to desserts, or featured as a garnish will add color and taste alternatives to your customers.

BEVERAGES

Customers are so conditioned to purchasing a beverage with their meal, that this category just deserves a mention. Listing the popular selections and their selling price will normally suffice. Space in this section should be reserved for merchandising specialty beverages that produce a high check average as well as high gross profit.

DESSERT WINES

CHÂTEAU RIEUSSEC, SAUTERNES
$8.50 *per glass*

MOSCATO d'ORO, ROBERT MONDAVI
$7.00 *per glass*

ALEXIS LICHINE, SAUTERNES
$5.00 *per glass*

FIGURE 5-11. Sample beverage menu.

LISTINGS

Once the categories have been decided, the next step is to determine what specific listings will be presented in those categories. This cannot be done in a haphazard manner of personal likes and dislikes. Many factors need to be taken into account. First and foremost are the demographics of the trade area. Popularity of the item and the selling price must fit the customer. The restaurant or food service operation must be able to properly produce the items from an equipment standpoint as well as the capabilities of the production and service staff. It must fit the commitment to offering nutritious, well-balanced meals. When these criteria have been satisfied, the menu listings must then be assembled and go through another series of tests before being placed on the final menu. This would include variety, balance, and composition. The best way to accomplish this is to use a menu pattern. By using this tool, the menu writer is assured of meeting all of the desired criteria.

VARIETY

It is imperative that each category listed have variety within its listings. Variety takes on many different connotations in connection with menus. There should be a variety of hot and cold, cooking methods, textures, shapes, sizes, and color—each with special meaning when applied to certain categories. Let's look at some specific examples.

Hot and Cold

This would apply to only a few categories. Vegetables and starches are normally served hot while salads, cheeses, and fruits are normally served cold. Appetizers, soups, and desserts, on the other

APPETIZERS

Fullers Cured Northwest Salmon Napoleon
$7.95

Roasted Quail with Grilled & Marinated Portobello Mushrooms
$8.75

Northwest Oysters with Green Apple Mignonette
Market Price

Smoked Lamb with a Dried Berry & Grapefruit Compote
$7.25

Pecan & Cornmeal Dusted Pacific Oysters with Chipolte Aioli
$7.75

Sautéed Sea Scallops with Tempura Onion Rings & Balsamic Rosemary
Vinaigrette
$8.95

Hudson Valley Foie Gras with Carmelized Belgian Endive & Rhubarb Compote
$13.50

Grilled Shrimp & Eggplant Lasagna
$7.50

Warm Sautéed Sweetbread "Nuggets" with Chimichurri
$6.95

SOUP AND SALADS

Saffron Scented Seafood Soup
$5.25

Sweet & Bitter Greens with
Roasted Beet & Shallot Vinaigrette
$5.95

Warm Spinach Leaves with
Smoked Duck & Honey Sesame Dressing
$7.25

Salad of Mixed Organic Greens
$4.95

Baby Romaine Spears with
Viejo Cheese, Calamari and Caesar Vinaigrette
$7.00

FIGURE 5-12. The complete menu of Fullers Restaurant located in the Seattle Sheraton Hotel and Towers, Seattle, Washington.

ENTREES

Mustard & Beer Marinated Pork Loin with Cumin and Curry
$18.25

Pan Seared Kasu Cod with Mango Chili Relish
$17.50

Garlic Stuffed Beef Tenderloin with Sweet Onion Merlot Sauce
$23.50

Northwest Halibut Roasted with
Smoked Onion & Sun-dried Tomato Vinaigrette
$18.50

Rosemary Glazed Farm Raised Chicken
with a Fig & Lentil Salad
$17.50

Tellicherry Peppered Tuna Steak Niçoise
$19.50

Sautéed Salmon with a Fennel Saffron Vinaigrette
$19.25

Venison Medallions with a Pear and Pepper Armagnac Sauce
$23.50

Grilled East Coast Scallops with Gingered Vegetables and Coconut Carrot Jus
$17.75

Rack of Ellensburg Lamb with a Currant Star Anise Sauce
23.50

Roasted Atlantic Monkfish with Lobster Sauce
$18.50

PRIX FIXE MENU

A sampling of Fullers' most popular selections

Fullers Cured Northwest Salmon Napoleon

Saffron Scented Seafood Soup

Wild Greens with Roasted Beet & Shallot Vinaigrette

Northwest Halibut Roasted with
Smoked Onion & Sun-dried Tomato Vinaigrette

Rack of Ellensburg Lamb with a Currant Star Anise Sauce

Fullers Dessert Sampler

$42.50

Fullers is pleased to offer a non-smoking environment.

FIGURE 5-12. *(Continued)*

FIGURE 5-13. The complete menu of the Bristol Bar and Grill on the Country Club Plaza, Kansas City, Missouri. (*Courtesy of Gilbert/ Robinson Inc., owner and operator of The Bristol.*)

Appetizers

FRESH OYSTERS *today's selection, half dozen* *5.95*

COCKTAIL OF JUMBO SHRIMP *with tangy cocktail sauce and fresh horseradish* *6.95*

SCAMPI SAUTE *in seasoned garlic butter* *5.95*

STEAMED MAINE MUSSELS *in white wine broth* *5.95*

ESCARGOT *baked in seasoned garlic butter* *5.25*

SWORDFISH SOFT SHELL TACOS *with spicy sour cream,*
tomato-basil and avocado salsas *5.95*

CRISP FRIED CALAMARI *with Anaheim chili aioli* ....*half order 3.75*............*5.95*

CLAM CHOWDER *New England-style* ....*cup 2.95* ....*bowl 3.95*

CREOLE GUMBO *spicy New Orleans-Style* ....*cup 2.95* ....*bowl 3.95*

Salads

HOUSE SALAD *seasonal greens, fresh mushrooms, croutons, roasted nuts,*
feta cheese and tomato. Tossed with a honey-balsamic vinaigrette *3.95*

A SALAD OF FRESH SPINACH *crisp bacon, croutons,*
sweet red onion and hickory-smoked almonds with a warm bacon dressing..................*3.95*

A SALAD OF SLICED TOMATOES AND RED ONION
herb vinaigrette.................................*2.95*   *with bleu cheese* *3.75*

CAESAR SALAD *garlic, olive oil and parmesan cheese* *2.95*

GRILLED SEA SCALLOPS & SHRIMP SALAD *seasonal greens, mushrooms,*
double-smoked bacon, Fontina cheese and bell pepper with an herb vinaigrette *9.95*

GRILLED CHINESE CHICKEN SALAD *seasonal greens, assorted julienne vegetables,*
bean sprouts, mushrooms, snow peas and toasted almonds with a light sesame dressing *7.95*

Pastas & Sandwiches

GRILLED CHICKEN & PASTA *spicy red pepper cream sauce*
tossed with linguine. Garlic cheese toast *8.50*

GRILLED BREAST OF CHICKEN *melted mozzarella and crisp hickory-smoked bacon*
on a toasted roll with dill-mustard mayonnaise. With cole slaw and French fries *7.95*

LINGUINE & SHRIMP *tossed in a light broth with fresh basil*
and diced tomatoes. Garlic cheese toast...*9.25*

CHEDDAR BURGER *grilled fresh ground chuck on a toasted roll.*
With cole slaw and French fries *6.95*
    With crisp hickory-smoked bacon strips ....*Add .25*

FRESH FISH SANDWICH *mesquite-grilled on a toasted roll. Served with*
cole slaw and French fries. Your server will tell you today's fresh fish selection *8.95*

Desserts

SOUR CREAM APPLE PIE *with walnut streusel topping* *3.95*
    With ice cream ....*Add .50*

HOMEMADE NEW YORK-STYLE CHEESECAKE *3.75*
    With fresh strawberries in sauce..*Add .50*

CARROT CAKE *3.75*

CHOCOLATE EXTREME CAKE *with coconut cream anglaise*.................................*3.95*

DEEP DISH KEY LIME PIE *3.95*

FRESH BERRIES...*market*

"HAAGEN DAZS" VANILLA ICE CREAM
with chocolate chip cookie...*2.95*

FIGURE 5-13. *(Continued)*

This space is used for "Daily Fresh Sheet"

Specialties

*Our Specialties are served with vegetable and your choice of
roasted garlic mashed potatoes and gravy, wild rice pilaf, steamed new potatoes or shoestring fries.*

FIRE ROAST "FLATTENED" CHICKEN *with roasted garlic mashed potatoes,
natural gravy and fresh vegetable saute*...*10.95*

SAUTEED FRESH SEA SCALLOPS *with chef's seasoned butter* *15.75*

TRIO COMBO *crisp-fried shrimp, scallops and jumbo lump crabcake with a trio of sauces* *16.95*

GRILLED SHRIMP & SCALLOP PASTA *spicy tomato sauce and cream. With vegetable* ..*13.95*

SHELLFISH CIOPPINO *fresh fish, sea scallops, Maine Mussels and Gulf Shrimp
in a red wine tomato-herb sauce. Garlic cheese toast* *14.95*

LOBSTER TAIL *broiled or steamed*...*19.95*

JUMBO SHRIMP *crisp-fried. With traditional cocktail sauce* *15.95*

JUMBO LUMP MARYLAND-STYLE CRABCAKES...................................*17.95*

MIXED GRILLE *jumbo sea scallops and shrimp over sauteed savoy spinach and grilled Mahi Mahi with
tomato-basil salsa*...*16.95*

Steaks & Combinations

*Served with vegetable and your choice of
roasted garlic mashed potatoes and gravy, wild rice pilaf, steamed new potatoes or shoestring fries.*

*To continue with our tradition of excellence, along with our seafood, we offer Certified Angus Beef. Only top of the U.S.D.A. prime
and choice grades are labeled and sold under the Certified Angus Beef trademark. Carefully aged and cut to our rigid quality specifications,
the C.A.B. label is your guarantee of fresh Certified Angus Beef, never frozen.*

FILET MIGNON *(8 oz.)* *17.95*

KANSAS CITY STRIP *(14 oz.)* *19.95*

FILET MIGNON *(6 oz.)* **& BROILED OR STEAMED LOBSTER TAIL**...............*29.95*

FILET MIGNON *(6 oz.)* **& JUMBO FRIED SHRIMP**.....................................*18.95*

FILET MIGNON *(6 oz.)* **& MARYLAND-STYLE CRABCAKE**........................*19.95*

In consideration of all our guests, cigar and pipe smoking is permitted only at the bar.

FIGURE 5-13. *(Continued)*

PALM TERRACE RESTAURANT

◇◇◇◇◇

APPETIZERS

Norwegian Smoked Salmon Roll filled with
Potato, Sevruga Caviar, and Fresh Herbs in Sour Cream
$12.50

Casserole of California Vineyard Snails in a Merlot Wine and Garlic Sauce
$12.00

"Salad Gourmande"
Louisiana Crayfish, Grilled Sea Scallops, Foie Gras, Asparagus, and Wild Mushrooms
on a bed of Mesclun and Herbs, Banyuls Wine Vinegar and Truffle Oil Dressing
$13.00

Quick Fried Quail over Frisée Salad with Roasted Garlic and Truffles
$14.00

Maine Lobster Croustillant with an Oriental Salad
$13.00

Polenta and Farm Goat Cheese Tarte with
Glazed Onion and Fresh Tomatoes with Basil Oil
$11.00

Sautéed Fresh Duck Foie Gras with Grapes in a Black Muscat Wine Sauce
$16.50

California Baby Field Greens with Aged Red Wine Vinaigrette
$8.50

A Sauté of Spring Wild Mushrooms in Brioche, Madeira Wine infusion
$11.50

SOUP

Chilled Vine Ripe Tomato Soup with Lobster Medallions and Basil Sorbet
$9.50

Fresh Green Asparagus Soup with Morel and White Asparagus Flan
$8.50

The Palm Terrace is pleased to provide Italian mineral waters for our guests:
FONTE LIMPIA NON-CARBONATED MINERAL WATER *(1000 ml)* $4.50
SAN PELLEGRINO SPARKLING MINERAL WATER *(750 ml)* $4.50
TY NANT ORIGINAL NATURAL SPRING WATER *(25 fluid oz.)* $5.50

FIGURE 5-14. The complete menu of the Palm Terrace Restaurant located in the Palazzo Hotel, U.S. Virgin Islands.

FISH AND SEAFOOD

Roasted Sea Scallops with a Verjus Ravigote Dressing,
Fresh Field Salad, and Root Vegetable Chips

$27.00

Sautéed Dover Sole Filets with Dungeness Crab Meat Millefeuille
in a Lobster Sauce and Tarragon Oil

$28.00

Seared Canadian Salmon Filets and Root Vegetable filled Smoked Salmon Ravioli
with Green Lentils in a Fine Herb Vinaigrette

$28.00

Northern Atlantic Black Sea Bass Filets with
Caribbean Fruits in a mild spicy sauce

$27.00

Fresh Atlantic Turbot cooked in a Potato Crust
with Porcini Mushrooms and a Merlot Wine Sauce

$28.00

Grilled Gulf Shrimp in a Roast Garlic Sauce and Red Chili Oil

$26.00

MEAT AND POULTRY

Roasted Half Free Range Chicken
with a Confit of Garlic and Shallots and a Medley of Vegetables

$25.00

Sautéed Magret of Moulard Duck with
Pineapple in a Vanilla Scented Szechwan Pepper Sauce

$26.00

Medallions of Loin of Veal with Fresh Oregon Morels and Asparagus

$28.00

Medallions of Beef Tenderloin in a Light Roquefort and Aged Red Port Sauce

$28.00

Oven Roast Loin of Spring Lamb in Moroccan Spice Crust
with a Vegetable and Lemon Couscous

$29.50

Roasted Rib of Beef "Marchand de Vin", Vegetables Bouquetière

$56.00 (2 Persons)

Any entree can be prepared plain broiled, grilled, or poached without sauce upon request

GRATUITY IS NOT INCLUDED, 15% IS CUSTOMARY IN THE UNITED STATES FOR GOOD SERVICE.

FIGURE 5-14. *(Continued)*

P A L M   T E R R A C E   R E S T A U R A N T

◊ ◊ ◊ ◊ ◊

D E S S E R T
$8.00

A N I S   C R E M E   B R U L E E
Star Anis Flavored Custard with a Caramelized Crust

P A S S I O N   F R U I T   S O U F F L E
A rich Custard flavored with fresh Passion Fruit Juice folded into an Italian Meringue,
then baked and served with a Mango Coulis

F R E N C H   A P P L E   T A R T
With Caramel Sauce and Vanilla Ice Cream

C H O C O L A T E   C A R A C A S
Fine Chocolate Sponge Cake layered with a Chocolate Mousse and Caramelized Bananas,
covered with an Italian Meringue and served with a Rum Crème Anglaise

C R E P E S   S U Z E T T E
Warm Crêpe filled with Banana Ice Cream surrounded by Citrus Fruit,
a Grand Marnier Orange Sauce, and Banana Spice Infusion

" M I N E S T R O N E "   O F   F R E S H   T R O P I C A L   F R U I T S
Tropical Fruits sitting on a Spiced Tomato and Vanilla Infusion Broth,
served with a Fromage Blanc Ice Cream and a Crispy Cookie

S O R B E T S   A N D   I C E   C R E A M S

◊ ◊ ◊ ◊ ◊

D E S S E R T   W I N E S

C H Â T E A U   R I E U S S E C ,   S A U T E R N E S
$ 8 . 5 0 *per glass*
M O S C A T O   d' O R O ,   R O B E R T   M O N D A V I
$ 7 . 0 0 *per glass*
A L E X I S   L I C H I N E ,   S A U T E R N E S
$ 5 . 0 0 *per glass*

FIGURE 5-14. *(Continued)*

hand should contain a variety of both hot and cold offerings. Too often, these listings are almost always exclusively hot or cold. With so many choices, there is no reason that these items should be one dimensional.

Cooking Methods

Regardless of whether an item is served hot or cold, odds are that it has gone through a cooking process. The exceptions to this would be raw fruits, vegetables, marinated fresh fish and seafood, and steak tartar. The smart menu writer would assure that there is a variety of cooking methods in each category. Failure to do so would result in a dull, one-dimensional menu. Let's analyze the key categories where different methods can be employed. Deep fat frying for breaded vegetables; boiled and chilled shrimp or crab claws; sandwiches could include deep fried, grilled, broiled, and roasted (some hot, some cold). For hot entrees consider adding braised and sauteed to the traditional methods. Cold entrees would follow basically the same methods. Desserts—frozen, baked. With all of these methods and varieties available, why should any menu be dull and one dimensional?

Texture

There are many textures in the foods we eat and a variety of these textures are important when selecting various listings to place on the menu. A solid, chewy texture is found in meats such as steaks or roasts. A soft, mushy texture is inherent in whipped potatoes or puddings. Casserole items might tend to have a liquid texture for their base as would listings that contain a sauce. Cooked vegetables, if they are properly prepared, would have a slight crispness to them, while raw vegetables would have a definite crunch. A variety of these and other textures throughout a meal would make it a more interesting experience than would a meal with only one or two textures.

Shapes and Sizes

Shape and size appeal to the eye. An attractively presented plate will appeal to a customer more than a dull plate and will psychologically taste better too. An entree of medallions of beef, pommes Anna, and sliced harvard beets would contain all circles and as such would not be very appealing. In addition to varying the shapes and sizes on a menu, remember that the shape of food should always be as natural as possible. With the proliferation of prefabricated foods on the market, it is easy for the menu planner to forget this fact. A breaded fish square on a plate is not nearly as attractive as a fillet.

Color

Although shape and size are important, color will do more for eye appeal than anything. Consider this: If a menu is properly prepared with a variety of shapes, sizes, and color, the plate would need no garnish. The result would be less labor to prepare the plate and less food cost. There are many beautiful, bright, vivid colors that occur naturally in foods. Use them to your advantage. Unfortunately, there are also many dull bland colors inherent in foods. It would not be prudent to eliminate these foods as many of them are quite popular. A careful blend is the key to a colorful plate. Take, for example, a simple pork chop. If we were to serve this with potatoes au gratin, buttered corn, and a ramekin of applesauce, we would have dull like you wouldn't believe. But by substituting potatoes O'Brien, tiny LeSeur peas, and a spiced crabapple, we would then create a plate with substantially more eye appeal than its predecessor.

Balance

Balance takes on many different connotations when used in conjunction with menu planning. The same criteria that were utilized in association with variety, would be used when discussing balance. We need to have a good balance within each category listed on the menu, balance of items, temperatures, cooking methods, textures, shapes, sizes, and color. To illustrate balance, let's analyze the hot entree category of the menu.

Balance of items in hot entrees would include meat, poultry, and fish/seafood. Breaking this down further, it would be necessary to have a balance of meats, i.e., beef, veal, pork, and lamb. Likewise, in poultry, include chicken, turkey, and possibly game such as quail or pheasant. Fish and seafood should also have a balance. Including some or all of these items automatically gives us variety; however, we do not want to become one dimensional with an overabundance of one particular type of item. An exception to this, of course, would be a specialty restaurant where one type of food would be predominant. A steak house, for instance, should be unbalanced with beef. Other selections may or may not be offered. However, it should be remembered that this is an exception and the rule would be to have a balanced variety within this category.

Temperature within the hot entree category would be a nonentity as it would be assumed all hot entrees would be served hot. Cooking methods, on the other hand, should be considered. When variety was considered we talked about roasting, broiling, grilling, and braising. Not only is it important to have a variety of these cooking methods, it is also important to strike a balance between them.

Texture balance is also important. Entrees of solids such as steaks and roasts, semi solids such as croquettes and loafs, and extenders such as stews and casseroles, should be listed in a manner as to achieve balance. Shapes, sizes, and colors would also be handled in a like manner.

COMPOSITION

Composition refers to the makeup of the plate itself. Consideration of composition needs to be taken into account when writing menus in which the customer has no choice. Banquets, institutions, school lunches, and in-plant cafeterias are all areas where composition becomes important. In operations where the customer can choose which items they prefer with each other, composition then is taken out of the hands of the menu writer and becomes the choice of the customer. In considering plate composition, all of the criteria heretofore mentioned must be taken into consideration. The plate should have variety and balance. Various cooking methods should be used. Textures are important. We would not want, for example, a plate of chicken a la king with scalloped potatoes and harvard beets all running together. Shape, size, and color also come into play. All of these criteria need to be carefully analyzed before writing a menu.

DESCRIPTIVE TERMINOLOGY

Descriptive terminology is used on a menu for two reasons, first, to explain a product and second, to sell that product. While these functions would appear to be among the duties of the service personnel, don't count on it. The other evening, while dining in a fine restaurant, the maitre d' commented while seating us that the waiter would explain the chef's selection for the evening as well as the soup du jour. The waiter did neither. Nor was a wine offered or even suggested and no attempt was made to sell a dessert. The waiter did not know the contents of several of the dishes. The point is, unfortunately, that you cannot count on your service personnel to sell or explain, no matter how well trained. The menu must do it. If both the menu and the service personnel sell and explain, that's a plus.

EXPLAINING

Many menu items are confusing to the customer. If they don't understand what a particular dish is made of, they won't order it. While the majority of your customers may understand a listing, others won't. The assumption must be made that *all* of your customers won't understand *any* listing and all listings should be fully described. All too often restaurant owners and managers seeing the same items over and over forget that some customers may not understand them.

For example, take an item like beef stroganoff. Ask a group of people what it is. Very few will be able to answer you. Simply listing beef stroganoff on the menu will not get the job done. Many people will avoid ordering it not knowing that the ingredients could be some of their favorite foods and that they would thoroughly enjoy this dish, if it were properly explained. Next, ask a group of chefs how they prepare beef stroganoff. Prepare yourself for a difference of opinion. Some use tenderloin tips, others stew beef, still others use miscellaneous cuts from leftovers. How much and what kind of spices? Some more. Some less. How do they serve it? En casserole, over buttered noodles, with or without caraway seeds? Wide noodles, narrow, dumpling style? Odds are, you won't get two identical answers. That's one of the things that makes our industry so great—individuality. Even if your customers know what beef stroganoff is, they do not know how your restaurant or your chef prepares it. It must be explained to them in order for that item to sell.

Take an item that 99.94 percent of the population know and understand. Steak. Simply listing steak doesn't tell the customer everything they need to know about that item. What kind of steak? Strip. *Strip steak.* What style of strip steak? New York. *New York strip steak.* How is it cooked? Broiled. *Broiled New York strip steak.* How is it broiled? Charcoal. *Charcoal broiled New York strip steak.* What is its size? 12 oz. *Charcoal broiled 12 oz. New York strip steak.* Now we have a menu listing. All of these questions go through the customer's mind when making a decision. If the menu doesn't answer these questions, they will ask the service personnel with delay and possibly confusion resulting. Anticipate these problems when writing the menu. Describe fully and accurately each menu listing. As we will learn in Chapter 6, accuracy is a must.

SELLING

By describing the item, the task of writing the menu is semicomplete. The selling of that item must now be accomplished. To have a truly complete menu listing, the item must be fully described as well as romanced in order for it to be sold.

In selling or romancing an item, the listing must sound so good that the customer can't pass it up. To do this, the use of adjectives, used profusely, is employed. Here simple wording is not enough. Use a complete sentence, maybe two, to sell the item. For instance, the steak in the previous example becomes:

NEW YORK STRIP STEAK
A generous 12 oz. portion of USDA. Choice well marbled beef carefully charcoal broiled to your specifications.

Thus we have a complete menu listing. It both explains and sells the item.

Writing descriptive terminology on menus is not easy nor is it easily taught. It comes primarily from experience, both in the industry and the classroom. Students often ask why they need liberal arts in addition to the technical courses. Here is a perfect example. Skills learned in a communications class or a creative writing class will go a long way in aiding a person who must write menus as a part of their job. Figure 5-15 contains some key words used in menu writing. Take these, add some of your own, and go to work. Practice makes perfect, and soon you will find that this task is in reality very easy.

An often-asked question is if every item on the menu is written in such a way that the customer cannot pass it up, won't this confuse the customer? The answer to that is an emphatic, NO! Customers will immediately eliminate an item they personally dislike. Even if you are a Pulitzer Prize winning writer you will not convince a person to order lamb if they do not like lamb. From a correctly written menu the customer can choose from several items they cannot pass up. One will be selected with the thought that they will return to try the others. Thus, a properly written menu will have a residual effect, repeat business. Of course, the item selected must be properly prepared and meet the customer's expectations or the whole effect is blown.

Most menus are written with descriptive terminology limited strictly to entrees. Appetizers, soups, side orders, and desserts are simply listed. This is a mistake as our definition of descriptive terminology is to explain and sell. When people come into a food service establishment, they are probably going to order an entree regardless of how it is written or described. What needs to be sold is add ons, those items which increase the average check. By using descriptive terminology to sell appetizers, soups, side orders, and desserts, we can accomplish just that. Thus, we cannot properly write just part of the menu; we must do a complete job. Descriptive terminology should be used on all of the menu. This includes the headings or category listings. Choose headings that tie into the theme of the restaurant.

FIGURE 5-15. Descriptive wording for menus.

Abundance	Appeal
Abundant	Appealing
Accented	Appetite
Accentuated	Appetizing
Accompanied	Arrangement
Accompaniment	Array
Additional	Aroma
Adorned	Aromatic
Adventure	Assorted
Aflame	Assortment
Al Dente	Attractive
Alternate	"Au jus naturel"
Alternative	Authentic
Ambrosiac	Awesome
Ambrosial	Baby
Ample	Baked

FIGURE 5-15. (Continued)

Barbecued	Culinary
Basted	Dainty
Batter dipped	Delicacy
Beautiful	Delicious
Beautifully	Deliciously
Beginning	Delicate
"Best"	Delicately
Beverage	Deep fried
Big	Deglazed
Blackened	Delectable
Blanched	Delight
Bland	Delightful
Blend	Deluxe
Blooming	Diced
Bonne bouche	Dieter's
Boned	Dimension
Boneless	Discriminating
Bordered	Discriminatingly
Bountiful	Discriminative
Bouquet	Display
Braised	Distinctive
Brandied	Distinguished
Brilliant	Divine
Broiled	Dressed
Buffet	Dusted
Buttered	Elegantly
Butterflied	Enhanced
Candied	Enchanting
Capped	Enjoyment
Carefully	Entire
Carved	Entrenched
Catch	Epicurean
Celebrated	Epicure's
Celestial	Essence
Charbroiled	Excellent
Chilled	Exceptional
Choice	Exciting
Chunks	Exotic
Classic	Extra-fine
Coals	Extra-flavor
Coated	Extra lean
Coddled	Extraordinary
Combination	Extra thick
Colorful	Extravaganza
Colossal	Fabulous
Complemented	Famous
Compote	Fancy
Concoction	Fanfare
Cooked	Favorite
Covered	Featuring
Creamed	Festive
Creation	Fiery
Creative	Filled
Crisp	Finale
Crisped	Finely
Crispness	Finest
Crisply	Finished
Crispy	Flakey
Cuisine	Flamed

FIGURE 5-15. *(Continued)*

Flaming	Imported
Flavor	Impressive
Flavored	Incredible
Flavorful	Individual
Florentine	Inexplicable
Fluffy	Interlaced
Forte	Jardiniere
Fragrant	Jelled
Framed	Jellied
Fried	Juicy
Fresh	Julienne
Freshly	Jumbo
Frosted	Kosher
Frosty	Laced
Frothy	Large
Frozen	Lavish
Full flavored	Layered
Gaily	Lean
Garden	Liberal
Garnished	Light
Garniture	Lightly
Gastronomy	Liking
Gems	Live
Generous	Magnificent
Genuine	Magnifico
Gigantic	Marinated
Glazed	Marvelous
Golden	Matchless
Goodness	Medallions
Gourmet	Medley
Graced	Melt away
Gracious	Melted
Grade	Mid-western
Gran deur	Mild
Grand	Milk fed
Grated	Minced
Green	Miniature
Greens	Minted
Grill	Minute
Grilled	Mixture
Haute cuisine	Moist
Healthful	Morsels
Healthy	Most
Heart warming	Mound
Hearty	Mounds
Heavenly	Mouthwatering
Herbed	Natural
Hickory smoked	Nectarous
Highest	Nested
Highlighted	New
Hint	"New-fashioned"
Home style	Notable
Honey cured	Nourishing
Honeyed	Novel
Hot	Numerous
Iced	Old-fashioned
Ideal	Open-faced
Imagination	Original
Impeccable	Oven baked

FIGURE 5-15. (Continued)

Over flowing	Sizzled
Palatable	Skewered
Palate	Skillfully
Pan broiled	Sliced
Parchment	Slow roasted
Parsleyed	Small
Particular	Smooth
Permeating	Smothered
Perfect	Soft
Perfection	Softly
Petite	Softened
Piping hot	Soothing
Piquant	Sparkling
Plain	Special
Pleasing	Specially
Plentiful	Specialty
Plump	Spectrum
Poached	Spiced
Popular	Spicy
Potpourri	Spirited
Preference	Splendid
Premium	Spread
Prepared	Spring
Preserved	Sprinkled
Prime	Steamed
Properly aged	Steaming
Pure	Stewed
Quality	Stir fry
Quick	Strips
Radiant	Stuffed
Ragout	Succulent
Rainbow	Sugar cured
Rare	Sultry
Refreshing	Sumptuous
Refined	Super fine
Regal	Superb
Renowned	Superior
Reputable	Supreme
Rich	Supremely
Ripened	Surprising
Roast	Sweet
Roasted	Sweetness
Robust	Sweltering
Sauce	Tableside
Sauteed	Tangy
Sassy	Tantalizing
Savory	Taste
Savorous	Tasteful
Scented	Tasty
Seasonal	Tempting
Select	Tender
Selected	Tenderized
Selection	Tenderly
Sensational	Textured
Shredded	Thick
Silky	Thin
Simmered	Thrill
Simple	Throughout
Sizzling	Tidbit

FIGURE 5-15. *(Continued)*

Tiny	Utmost
Topped	Variation
Torrid	Variety
Toasted	Vine ripened
Totally	Warm
Touch	Warmed
Tremendous	Warming
Trimmed	Warm weather
Tropical	Wedges
Ultimate	Whipped
Uncommon	Whole
Uncommonly	Wholesome
Undefinably	Winter
Unequalled	Wonderful
Unique	Wondrous
Unparalled	Wrapped
Unprecedented	Young
Unsurpassed	Zest
Unsurpassable	Zesty
	Zippy

NEGATIVE TERMINOLOGY

All too often menus contain wording that can best be described as negative terminology. Although written in a positive framework, they still have negative overtones. They do nothing more than have a negative psychological effect on the customers and, therefore, destroy all of the positive effects that the menu writer has attempted to convey to the customer. Some examples of negative terminology are *Roquefort dressing, 50¢ extra. Fifteen percent gratuity will be added to your check. No shoes, no shirts, no service.* Don't undo all of the positive selling by a negative comment.

CONCLUSION

It's mind boggling. By now the reader is saying, "I didn't know writing a menu could be this complicated." Let's review. Pick the categories that you want to serve. Draw up a list of items that you want to sell in each category. Check for variety, balance, and composition. Make changes where necessary. Once the listings are complete, describe and sell those items using descriptive terminology. It's just that simple.

FIGURE 5-16. Foreign wording for menus.

A La. (French) According to the style of.

A La Carte. (French) Signifies each course is priced separately.

A La King. (French) A dish in a rich cream sauce containing mushrooms, pimentos, green peppers and usually sherry.

FIGURE 5-16. (*Continued*)

A La Mode. Usually refers to ice cream on top of pie but may be other dishes served in a special way.

A La Provencale. (French) Dishes with garlic and olive oil.

A La Rousse. (French) The Russian way.

Al Dente. (Italian) Term used to describe pasta and rice cooked until tender but not soft, firm enough to be felt between the teeth—literally, "to the tooth."

Agneau. (French) Lamb.

Aglaise. (French) In the English style.

A L'Orange. (French) In an orange sauce.

Amandine. (French) Made with or garnished with almonds.

Antipasto. (Italian) Assorted hors d'oeuvres served before the main course, literally, "before the pasta."

Aspic. (French) A clear, savory jelly made from meat or vegetable stock used to mold cold meat, fish, poultry or vegetables, or to garnish same.

Au Beurre. (French) With or cooked in, butter.

Au Gratin. (French) Food covered with a sauce, sprinkled with crumbs or cheese and baked or browned in oven or boiler.

Au Jus. (French) Literally with juice—refers to meat dishes served with their natural juices.

Au Lait. (French) With milk.

Baba Au Rhum. (French) Cake that has been soaked in rum after it's been baked.

Baguette. (French) Long loaf of French bread.

Beurre. (French) Butter.

Bearnaise sauce. (French) A thick sauce made with shallots, tarragon, thyme, bay leaf, vinegar or wine and egg yolks.

Bechamel. (French) A basic white sauce made with butter, flour and milk.

Beignet. (French) A doughnut or light sweet or savory fritter.

Biscotti. (Italian) All anise-flavored cookies.

Biscuit Tortoni. (Italian) Dessert made of egg whites, whipped cream and topped with chopped almonds.

Bisque. (French) Thick cream soup or puree, usually of shellfish, bivalves and crustaceans.

Blancmange. (French) A puddinglike dessert flavored with almonds or vanilla and shaped in a mold—literally "white food."

Blanquette. (French) White, cream stew (ragout) based on lamb, chicken or veal.

Boeuf. (French) beef.

Boeuf Bourguignon. (French) Braised beef prepared in the style of Burgundy, with small glazed onions, mushrooms and red wine.

FIGURE 5-16. *(Continued)*

Bordelaise. (French) Brown sauce made with wine and bone marrow.

Bouillabaise. (French) A provence fish soup-stew dish cooked in either water or wine with garlic, parsley, oil and tomatoes—the ingredients vary with the restaurant.

Boulangere. (French) A style of cooking potatoes beneath roasting meat.

Bourguignonne. (French) Pertaining to Burgundy wine flavored sauces and a garnish or lardons, mushrooms, and pearl onions.

Brochette. (French) A skewer—anything cooked on a skewer may be called a "brochette".

Buche De Noel. (French) A special Christmas cake made to look like a yule log.

Cacciatora, Alla. (Italian) Prepared in the style of a hunter, with mushrooms, herbs, shallots, tomatoes, wine, etc.

Cafe. (French) Coffee.

Cafe Cappuccino. (Italian) Coffee with whipped cream topping and cinnamon flavor.

Cafe Glace. (French) Cold coffee with whipped topping.

Calamari. (Italian) Squid.

Calzone. (Italian) Pastry crust with ham and cheese.

Canape. (French) A toasted slice of bread—can be topped with a variety of spreads and used as an appetizer.

Cannelloni. (Italian) Meat stuffed rolls of pasta, baked.

Cannoli. (Italian) Custard filled pastry in a tubular shape with candied fruits and rum flavoring, sometimes sprinkled with powdered sugar.

Capanata. (Italian) A mixture of eggplant, onions, and tomatoes.

Cappelli D'Angelo. (Italian) A very thin noodle—literally means "angel hair."

Champignons. (French) Mushrooms.

Chanterelles. (French) A type of mushroom.

Chanteaubriand. (French) Thick slice of steak, classically grilled and served with a garnish of potatoes cut in strips and with a Bearnaise sauce.

Chantilly Cream. (French) Vanilla whipped cream.

Chantilly Sauce. (French) Hollandaise sauce with whipped cream.

Chasseur. (French) Prepared and served in a tomato sauce with mushrooms, wine, etc.—literally "hunter style."

Coquille. (French) Shell.

Coquille St. Jacques. (French) Scallops in a shell.

Creole, A La. (French) Prepared with rice.

Coulis. (French) Thick soups made with crayfish, lobster, prawns and other crustaceans.

Coupe. (French) A shallow cup made of glass or silver, usually on a low stem, used for serving ices or fresh fruit salad.

FIGURE 5-16. *(Continued)*

Croustade. (French) A dish made with flaky puff pastry shell or from bread that has been hollowed out.

Demitasse. (French) A small cup of coffee served after dinner.

Dijonnaise. (French) A sauce of egg yolks, Dijon mustard, salt and pepper beaten with oil and lemon juice to the consistency of mayonnaise.

Du Jour. (French) Of the day.

Duxelles. (French) Mushrooms chopped and sauteed in butter and oil, mixed with onions, shallots and a bit and wine and parsley and sometimes breadcrumbs.

En Coquille. (French) Served in a shell, usually a rich, creamed seafood dish.

En Crote. (French) Baked in a pastry crust.

Entremets. (French) All side dishes. Also, the various sweet desserts served after the cheese course.

Escalopes. (French) Boneless slices of meat or fish, usually fried in butter.

Escargots. (French) Snails cooked in an aromatic garlic-butter-parsley mixture, usually served in their shells but sometimes in mushroom caps.

Fagioli. (Italian) Dried white beans.

Farci. (French) Literally—stuffed.

Fettuccine. (Italian) Ribbonlike pasta, about 1/4" wide.

Fettuccine Al Burro. (Italian) Noodles with melted butter.

Fettuccine Alfredo. (Italian) Noodles tossed with butter, cream and Parmesan cheese.

Filet De Beouf En Crote. (French) Filet of beef in a pastry crust.

Filet Mignon. (French) Small choice cut of beef prepared by grilling or sauteeing.

Fines Herbes. (French) Fresh, finely chopped parsley, alone or in combination with chives, tarragon, chervil and other herbs.

Flambe. (French) To flame—applies to foods which are doused in warm spirits and ignited just before serving.

Florentine, A La. (French) Foods cooked in this style, usually eggs, fish, or poultry, are put on spinach, covered with mornay sauce and sprinkled with cheese.

Foie Gras. (French) The livers of especially fattened geese and ducks.

Fondue. (French) Literally, "melted," and indicating roasted or melted cheese.

Fricassee. (French) Today, a method of preparing poultry and sometimes veal in a white sauce.

Fromage. (French) Cheese.

Frappe. (French) Iced drinks and desserts made from fruit juices and frozen to a mushy consistency. Literally—"iced."

Fruits De Mer. (French) Seafood served cold in salads or hot in special sauces. Literally—"fruits of the sea."

FIGURE 5-16. *(Continued)*

Fume. (French) Smoked.

Galantine. (French) Boned game, poultry or meat, stuffed and reshaped—steamed or poached, served hot or cold, sometimes in aspic.

Gelato. (Italian) Ice cream.

Genoise. (French) A rich cake using eggs as its leavening agent.

Gateau. (French) Cake.

Genovese, Alla. (Italian) With pine nuts, cheese, basil, garlic and other herbs.

Gnocchi. (Italian) Small dumplings.

Grissini. (Italian) Break sticks.

Hollandaise. (French) Hot sauce of egg yolks, butter, lemon juice and seasonings, served with vegetables and fish.

Homard Saute. (French) Chunks of lobster sauteed in butter with herbs added.

Hors D'Oeuvres. (French) Appetizers, hot or cold.

Insalada. (Italian) Salad.

Jardiniere, A La. (French) Garnished with fresh vegetables, served with roast, stewed or braised meat and poultry—the vegetables may be broiled or glazed and are placed around the meat.

Julienne. (French) Meat or vegetables cut into thin strips.

Lasagna Verdi Al Forno. (Italian) Green lasagna baked in a meat sauce.

Legumes. (French) Vegetables.

Linguine. (Italian) Narrow noodles.

Lyonnaise. (French) Prepared with onions.

Maitre D'Hotel Beurre. (French) Seasoned butter with fresh parsley and lemon, served with grilled foods.

Manicotti. (Italian) Large pancake like noodles that are stuffed and baked with a sauce.

Marinara. (Italian) Sauce made with tomatoes, olives and garlic, no meat.

Marzipan. (German & French) Sugar, almond, egg white paste candy shaped into various forms.

Medaillon. (French) Food cut into a round or oval shape.

Meuniere. (French) Method of preparing fish. Seasoned, floured and fish fried in butter and served with lemon juice, parsley and melted butter.

Milanese, Alla. (Italian) Coated with bread crumbs and cooked in butter.

Minestrone. (Italian) A thick vegetable soup with pasta.

Mornay Sauce. (French) A cream sauce with cheese added.

Mousse. (French) A light and airy dish made with cream and eggs and the addition of fish, chicken, fruits or chocolate.

Mousseline. (French) Hot or cold molds or sauces as well as certain desserts which have been lightened and enriched with whipped cream.

Noir. (French) Black.

FIGURE 5-16. *(Continued)*

Noisettes. (French) In combination with other words, small round cuts of meat, vegetables, etc.

Normande. (French) With oyster juice—used with fillet of sole.

Oignons. (French) Onions.

Oreganato. (Italian) Baked with oregano.

Orzo. (Italian) Rice shaped pasta.

Osso Buco. (Italian) Veal shank stewed in tomatoes and wine.

Palmier. (French) Pastry formed from many horizontal layers, then baked with powdered sugar glaze.

Papilloie, En. (French) Baked in buttered parchment, aluminum foil or other paper to retain juices of foods.

Parplit. (French) Light, sweet ice of various flavors.

Parmigiano, Alla. (Italian) Prepared with Parmesan cheese.

Pasta Verde. (Italian) Spinach noodles.

Pénne. (Italian) Short, tubular pasta.

Pastina. (Italian) Very small macaroni, usually used in soups.

Páte. (French) Dough pastry. Originally the term *pate* was applied only to a meat or fish dish enclosed in a pastry and baked; now it describes any dish of ground meat or fish baked in a mold that has been lined with strips of bacon.

Pate Maison. (French) A pate unique to a particular restaurant.

Patissier. (French) Pastry chef.

Pauplettes de Sole. (French) Slices of sole which are stuffed and rolled.

Pesto. (Italian) Paste or sauce made from fresh basil, garlic, cheese and olive oil.

Petit. (French) Small.

Petits Four. (French) Bite sized iced or fondant coated and decorated little cakes and confections.

Petits Pois. (French) Small green peas.

Petite Marmite. (French) A strong consomme with beef, chicken and vegetables.

Piccante. (Italian) Highly seasoned.

Piece De Resistance. (French) Main dish.

Pizzaiola. (Italian) Sauce of tomato, garlic and marjoram.

Plat Du Jour. (French) Specialty of the day.

Pois A La Francaise. (French) Peas cooked with lettuce leaves and onions.

Poisson. (French) Fish.

Potage. (French) Soup, usually thickened.

Pots De Creme. (French) Small individual pots of rich, mousselike cream—vanilla, chocolate, coffee—served chilled, sometimes with whipped cream.

FIGURE 5-16. *(Continued)*

Printaniere. (French) Garnish of spring vegetables cut in small dice.

Profiteroles. (French) Small round cream puffs filled with custard, ice cream or creme patissiere and glazed or sauced in chocolate.

Quenelles. (French) Dumplings made with either fish or meat.

Quiche. (French) Unsweetened custardlike tart or pie with various fillings.

Radicchio. (Italian) Red lettuce.

Ragout. (French) A dish made of meat, poultry or fish that has been cut up and browned, with or without vegetables.

Ragu. (Italian) May mean a sauce or a meat stew with garlic, tomatoes and herbs.

Ratatouille. (French) A dish of eggplant, zucchini, tomatoes, and onions stewed in olive oil with garlic, served hot or cold.

Ravioli. (Italian) Envelopes of pasta that are stuffed with either meat or cheese and eaten in soup or with a sauce.

Rigatoni. (Italian) Large macaroni shaped pasta which is grooved.

Risotto. (French & Italian) Rice baked in a chicken stock.

Risotto Alla Milanese. (Italian) Risotto with saffron, Parmesan cheese and ham added.

Robert Sauce. (French) Sauce of onion, white wine and mustard; served with grilled pork dishes.

Rossini. (French) Garnished with truffles and poie gras.

Roulade. (French) A rolled piece of thin meat.

Rugola. (Italian) Field lettuce.

Sabayon. (French) Dessert served in glasses with whipped egg yolks, vanilla, sugar, sherry, white wines.

Salad Nicoise. (French) Potatoes, string beans with an oil and vinegar dressing, trimmed with olives, capers, anchovies and tomatoes.

Salsa Alla Millanese. (Italian) Sauce of ham and veal cooked in butter with fennel and wine.

Saltimbocca. (Italian) Slices of veal seasoned with sage.

Sauce Soubise. (French) Cream sauce with onion, puree added.

Sauerbraten. (German) Rich dark pot roast with a sweet and sour gravy usually made with ginger snaps.

Scalloppine. (Italian) Thin slices of meat, most usually of veal.

Scalloppine Alla Florentina. (Italian) Thinly sliced veal on spinach with a white sauce.

Scampi. (Italian) Shrimp.

Schnitzel. (German) Cutlet, usually veal.

Schnitzel A La Holstein. (German) Cutlet topped with baked often with anchovies, capers, smoked salmon or mushrooms.

FIGURE 5-16. *(Continued)*

Souffle. (French) Dish made with pureed ingredients, egg yolks and stiffly beaten egg whites, and may be made with vegetables, fish, meat, fruit, nuts, etc. served as an appetizer, a main dish or a dessert.

Spaitzle. (German) Tiny dumplings of egg-four nature, noodlelike, pressed through a colander into boiling water or soup.

Spaghetti Al Burro. (Italian) Spaghetti with butter.

Spaghetti Alla Carbonara. (Italian) Spaghetti tossed with oil, eggs, bacon and cheese.

Spumone. (Italian) Dessert of ice cream, candied fruits with whipped cream and nuts.

Steak Au Poivre. (French) Steak made with crushed peppercorns.

Steak Tartare. (French) Uncooked raw steak which is seasoned and served with a raw egg yolk on top and capers, chopped onions, and parsley on the side.

Terrine. (French) Meat, fish, or fowl chopped finely, baked in a dish called terrine, and served cold; often called páte in the U.S.

Timbale. (French) Large or small case of pastry crust, deep-fried noodles or julienned potatoes or a hollowed brioche. Also a jellied mold containing vegetables used to garnish meats.

Torte. (German) Extremely light, delicate cake baked in round layers and filled with whipped cream, fruit, chocolate, other icings, jams, jellies. (Includes sacher, limzer, dobos and black forest cherry. Also, a flan or tart with filling. In the U.S., commonly cake in which the flour has been replaced by breadcrumbs or cookie crumbs and finely ground nuts.

Tortellini. (Italian) Meat or cheese or other stuffed twisted pasta.

Tournedos. (French) A small slice of beef, round and thick, from the heart of the fillet of beef—sauteed or grilled.

Tournedos Rossini. (French) Tournedos sauteed in butter and arranged on toast, a slice of foie gras and truffles tops the meal, covered with a sauce overall.

Truffe. (French) Truffle, a famous fungus that grows underground.

Veloute. (French) Smooth white sauce, made with veal or chicken stock, egg yolks, and cream.

Vermicelli. (Italian) Long thin threads of pasta, finer than spaghetti.

Vichyssoise. (French) A cream soup of leeks, potatoes and chicken broth, served cold.

Vinaigrette. (French) Mixture of oil and vinegar, seasoned with salt and pepper, and at times herbs.

Zabalione. (Italian) A thick frothy dessert composed of egg yolks, sugar and Marsala wine, served hot or cold. Also a sauce similarly composed for puddings, bombes etc.

FIGURE 5-16. *(Continued)*

Zeppole. (Italian) A type of fritter.

QUESTIONS

1. Meeting all of the criteria in the chapter, write out six menu listings for each of the 13 categories.

2. Define in your own words the following terms as they apply to menu planning.
   a) Variety
   b) Texture
   c) Size and shape
   d) Color
   e) Balance
   f) Composition

3. Rewrite the following menu listings using descriptive terminology. Consult a recipe book if you are unfamiliar with the items.
   Fruit Compote
   Shrimp Cocktail
   Sauerbraten
   Roast Loin of Pork
   Finnan Haddie
   Lobster Newburg
   Peas
   Duchess Potatoes
   Chef's Salad
   Strawberry Mousse

CHAPTER SIX

Truth in Menu

OBJECTIVES
- To understand the importance of accurately describing menu listings.
- To learn the eleven sections of the accuracy in menu position paper adopted by the National Restaurant Association.

IMPORTANT TERMS   Representation of:

Quantity	Quality
Price	Brand names
Product identification	Points of origin
Merchandising terms	Preservation
Preparation	Verbal presentation
Visual presentation	Nutritional claims

In the preceding chapter, you learned that descriptive terminology is an important element in creating menus. Equally important is the *Truth in Menu* concept. Also known as *accuracy in menu offerings* and *truth in dining,* it concerns itself with accurate menu listings. An overzealous menu writer using flowery descriptive terminology could (and many do) unwittingly mislead the customer. In a recent Gallup survey, it was noted that one out of every five restaurant patrons felt that menus were misleading or dishonest.

Because of misleading menu listings on the part of unscrupulous or naive operators, some states have enacted legislation to thwart such maneuvers. California, for example, created legislation in 1974 to prohibit inaccurate menu listings. The law is enforced on a county-to-county basis. Thousands of cases, involving chains as well as independent operators, have been prosecuted and the owners fined as a result of this bill. The city of Chicago has also enacted similar legislation with like results.

In a speech before the International Society of Restaurant Association Executives, Dr. Bailus Walker outlined a survey taken in Washington, D.C. Results of a review of 350 menus in various restaurants in that city clearly pointed out that many contained violations. Over 85 percent of the restaurants that listed beef as "prime" could not substantiate that claim. One hundred percent listed shrimp as fresh when it was, in fact, frozen. Fifty per-

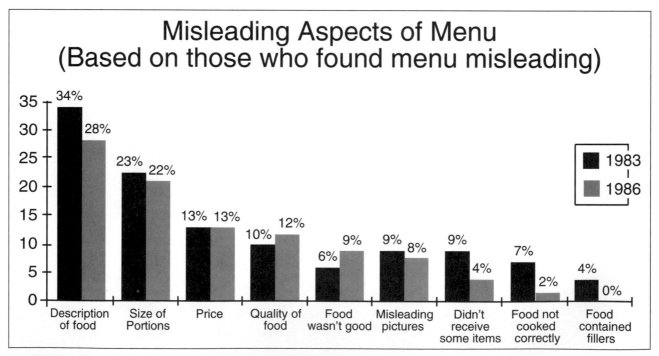

FIGURE 6-1.   Percentage of persons surveyed who felt that a menu was misleading or dishonest and what aspect of that menu was misleading. (*Data courtesy of the National Restaurant Association, Washington, D.C.*)

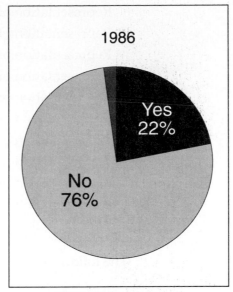

FIGURE 6-1. Continued.

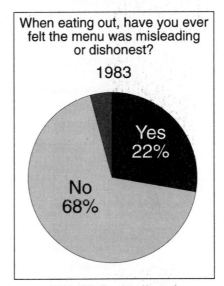

FIGURE 6-1. Continued.

cent of the restaurants listed delicatessen products as Kosher when they were not.[1] The list goes on and on. Because of enacted legislation in some states and impending legislation in many others as well as in Congress, the National Restaurant Association decided to tackle the problem. An Accuracy in Menu position paper was prepared and adopted in February 1977. It contained 11 sections. There were:

[1]Walker, Bailus Jr., Ph.D., M.P.H., *A Survey of the Accuracy of Menus in Public Eating Establishments in the District of Columbia.*

Representation of Quantity

Representation of Quality

Representation of Price

Representation of Brand Names

Representation of Product Identification

Representation of Points of Origin

Representation of Merchandising Terms

Representation of Means of Preservation

Representation of Food Preparation

Representation of Verbal and Visual Presentation

Representation of Dietary or Nutritional Claims

The following is a reprint of the Accuracy in Menus paper.

ACCURACY IN MENUS

Introduction

Every food service operator is acutely aware that success is based upon providing customer satisfaction. A keystone in this effort is the accurate representation of the products served. This truthful representation involves not only the printed menu, but also photographs, graphic illustrations, and other printed materials, as well as verbal depiction by employees.

The founders of the National Restaurant Association recognized this in 1923 when adopting its Standards of Business Practices. These standards appearing on the inside front cover, have been repeatedly endorsed and employed by NRA members in the conduct of their business. In February 1977, the NRA Board of Directors reaffirmed the position by adopting the statement "Accuracy in Menu" (reproduced at the end of the chapter).

This publication has been developed to assist the food service operators in properly representing the foods offered for sale in their restaurant. The specific types of errors are limitless and this guide describes some of the most likely kinds of mistakes.

The ultimate responsibility for accuracy in representing your menu offerings rests with you. Creativity and appealing merchandising is in no way restricted, but description and phrases must accurately reflect the food served. Be certain you can substantiate your written and spoken words with product, invoice, or label.

Representation of Quantity

Proper operational procedures should preclude any concerns with misinformation on quantities. Steaks are often merchandised by weight, and the generally accepted practice of declared quantity is that prior to cooking.

Obviously, double martinis are twice the size of the normal drink, and if jumbo eggs are listed it means exactly that—as "jumbo" is a recognized egg size. Petite and super-colossal are among the official size descriptions for olives. However, the use of terms such as "extra large salad" or "extra tall drink" may invite problems if not qualified. There is no question about the meaning of a "three-egg omelette" or "all you can eat." Also, remember the implied meaning of words—a bowl of soup contains more than a cup of soup.

Representation of Quality

Federal and state standards of quality grades exist for many restaurant products including meats, poultry, eggs, dairy products, fruits, and vegetables. Terminology used to describe grades includes Prime, Grade A, Good, No. 1, Choice, Fancy, Grade AA, and Extra Standard.

Care must be exercised in preparing menu descriptions when these words are used. In certain uses, they imply certain quality. An item appearing as "choice sirloin of beef" connotes the use of USDA Choice Grade Sirloin of Beef. One recognized exception is the term "prime rib." Prime rib is a long established, well understood and accepted description for a cut of beef (the "primal" ribs, the 6th to 12th ribs) and does not represent the grade quality, unless USDA is used in conjunction.

Because of our industry's volume use of ground beef, it is well to remember the USDA definition: Ground beef is just what the name implies. No extra fat, water, extenders, or binders are permitted. The fat limit is thirty percent. Seasonings may be added as long as they are identified. These requirements identify only product ground and packaged in federal or state inspected plants.

Representation of Price

If your pricing structure includes a cover charge, service charge, or gratuity, these must be appropriately brought to your customer's attention. If extra charges are made for requests such as "all white meat" or "no ice drinks," these should be so stated at the time of ordering.

Any restrictions when using a coupon or premium promotion must be clearly defined.

If a price promotion involves a multi-unit company, clearly indicate which units are participating.

Representation of Brand Names

Any product brand that is advertised must be the one served. A registered or copyrighted trademark or brand name must not be used generically to refer to a product. Several examples of "brand" names of restaurant products are:

Armour Star Bacon, Sanka, Log Cabin Syrup, Coca-Cola, Seven-Up, Swifts Premium Ham, Pepsi-Cola, Starkist Tuna, Ry-Crisp, Jell-O, Heinz Catsup, Maxwell House Coffee, Chase and Sanborn Coffee, Kraft Cheese, Tabasco Sauce, Ritz Crackers, Seven and Seven, Miracle Whip.

Your own "house" brand of a product may be so labeled even when prepared by an outside source, if its manufacturing was to your specifications. Containers of branded condiments and sauces placed on a table must be the product appearing on the container label.

Representation of Product Identification

Because of the similarity of many food products, substitutions are often made. These substitutions may be due to nondelivery, availability, merchandising considerations, or price. When such substitutions are made, be certain these changes are reflected on your menu. Common substitutions are:

Maple syrup and maple flavored syrup
Boiled ham and baked ham
Chopped and shaped veal patty and veal cutlet
Ice milk and ice cream
Powdered eggs and fresh eggs
Picnic style pork shoulder and ham
Milk and skim milk
Pure jams and pectin jams
Whipped topping and whipped cream
Turkey and chicken
Hereford beef and Black Angus beef
Peanut oil and corn oil
Beef liver and calves liver
Cream and half & half
Non-dairy creamers or whiteners and cream
Ground beef and ground sirloin of beef
Capon and chicken
Standard ice cream and French style ice cream
Cod and haddock
Noodles and egg noodles

Light meat tuna and white meat tuna

Pollack and haddock

Flounder and sole

Cheese food and processed cheese

Cream sauce and non-dairy cream sauce

Bonita and tuna fish

Roquefort cheese and bleu cheese

Tenderloin tips and diced beef

Mayonnaise and salad dressing

Margarine and butter

Representation of Points of Origin

A potential area of error is in describing the point of origin of a menu offering. Claims may be substantiated by the product, by packaging labels, invoices, or other documentation provided by your supplier. Mistakes are possible as sources of supply change and availability of product shifts. The following are common assertions of points of origin:

Lake Superior Whitefish	Bay Scallops
Idaho Potatoes	Gulf Shrimp
Maine Lobster	Florida Orange Juice
Imported Swiss Cheese	Smithfield Ham
Danish Bleu Cheese	Wisconsin Cheese
Louisiana Frog Legs	Alaskan King Crab
Colorado Brook Trout	Colorado Beef
Florida Stone Crabs	Long Island Duckling
Chesapeake Bay Oysters	

There is widespread use of geographic names used in a generic sense to describe a method of preparation or service. Such terminology is readily understood and accepted by the customer and its use should be restricted.

Examples are:

Russian Dressing	French Toast
New England Clam Chowder	Country Fried Steak
Irish Stew	Denver Sandwich
Country Ham	French Dip
French Fries	Swiss Steak
Danish Pastries	German Potato Salad

Russian Service	French Service
English Muffins	Manhattan Clam Chowder
Swiss Cheese	

Representation of Merchandising Terms

A difficult area to clearly define as right or wrong is the use of merchandising terms. "We serve the best gumbo in town" is understood by the dining-out public for what it is—boasting for advertising's sake. However, to use the term "we use only the finest beef" implies that USDA Prime Beef is used, as a standard exists for this product.

Advertising exaggerations are tolerated if they do not mislead. When ordering a "mile-high pie," a customer would expect a pie heaped tall with meringue or similar fluffy topping, but to advertise a "foot-long hot dog" and to serve something less would be in error. Mistakes are possible in properly identifying steak cuts. Use industry standards such as provided in the National Association of Meat Purveyor's *Meat Buyer's Guide.*

"Homestyle," "homemade style," or "our own" are suggested terminology rather than "homemade" in describing menu offerings prepared according to a home recipe. Most food service sanitation ordinances prohibit the preparation of foods in home facilities.

If using any of the following terms, be certain you can qualify them.

Fresh Daily	Corn Fed Porkers
Fresh Roasted	Slept in Chesapeake Bay
Flown in Daily	Finest Quality
Kosher Meat	Center Cut Ham
Black Angus Beef	Own Special Sauce
Aged Steaks	Low Calorie
Milk Fed Chicken	

Representation of Means of Preservation

The accepted means of preserving food are numerous, including canned, chilled, bottled, frozen, and dehydrated. If you choose to describe your menu selections with these terms, they must be accurate. Frozen orange juice is not fresh, canned peas are not frozen, and bottled applesauce is not canned.

Representation of Food Preparation

The means of food preparation is often the determining factor in the customer's selection of a menu entree. Absolute accuracy is a must. Readily understood terms include:

Charcoal Broiled Deep Fried
Sauteed Barbecued
Baked Smoked
Broiled Prepared from Scratch
Roasted Poached
Fried in Butter

Representation of Verbal and Visual Presentation

When your menu, wall placards, or other advertising contain a pictorial representation of a meal or platter, it should portray the actual contents with accuracy. Examples of visual misrepresentations include:

- The use of mushroom pieces in a sauce when the picture depicts mushroom caps.
- The use of sliced strawberries on a shortcake when the picture depicts whole strawberries.
- The use of numerous thin sliced meat pieces when the picture depicts a single thick slice.
- The use of five shrimp when the picture depicts six shrimp.
- The omission of vegetables or other entree extras when the picture depicts their inclusion.
- The use of a plain bun when the picture depicts a sesame topped bun.

Examples of verbal misrepresentation include:

- If a waiter asks "sour cream or butter with your potatoes" when, in fact, an imitation sour cream or margarine is served.
- A waitress' response "the pies are baked in our kitchen" when, in fact, they are a purchased prebaked institutional pie.

Representation of Dietary or Nutritional Claims

Potential public health concerns are real if misrepresentation is made of the dietary or nutritional content of food. For example, "salt free" or "sugar free" foods must be exactly that to assure the protection of your customers who may be under particular dietary restraints. "Low calorie" or nutritional claims, if made, must be supportable by specific data.

To list menu items accurately should be a priority with all professional food service managers, whether or not it is law in your jurisdiction. Not to do so can result in customers' dissatisfaction and, consequently, lost sales. The original intent of misrepresenting a menu listing to obtain increased sales is reversed when the patron discovers that what was ordered was not what was received.[2]

[2]*Accuracy in Menus.* National Restaurant Association, Washington, D.C., February 1977.

Some critics of Accuracy in Menus maintain that it takes away from the ability to sell via the use of descriptive terminology. This could not be farther from the truth. There are thousands of words available to describe, romance, and sell food. Use them. Whet the customer's appetite with what they are going to get, not what they think they are going to get.

A POSITION STATEMENT OF THE NATIONAL RESTAURANT ASSOCIATION

The food service industry has long recognized the importance of accuracy in describing its products, either on menus, and through visual or oral representation, both on ethical grounds and from the standpoint of customer satisfaction. The National Restaurant Association incorporated standards of accuracy in all representations to the public in its Standards of Business Practice, originally adopted by the Association in 1923. We reaffirm and strongly support the principles therein expressed.

"Truth in dining" or "truth in menu" laws and ordinances have been proposed in some government jurisdictions, and in few cases adopted, in the belief that representations on restaurant menus present a unique problem in consumer protection. The National Restaurant Association believes that such legislation is unnecessary as federal, state, and many local governments have laws and regulations prohibiting false advertising and misrepresentations of products, and providing protection from fraud. In an industry such as ours, where economic survival depends upon customer satisfaction, misrepresentation is most affectively regulated by the severe sanction of customer dissatisfaction and loss of patronage.

To be equitable, the complexity of such legislation would be staggering. It is conceivable that standardized recipes for each menu listing would be required if regulatory refinement followed its logical course. The problems of enforcement, and proof if due process is observed, would be monumental, if not impossible.

The "truth in dining" movement is not confined to the proposition that restaurant menus be absolutely accurate in their representations. Legislation and ordinances have been proposed that would require the identification of a specific means of preservation, method of preparation or statement of food origin. Such requirements could unjustly imply that certain foods, processes, or places of origin are unwholesome or inferior.

Government action must be confined to problems where its intervention can be effective and at a cost commensurate with the benefits to be gained. Adopted February 1977.[3]

[3]*Position Statement of the National Restaurant Association.* National Restaurant Association, Washington, D.C. February 1977.

CONCLUSION

Descriptive terminology is important to explain and sell menu listings, however, the menu writer should not be caught up in overstating their case. Accurate menu descriptions result in a satisfied customer receiving the product expected. It also improves the confidence of the public toward the restaurant industry. Tell the truth. It's just that simple.

QUESTIONS

1. Discuss why "truth in menu" is important to an individual restaurant and the industry as a whole.
2. In your own words, describe and analyze each of the 11 truth in menu concepts.
3. In your own operation (or one in which you work), list all truth in menu violations or potential violations.
4. Analyze the menus of several competitors. See if you can spot any potential truth in menu violations.

CHAPTER SEVEN

Menu Layout and Printing

OBJECTIVES
- To explore the various styles of menu covers and explain their importance to the overall ambience of the restaurant.
- To learn the proper layout techniques for the headings, subheadings, listings, and descriptive terminology for food as well as alcoholic beverage listings.
- To understand basic principles of printing techniques and terminology in order to communicate with the printer.

IMPORTANT TERMS

Menu cover	Lamination
Menu layout	Prime space
Institutional copy	Clip-ons
Type styles	Points
Leading	Upper case
Lower case	Proot
Desktop publishing	

INTRODUCTION

For most people, at this stage of menu development, the hard work is over and the fun is about to begin. With the layout and printing of the menu, your imagination and artistic talents can go wild. There are, of course, certain criteria which must be followed, but overall the possibilities are endless, limited only by one's daring or lack thereof.

COVER

The cover of your menu is vital to the aesthetic strategy of your operation in that it should immediately convey the overall theme of your restaurant to the customer. That old adage you can't tell a book by its cover, does not apply here. Conversely, what you want to know about a particular restaurant should be conveyed by the cover. Clues as to theme, price range, decor, and cooking style should all be at least hinted at by the cover. It is the symbol of your identity and also ties together the various nuances of your restaurant.

STYLE OF COVERS

There are a multitude of menu cover styles from which to choose. Some of the more popular types are padded, custom designed, insert, laminated, and paper. The most expensive are the padded and custom designed covers.

Padded Covers

Padded menu covers are made with either a light board or very heavy cardboard, covered with a plastic material resembling leather, and then stuffed with material to give them a padded effect. They are quite heavy. Several variations are available in addition to the imitation leather, such as suede, velvet, and real leather. Because of the special materials used, the printing on these covers is limited to a logo and/or the name of the establishment. The inside of these menus consists of heavy linen-type paper on which the various listings are printed and held in place by a ribbon, cord, or stick tape going down the center fold of the cover. These inserts are changed as often as the listings and selling prices dictate. While padded covers are very expensive, they are durable and will last a long time when properly cared for. Changes to the menu are made on the inserts only and one cover can go through many insert changes.

Custom Designed Covers

Custom designed covers are limited only to the designer's imagination. The variations, their size, shape, and material are so numerous that, unfortunately, they can't all be listed.

While these types of menu covers are great conversation pieces for the customers and convey the theme quite appropriately, it should be remembered that they are quite expensive. Materials such as wood or metal which are oftentimes used are even more expensive than paper. Even if paper or cardboard is used, the special cutting process necessary to obtain an unusual shape or size involves a more costly process than a standard square or rectangle. However, the uniqueness of such a design might well outweigh the cost when measured against the increase in sales which result from such a bold and imaginative menu.

Insert-Type Covers

Insert-type covers are widely used and are less expensive than the previous two types. They follow the same principle as padded covers in that the cover is used repeatedly while the insert is changed as often as the menu items and prices dictate. The primary difference is the material used—a heavy cardboard which can be selected from several different styles including imitation velvet, leatherette, or a glossy finished card stock. There are several companies which specialize in this type of cover and the user can choose between many stock designs or have a customized design drawn by one of the company's artists. Obviously, a stock design would be less expensive, but remember that the cover is a reflection of the restaurant's theme and decor. If a suitable stock design is compatible to the theme and decor, fine. If not, it would well be worth the extra money to have it custom designed. The cover will be used many times and the dollars spent become infinitesimal with use, especially in light of a menu which is appropriate for your operation.

Laminated Covers

Laminated covers are very popular in informal settings, such as coffee shops. Lamination is a process in which the menu, usually a durable cardboard, is covered with a clear plastic coating in order to protect it. Thus, when a menu becomes soiled or greasy, it can simply be wiped off and used over again. With this process the entire menu, cover and inside, is printed on the cardboard. It can be folded in the middle, creating a four-page menu or in thirds creating in effect a six page menu.

STARTERS

Tater Skins	3.95		**Santa Fe Dip**	2.95

Tater Skins   3.95
Crisp fried tater skins under Jack and Cheddar cheeses, bacon bits and scallions.

Chicken Quesadillas   4.95
Two grilled tortillas filled with spicy chicken, melted Jack and Colby cheese. Served with guacamole, sour cream and salsa.

Onion Rings   2.50
A hefty portion of steak cut, batter fried rings.

'shrooms   2.25
Jumbo mushroom caps filled with herbs, garlic and cheese. Breaded and fried. Served with creamy horseradish dip.

Buffalo Chicken Wings   2.95
Hot and spicy wings cooked just right then served up with a Bleu cheese dip.

Santa Fe Dip   2.95
Crispy corn tortillas topped with spiced ground beef, refried beans, diced tomatoes and onions, smothered with a Cheddar cheese sauce.

Chicken Fingers   5.25
White meat chicken strips breaded and fried to a golden brown. Served with a tangy BBQ sauce.

Mozzarella Stix   2.95
Six luscious Mozzarella stixs breaded and fried. Served with marinara sauce.

Flautas   4.95
Shredded beef and spicy chicken rolled in a corn tortilla then fried to perfection. Served with salsa and sour cream.

Crestwood Tid Bits   3.95
Tater skins, nachos and flautas. A great combination.

FIGURE 7-1. A unique menu presentation with each category folding down and the drink and dessert categories on the back. (*Courtesy of the Crestwood Country Club, Pittsburg, Kansas*).

SPECIALTIES

Chimichanga   9.95
Your choice of beef, chicken or seafood blended with cheese, scallions and mild sauce in a golden fried flour tortilla. Topped with lettuce, diced tomato and guacamole.

Sizzling Fajitas   8.95
Char-grilled beef or chicken with bell peppers, red onion, guacamole, sour cream, Cheddar cheese and mild salsa. Served on a sizzling platter. Beef, chicken or combination.

Southwestern Torte   7.95
Spicy ground beef, cheese and a special Rio Grande sauce layered between corn tortillas, baked then topped with lettuce and diced tomato. Served with refried beans and salsa.

Shrimp and Fettuccine Primavera   10.25
White Gulf Shrimp sauteed with fettuccine noodles, vegetables and garlic in a white wine sauce topped with Parmesan cheese.

Straw and Hay   8.50
Green and white pasta tossed with green peas, prosciutto ham in a three cheese sauce.

Flying Angel   8.95
Grilled marinated chicken breast combined with diced tomato, sweet peppers, mushrooms, onion and herbs on a bed of angel hair pasta.

TAKEN TO FLIGHT

Chicken Breast Dijon   8.50
Charbroiled boneless chicken breast cooked to perfection and delightfully topped with a Dijon mustard and white wine sauce.

Cashew Chicken   8.50
Tender strips of boneless chicken breast breaded, deep fried and topped with our special sauce, cashews and chives nested on a bed of rice pilaf.

Chicken Cordon Bleu   8.95
Boneless chicken breast breaded with fresh bread crumbs then filled with ham and Swiss cheese, baked in our own Cheddar cheese sauce.

FROM LAND AND SEA

Kansas City Strip   8 oz. 10.95   12 oz. 12.95
The finest U.S.D.A. prime beef. Carefully charbroiled to your specification.

Chopped Sirloin   7.95
7 oz. of lean ground beef, charbroiled and garnished with an onion ring.

Chicken Fried Steak   7.25
Lightly hand breaded, country fried and topped with cream gravy.

Jumbo Gulf Shrimp   9.95
Deep fried to perfection or broiled with herbs. Served with cocktail sauce or tartar sauce.

Pittsburg Filet   6 oz. 10.95   8 oz. 12.95
The Pride of Pittsburg, juicy choice tenderloin cut to order and charbroiled to your satisfaction.

Beef Bourguignon   10.25
7 oz. of tenderloin tips blended with onion, mushrooms and bordelaise sauce then finished with burgundy wine.

Baby Beef Liver Lyonnaise   6.95
Dusted in flour then sauteed with julienne strips of onion and green pepper.

Filet of Sole   8.95
7 oz. of white boneless sole broiled with lemon pepper and lemon juice to flaky perfection.

All entrees are served with a house salad or soup, the appropriate potato, vegetable du jour, and our homemade rolls.
May we suggest a loaf of cinnamon bread to enhance your dining pleasure.

FIGURE 7-1. *(Continued)*

Crestwood Burger   3.95
5 oz. of lean ground beef cooked the way you like. Served on a toasted bun with fries. Topped with bacon or cheese add 25¢ each.

Teriyaki Burger   3.95
Our 5 oz. patty broiled with teriyaki sauce, served on a toasted bun, accompanied by stir fry vegetables.

Mushroom Burger   4.25
Sauteed mushrooms, onions and melted Swiss cheese top our charbroiled burger on a toasted bun. Served with fries.

California Burger   4.95
A butter toasted bun topped with 5 oz. of lean ground beef. Charbroiled to your liking. Dressed with cool avocado slices and alfalfa sprouts.Served with fries.

Club Sandwich   4.95
Triple decker of bacon, turkey, lettuce, tomato on toasted whole wheat. Served with a juicy dill spear and fries.

Hot Stacked Beef & Cheese   5.95
Sliced roast beef with sauteed onions, mushrooms and melted Swiss cheese on a Hoagie bun, served with Au Jus and fries.

Grilled Ham & Cheese   4.25
Lean shaved ham with your choice of cheese on whole wheat bread with fries.

Reuben Sandwich   4.95
Lean corned beef, sauerkraut and Swiss cheese on buttered grilled rye bread. Served with fries.

Chicken Breast Sandwich   6.95
A tender grilled chicken breast topped with bacon and Monterey Jack cheese on a Kasier roll. Served with fries.

Crestwood Omelet   4.25
A fluffy three egg omelet with your choice of three ingredients, country fries and toasted whole wheat.

Build a Pizza   3.50
Start with a 6 inch crust topped with sauce and a blend of cheese and you pick everything else you want 25¢ per item.

American Cheese	Mushrooms	Bell Pepper	Pepperoni
Swiss Cheese	Onions	Sausage	Black Olives
Cheddar Cheese	Tomatoes	Ham	Ground Beef

Cakes for all occasions are made upon request. Contact us for all of your catering needs. We provide the best for you for all private parties, weddings and receptions.

FIGURE 7-1.   *(Continued)*

French Onion			Soup of the Day		
Sauteed onions simmered in rich beef stock and sherry, topped with a crouton and melted cheeses.	Cup Bowl	1.25 1.95	Made in our kitchen daily from the freshest ingredients.	Cup Bowl	1.95 2.50

Cinnamon Bread   Mini   .50
Bill's homemade cinnamon bread baked   Large   1.50
daily into mini loaves or large for the
whole family.

Cobb Salad   4.95
Cold crisp iceberg lettuce tossed tableside with tomato, egg, cheese, black olives, ripe avocado and your choice of dressing.

Monterey Seafood Salad   5.25
Flaked salmon, bay shrimp, artichoke hearts, sliced mushrooms, black olives and wedges of tomato on a bed of mixed greens.

Crestwood Chef Salad   4.25
Thin sliced ham, breast of turkey, black olives, hard boiled egg, Swiss and American cheeses on a bed of crisp mixed greens.

Seafood Salad Supreme   5.25
Freshly tossed lettuce accompanied by baby bay shrimp and crabmeat with tomato wedges, sliced egg and a ring of green pepper.

Taco Salad   4.25
Iceberg lettuce topped with seasoned ground beef, diced tomato, cheese, guacamole and sour cream in an edible shell. Served with salsa.

Fresh Fruit Salad   4.25
A bountiful array of seasonal fruits served with our sensational poppy seed dressing.

Pasta Salad   4.25
Bow tie pasta tossed with peppers, broccoli, cauliflower, carrot strips, sundried tomato in a special balsamic vinegar dressing.

FIGURE 7-1. *(Continued)*

SPECIALTY DRINKS

Lime Daiquiri
Strawberry Daiquiri
Pina Colada
Strawberry Colada
Crestwood Surfer
Butter Nip
Snowshoe
Fuzzy Navel
Attitude Adjuster

Rich, thick ice cream drinks served tall with special blends of liqueurs.

Kansas Tumbleweed
California Pink Squirrel
Italy's Golden Cadillac
Brandy Alexander
Grasshopper

BOTTLED BEERS

DOMESTIC

				IMPORTED
Bud	Busch Light	Coors Dry	Michelob Light	Corona
Bud Light	Coors	O'Douls	Michelob Dry	Heineken
Bud Dry	Coors Light	Michelob	Miller Light	Moosehead
Busch				

PREMIUM WINES

We carry a fine selection of wines to enhance your dining pleasure. Ask your server for our complete wine list.

Wine By The Glass. . . . . California Taylor. . . . . Chablis   Burgundy
                                                    White Zinfandel   Chardonnay

                          Riunite. . . . . Lambrusco   Rosato
                                                   Bianco

BEVERAGES

Pepsi, Diet Pepsi, Teem.	.75
Iced Tea.	.60
Hot Tea.	.60
Coffee, regular and decaf.	.60
Milk.	.75
Hot Chocolate.	.60
Perrier.	1.25

AFTER DINNER DRINKS

Served in warm snifters for the best aroma and flavor.

Grand Marnier. 3.50
   A fine cognac with a hint of orange

B & B. 3.50
   A delicate balance of Benedictine liqueur and fine French brandy.

Drambuie. 3.50

SWEETS

Cheesecake. 2.50
   Classic New York style. Rich and creamy, with fruit topping.

Turtle Pie. 2.95
   Rich Praline Pecan ice cream in a chocolate cookie crust, layered with tawny carmel, garnished with a rippling fudge border and pecan halves.

Ice Cream. 95

? ? At the whim of the chef, we may have a special dessert today. Ask your server.

Gourmet Cake. 3.25
   A changing variety of deluxe gourmet cakes. All are rich and luscious. Ask about today's selection.

Sherbert. 95
   Cool and delightful, orange, lime or pineapple.

Crestwood Sundae. 3.25
   Combine two scoops of vanilla ice cream, cover with hot fudge sauce and warm caramel and top it off with whipped cream, nuts, maraschino cherry and a French cookie.

CRESTWOOD COUNTRY CLUB, Pittsburg, Kansas 66762
WILLIAM H. ASKEW, Executive Chef

FIGURE 7-1. *(Continued)*

While the laminated menu is durable, it is a fairly expensive process. Therefore, this style should only be used in restaurants where the listings are permanent and price changes are not anticipated with any regularity. If this is the case, because of its extended use, the cost becomes quite reasonable over the long run.

Paper Covers

The paper menu and cover have become very commonplace in many restaurants. The primary reason behind this is that it is low in cost. Once the cost of setting the type is paid for, it is relatively inexpensive to make minor changes. In a time when food costs are fluctuating rapidly, selling prices on the menu can be changed with small printing charges. Furthermore, little cost is involved in changing menu listings. A new operation, in particular, would be wise to print its first menu on paper until best-selling listings are determined. Another advantage to paper menus is that they are economical enough to be given away to customers. In fact, they are a very reasonable means of advertisement and when they become soiled or greasy, they can simply be discarded. Thus, established restaurants, as well as new ones, find this particular style to their liking.

The type of menu cover chosen will depend on several factors: the type of restaurant involved, the style of service, the price range of that restaurant, and cost. A fine dining restaurant or private club could opt for an elegant menu with a padded cover, while a fast food operation would prefer a giveaway style printed on paper. Certainly, cost will enter the picture based upon the budgetary restrictions set aside for menu printing. Whichever avenue is pursued, choose or design a cover that has style, that ties together the theme of your restaurant, and reflects its decor.

THE LAYOUT

Once the cover has been chosen, attention should be given to the layout of the inside of the menu. There is a right way and a wrong way to accomplish this.

The first consideration is the sequence of the headings. The headings are merely the names of the various categories covered in Chapter 5. They are:

- appetizers
- soups
- salads
- cold entrees

- hot entrees
- vegetables
- sandwiches
- side dishes
- starches
- desserts
- cheeses
- fruits
- beverages

Selecting Category Names

After the decision is made as to which categories will be used, the names of these categories or headings are listed on the menu. The majority of restaurants simply use the name of the category as its heading, but with a little imagination and foresight, these can be changed to offer variety or to tie in with the theme of your restaurant. For example, instead of using the word appetizers as a heading, why not us "Starters" or "Before the Feast." One restaurant with a racing theme headed appetizers as "Gentlemen—Start Your Engines."

With some imagination, a standard generic menu can become an individualized piece of work, one that excites the customer into looking at all of the categories and, consequently, ordering additional items. The longer the customers read the menu, the more likely they are to order a meal complete with opening and closing selections. Whether you use the proper name of the category or come up with an imaginative one, the sequence of the headings must be in, or close to, the order given above. This creates a smooth flow to the menu and leads the reader on a logical course to choose their meal. Exceptions to this rule are possible, however, as one may opt to place sandwiches in front of entrees or soups before appetizers. Whether or not certain headings are changed, the smooth flow rule must never be violated.

Use Subheads When Listing Entrees

Occasionally it will be necessary to have subheadings listed under main headings—most likely in the entree category. Under the entree headings, subheadings could include, but not be limited to, meat, poultry, fish, and seafood. Under the headings and subheadings come the actual menu listings. These should be presented in no particular order; however, you should group like items together. For example, under the heading entrees, subheading beef, the steaks would be listed together instead of mixing them throughout the beef category. Do not list items in direct or inverse relation to selling price. In other words, avoid listing items with the most expensive first and going on down to the least expensive last. The reverse is also true. Products arranged by price will cause your customers to think in terms of price instead of taste and, in turn, will lower the average check of the establishment.

Under each listing on the menu is the descriptive terminology for that listing. As previously discussed, descriptive terminology is used to explain and sell the product and the product must be described truthfully and accurately. Many menus do not recognize this fact, leaving the customer confused and undecided prior to ordering and angry if they do not receive what they anticipated. If the headings and listings on your menu are written in a foreign language to tie in with the theme, it is mandatory that the descriptive terminology be written in English. Some restaurants, particularly French, take on a snobbish attitude that the customer who doesn't understand French cuisine doesn't belong there in the first place. Don't drive customers away with this attitude (unless, of course, you've got more business than you can handle, in which case you might as well stop reading this book now). If you're still reading, use accurate, descriptive terminology on your menu.

Be Creative with Alcoholic Beverage Listings

Alcoholic beverages baffle many menu writers. Some stick them in some unused space on the menu, while others, not knowing what to do, totally ignore the problem—blissful ignorance. Alcoholic beverages can solve three problems. First, and most important, they are among the highest gross profit items of any product sold in the restaurant. Second, they relax the customer and break down inhibitions which in turn makes the meal more enjoyable. Third, they can cover up delays in seating and service. A famous restaurateur once said that giving a customer a drink was like giving a baby a rattle. Of course, this theory can and has been overdone with the result being a disgruntled rather than satisfied customer.

With the profit to be made on alcoholic beverages, the obvious solution is to get them on the menu. In placing them, the same criteria that were used to arrange the food category headings would be used. That is, they should be listed in proper sequence with a smooth flow to guide the customer through the meal. There are three menu categories of alcoholic beverages, before dinner drinks, wine with the meal, and after dinner drinks.

Before-dinner Drinks. Before-dinner drinks would be listed prior to the appetizer. In addition to listing popular drinks such as highballs, some creative house specialty blended drinks should also be listed. These bring a higher selling price and, consequently, a higher gross profit. Merchandise them in special glasses with unusual garnishes. Feature them on the menu with appealing pictures.

Wine. Wine, while the fastest growing beverage in America, is still misunderstood by many people. Because of this fact, descriptive terminology is imperative—primarily to explain. Tell about the flavor, whether it is light or heavy, or sweet or dry, to assist the customers in a selection they will enjoy. Since wines are consumed primarily with the meal, they should be listed immediately adjacent to the entrees. Inasmuch as we are interested in educating the public, perhaps a selected wine should be listed with each entree. Conversely, the wine list could explain those wines which add enjoyment to certain entrees. The point is that the menu must break down the customer's resistance, due to lack of knowledge, to ordering wine by informing, educating, and leading them into a proper selection.

After-dinner Drinks. After-dinner drinks would obviously be listed adjacent to or after desserts. The same theory would apply here as applied to the before-dinner drinks. In addition to listing the obvious, try some blended ice cream creations that can become house specialities and properly mechandise them for added profit.

At the beginning of this dissertation on alcoholic beverages, it was stated that they do three things. Consider one more—they are add-ons. By handling them correctly on your menu, they can increase the average check. Be careful not to overdo it, however. While we have been discussing ways to increase sales by selling alcoholic beverages, we must do so in a responsible manner. Enticing customers to become intoxicated is not the point. Enticing them to have a good time and enjoy themselves is. Proper menu merchandising will accomplish the latter, while responsible bar service will ensure that the former does not happen.

PUTTING IT ALL TOGETHER

The menu is now starting to take shape. The categories have been decided, the headings and subheadings chosen, the listings selected, and the descriptive terminology written. Assuming the order is correct, the menu takes on a good flow leading the customers to the choices they will select.

Using Prime Space Properly

When placing all of these on the menu itself, one more factor needs to be taken into consideration—prime space. When the customer opens the menu, the spot that their eyes hit first is known as the

Stephenson's
Home of the famous

Old Apple Farm Daiquiri

For your drinking pleasure we have created this rum drink —
served in a frosted, king size glass —
plenty of authority in this drink.
Your choice of Plain, Apple, Strawberry, Peach or Banana

Farm Size Martini's and Manhattan's

Old Apple Farm Fresh Fruit Wine Punch

This is the way they used to make punch — delicious!
Glass or Carafe

Marguerita

The Apple Farm version of the famous
Tequila drink South of the border.

Stephenson's Missouri Apple Wine

Made from apples grown right here on our farm.
Glass or Bottle

Open every day — 11:30 a.m.
Come as late as 10:00 p.m. Monday thru Thursday
11:00 p.m. Friday and Saturday
9:00 p.m. Sunday
for complete service

FIGURE 7-2. Excellent merchandising of high gross profit "add-on" drinks. Before-dinner drinks are on the cover with after-dinner drinks on the back. The wine list is an insert in the middle of the entree section. (*Menu courtesy of Stephenson's Old Apple Farm Restaurant, Kansas City, Missouri*)

After Dinner

Coffee Calypso

A secret ingredient and topped with whipped cream.

Florentina

This is Galliano liqueur blended with french vanilla ice cream into a delicate, delicious dessert drink.

Hot Cider in Tuaca Liquor	Sambucca
Cherry Heering	Grasshopper
Galliano	Black Russian
Kuhlua	Brandy Alexander
Brandy	Irish Coffee
Creme de Menthe	Rusty Nail
Courvoisier V.S.O.P.	Stinger
Bailey's Irish Cream	Drambuie

To Our Guests:

As expenses continue to rise we have to adjust menu prices from time to time. We still, however, want to give you the best value possible without sacrificing quality or quantity.

Our object, as always, is to be one of Americas finest restaurant and one our community is justly proud. We pledge as in the past to cook everything from scratch. We smoke our own meats and poultry over hickory and apple wood. We do our own baking, making hot light yeast rolls, fresh apple pie and dumplings. We make our own sauces, salad dressings, relishes, apple butter and squeeze our own cider.

We purchase the finest ingredients, meat, produce and supplies available. We will continue to serve you with friendly, polite, gracious service in a pleasant, casual and comfortable surroundings.

We always hope you will have a memorable visit and think of Stephenson's as a place you would want to take friends. If there is anything we can do for you please let us know.

Rick Stephenson, Manager

FIGURE 7-2. *(Continued)*

May We Suggest a Bottle of Wine?

Champagnes and Sparkling Wines

Bin #		Bottle
32	**Korbel Brut**	**21.00**
	A most popular sparkling wine	
33	**Domaine Chandon Blanc de Noir**	**23.00**
	Deliciously fruity sparkling wine	
34	**Moet Dom Perignon (Vintage) (French)**	**105.00**
	True French champagne at its umcompromising best	
35	**Villa Banfi Asti Spumante (Italy)**	**16.00**
	Sparkling light and delicate	
36	**Freixenet**	**13.00**
	A white sparkling wine from Spain	

Red Table Wines

26	**Baron Phillipe De Rothschild Mouton Cadet**	**15.00**
	Light and fruity	
27	**Louis Jadot Beaujolais Villages**	**15.00**
	A versatile wine that enhances steaks and chops	
28	**Inglenook Cabernet Sauvignon**	**16.00**
	Medium bodied with excellent balance	
29	**Beaulieu Vineyard Cabernet Sauvignon**	**15.00**
	This rich elegant wine is praised for its depth of flavor and intense bouquet	
30	**Robert Mondavi Cabernet Sauvignon**	**28.00**
	Classically styled California Cabernet Sauvignon showing a supple texture and elegant flavor	
31	**Fetzer Zinfandel**	**12.00**
	Medium bodied red wine with a spicy characteristic and a fruity bouquet	

Rose Table Wines

24	**Lancers Rose**	**10.00**
	Light, semi-dry and fruity	

Stephenson's Missouri Apple Wine
Made from apples grown right here on our farm

Glass	Bottle
2.95	8.95

White Table Wines

Bin #		Bottle
10	**Simi Chardonnay**	**23.00**
	Prized by wine lovers the world over, a stylishly dry and complex wine	
11	**Robert Mondavi Chardonnay**	**25.00**
	Exhibiting a unique depth of flavor	
12	**Chateau Ste Michelle Chardonnay**	**19.00**
	A dry complex wine	
13	**Inglenook Sauvignon Blanc**	**15.00**
	A soft, crisp taste	
14	**Robert Mondavi Fume Blanc**	**17.00**
	A rich fruity aroma, full bodied	
15	**Chateau Ste Michelle Gewurztraminer**	**12.00**
	A crisp, dry, medium bodied wine	
17	**Simi Chenin Blanc**	**13.00**
	Light bodied and semi dry	
18	**Baron Phillipe De Rothschild Mouton Cadet Blanc**	**15.00**
	Delicate, dry and crisp	
19	**Kendall-Jackson Sauvignon Blanc**	**15.00**
	Crisp, fresh and fragrant	
20	**Louis Jadot Pouilly Fuisse**	**34.00**
	A distinct, rich quality	
21	**Rudolf Muller Piesporter Goldtropfchen Qba**	**15.00**
	Light, gold in color	
22	**Blue Nun Liebfraumilch**	**11.00**
	Light, fruity and semi dry	
23	**Sutter Home White Zinfandel**	**11.00**
	Blush-colored with a fresh bouquet.	

A Glass or Carafe of Wine
Special Premium Wines by the Glass

Chateau Ste Michelle Chardonnay	4.25
Rudolf Muller Piesporter	4.25
Blue Nun Liebfraumilch	3.75
Sutter Home White Zinfandel	3.75
Louis Jadot Beaujolais	3.75
Inglenook Cabernet Sauvignon	4.25
Freixenet	3.75

House Wines - Robert Mondavi

	Glass	Carafe
California Sauvignon Blanc	3.25	9.95
California Gamay Rose	2.95	8.95
California Cabernet	3.95	12.95

FIGURE 7-2. *(Continued)*

prime space. Studies have shown that the customer is more likely to order what is seen first. Thus, the prime space on the menu becomes an extremely important merchandising area. Many people are ignorant of this fact, because few menus use it to their advantage. The prime space is determined by the type of menu. On a two-page menu, it is located in the middle of the right-hand page. On a three-page or a single menu, it is in the center of the upper third of the menu.

Since this is the predominant area, it stands to reason that the menu writer should place the item that they most want to sell in this spot. Quite naturally this item should be popular and bring the restaurant a high gross profit. If the listing is unpopular, it would defeat the purpose. If the customer does not like sauteed lamb kidneys, no matter how well it is merchandised they will not buy it. Also, if the restaurant does not realize a good profit margin, then why display such a listing in the predominant area? One more thing, do not waste this space to list the house specialty. Use it for something else that you want to sell. If the restaurant is famous for Prime Rib, the customer already knows that. Don't use prime space to state the obvious.

Boxes or borders should be used to outline and accentuate those items that you want to sell the most. They should always be used in prime space, but can be used elsewhere on the menu. A word of caution. Don't overdo borders as they tend to lose their effectiveness. A maximum of three boxes per page should be used.

With the criteria stated for prime space, it should be fairly obvious that an entree would be listed. When discussing a high gross profit item, we are talking about dollar gross profit, not percent. To get the menu to flow properly, with the correct order of categories, and to end up with the entree section in the prime space is sometimes quite tricky. Quite often it takes work and imagination to make this happen. The result will pay dividends to the person who perseveres.

Using Leftover Space—Institutional Copy

With the menu properly laid out, the next point of business becomes what to do about the leftover space. This space can be used for institutional copy—stories about the restaurant, the area, or an explanation of the theme make up institutional copy. This copy goes hand in hand with the cover of the menu. Institutional copy ties all of the loose ends together to make the restaurant, its theme, location, and the meal a total experience for the customer. It can be written on the back of the menu, toward the front, or interspersed throughout. Good institutional copy separates an ordinary, mundane food list from an outstanding menu.

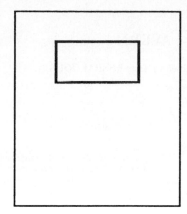

Prime Space on a One Page Menu

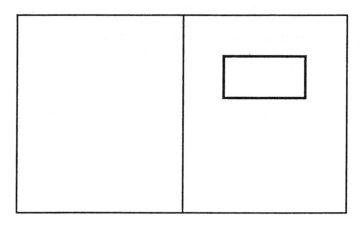

Prime Space on a Two Page Menu

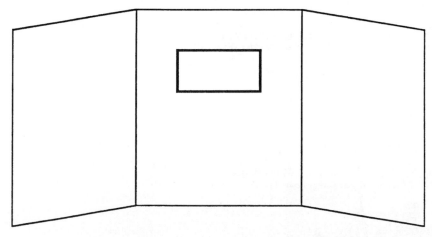

Prime Space on a Three Page Menu

FIGURE 7-3. Proper use of prime space.

EVENING FARE
Christiana Campbell's TAVERN

Giving Satisfaction to TRAVELERS and TOWNSPEOPLE with a Taste for SEAFOODS

APPETIZERS

Captain *Rasmussen's* Clam CHOWDER
1.95

Cherrystone CLAMS on the Half Shell
One-Half Dozen   One Dozen
4.95   8.25

Colonial PASTY
A Mixture of MEATS and SPICES
in a Pastry SHELL
2.50

SOUP of the Day
1.75

Blue Point OYSTERS on the Half Shell
One-Half Dozen (offered seasonally)
6.95

ENTRÉES

SMALL TENDERLOIN AND CRAB IMPERIAL
Backfin CRAB Imperial and
Broiled Tenderloin of BEEF
served with Russet POTATOES, a Pumpkin FRITTER,
and a VEGETABLE
21.25
Suggested WINE: Bin No. 84 (Red) or No. 194 (White)

THE GLOUCESTER DINNER
Captain *Rasmussen's* Clam CHOWDER
Southern Skillet-Fried CHICKEN
served with *Virginia* HAM, a Pumpkin FRITTER,
and a VEGETABLE
Choice of BEVERAGE   Choice of ICE CREAM
18.45
Suggested WINE: Bin No. 93

A MADE DISH OF SHRIMPS, SCALLOPS, AND LOBSTER
SHRIMPS, SCALLOPS, and LOBSTER combined with
Fresh MUSHROOMS, TOMATOES, Green PEPPERS,
and ONIONS
sautéed in SHERRY and served with RICE
20.45
Suggested WINE: Bin No. 122

CHESAPEAKE BAY JAMBALAYA
A Combination of SCALLOPS and SHRIMPS
braised in a Spicy Tomato SAUCE
and served over RICE
18.95
Suggested WINE: Bin No. 47

CHRISTIANA CAMPBELL'S CRAB CAKES
served with *Virginia* HAM,
Russet POTATOES, and a
VEGETABLE
18.95
Suggested WINE: Bin No. 98

WALLER STREET SELECTION

The CHEF'S nightly Choice
Priced daily

BROILED RIB EYE STEAK
served with Braised Sliced Fresh
MUSHROOMS, Baked POTATO, and a
VEGETABLE
18.75
Suggested WINE: Bin No. 19

MRS. *CAMPBELL'S* SEAFOOD PLATTER
A Combination Platter of Fried SHRIMP,
SCALLOPS, and Broiled FLOUNDER with CRAB Imperial,
Russet POTATOES, and a VEGETABLE
20.25
Suggested WINE: Bin No. 105 or No. 159

CHICKEN *CHRISTIANA*
Fillet of CHICKEN Breast with
CRABMEAT and White Wine SAUCE
served with a VEGETABLE
17.45
Suggested WINE: Bin No. 93

All Selections are served with

Campbell's Cabbage SLAW   SPOON BREAD   Drop BISCUITS   Sweet Potato MUFFINS

BEVERAGES

Hot COFFEE or Hot TEA 1.25   Iced TEA or LEMONADE .95
Serving *Christiana Campbell's* Tavern Orange Pekoe TEA

Please, NO SMOKING inside the Tavern.   4/93

FIGURE 7-4. Excellent use of prime space on a one-page menu. The two featured entrees are highlighted by boxes on the upper part of the page. (*Menu courtesy of Christiana Campbell's Tavern, Colonial Williamsburg, Williamsburg, Virginia.*)

FIGURE 7-5. A menu from the Victoria Dining Room with institutional copy on the inside front cover. (*Courtesy of Chateau Lake Louise, Alberta, Canada*)

Using Clip-ons

Clip-ons are used on menus in all styles of restaurants. While some operations disdain the use of clip-ons, the degree of success with such an advertising medium is dependent upon how they are used. Clip-ons are predominant on low- to moderate-priced menus and are seen less frequently on high-priced menus. The rationales behind using clip-ons are many. They can be used to test new products to see if they will sell. They can also be used to feature either low-priced specials or high gross profit items. They are an excellent means of selling leftovers, which otherwise could not be merchandised on a predetermined printed menu. If it is the restaurant's philosophy that clip-ons are a good merchandising tool, then proper planning for them must be executed when the menu is laid out. All too often, clip-ons cover up important listings on the menu. Few customers will lift up a clip-on to see what is underneath; therefore, those items cannot be expected to sell well. When

Victoria Dining Room

JEWEL OF THE ROCKIES

Lake Louise was discovered by the late Tom Wilson in 1882. Tom was at that time emplc
Maj. Rogers who was surveying for the Canadian Pacific Railway which was under constr
at that time. Lake Louise was named after Princess Louise, in 1884, who was the wife
Lorne, the Governor General of Canada, and also the daughter of Queen Victoria. The te
Louise during the year averages 1 degree celcius to 5 degrees celcius. The altitude of La
feet above sea level. The dimensions of Lake Louise are 1½ miles long, ¾ miles wide; ƒ
The colouring of the lake is due to the depth and the fine mineral deposits of Glacial
carried down from the Victoria Glacier.

The Victoria Glacier is 6 miles from the Chateau Lake Louise. The upper Glacier is 200 tc
while the lower Glacier is 400 to 500 feet in depth. Lake Agnes is located 2½ miles by trail
at an altitude of 6,885 feet. There is a Tea House at the lake which was built in 1908. Tl
reconstructed in 1981. A trail from the Chateau takes you to the Tea House, and can ei
horse ridden. The Plain of Six Glaciers is 4 miles from the Chateau Lake Louise at an alti
This site also boasts a Tea House which was built by the Chateau Lake Louise in 1925, a
by foot or on horse back.

There have been four different buildings of the Chateau. They are as follows:

Original Chateau built	1890
Chateau burned completely	1892
Chateau rebuilt	1893
Wooden building constructed	1900
Paynter Wing constructed	1913
Wooden building burned	1924
Barrett Wing constructed	1925
Major Exterior Renovations	1985
Glacier Wing constructed	1987

FIGURE 7-5. (*Continued*)

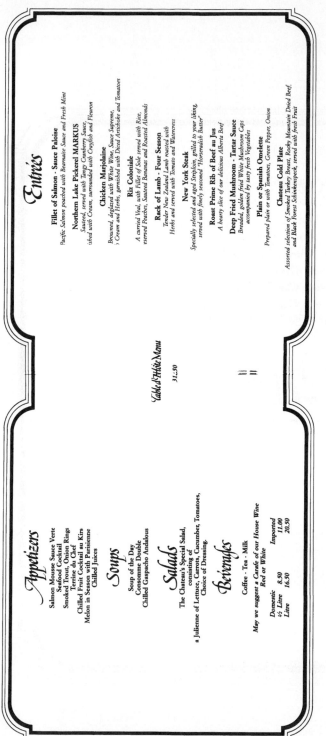

FIGURE 7-5. (*Continued*)

Desserts

Kahlua Parfait
Today's Pie, plain or à la mode
Canadian Cheddar Cheese with Grapes & Biscuits
Black Forest Cake
Vanilla or Chocolate Cheese Cake
Passion Fruit Cake
Fresh Fruit in Season

Special Coffees

Monte Cristo   4.75
Rich black coffee together with Kahlua (¾ oz.),
Curacao (¼ oz.) and fresh cream.

Blueberry Tea   4.75
Take a little break from coffee and try fine Earl Grey tea
with Grand Marnier (¾ oz.), Amaretto (¼ oz.), and fresh cream.

Spanish   4.75
The perfect blend of smooth Brandies (1 oz.), Kahlua (½ oz.),
coffee and fresh whipped cream.

Irish   4.75
The old country traditional of Irish Whiskey (1 oz.),
Irish Mist (½ oz.), coffee and fresh whipped cream.

The Princess Louise Coffee   5.00
The perfect blend of Grand Marnier, Amaretto and Kahlua
with special blend coffee, fresh cream and shaved chocolate.

FIGURE 7-5. *(Continued)*

planning a menu that will use clip-ons, the space underneath them should have either some artwork or institutional copy rather than menu listings. Do not leave the space blank. If you do not use clip-ons during a particular day or meal period, the menu will look incomplete to the customer. Clip-ons should be printed on the same type paper as the menu and use the same style of type. They may be bordered to attract attention and should always be clean and fresh, never dirty or greasy.

PRINTING THE MENU

Once the style and overall layout of the menu has been determined, the next step is to have it printed. Many decisions must be made which will affect the final outcome. First and foremost a reliable printer must be selected, as their knowledge and expertise will not only speed up the process but will also dictate the quality of the finished product. This is important as all of the previous efforts will be for naught if the menu is not properly printed. One of my first consulting jobs was to develop a menu for a resort. The items are carefully selected, formulas developed, the costs were figured, selling prices determined, and the proper layout completed. The client was satisfied and sent it to his printer. The results were embarrassing. The styles and size of type, spacing, type of paper, and colors were all wrong. All of my efforts and the client's money were wasted. Since that time, total control of the menu development process, including printing, has produced improved results.

The printing industry is a large one. Select a printer who has experience with menus. Analyze their work. Develop a strong line of communication so that each person knows exactly what is to be done. As previously stated, many decisions must be made, including the paper to be used, the size and shape, the style of type, and the artwork.

Paper

The paper or paperboard chosen for the menu will normally run 30 percent of the finished cost, but could run as high as 50 percent depending upon the product selected. The characteristics of the paper will, to a large degree, influence the finished appearance of the menu. Since there is an almost infinite number of possibilities affecting paper characteristics, it is important that the menu planner work closely with the printer in selecting the proper paper. Several factors need to be considered: weight, strength, color, and coating.

Paper is manufactured and identified by its basis weight, that is, the weight in pounds for 500 sheets of the basic size for that particular grade. For example, book paper varies in basis weight from

50-100 pounds. Do not confuse weight with strength. While weight has some bearing on strength, the strength of paper is more dependent on the fiber used. Generally speaking, the stronger papers have more long pulp fibers than do papers of lesser strength. Color is important as it affects the readability of the color of type used.

Type is most easily read on a soft white paper. The type of coating will also affect the final outcome of the menu. While some papers are not coated at all, those that are have finishes from dull to very glossy and everything in between. Do not confuse laminated menus with those printed on high gloss paper. Lamination is a process which takes place after the menu is printed to give it protection and durability.

After the paper is selected, one more consideration must be made—size. Paper used for printing purposes comes in large sheets of varying sizes. Upon selecting a particular type of paper, inquire into the size of the sheets that are available. Compare the proposed size of the menu to the most economical size sheet available. Normally several menus can be printed on one sheet of printing paper. It is entirely possible that by changing the size of the menu slightly, more menus can be printed using fewer sheets. This is important because, as stated earlier, the paper can equal up to 50 percent of the cost. For example, a common size printing sheet is 17-1/2" by 22-1/2". If you desired to have a menu page that measured 9" by 11", you could print one two-page menu per sheet. If on the other hand, the menu page was reduced 1/2" to 8-1/2" x 11", two two-page menus could be printed, thus reducing your paper cost by 50 percent.

This is but one example. Because of the many sizes of printing sheets available, consult with the printer about the desired size of the menu versus the size of the printing sheets for the most economical approach. Sometimes aesthetics need to be measured against cost. If it is vitally important that the menu be a certain size or take on a particular shape to emphasize a theme, then cost should become less of a factor and the design should dominate your planning.

Color

In conjunction with the paper selected for the menu, a decision must be made with regard to color. Of course, the basic black ink on white paper is least expensive. However, for a very slight increase in cost, colored ink on a colored paper could be used. As the number of colors increases, so does the cost. The reason for this is that additional press runs must be made. To achieve various colors, a printer uses four basic inks (colors). As the menu goes through the press, each run with a different ink, different colors will be produced. Thus, the four basic inks will produce virtually every imaginable color. The

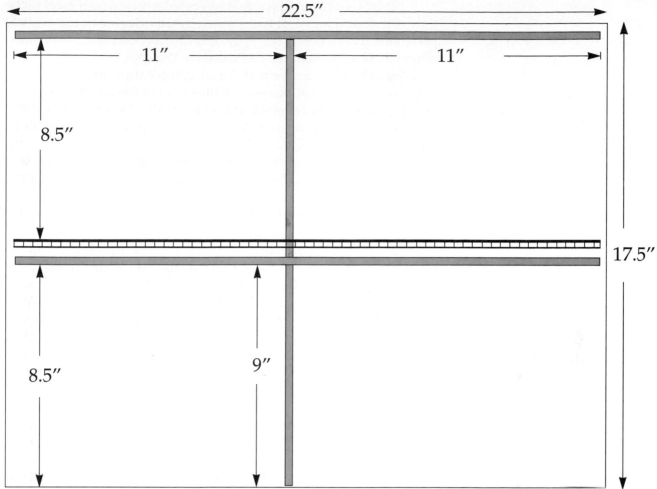

FIGURE 7-6. Illustration showing how a large sheet of printing paper is reduced to smaller sizes. Notice how a common size will give more menus per page.

overall aesthetic value of the menu will be greatly influenced by the proper selection of paper color and the combinations of inks.

Type

There are many different styles of type from which to choose. To simplify matters, they can be placed into classes of which the most common are old style, modern, transitional, square serif, sans serif, script, text letters, and decorative types. While these classifications in no way cover all of the styles, it is a useful breakdown which covers a wide variety of types.

Old style is patterned after letters used on classical Roman inscriptions. It is a very readable style of type because the letters are open, wide, and round. This would be an excellent choice for the descriptive terminology and the institutional copy on the menu.

Modern is a class of type that refers to its style as opposed to the time it was developed. It has a much greater degree of mechanical perfection than the old style type. It is also a good choice for menus where there are a multitude of words in the copy.

Transitional is a group that is a combination of the first two classes—old style and modern. While most of the characteristics of old style have been retained, it is less sturdy. As is the case of the first two classes, it is an excellent choice for the wordier portions of the menu.

Square serif is a contemporary style of type that has a blocked or square look to it and has more uniform strokes. This class should be used in category headings or for the listing of items. Because of its style, it should not be used for institutional copy as it becomes difficult to read when grouped together.

Sans serif, while similar to square serif, is cleaner and has a simpler design. It is a comparatively new type and is also useful used for headings and product listings.

Script is a style of type that is used to simulate handwriting or hand lettering. It is commonly used on invitations or announcements. As far as menus are concerned, it is very popular for category headings.

Text letters resemble the hand drawn letters of early scribes. It is quite often selected for religious documents, certificates, and diplomas. It would be an excellent choice for restaurants which have an old world theme such as seafaring or Old English. It should, however, be used only for category headings or product listings as it becomes difficult to read when used for menu copy.

Decorative types are designed to express different moods and may appear eccentric at times. Primarily used to command attention, they are a good choice to headline boxed or bordered items on the menu. They can also be used for headings and listings.

Type selection should be done carefully. The styles chosen can reinforce the theme of the restaurant that is being carried out on the menu. Limit the selection to one or two styles, one for headings and item listings and one for copy. Too many classes of type on one menu will make it appear cluttered and confusing. Check with your printer to see what styles are available to select from.

In addition to selecting the styles of type, there are other decisions to be made regarding the printing of the menu. They include the size of the type, letter spacing, and leading.

The *size of type* is measured in points with 72 points equaling an inch. Normally type is available from 6 to 72 points. When selecting the size of type for a menu, 12 points should be considered the minimum, and then only for institutional copy or for descriptive terminology. While 12 points is relatively large for copy, it should be remembered that most restaurants have a lighting level that is more conducive to dining and atmosphere than it is to reading. Headings and item listings should be 18 points or more. In addition to select-

Avant Garde	Gill Sans
Baskerville	Goudy
Bellevue	Helvetica
Blippo Black	**Hobo**
Bookman	*Kauflinn*
Brittanic	Korinna
Broadway	*Mural Script*
Brody	**Old Towne**
Brush Script	Optima
Century Schoolbook	Palatino
Chaucer	*Park Avenue*
City Medium	**Sans Extended**
Clarendon	Souvenir
Clearface Gothic	Square Serif
Cooper Black	Tekton
Copperplate	Times New Roman
Eurostile	University Roman
Flare Gothic	*Vivante*
Frugal Sans	Windsor
Garamond	*Zapf Chancery*

FIGURE 7-7. Type styles

ing the size of type, a decision will have to be made as to whether to use upper case, lower case, or both. *Upper case* is printers' terminology for capital letters, *lower case* is small letters.

Another consideration is the letter spacing and leading. *Letter spacing* is just what the name implies, the amount of space between letters. Spacing affects readability. It also allows you to fill an empty area of the menu. It is best to leave the letter spacing to the judgment of the printer. *Leading*, on the other hand, is the amount of space between the lines. Like type size, it is also measured in points. Again, because of the amount of light in most restaurants, three points of leading is recommended.

Artwork

Another decision to be made is whether or not to employ artwork on the menu. Many menus have no artwork at all, using strictly printed copy, while others use art quite extensively. Because artwork increases the cost of the menu, you should decide if the use of artwork will enhance the overall impression of the menu. Certainly, it could be used to enhance the theme of the restaurant or to highlight certain areas of the menu or both. However, is it cost effective?

Larger printing firms have artists on their staffs who can provide this service. If a small printing firm is used, the artwork will have to be supplied. This can be obtained from a commercial art firm or by a freelance artist. It is generally helpful if the artwork supplied to the printer is camera ready copy.

The Proof

Now the printer goes to work. The menu is laid out and typeset according to specifications. The result is a *proof*—a copy of what the menu will look like. Examine the proof carefully. Check for misspelled words, accurate phrasing, punctuation, and correct pricing. Any errors that are not detected and corrected will appear on the final menu. Avoid massive changes as this will add to the cost. If the work to this point was performed accurately with good communication with the printer, the changes should be minor in nature. Remember, it is imperative to check for accuracy before approving the proof for final printing.

After the proof has been approved, the last decision to be made is how many menus should be printed. While approximately 30 percent of the menu cost is in paper, about 50 percent of the cost is in typesetting and plate preparation. Since this is a one-time cost, it stands to reason that the more menus printed, the lower the cost for each menu. However, don't be misled by false economics. For example, if you need 100 menus at a cost of $3 each ($300 total), don't order 1,000 at a cost of $1.50 each ($1,500 total).

While the quantity to order would vary from operation to operation, depending on specific circumstances, some rules of thumb can be established. In restaurants where revisions are not anticipated due to fluctuating prices or item changes for a period of six months or longer, two and a half times the number of seats would be the normal amount to purchase. In restaurants where revisions

APPETIZERS

Chicken Fingers
Lightly breaded and seasoned chicken breast tenderloin deep-fried to a golden brown. Served with barbecue sauce or honey-mustard dressing. $3.45

Deep-Fried Mushrooms
Plump and juicy breaded mushrooms, fried light and golden. Served with country ranch dressing for dipping. $2.45

Seasoned French Fries
Our famous French fries, seasoned to perfection. $1.45

Mozzarella Cheese Sticks
Breaded and deep-fried golden brown and served with marinara sauce for dipping. $3.25

Country Onion Rings
Cut large, breaded with our special batter and fried golden. $1.95

SOUPS

Old-Fashioned Calico Bean Soup® 💙
A Country Kitchen® specialty. A hearty combination of seven different beans, smoked ham and special seasonings.
Cup $1.25   **Bowl** $1.75

Soup of the Day
Ask your server for today's selection.
Cup $1.25   **Bowl** $1.75

Chili
Hearty chili prepared with just enough spices. Topped with cheddar cheese and served with crackers.
Cup $1.95   **Bowl** $2.45

Soup and Salad 💙
A bowl of Calico Bean Soup® served with our tossed green salad. $3.25

Soup and Sandwich
A bowl of Calico Bean Soup® served with today's featured sandwich. $4.25

SALADS

Grilled Chicken Breast Salad 💙
A mound of crisp garden greens topped with grilled marinated chicken breast, tomatoes, green onions, mushrooms, green peppers and croutons. Served with your choice of dressing and a dinner roll. $5.45

Taco Salad
Spicy taco meat, cheddar cheese, tomatoes, black olives, onions, sour cream and guacamole served over crisp garden greens in a giant tortilla shell. Served with salsa and a dinner roll. $5.25

NEW Country Club Salad
Salad greens topped with chunks of turkey and ham. Garnished with egg and tomato wedges, shredded cheddar cheese and bacon. Served with your choice of dressing and a dinner roll. $4.95

Beef or Chicken Fajita Salad
Grilled seasoned beef or chicken strips, cheddar cheese, black olives, green peppers, green onions, tomato, guacamole and sour cream on crisp garden greens. Served with tortilla chips, salsa and your choice of dressing. $5.45

Salad Bar (Where Available)
Salad bar as a meal in itself. $4.50
With any sandwich. $1.75
With entrée as substitute for tossed salad. $ .95

Indicates Country Kitchen® specialties.
Right Choice™ – For guests concerned about a healthy diet.
💙 Less than 400 calories.
💙 Less than 100 mg. cholesterol.
💙 Less than 1000 mg. sodium.
💙 Meets guidelines without French fries.

FIGURE 7-8. Notice how the artwork on this menu ties in with the decor of the restaurant. (*Menu and photograph courtesy of Country Kitchen, Country Hospitality Corporation, Minneapolis, Minnesota*)

SANDWICHES

All of our sandwiches and burgers (excluding All-American Hot Sandwich) are served with seasoned French fries and pickles.

Deluxe Clubhouse
A triple-decker of sliced turkey, ham, crisp bacon, Swiss cheese, tomatoes and lettuce. Served with mayonnaise on your choice of toast. $5.45

Country Clubhouse
A triple-decker with sliced turkey, crisp bacon, lettuce and sliced tomatoes. Served with mayonnaise on your choice of toast. $4.95

French Dip ♥.
Thinly-sliced roast beef served on a French roll. Accompanied by au jus for dipping. $5.25

Philly Beef and Cheese ♥.
Thinly sliced beef grilled with onions and mushrooms served on a French roll with lots of melted mozzarella cheese. $5.45

Reuben Sandwich ♥.
The classic combination of corned beef, Swiss cheese, sauerkraut and Thousand Island dressing served on grilled caraway rye bread. $5.25

Barbecued Chicken Sandwich
Boneless chicken breast, grilled and topped with barbecue sauce, Swiss cheese and bacon. Served on a toasted Kaiser roll. $5.25

Smothered Chicken Melt
Grilled chicken breast smothered in mozzarella cheese, onions, tomatoes and mushrooms on grilled Parmesan sourdough. $5.25

Fish Fillet
Lightly breaded fish fillet, fried golden brown and topped with American cheese. Served on a French roll with lettuce and tartar sauce. $4.95

Indicates Country Kitchen® specialties.
Right Choice™ – For guests concerned about a healthy diet.
♥ Less than 400 calories.
♥ Less than 100 mg. cholesterol.
♥ Less than 1000 mg. sodium.
♥ Meets guidelines without French fries.

Chicken Breast Sandwich ♥.
Grilled chicken breast, on a toasted Kaiser roll with lettuce and tomato slices. Served with mayonnaise. $4.95

Chicken Bacon Melt
Grilled chicken breast smothered in American cheese, topped with bacon and tomato on grilled Parmesan sourdough. $5.25

All-American Hot Sandwiches ♥
Your choice of roast beef, meat loaf or sliced turkey mounded on fresh bread. Served with mashed potatoes and gravy. $4.25

BURGERS

Country Boy®
Our famous double-decker hamburger served on a toasted roll with cheese, tomato, lettuce and special sauce. $3.95

Classic Hamburger ♥. w/o bacon
A third-pound of ground beef topped with lettuce, tomato and mayonnaise. Served on a toasted Kaiser roll. $4.25
With Swiss, cheddar or American cheese add $.20
With bacon add $.70

Barbecue Burger
Our beef hamburger topped with grilled ham, Swiss cheese, lettuce and tomato. Served with barbecue sauce. $4.65

Mushroom Cheeseburger ♥.
The classic beef hamburger topped with American and Swiss cheese, mushrooms, lettuce, tomato and mayonnaise. $4.65

Patty Melt
An all-time favorite. A beef hamburger topped with American cheese, Swiss cheese and sautéed onions. Served on grilled caraway rye bread. $4.65

FIGURE 7-8. *(Continued)*

Each meal (excluding pasta and stir fry dishes) includes a choice of potato or rice pilaf, today's vegetable, a warm dinner roll and a salad.

CHICKEN

Smothered Chicken 💜
Boneless chicken breast, grilled with onions and mushrooms and covered with melted mozzarella cheese. $6.25

Grilled Chicken 💜
Marinated, boneless chicken breast grilled to perfection. $5.95

🌲 **Country Fried Chicken**
Our special recipe. Fried crisp and golden on the outside, moist and tender on the inside. $5.95

Chicken Parmigiana 💜
Tender boneless chicken breast, served over pasta and topped with marinara sauce and mozzarella cheese. Served with a salad and garlic toast. $6.25

Chicken Finger Dinner
Six chicken fingers, lightly breaded and deep-fried. Served with honey-mustard or barbecue sauce. $5.45

SEAFOOD

Shrimp Scampi
Shrimp sautéed in garlic flavored sauce and served over pasta. Accompanied by a salad and garlic toast. $6.25

Rainbow Trout 💜
Tender boneless rainbow trout fillet, butterflied and grilled to perfection. Served with tartar sauce. $6.45

Country Breaded Shrimp 💜
Lightly dusted shrimp deep-fried to a golden brown. Served with tangy cocktail sauce. $5.95

Fillet of Fish
Lightly breaded fried fish fillets. Served with tartar sauce. $5.95

STEAKS

New York Strip Steak
U.S.D.A. Choice 10 oz. strip steak grilled to your liking. Garnished with onion rings. $9.95

Rib Eye Steak
U.S.D.A. Choice 8 oz. rib eye steak, grilled to your liking. Garnished with onion rings. $8.95

Top Sirloin Steak
U.S.D.A. Choice 6 oz. top sirloin steak, grilled to your liking. Garnished with onion rings. $6.95

SPECIALTIES

🌲 **Beef or Chicken Stir Fry**
Specially seasoned beef or chicken stir fried with oriental vegetables on a bed of rice pilaf. Served with teriyaki sauce, salad and warm dinner roll. $5.95

Old-Fashioned Meat Loaf
A Country Kitchen® favorite. Baked and topped with rich gravy. $5.45

Country Turkey Dinner
Sliced breast of turkey with cranberry sauce. Served with our delicious stuffing and gravy. $5.45

Country Fried Steak
Select beef, pounded thin, lightly breaded and fried golden. Served with country gravy. $5.75

Spaghetti with Meatballs 💜
The classic Italian favorite! Served with a salad and garlic toast. $4.95

Baked Lasagna 💜
Lasagna noodles layered with Ricotta cheese and a classic-style tomato sauce with sausage; topped with mozzarella cheese. Served with a salad and garlic toast. $5.95

🌲 Indicates Country Kitchen® specialties.
Right Choice™ – For guests concerned about a healthy diet.
💜 Less than 400 calories.
💜 Less than 100 mg. cholesterol.
💜 Less than 1000 mg. sodium.
💜 Meets guidelines without French fries.

FIGURE 7-8. *(Continued)*

KIDS' MEALS

For kids under 10, we have special reduced portions. Each meal includes choice of small juice, soft drink or a special dessert.

NEW *Kids' beverages are served with a fun collectible, re-useable, spill resistant cup which is yours to take home.*

BREAKFASTS

 Lil' Stack ♥
Piping hot Country Kitchen® pancakes served with crisp bacon and warm syrup. $2.25

Cakes and Egg
One farm-fresh scrambled egg, crisp bacon and pancakes served with warm syrup. $2.25

Kids' French Toast ♥
Two slices of French bread dipped in egg batter and grilled golden. Served with crisp bacon and warm syrup. $2.25

LUNCH AND DINNER

Grilled Cheese Sandwich
An American cheese sandwich grilled golden brown. Served with crisp seasoned French fries. $2.25

Kids' Burger ♥.
Our special hamburger served on a toasted bun with seasoned French fries. $2.25

Spaghetti with Meatballs ♥
Kids' favorite! Served with a slice of toast. $2.25

Fillet of Fish
A golden flaky fish fillet served with seasoned French fries and toast. $2.25

Country Fried Chicken Strips ♥.
Tender chicken filet strips deep-fried and served with seasoned French fries, choice of dipping sauce and toast. $2.25

Corn Dog
The original ▒▒ corn dog, served with seasoned French fries. $2.25

NEW **Peanut Butter and Jelly Sandwich**
Everyone's favorite sandwich, made with Smucker's peanut butter and grape jelly, served with seasoned French fries. $2.25

FOR OUR SENIOR GUESTS

Specially planned smaller portions for those over sixty. For dinner, each meal (excluding pasta dish) includes your choice of potato or rice pilaf, vegetable of the day, a cup of soup or tossed green salad and a warm dinner roll.

One Egg Any Style ♥
With two strips of bacon, toast and juice. $2.95

 A Short Stack of Pancakes ♥
Our famous pancakes with warm syrup, sausage and juice. $2.95

French Toast
Thick slices of French bread dipped in egg batter and grilled golden. Served with crisp bacon, warm syrup and juice. $3.25

A Cup and a Half
A cup of our soup and today's half sandwich. $3.25

Hamburger ♥.
With seasoned French fries. $3.45

Spaghetti with Meatballs ♥
Served with garlic toast. $3.95

 Country Fried Chicken
Two pieces, crisp and tender. $4.25

Roast Turkey Dinner
With sage stuffing and cranberry sauce. $4.25

Fillet of Fish
Served with tartar sauce. $4.25

Chopped Beef Steak
A third-pound of ground beef topped with a golden onion ring. $4.25

Baked Meat Loaf
Topped with rich gravy. $4.25

🍳 Indicates Country Kitchen® specialties.
Right Choice™ – For guests concerned about a healthy diet.
♥ Less than 400 calories.
♥ Less than 100 mg. cholesterol.
♥ Less than 1000 mg. sodium.
♥. Meets guidelines without French fries.

FIGURE 7-8. *(Continued)*

BEVERAGES

Soft Drinks
Free refills. $ .95

Milk $ .95

Coffee
We serve a bottomless cup of the best coffee in town. Regular or decaffeinated.

Iced Tea
Free refills. $ .85

Hot Tea
Free refills. $ .85

Lemonade
Free refills. $ .95

Hot Chocolate
Free refills. $ .85

BEER AND WINE
(Where Available)

Country Kitchen®
Marks of Quality

We use only Grade AA eggs, real dairy Half and Half creamers, Grade A garden vegetables and U.S.D.A. Choice steaks. We proudly serve such nationally famous quality brands as Heinz Ketchup, Smucker's jams and jellies, Uncle Ben's Rice, Oscar Mayer meats and more. In the interest of your health, we also serve 2% lowfat milk and all of our fried and grilled foods are cooked with cholesterol-free oils.

Give a Gift That's
Always In Good Taste

Country Kitchen® restaurant Gift Certificates make an excellent, thoughtful gift for any occasion – holidays, birthdays, anniversaries or as business gifts. They can be redeemed at any participating Country Kitchen® restaurant in the U.S., Canada or Puerto Rico. To purchase, see the cashier or ask your server.

DESSERTS

Down-Home Apple Dumpling
A tangy, sweet apple, baked in a pastry shell and topped with cinnamon sauce and served a la mode with cinnamon or vanilla ice cream. $1.75

Hot Fudge Cake
Creamy vanilla ice cream layered between slices of rich chocolate cake. Drizzled with hot fudge sauce, crowned with whipped topping. $1.75

Pecan Pie $1.45

Special Recipe Pies – *Baked Fresh Daily*
Fruit pie, served hot. $1.35
A la mode. $1.75
Cream pie. $1.45

Ice Cream Sundaes
Two scoops of ice cream covered with your choice of hot fudge, butterscotch, chocolate or strawberry sauce. Topped with whipped topping. $1.75

Strawberry Twinkie® Shortcake
A tender cream-filled Twinkie®, sliced and topped with vanilla ice cream, sweetened strawberries and whipped topping. $1.95

Hot Fudge HoHo®
Two cream-filled HoHos® topped with vanilla ice cream, hot fudge and whipped topping. $1.95

Twinkie® and HoHo® are registered trademarks of The Continental Baking Company.

Indicates Country Kitchen™ specialties.
Right Choice™ – For guests concerned about a healthy diet.
♥ Less than 400 calories.
♥ Less than 100 mg. cholesterol.
♥ Less than 1000 mg. sodium.
♥ Meets guidelines without French fries.

FIGURE 7-8. *(Continued)*

JUICES

Chilled Orange, Grapefruit, Tomato or Apple Juice $.95

SKILLET BREAKFASTS®

Farm Skillet®
Seasoned hash browns, topped with two eggs, sausage, onions and green peppers. Served with toast and jelly. $4.75

Skillet Scramble®
Two scrambled eggs and grilled ham served on a bed of seasoned hash browns, topped with tangy cheese sauce. Served with toast and jelly. $4.75

Fiesta Skillet®
Seasoned hash browns combined with taco meat, topped with two eggs, shredded cheese, diced tomatoes and green peppers. Served with a side of salsa, sour cream, toast and jelly. $4.75

Double-Up Skillet®
Two eggs, two strips of bacon and two slices of French toast on a bed of seasoned hash browns. Served with warm syrup. $4.75

Southern Skillet
An old favorite! Sausage patties on biscuits, with two eggs. Served with country sausage gravy on the side. $4.75

OMELETTES

Our omelettes are made with three eggs and served on a bed of seasoned hash browns, accompanied by toast and jelly.

Simply Eggs™ Garden Omelette
Stuffed with broccoli, tomato, mushrooms, onions and green peppers. $4.95

Western Omelette
Sautéed ham, onions and bell peppers combined with eggs and American cheese and topped with cheese sauce. $4.95

Ham and Cheese Omelette
Fresh ham and cheese combined into the classic omelette and topped with cheese sauce. $4.95

Mushroom and Cheese Omelette
Sautéed mushrooms and American cheese folded into an omelette and topped with cheese sauce. $4.75

PANCAKES

Best Pancakes in Town
Our famous pancakes are light and fluffy with a hint of sugar and vanilla. Served with your choice of bacon, ham or sausage and warm syrup.
Full stack. $4.25
Short stack. $3.75

Cakes and Eggs
Two eggs, two pancakes and two slices of crisp bacon. Served with warm syrup. $3.75

Blueberry Pancakes
Our light fluffy pancakes filled with blueberries and cooked golden. Served with your choice of breakfast meats and warm blueberry compote or syrup. $4.75

Indicates Country Kitchen® specialties.
Right Choice™ – For guests concerned about a healthy diet.
Less than 400 calories.
Less than 100 mg. cholesterol.
Less than 1000 mg. sodium.
Meets guidelines without French fries.

FIGURE 7.8. *(Continued)*

COUNTRY CLASSICS

Country Eggs
Two eggs any style, seasoned hash browns, toast and jelly. $2.95

Everybody's Favorite
Two eggs any style, seasoned hash browns, toast and jelly. Served with your choice of bacon, ham, sausage or a grilled beef patty. $4.45

Country French Toast
Thick slices of French bread dipped in egg batter and grilled golden. Served with bacon, ham or sausage and warm syrup. $4.45

Simply Eggs™ Breakfast ♥
Scrambled Simply Eggs™ served with fresh fruit and a warm muffin. $4.75

Country Fried Steak and Eggs
Tender beef, lightly breaded and fried. Served with two eggs, seasoned hash browns, country gravy, toast and jelly. $4.95

Steak and Eggs
Two eggs, seasoned hash browns and two slices of toast and jelly with a 6 oz. U.S.D.A. Choice top sirloin steak. $5.95
With an 8 oz. U.S.D.A. Choice rib eye steak. $7.95
With a 10 oz. U.S.D.A. Choice New York strip steak. $8.95

SIDE ORDERS

Hot or Cold Cereal ♥
Served with fruit, a freshly baked muffin and milk. $3.25

Oscar Mayer Bacon or Sausage ♥ $1.95

Ham ♥ $1.95

Seasoned Hash Brown Potatoes ♥ $1.45

English Muffin ♥ $ .95

Giant Sweet Roll ♥
Glazed or caramel, served warm. $1.45

Toast ♥ $ .95

Freshly Baked Muffin ♥ $1.25

Fruit Medley ♥
Served with a freshly baked muffin. $3.25

Biscuits and Gravy $2.25

Country Kitchen® restaurant's famous breakfasts are served all day. Ask your server for today's breakfast specials. We serve [Oscar Mayer] products.

For our guests concerned about diet, we offer Simply Eggs™. Simply Eggs™ is a great tasting, real, whole egg product that has 80% less cholesterol than shell eggs. Simply Eggs™ is available as a substitute on any breakfast. Simply Eggs™ is a registered trademark of Michael Foods, Inc.

🍳 Indicates Country Kitchen® specialties.
Right Choice™ – For guests concerned about a healthy diet.
♥ Less than 400 calories.
♥ Less than 100 mg. cholesterol.
♥ Less than 1000 mg. sodium.
♥ Meets guidelines without French fries.

FIGURE 7-8.   *(Continued)*

FIGURE 7-8. *(Continued)*

are made on a more timely basis, such as seasonally, two times the number of seats would be the norm. There are exceptions to this rule and knowledge of the operation is essential if modifications are to be made.

Some students would question why one would print more menus than seats. The answer is simple. Menus get soiled, torn, and stolen. There is little that can be done to correct the first two problems, but to reduce theft, reproduce a copy of the menu on a regular sheet of paper. These can be used as handouts and are an excellent form of advertisement at a very reasonable cost.

DESKTOP PUBLISHING

An alternative to having a printer create the layout, typesetting, and artwork on your menu would be to use *desktop publishing*. This could be very cost effective assuming that your restaurant already has a computer. If not, the purchase of hardware, CRT, printer, and software would more than offset the savings that could be derived unless the system were to be used for other functions such as accounting, inventory, and cost controls.

In addition to saving money on menu costs, a computer developed menu can allow you to react quickly to price changes in the marketplace, change menu items as customer demand fluctuates, take advantage of seasonal items, and run holiday or special event promotions. An additional advantage would be to tie the menu to an analysis method (Chapter 15) so that you could quickly determine what adjustments are needed on your menu mix to improve profitability.

FIGURE 7-11.   An example of a menu cover and copy developed by using desktop publishing software on a computer. (*Courtesy of Patricia Bors*)

◄··■ STARTERS ➤··➤

Batter Fried Veggies ....$.
   Zuchinni, mushrooms and cauliflower deep fried in our special blend of herbs and seasonings.

Chilled Shrimp Cocktail ....$.
   Fresh popcorn shrimp served up with a special Louisiana style marinara sauce.

Nachos ....$.
   Spicey cheese sauce and mild or hot picante sauce over fresh crisp corn tortilla chips.

Big Nachos ....$.
   Shredded seasoned beef, refried beans, spicey cheese sauce, topped with tomatos, onions, sour cream, guacamole, and olives on corn tortilla chips.

Potato Skins ....$.
   Topped with cool sour cream, hot melted cheese sauce, crisp crumbled bacon, and sprinkled with chives. Four to a plate.

Vegetables and Dip ....$.
   Cool crisp carrots, cucumber, green pepper and celery sticks with a creamy dill dip.

·············· Soups ··············

	cup	bowl
Homestyle Steak Soup	$.	$.
Broccoli Cheese Soup	$.	$.
French Onion Soup	$.	$.
Boston Clam Chowder	$.	$.

·············· Salads ··············

	dinner	entree
Garden Salad	$.	$.

   Traditional tossed salad of iceberg lettuce, tomato wedges, carrots, celery, green peppers, cucumber, and onion.

| *Chef's Salad* | $. | $. |

   Paper thin sliced ham, breast of turkey, eggs, black olives and American swiss cheese with tomato wedges on salad greens.

| *Chicken Avocado Salad* | $. | $. |

   Chunks of smoked chicken, ripe avocado, tomato, and peas tossed with sprouts and peanuts and our special herb dressing.

| *Oriental Vegetable Salad* | $. | $. |

   Eight different vegetables, toasted almonds and chow mein noodles with sesame seed dressing.

◄··■ ENTREES ➤··➤

Sirloin Strip Steak ....$.
   8 oz. of choice sirloin, served with garlic butter or sour cream.

Grilled Filet of Sole ....$.
   Lightly seasoned with lemon butter.

Batter Fried Shrimp ....$.
   6 huge gulf shrimp deep fried in our own blend of special seasonings and served with a tangy marinara sauce.

Lasagna ....$.
   Spicey Italian sausage layered with three different cheeses, tomato sauce and pasta.

Stuffed Breast of Chicken

A generous chicken breast portion filled with tomatoes, fresh mushrooms and a delicious blend of herbs, baked to tender perfection and topped with golden toasted parmesan cheese. A house specialty.

$.

Mexican Platter ....$.
   Choice of chicken or beef taco and burrito, beef and bean tostada, and a cheese enchilada.

Accompaniments		Beverage	
French Fries	$.	coffee	$.
Baked Potato	$.	hot tea	$.
Onion Rings	$.	iced tea	$.
Wild Rice		soft drinks	
with mushrooms	$.	$.	$.
Refried Beans	$.	lemonade	
Steamed vegetables	$.		$.
		shakes	$.

◄··■ DESSERTS ➤··➤

Black Forrest Cake	$.	Ice-Cream
Chocolate Mousse Pie	$.	$.
Deep Dish Apple Pie	$.	
Cheesecake	$.	

   with cherries, blueberries, strawberries or raspberries.

Hot Fudge Brownie Sundae ....$.

FIGURE 7-11. *(Continued)*

Giorgio
Restaurant
Weekly Special

11:30 am to 1:30 pm

Monday
Lettuce & Tomato Salad
Cornish Hens with Brazil Nut Stuffing
Peas, Onions, and Mushrooms
Cherry-Almond Torte

Tuesday
Creamy Mushroom Soup
Pork Chops with Creamy Rice & Peas
Assorted Pickles or Spiced Apple Rings
Pound Cake with Fresh Strawberries & Whipped Cream

Wednesday
Tossed Green Salad
Swiss Cubed Steaks & Brussels Sprouts Piate
Twice Baked Potatoes
Cheesecake with Strawberry Topping

Thursday
Fruit Salad with Honey Dressing
Chicken Breast with Wine & Mushrooms
Bacon - Cheese Stuffed Potatoes
French Green Beans
Apple Pie with Whipped Cream

Friday
Boston Lettuce with Dill and Vinegar Dressing
Shrimp in Butter Sauce
Flavored Rice
Zucchini & Tomatoes
Cranberry Ice Cream Pie

FIGURE 7-12. A menu showing the daily specials for the week is another example of desktop publishing. This menu used Design CAD 2-D, Microsoft Word, and MoreFonts for DOS. (*Courtesy of the Hospitality Management Program, Fort Leavenworth Disciplinary Barracks, Leavenworth, Kansas*)

If an entire system (hardware and software) is to be purchased, make sure it will handle a multiplicity of functions in your restaurant, not merely menu development. If a computer is in place, all you will need to purchase is the software. Two packages will probably be needed; one for the text, and one for artwork. Your computer dealer can assist you in selecting the proper software for your particular brand of computer.

Another factor to consider is the printer as it will affect the quality of the finished menu more than anything. There are three styles of printers, dot-matrix, letter quality, and laser. The first two will not give high quality results, while a laser printer will develop a menu that is so close to a typeset menu that the average customer will not notice the difference.

In creating your own menu with desktop publishing, you can do the entire project—cover and inside text—yourself. Another option would be to just do the text and purchase a cover from one of several menu companies that have created covers specifically for computer-developed menus.

Once you have developed your menu, it will still be necessary to take it to a printing company if a large number of copies are needed. The costs of reproducing the menu will be the same as if it were typeset. What you have saved is the cost of typesetting plus you now have a menu which is exactly the way you want it.

CONCLUSION

Once the items have been selected and priced, a critical point is reached—the layout and subsequent printing of the menu. Select a style that fits the restaurant. The cover, the inside layout, and the institutional copy should reinforce the theme and ambience of the restaurant. Work closely with the printer and use his knowledge and expertise. The result will be a menu of which you can be proud and more importantly which will sell products and make a profit. It's just that simple.

QUESTIONS

1. Explain in your own words:
   Lamination
   Headings
   Institutional copy
   Prime space
   Clip-ons
   Points
   Upper case
   Leading

2. Pick a restaurant theme. Tell what type of cover you would design, what headings and subheadings you would use, what would be merchandised in the prime space, and write the institutional copy.

3. Referring to question two, tell what style of type and size in points you would use for your headings, subheadings, descriptive terminology and institutional copy.

CHAPTER EIGHT

Fast Food

OBJECTIVES
- To know that the key to fast food menus is simplicity.
- To understand how speed, holding qualities, packaging and minimum handling of products is important in menu planning.
- To learn the importance of standardization of menu items.
- To appreciate the role of test marketing in menu selection.
- To learn how the menu interrelates to other facets of the fast food industry such as concessions, delis, drive thrus and delivery.

IMPORTANT TERMS:

KISS	Standardization
Test marketing	Concessions
Holding qualities	

INTRODUCTION

When we think of fast food, we most often think of the major players, e.g., McDonalds, Pizza Hut, Taco Bell, and so on. While the dominant force in this segment of the food service industry is in the national and regional chains, there are many small independent operators who compete successfully in this market. In addition to the typical stereotype of fast food, there are other components of this part of our industry. Concession stands in sports arenas, small neighborhood delis, drive thrus, home deliveries, gourmet boxed to go, and hot food take-outs in supermarkets all comprise a portion of this segment. While there are only a few principles involved in menu planning for fast food operations, those that do exist are important.

SIMPLE AND LIMITED

The key to writing a fast food menu is simplicity. The president of a successful chain has a sign behind his desk that says, "KISS"—translated "Keep it simple, stupid." Good advice! However, he should have added "limited." That is, the menu should be simple to prepare and serve as well as limited in the number of menu items.

The reasons behind keeping the menu simple and limited are many—the most important one being speed. Fast food operations are, for the most part, in the low-price range. With today's high fixed costs and high labor costs, the only way for a restaurant to survive is with equally high sales. Therefore, if the menu has a low selling price, it must depend on a high turnover rate to achieve high volume. Thus, speed becomes important. For without it, high turnover and, consequently, high volume cannot be realized. To realize speed, any item placed on the menu must fit these following criteria. First, it must involve minimum handling by the production staff. Second, it must have the ability to withstand holding and at the same time maintain an acceptable quality level as most fast food items are pre-cooked. Third, it must require minimum handling by the service staff. If a potential menu item can't be put directly into a bag or box by the service personnel, forget it—it will slow down service.

While speed is the primary reason for keeping the menu simple and limited, there are several other factors that benefit from this key criterion. One important benefit is a low inventory. With a limited menu, less product will have to be kept in storage than would be the case with an extensive menu. With less inventory, the restaurant has a higher turnover of goods and, consequently, a better cash flow. Also, with a simple, limited menu a lower skill level of personnel is necessary. Thus, a totally unskilled person could be trained (in a relatively short period of time) to produce and/or serve the menu. The primary benefit from this factor is a lower wage per hour resulting in a lower total payroll. It would also allow these unskilled people to produce an acceptable product that meets the company's standards and the customer's expectations. Finally, a limited menu takes away from customer indecision, which greatly slows down service. You have all heard the old story of why a restaurant owner only carried vanilla ice cream. "If I added chocolate, it would take the customer forever to decide." While this may not be totally valid, there is some truth to it. A limited menu definitely speeds up service.

STANDARDIZATION

Another important criterion in writing fast food menus is the ability of an item to be standardized—one of the key features of chain operations. The independent can follow the same approach. That is, the product must be of the same quality and quantity time after time. Therefore, when deciding on a menu item, determine if the product can be controlled. For example, if an operation were deciding between adding a 4 oz. hamburger to the menu or a 3 oz. roast beef sandwich, in terms of control, they should opt for the hamburger. A preformed 4 oz. hamburger patty can be obtained from any meat packer. With this item, there is no question. A 4 oz. (precooked weight) hamburger will be served each and every time one is ordered. With the roast beef sandwich, on the other hand, many things can go wrong in terms of control. Each roast will differ in its fat to lean ratio. Cooking times and temperatures will vary. Each roast will have different weights. In other words, the yield will not be constant. If a precooked roast were purchased, this would solve part of the problem, but what about portion control? Can the server be counted on to put exactly 3 oz. of sliced beef on a sandwich each and every time? Probably not. Fast food standards need to be precise and exact. If a standard calls for three pickle slices on a sandwich, it doesn't mean two or four; it means three—period! As soon as a person starts thinking that four pickle slices would be better, they become dangerous to the organization. Each menu item must be explored by the menu writer for possible variations by the server. The less variations, the better.

Finally, we must consider the equipment. As you know, the restaurant must have the proper equipment and the capacity to produce the item. Consider the following anecdote concerning a fast food chain. This chain decided to add cole slaw to its menu. A formula was developed, costs were established, a selling price determined, and purchasing specifications written. This material was sent to the stores in the field. They forgot, however, one thing—the equipment necessary to produce the cole slaw. As one executive from this company put it, "Things got so bad, we had managers chopping cabbage on their desks." While making sure that the proper equipment is available may seem obvious, even the largest companies can make mistakes. Don't let this happen to you.

Once a menu item is decided upon, it should be test marketed. After all, a menu is written for the customer. It may be perfect for the restaurant, but if it is not accepted, all is for naught. Each fast food chain has certain markets they designate as test markets. Normally these markets are typical, demographically, of the country as a whole. A new menu item is tested in these markets to determine customer acceptance. If it passes the test, the item is then introduced chainwide. If it fails, it goes on the shelf. Not only is customer acceptability tested, but also the effect it has on the total product mix of the store. Assume, for example, that if the new item has a lower gross profit than another menu listing and also takes sales away from that particular listing, the results would lower total gross profit. The new item, even though the customers bought it, would be totally unacceptable to the chain. Independent fast food operations, even though they don't have test stores, should also carefully test new items, via blackboards, table tents, or point of purchase signage before making them a permanent part of the menu.

Once a new menu listing has passed its test, it is then marketed throughout the chain. The marketing function in fast food restaurants will determine more than anything which items on a menu will sell. Two criteria are used to determine which items to market—those items that have a high gross profit, and new items that will bring new customers into the store. Feature these items in your advertising.

Originally, fast food restaurants started out with only one or two items on their menus. Their efforts were concentrated on expanding their chains across the country. While the chains were expanding, new companies entered the market. This led to overcrowding and, in some cases, market saturation. As this happened, the byword became increased store sales. With expansion less prevalent in the chain's total sales, the only place left to obtain increases was with each individual store contributing more. To achieve this, the fast food companies looked to the menu. Slowly and carefully adding new items to reach a greater market, they increased store sales by menu changes appealing to a broader base.

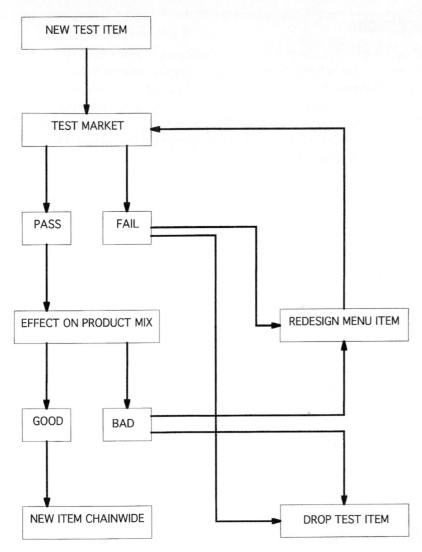

FIGURE 8-1. New item test model.

In addition to this, they expanded their hours of operation with the addition of breakfast. At first, only a few chains experimented with this novel idea, then one by one the others fell into line with virtually every fast food restaurant now serving breakfast.

What is a limited menu? That's a good question because even the experts can't agree. Some chains still cling to the few menu items, while others, even though they classify themselves as fast food, resemble mini coffee shops. How far will the chains go with menu expansion? How far can they go before the concept of simple and limited menus with fast service is destroyed? As of this writing, these questions go unanswered.

One observation, however, is clear. The pendulum swings back and forth. Fast food companies add to and delete from their menus. During one period, the byword is menu expansion. During another period, it is back to basics with limited offerings. Perhaps this youngest segment of our industry is still trying to find itself.

CONCESSIONS

Food service in sports arenas and stadiums is big business. Many of the newer ones have fine dining or theme restaurants, catering service to luxury boxes, as well as the familiar concession stands. The concepts of menu planning for the restaurants have been covered in a previous chapter and delivery to the private boxes follow the same principles as would a hotel room service menu. The concession stands likewise conform to the same rules for fast food with a few minor additions.

In addition to limited, simple standardized and fast, concession stands need to be concerned with volume. For the average ballgame or concert, they must obtain their sales in 4–6 hours. This makes the previously mentioned principles paramount to success. The menu selections must also take into account the fact that people are there for a good time, to have fun, and nutritious healthful food be damned. Nachos, popcorn, hot dogs, pizza, ice cream, cotton candy, peanuts, beer and soda are the staples. It must taste good, be sold quick and be easily packaged.

Packaging is very important not only for the ease of the customer or vendor in delivery to the seats, but in many cases for cost control. Most concessionaires control their costs by strict inventory control. Hot dogs, buns, popcorn boxes, soda and beer cups, packs of peanuts, and the like are all counted prior to and after the event to ascertain what the sales should be by product. These are added together for total sales and should equal the cash sales of that particular stand.

DELIS

Delis refer to the small operations that limit their sales to cold meats, salads, breads, and pastries and are not to be confused with the large delicatessens found in most major cities. These resemble more of a coffee shop or theme restaurant and, thus, would follow those menu principles.

Delis are, in reality, two businesses: fast food and bulk sales. The fast food aspect follows those concepts of menu planning with one exception—most of the sandwiches are prepared to order, as well as the salads sometimes being packaged to order. Thus, speed is less of a factor than is quality and the satisfaction of the customer who is able to choose his own ingredients.

Bulk sales are an important part of the overall sales mix of a deli. Meats and cheese sold by the pound, salads sold by the pint, quart, or pound, and bakery products sold by the dozen make up a large part of the business. Meat, cheese, and vegetable

FIGURE 8-2. Example of a drive-through menu. (*Courtesy of Pizza Hut, Inc., Wichita, Kansas*)

platters are also sold, and many delis have an extensive catering business as well.

Paramount to menu planning in delis is the ability of the products to retain freshness as well as taste.

DRIVE THRU, DELIVERY, AND BOXED TO GO

While we are dealing with three totally different concepts here, they all have two things in common with regard to menu planning: The items selected for the menu must have the ability to be packaged for easy handling, and they must have the capacity to hold temperature and quality over a period of time. While drive thru and delivery are for the most part an extension of existing fast food operations, they offer a new challenge to the menu planner. *Drive thru* patrons must have access to the regular menu and, therefore, packaging becomes of utmost importance to the entire menu. *Delivery,* on the other hand, may or may not be offered by a company depending on whether or not its menu can withstand holding qualities for a period of 30 minutes or more.

Boxed to go is the newest segment of our industry and caters to the working person who does not have the time or inclination to cook, but would prefer to eat at home rather than in a restaurant. These operations are found in storefronts, supermarkets, and as extensions of established restaurants. In addition to offering menu selections that have holding qualities and can be readily packaged, these items also should be microwaveable.

CONCLUSION

Fast food restaurants should carefully choose menu items for simplicity. Simple to prepare, package, and serve. The menu should be limited with careful attention to standardization. The less room for error, the better.

In the summary of previous chapters, the concluding comment has been "It's just that simple." In this chapter, it is fact. It's just that simple.

QUESTIONS

1. Discuss the relationship between simplicity, sales, and profit in the fast food industry.

2. Choose a fast food restaurant in your area and develop a new menu item using the skills you learned in this chapter.

3. Develop a fast food menu for a new trend or type of cuisine that is not represented in the fast food industry.

4. In your opinion, have the fast food chains gone too far with menu expansion or are they justified with this expansion? Defend your answer with concrete examples.

CHAPTER NINE

Coffee Shop Menus

OBJECTIVES
- To understand that moderate is a key word for coffee shop menus in terms of pricing, staff skill levels, and complexity of listings.
- To develop menus that have regional appeal.
- To appreciate the importance of variety and balance.
- To generate menus that have the familiar listings as well as innovative and "cutting edge" listings.

IMPORTANT TERMS

Moderation	Balance
Variety	Check average
Three-in-one menu	

INTRODUCTION

Coffee shops menus are as diverse as coffee shops themselves. Although some coffee shops offer little other than breakfast items during early morning hours, most coffee shops provide breakfast, lunch, and dinner. Some are even open 24 hours a day. In addition to the main meals, many of these shops offer snacks, fountain items, and late suppers. Coffee shop size and style vary considerably from the simple, small diner to the heavily decored California coffee shop often seating 200 or more. Although many coffee shops today are free standing units, an equal number share space in a variety of settings—hotels, truck stops, diners and shopping malls among others.

GENERAL PRINCIPLES

If one word had to be chosen to describe coffee shop menus, it would have to be moderation. The range of selling prices, the menu items themselves, the skill level of the kitchen and service personnel, and the descriptive terminology are all moderate. However, do not confuse moderate with plain or boring. Nothing could be farther from the truth. Coffee shop menus can be exciting and trendy as well as moderate.

Because each coffee shop serves a unique market, the menu writer must know and understand the clientele. The principles presented in this chapter will cover the majority of coffee shops and, therefore, will cover a wide range of demographics. Usually, prices are in the low to moderate range. Care must be exercised in this area because we are dealing with a dual-edged sword. The object is to create as high a check average as possible to ensure profitability, but at the same time keep the selling price within the range of our clientele.

The skills of the cooking as well as the service staff are frequently limited. Therefore, the menu items should be uncomplicated. The kitchen staff should not be requested to prepare an item that they have not been properly trained to produce. To have them do so would result in disaster, dissatisfied customers, and lost sales. The service personnel, likewise, should not be expected to perform at high levels of achievement or possess much sales ability. The menu, while simple, must sell the customer. Do not expect your service personnel to do it for you.

One of the objectives in coffee shops is a high table turnover and, therefore, the menu items should reflect this. They should either be ready to serve listings or short order items. Ready to serve items are prepared ahead by the kitchen staff and are available for service when the customer orders them. Some examples include beef stew, soup, and chicken a la king. Short orders, on the other hand, are prepared to order within a relatively short period of time—for example, eggs, hot cakes, hamburgers (cooked to order), or sandwiches. Even one item on the menu that takes an extraordinary amount of time to prepare or requires extensive handwork could very easily slow table turnover. This is bad for both the coffee shop in decreased sales and for the customer in an unnecessary wait.

Another element to consider in coffee shop menus is the terminology used on the menu. Because the food and setting of a coffee shop are both relatively simple, the menu should be equally uncomplicated. Foreign terms should be avoided and the terminology should be kept modest. This does not mean, however, that descriptive terminology should be avoided. Nothing could be farther from the truth. Simple but exciting words that describe and sell should be used, as the menu must create sales. As stated before, the service staff has limited training, limited experience, and limited time.

Both hospitality management students and patrons frequently observe that coffee shop menus are quite dull and include common items that one can get in any other establishment. Such menus lack imagination. Although coffee shop menus should be simple and uncomplicated, they do *not* have to be dull! When writing your menu, feature some items that are peculiar to your particular region as well as some new and exciting items. However, you must balance interest and excitement with simplicity and efficiency. You must remember the people involved with your operation—the staff and its skills, the clientele, and its potential.

Unusual, new, and exciting items produced by your staff will add sales to any coffee shop. If the skill level is not sufficient, try incorporating some convenience foods for menu variety. To test new items to see if they will work in your restaurant, the clip-on is one method of experimenting. Another method is taste testing with your present customers. Give each one a small sample and note their reactions. If favorable, then a new menu item has been created. In addition to trying out new items, clip-ons can also be used for using leftovers. When using clip-ons, remember that the paper that they are printed on should match the paper of the menu both in style and color. Clip-ons should always be clean, neat, and typed (not handwritten) with the price also typed. Too often, the entire menu is destroyed by tacky, greasy clip-ons.

BREAKFAST

Let's take a look at the actual makeup of coffee shop menus starting with breakfast. The population is not consistent in its attitude toward breakfast. Many people subscribe to the notion that breakfast is the most important nutritional meal of the day, while others are content to have a cigarette and a cup of coffee to get them going. Certainly, people are always in a hurry at breakfast. Whether they overslept or had to take the kids to school, or are even on schedule, they must be at work on time, so they have very little time for breakfast. On the other hand, the senior citizen contingent has the time to socialize and quite often does over breakfast. Theirs is a steady market which gives the restaurant a consistent money sales volume. Therefore, the menu writer must take into account speed of service and variety in order to cover everyone. Increasing the difficulty of the task is the fact that the majority of breakfast items are cooked to order.

The makeup of the menu should include a la carte items, as well as club breakfasts, which are nothing more than combinations of a la carte items. Club breakfasts or specials are usually complete and should include an appetizer such as a fruit or juice as well as an entree with potatoes, toast, and beverage. Club breakfasts are cheaper as a package than ordering each individual item a la carte. Since customers have come to expect a value or a price bargain, feature club breakfasts! The menu itself should be set up in headings with the following categories: juices, fruits, cereals, eggs, meats, griddle cakes, waffles, side orders, bakery items, and beverages.

Juices

The most common juice, of course, is orange juice and should by all means be on the menu. How you handle orange juice will depend upon your particular situation and accessibility to fresh Florida and California oranges. It can either be canned, frozen, or fresh squeezed. Canned juice is a rather undesirable product and should be avoided. Frozen orange juice, on the other hand, is a very tasty, economical, and efficient product and is used in most operations. In restaurants where you can get the extra price, fresh squeezed orange juice is advisable and even mandatory if the location is convenient to the orange growing area of the country. Other juices that you would want to consider would be tomato, V-8, cranberry, pineapple, grapefruit, apple, and prune juice. The variety and types of juices that you put on the menu depend on your customer. For example, in areas where you have a lot of elderly people, prune juice is an excellent seller. However, in other areas where you are dealing primarily with younger people or blue collar workers, it is a very slow seller.

Fruit

The fruit category requires considerable care and common sense. List only those items which are in season most of the year, for example, a banana or half a grapefruit. In some areas of the country there is an excellent selection year round and, therefore, this is not a problem. However, in other areas fresh fruits are not available year round. Nothing is more tacky on the menu than the line "Fresh fruits in season—ask your waitress." Items such as cantaloupe, honeydew melons, fresh strawberries, when they are in season, would be best advertised to your customer by a table tent or by the waiter or waitress suggesting these items to the customer. Listing them on the menu and then not having them available for sale will create bad feelings. Several frozen fruits have very good product acceptability and could be used year round on the menu. In some areas and some locations canned fruits will work. For something different why not try a fresh fruit compote on your menu? Describe it as a "medley of fresh fruits carefully selected by our Chef." Do not be specific as to the content or you will be right back to the aforementioned problem. Garnish it with something unusual such as kiwi fruit or star fruit.

Breakfast menus are sort of a mundane thing with every operation selling basically the same items. The fruit category is an area where you can add unusual items to your menu to give something different that the competition does not have. When using fresh fruit, be careful with the types of fruits that you list and the amount you purchase, as they are perishable. Any items that have to be thrown out or discounted will directly affect the food cost of your restaurant.

Cereals

Cereals are listed on the menu as hot or cold. Hot cereals have severely declined in popularity in the past several years although they are still popular with older people. Whether or not you list hot cereals on the menu depends on your customer and the amount of the product you could sell. Dry cereals are still fairly popular and a wide assortment can be had by ordering the "variety" pack. They are fast, easy to service, and should be used on breakfast specials where speed is of the essence. Cereals can be served with either milk or with half and half or, if you are featuring a diet combination, with skim milk. If there is an extra charge for half and half, it should be so stated on the menu. An excellent way to increase the average check in a breakfast operation is to add fruit to the cereal such as bananas, which are available year round, and also seasonal items such as strawberries. Also, you might try a continental breakfast of coffee, juice, and a roll. If reasonably priced, it will sell.

Eggs

Eggs are the mainstay of the breakfast to many people. They can be prepared many ways: fried, sunny side up, over easy, boiled, scrambled, shirred, poached, and the ever popular omelette. Omelettes are an excellent way to increase the average check of an operation. You can list several on you menu. Why not have the customer create his own omelette? Very simply list the basic price of the omelette on the menu and beneath that list the ingredients so that the customers can choose their favorite, such as ham, sausage, bacon, onion, green pepper, mushroom, and cheese. The egg category on the menu can feature some new and exciting items. If your kitchen staff has the skill level, try eggs benedict. If not, try two poached eggs with two slices of Canadian bacon on English muffins. Mexican food is fast gaining in popularity in this country, so why not try Huevos Rancheros, or a breakfast taco made up of scrambled eggs, pork sausage, green pepper, onion, and hash browns all mixed together and folded in a warm flour tortilla?

Meat

The meat category must include the three basics—ham, bacon, and sausage. Sausage can either be patties or links, frequently both. In order to give some variety to your menu, you could add steak, Canadian bacon, Italian sausage, or scrapple—a Pennsylvania Dutch favorite made from pork and cornmeal.

Waffles and Griddle Cakes

The next category, waffles and hot cakes, also includes French toast. One thing to remember on waffles—in most operations they are very good sellers; however, you would be wise to check the skills of your kitchen staff to see if they could adequately produce this item. If you are serving an excellent product, you could stack up your kitchen with back orders. Be advised to check the cooking skills of your employees, equipment available, and product flow of your kitchen before adding this item to your menu. Hot cakes and French toast are relatively easy to prepare and do not take a great deal of time. Sales appeal can be added to these items by offering a variety of syrups and toppings. For a change, try fresh frozen peaches or strawberries on top of hot cakes or French toast .

Bakery

An operation can really excel in the bakery category. Sweet rolls, Danish, doughnuts, coffee cake, hot biscuits with butter and jam, or hot biscuits with gravy, cereal muffins such as bran, fruit muffins such as apple or blueberry, will greatly increase the sales of a restaurant. If you have a large operation with a bakery, this will be no problem. In small operations, you could check into the wide variety of convenience foods to increase the bakery section on your menu. There are many mixes on the market which make it relatively easy to produce some of these items. Do not forget basic items such as toast, which would be either white, whole wheat, or rye and also

English muffins. Bagels are an excellent seller in many areas, as are croissants, which have exploded onto the scene.

Side Orders

Side orders include potatoes, grits, or any other items you wish to sell that are not listed elsewhere on the menu. It is sort of a miscellaneous category.

Beverages

Beverages are basically self-explanatory and would include coffee, Sanka, tea, milk, buttermilk, chocolate milk, and hot chocolate.

CLUB BREAKFASTS

Club breakfasts are made up of combinations of a la carte items and should be all-inclusive with the possible exception of beverages. Some restaurants charge additional for beverages while others include it on the club breakfast. By all-inclusive, I mean including such items as potatoes or grits, and toast or English muffins with jelly. It is very tacky to have a nice assortment of club breakfasts with the words "hash browns extra." Club breakfasts should include such items as eggs with meat, omelettes with meat, and hot cakes, waffles, or French toast with meat. Eggs and omelettes with meat should include toast, jelly, and hash browns. Your menu should include one relatively fast club breakfast that a customer could be served in a short period of time, for example, scrambled eggs with diced ham, hash browns, toast, jelly, and coffee. Prepared ahead of time, these items are simply plated when the customer orders them. At least one club breakfast should be economical, clearly exhibited, a good price/value relationship. If so, then your customer might buy more than coffee and a roll. Furthermore, an economy club breakfast makes excellent advertising copy. An ideal item for such club breakfasts is hot cakes. Box in or otherwise highlight the highest gross profit club breakfast on your menu.

LUNCH AND DINNER

The next two sections to be examined, lunch and dinner have many inherent similarities so there meals will be discussed concurrently. For example, the menu categories are very similar. These include: appetizers, soups, salads, entrees, sandwiches, side orders, desserts, and beverages. Whether or not to include all of these listings for both meals depends on several factors.

First think about the *check average.* In a coffee shop where a higher check average is desired, it would be wise to include appetizers on both the luncheon and dinner menus. Conversely, it may be advisable to drop sandwiches, particularly on the dinner menu, as these tend to lower the check average.

Another factor, closely related to the check average, is the *clientele* we are attempting to serve. If the demographics dictate a predominantly blue collar clientele, the check average would be lower because appetizers and salads play a smaller role than in a coffee shop which caters to white collar clientele.

The *skill level* of the production staff will determine the number of categories you would use. With the advent of convenience foods it would be quite simple to include all categories even if the employee skill level is low.

The *operating philosophy* of the restaurant would also need to be considered. If the scope of the operation is limited, then all categories should not be used. If the coffee shop is complete, that is "being all things to all people," then a comprehensive menu should be your goal.

The categories chosen should create balance. Certainly, the menu should be nutritionally balanced. This is imperative in coffee shop menus as many of the customers served are the same patrons day after day. Although it is not our job to force nutrition on our customers, we have a responsibility to offer a nutritionally balanced meal. Customers decide for themselves how well they wish to eat. Other balances to consider are hot/cold, textures and cooking methods. Balance as a whole will be discussed later within each category. When you write a menu, balance forces you to compose an exciting, varied menu. A well-balanced menu will not be dull, repetitious, or uninteresting.

Some generalized statements on the differences between luncheon and dinner menus are in order. Items on luncheon menus should be lighter in terms of fat content than on dinner menus. Portion sizes should be smaller and, because of this, the selling price should be lower. The speed of preparation should also be taken into account. While breakfast menus focus on speed, lunch is a divided affair with some patrons in a hurry due to a limited lunch break, while others whose time is not restricted will demand a slower pace. Dinner, on the other hand, is almost always a more leisurely meal. To make sure the menu has balance and variety, a menu pattern could be used. This would predetermine the number of items in each category, their color, texture, cooking methodology, temperature, and so on. Menu patterns can be devised for any combination desired and their use assures that balance and variety are achieved.

Appetizers

In analyzing the various categories on the luncheon and dinner menus, let's start with appetizers. If the appetizer category is used, several selections should be offered, some hot, some cold. Balance should be sought between meat, seafood, fruit, and vegetables. Other food groups, such as cheese, could be included. Avoid using the same cooking technique on all hot items. Too many menus list only a variety of breaded or tempura battered vegetables—all fried. With the ever-increasing health conscious market, raw vegetables with a dip or a fresh fruit and cheese board are becoming very popular.

Soups

The second category, soups, is closely aligned with appetizers and, in many instances, is combined. The number and variety of soups listed depends on your particular operation; however, at least one, a soup du jour, is indispensable. When offering two or more soups, balance a clear soup with a cream or chowder-type soup. Of the clear soups, consommes are very popular. This category is critical to the success of your operation as many coffee shops have built a reputation on the quality of their soups and some have even become famous for a particular soup. Obviously, the best quality is obtained from preparing your own on your premises. Nothing is more insulting to a customer than to offer a bowl of canned soup for $1.50, when they can prepare it themselves at home for 30¢. Let your imagination run wild, creating new and exciting offerings for your customers. Soup is also an excellent food cost item, particularly when the cost is lowered even more by utilizing leftovers. Soups also offer menu versatility when used in combination with sandwiches and salads.

Salads

Salads are rapidly gaining popularity as diet-conscious Americans turn away from fried foods to more natural offerings. Salads are of primary importance in markets which cater to white collar and/or female clientele. Balance in the variety of salads offered is important and could include fruit, vegetable, and meat, poultry, fish, and seafood. Fresh fruit salads with cottage cheese or sherbet are excellent sellers in season. Because of their seasonability, they should be promoted via a table tent or clip-on. The most common salad and the top seller in many coffee shops is the familiar chef's salad. By all means, this should be on every coffee shop menu. Fresh spinach salad and tossed garden greens are also popular.

A word about salad dressings—make them distinctly yours. They are simple to make in large batches and have a good shelf life when properly refrigerated. Avoid factory-made dressings if at all possible, but if you must, at least alter them to obtain individuality. Cold meat platters sell year round. Chicken and tuna salad, whether arranged on a cold plate with other fresh vegetables or stuffed in a ripe tomato, are also good sellers. Try new ideas when building the salad section of your menu. The result should be increased sales.

Entrees

The entree section of your menu is the most important as this is the area that your entire operation will be judged by. It is critically important that the pricing structure fall within the framework of your demographic guidelines. Balance between the food groups is also important and should contain a variety of beef, veal, pork, lamb, poultry, and seafood. The only exceptions occur if one of these happens to be ethnically unacceptable in your trade area. Conversely, one of the groups may predominate your area and the selections would, therefore, be increased and highlighted on the menu. You must provide a variety of cooking methods, using roasting, broiling, sauteing, pan frying, grilling, and deep fat frying. As previously mentioned, fried and deep fat fried foods should be downplayed and broiled and baked items given more predominance than in the past.

The aforementioned food groups can be broken down further into solid, semi-solid, and extenders. Typical *solid* entrees include steak, pork or lamb chops, fried or baked chicken, and shrimp or fish filets. *Semi-solid* items include meat loaf, Salisbury steak, and ham or chicken croquettes. *Extenders* are casserole items such as beef stew, chicken a la king, ham and beans, and pasta. Each of these has its place on the menu; the solids get a high selling price increasing the check average but a low gross profit, while the semi-solids and extenders get a lower selling price, but a higher gross profit. Between the three, the result is a good product mix with a satisfying gross profit.

Sandwiches

The sandwich section of the menu is almost as critical in importance as is the entree section, especially for a coffee shop. Balance within the meat food group—beef, pork, poultry, variety meats, fish—is imperative. And so is a balance of temperature and cookery methods. Sandwiches familiar to your clientele should be featured, but include some variety with new or unusual items on your menu.

Side Orders

The side order section historically has been a miscellaneous area of the menu. If one did not know where to list an item, it automatically went to this section. Consider for a moment what side orders are, they are essentially add-ons. With proper merchandising on your menu, they can substantially increase your check average. Use them to complement your entree and sandwich sections with offerings that are compatible to these listings.

Desserts

The last section to be discussed, the dessert section, is frequently given only passing notice by otherwise good menu planners. In addition to the regular listings that are common to all coffee shops, give this section some flair. Pastries, tortes, eclairs, tarts, and fountain creations can pay dividends to the menu planner with imagination. If the skills of your kitchen staff or the proper equipment is lacking, try convenience foods. If it is properly planned and executed on the menu, you can increase the check average and also can create business, particularly during the slack hours.

MENU LAYOUT

Now that we have discussed the three meals on the coffee shop menu, the next problem concerns layout. As you can already see a coffee shop menu is really several menus combined into one, the most common approach in the industry today. Certainly, this is the most expedient, as well as the cheapest, way to approach the problem. In some operations this method creates a logistical problem in that it is not expedient to serve breakfast during a lunch rush. Whichever method you choose (i.e., one or separate menus) will be dictated by the individual needs particular to your restaurant.

ROOM SERVICE MENUS

An offshoot of the coffee shop menu is the room service menu that is used in all major hotels and those hotels with food service. While there are striking similarities between the two in that they both cover all meal periods and snacks, there are a few major differences that need to be studied.

Probably the most crucial part to room service is the facilities and staffing of this department. Due to the fact that it is quite expensive to maintain, many operations attempt to cut corners with disastrous results. Consider the fact that one member of the waitstaff can handle 20 to 30 seats in the coffee shop and turn them over relatively quickly, but it takes one person 10 to 15 minutes to assemble an order and deliver it to one room. That room service delivery should, if properly done, be delivered in a cart which would hold the temperature, either heated or chilled, of the product whereas a tray would suffice in the coffee shop. Because of its high cost and low sales volume, many operations will charge a higher selling price on the room service menu than for the same item on the

FIGURE 9-1. A complete coffee shop menu. (*Courtesy of Flagstar Corporation, operators of Denny's Restaurants, Spartanburg, South Carolina*)

Moons Over My Hammy™ 4.59

The supreme ham and egg sandwich, made with Swiss and American cheese on grilled sourdough. Served with choice of hashed browns or French fries.

Day Breaks

You may substitute egg beaters, in any breakfast for an additional 25¢. Low-calorie syrup available upon request.

Southern Slam® 3.89

Two steamy, buttermilk biscuit halves, covered with rich, country sausage gravy and served with two eggs, two bacon strips and two sausage links.

All-American Slam™ 4.59

Three eggs scrambled with Cheddar cheese. Served with hashed browns, two sausage links, two bacon strips and choice of toast, buttermilk biscuit or English muffin.

Chicken-Fried Steak and Eggs 4.85

A southern specialty. Served with country gravy and hashed browns. Choice of toast, buttermilk biscuit or English muffin.

Look for this symbol for our famous signature entrees.

BEVERAGES

Denny's Mug O'Coffee™
Our famous private blend.

Regular or decaffeinated	.80
Hot Chocolate	.80
Hot Tea, Herbal Tea	.80
Freshly-Brewed Iced Tea	.95
Soft Drinks, Lemonade	.99
Milk:	
Regular (10 oz.)	.80
Large (16 oz.)	1.00
Juice:	
Orange, Apple, Grapefruit or Tomato	
Regular (10 oz.)	.89
Large (16 oz.)	1.29

Free refills on coffee, soft drinks, lemonade and tea.

OTHER POPULAR FAVORITES

Two-Egg Breakfast with Ham 4.40
Served with hashed browns and choice of toast, buttermilk biscuit or English muffin.

Two-Egg Breakfast 2.90
With four bacon strips or four sausage links 4.20

Steak and Eggs 5.99
U.S.D.A. Choice top sirloin steak and two eggs, served with hashed browns and choice of toast, buttermilk biscuit or English muffin.

GRIDDLE FAVORITES

Buttermilk Pancakes with Bacon or Sausage 3.45
Three fluffy pancakes served with warm, rich syrup and two bacon strips or two sausage links.
Buttermilk Pancakes 2.55

French Toast with Bacon or Sausage 3.65
Extra thick, batter-dipped and perfectly browned. Served with warm, rich syrup and two bacon strips or two sausage links.
French Toast 2.75

Belgian Waffle with Bacon or Sausage 3.65
A crisp, golden waffle served with warm, rich syrup and two bacon strips or two sausage links.
Belgian Waffle 2.75
Belgian Waffle Supreme 3.35
Covered with strawberry or blueberry topping and whipped cream.

BREAKFAST SIDES

Large Egg	.79	Bagel and Cream Cheese	1.30
Smoked Ham Slice	1.99	Buttermilk Biscuit	.85
Bacon or Sausage	1.95	Biscuit and Sausage Gravy	1.69
Hashed Browns	.99	Grits	.95
Toast or English Muffin	.85	Hot or Cold Cereal	1.10
Hot Cinnamon Roll	.99	Applesauce	.75
Blueberry Muffin	.99	Fresh Fruit in Season	1.00
NEW! Banana-Nut Muffin	.99	Mixed Fruit	1.00

FIGURE 9-1. *(Continued)*

International Slam 3.99

Two French toast halves and half of a golden Belgian waffle, served with two bacon strips, two sausage links and two eggs.

Original Grand Slam Breakfast 3.69

A Denny's original. Two buttermilk hotcakes, two eggs, two bacon strips and two sausage links.

Scram Slam 4.89

Three eggs scrambled with Cheddar cheese, mushrooms, green peppers and onions, then topped with diced tomatoes. Served with hashed browns, two sausage links, two bacon strips and choice of toast, buttermilk biscuit or English muffin.

French Slam 3.89

Four extra thick, batter-dipped halves of lightly browned bread, served with two eggs, two bacon strips and two sausage links.

All omelettes are served with hashed browns and choice of toast, buttermilk biscuit or English muffin.

Harvest Slam 3.99

Two whole wheat, apple, nut and spice hotcakes with rich apple topping. Served with two eggs cooked just the way you want them, two strips of bacon and two sausage links.

Veggie-Cheese Omelette 4.89

A fluffy three-egg omelette with sautéed onions, green peppers and sliced mushrooms, add Cheddar cheese and tomato slices, then top it with chopped green onions.

Ultimate Omelette 4.95

Three eggs wrapped around sautéed mushrooms, onions, sausage, bacon, green peppers and tomato. Topped with American cheese.

Mexican Omelette 4.99

A three-egg omelette filled with spicy ground beef and Cheddar cheese, topped with diced tomatoes. Served with salsa and sour cream.

Ham 'n' Cheddar Omelette 4.79

Diced ham and Cheddar cheese in a fluffy three-egg omelette.

Chili-Cheese Omelette 4.79

A three-egg omelette filled with Cheddar cheese and chili, then topped with even more chili and cheese.

Cereal Combo 3.55

Hot or cold cereal, with mixed fruit or banana and a regular-size glass of juice. Served with choice of toast, buttermilk biscuit, English muffin, blueberry muffin, banana-nut muffin or bagel.

LD63

FIGURE 9-1. *(Continued)*

Crispy Chicken Salad   4.99

Golden-fried chicken strips on a bed of mixed greens with diced tomato, Cheddar cheese, cucumber slices and bacon. Served in a crispy tortilla shell with honey mustard dressing on the side.
Add bowl of soup .... .99

Chef's Salad   4.89

Chunks of smoked ham and oven-roasted turkey breast, Cheddar cheese, black olives, egg and tomato over mixed greens. Served with bread.
Add bowl of soup .... .99

NEW! Grilled Chicken Caesar Salad   5.09

Tender pieces of grilled, lightly seasoned chicken breast served over a mixed bed of Romaine lettuce, Caesar dressing, croutons and shredded Parmesan cheese. Served with bread.
Add bowl of soup .... .99

Sandwiches &

All sandwiches and burgers are served with our large-cut French fries and pickle chips.

You may substitute seasoned fries in place of our regular fries for an additional 25¢.
Our 100% beef burgers are over 1/4 lb. (precooked weight).
We use only 100% soybean oil for frying.

The Works Burger   4.80

Two slices of American cheese, two strips of bacon, sautéed mushrooms, lettuce and tomato. Served with guacamole.
Add soup or salad .... .99

Bacon-Swiss Burger   4.50

A juicy hamburger with Swiss cheese, crispy bacon strips, fresh lettuce and tomato. Barbecue sauce on request.
Add soup or salad .... .99

Dennyburger Combo   4.79

Our all-American classic, with French fries and your choice of a bowl of soup, garden salad or Caesar salad.
With cheese, add .... .25

Dennyburger   3.80

With cheese, add .... .25

Patty Melt   4.30

The traditional patty melt with American cheese. Topped with sautéed onions on grilled rye.
Add soup or salad .... .99

Denny's features Coca-Cola® classic and other popular favorites.

LD63

FIGURE 9-1. *(Continued)*

Salads

Taco Salad 4.99

Spicy ground beef, Mexican-style beans, Cheddar cheese, black olives, tomato, guacamole and sour cream. Served over mixed greens in a crispy tortilla shell. Salsa on the side.
Add bowl of soup... .99

California Grilled Chicken Salad 4.99

A tender breast of chicken, grilled and sliced. Served over mixed greens with fresh cucumber, tomato, Cheddar cheese and chopped nuts. Honey mustard dressing on the side. Served with bread.
Add bowl of soup.................................99

Chicken Melt Slam™ 5.19

A grilled chicken breast between two slices of Monterey Jack cheese, tomato slices and crisp bacon on grilled sourdough.
Add soup or salad...................99

Tuna Melt Supreme 4.69

Tuna salad topped with tomatoes and bacon strips, then covered with melted American cheese, all on grilled Parmesan sourdough bread.
Add soup or salad....99

Look for this symbol for our famous signature entrées.

Roast Beef Deluxe 4.79

Thinly sliced roast beef with sliced tomatoes and melted American cheese on grilled sourdough. Thousand Island dressing on the side.
Add soup or salad.... .99

The Super Bird® 4.79

A Denny's original. Sliced turkey breast with Swiss cheese, bacon strips and tomato slices on grilled sourdough.
Add soup or salad ..... .99

The Club 4.79

The classic triple-decker. With sliced, oven-roasted turkey breast, bacon, lettuce and tomato on toasted white bread.
Add soup or salad................................99

Megamelt Slam™ 5.39

Thinly sliced ham and melted American cheese, topped with a layer of sliced roast beef, melted Monterey Jack cheese, mild green chiles and tomato slices, all on grilled sourdough. Served with French fries and coleslaw.
Add soup or salad 99

OTHER FAVORITES

Add soup or salad to any of these favorites for only 99¢. All sandwiches and burgers are served with our large-cut French fries and pickle chips.

Grilled Chicken Sandwich 4.60

Grilled breast of chicken, topped with lettuce and sliced tomato on an herb-toasted bun. Honey mustard dressing on the side.

Bacon, Lettuce and Tomato 3.70

Grilled Cheese on Sourdough 2.95

SIDES

NEW! Caesar Salad	1.65	Onion Rings	1.85
Garden Salad	1.65	Coleslaw	.99
Seasoned Fries	1.70	Bowl of Soup	1.65
French Fries	1.45	Bowl of Chili	1.99

Veggie-Cheese Melt 3.35

Fresh tomatoes, cucumber, guacamole and lettuce together with Monterey Jack, Swiss and American cheese on grilled multigrain bread.
Add soup or salad 99

FIGURE 9-1. *(Continued)*

Bowl of Chili 1.99
A hearty bowl of chili topped with shredded Cheddar cheese. Diced onions available on request.

Seasoned Chili Fries 3.09
A heaping basket of seasoned fries topped with chili and shredded Cheddar.

Mozzarella Sticks 3.75
Breaded and golden-fried. Served with a tangy tomato sauce.
Mini Order... 1.99

NEW! **Buffalo Wings** 3.99
A dozen spicy chicken wings served with celery sticks and your choice of bleu cheese or ranch dressing.
Mini Order 1.99

SOUP *of the* DAY

DAILY

Vegetable Beef 1.65
A hearty favorite at Denny's. With beef, barley and eight garden vegetables.

MONDAY

Chicken Noodle 1.65
With chunks of chicken, egg noodles, diced onions, celery and chopped parsley.

SIDES

NEW! *Caesar Salad*	1.65
Garden Salad	1.65
Basket of French Fries	1.45
Basket of Seasoned Fries	1.70
Basket of Onion Rings	1.85
Coleslaw	.99

BEVERAGES

Denny's Mug O'Coffee™
Our famous private blend.

Regular or decaffeinated	.80
Hot Chocolate	.80
Hot Tea, Herbal Tea	.80
Freshly Brewed Iced Tea	.95
Soft Drinks, Lemonade	.99
Milk:	
Regular (10 oz.)	.80
Large (16 oz.)	1.00
Juice:	
Orange, Apple, Grapefruit or Tomato	
Regular (10 oz.)	.89
Large (16 oz.)	1.29

Free refills on coffee, soft drinks, lemonade and tea.

Denny's features Coca-Cola classic and other popular favorites.

Chicken Strips 3.95
A basket of golden-fried chicken strips served with honey mustard dressing or tangy barbecue sauce.
Mini Order 2.49

Sampler 4.79
A delicious sampling of chicken strips, mozzarella sticks and onion rings. Served with a tangy tomato sauce and choice of barbecue sauce or honey mustard dressing.

Quesadilla 2.29
Diced tomatoes and mild green chiles, with melted Cheddar cheese, folded in a hot flour tortilla. Served with a side of sour cream, guacamole and salsa.

Chicken Quesadilla 4.29

Spicy Ground Beef Quesadilla 3.99

FIGURE 9-1. *(Continued)*

LIGHT LUNCH
COMBINATIONS

Served Monday through Friday, 11 a.m. - 2 p.m.

Fresh Garden or Caesar Salad
with Bowl of Soup   2.99

Sandwich with Choice of Bowl of Soup,
Garden Salad or Caesar Salad   3.89

Your choice of garden salad, Caesar salad or bowl of soup (vegetable
beef or soup of the day) and one of the following sandwiches: turkey
breast on wheat, tuna salad on white or ham and Swiss on rye.

Soups & Starters

We use only 100% soybean oil for frying.

*Cocktails, wine and/or beer may
be available at this restaurant.
Please ask your server.*

TUESDAY

Cream of Potato 1.65

Diced potatoes, green peppers,
celery, carrots and onions. With
a hint of bacon.

WEDNESDAY

Cream of
Broccoli   1.65

A creamy combination of
broccoli, cheese, celery and
onions, flavored with a
hint of garlic.

THURSDAY

Cheese   1.65

A delicious surprise.
Mild cheese, bacon,
diced celery and
green onion.

Nachos Supreme   2.99

Crispy tortilla chips topped
with spicy ground beef,
Mexican-style beans, Cheddar
cheese, green onions, diced
tomatoes, black olives,
guacamole and sour cream.
Salsa on the side.

FRIDAY

Clam
Chowder   1.65

Our famous prizewinning
chowder made with clams
and whitefish.

LD63

FIGURE 9-1. *(Continued)*

New York Steak 7.69

Over 1/2 lb. (precooked weight) of grilled U.S.D.A. Choice strip steak. Served with hot vegetable of the day and choice of potato or rice pilaf.

Fried Chicken 6.09

One-half chicken, southern-fried to a crispy golden brown. Served with hot vegetable of the day and choice of potato or rice pilaf.

All entrees are served with bread and choice of soup, garden salad, Caesar salad, coleslaw or fruit.

Dinner At Denny's

Dinners served from 11 a.m. Baked potato served from 4 p.m. - 10 p.m. only.

We use only 100% soybean oil for frying. Denny's features Coca-Cola® classic and other popular favorites.

Roast Beef Dinner 5.99

The classic American meal. Hot roast beef on white bread, with a generous helping of mashed potatoes, both covered with rich brown gravy. Served with hot vegetable of the day.

Steak and Shrimp 7.79

U.S.D.A. Choice top sirloin with six large, golden-fried shrimp. Served with a zesty cocktail sauce, hot vegetable of the day and choice of potato or rice pilaf.

Liver with Bacon and Onions 5.29

Two slices of beef liver, lightly seasoned and grilled, then topped with onions and two bacon strips. Served with hot vegetable of the day and choice of potato or rice pilaf.

Cocktails, wine and/or beer may be available at this restaurant. Please ask your server.

Roast Turkey and Stuffing 5.99

Sliced, oven-roasted turkey breast, layered over savory stuffing with rich gravy. Served with hot vegetable of the day and choice of potato or rice pilaf. Includes cranberry sauce.

FIGURE 9-1. (*Continued*)

Chicken Strip Dinner 5.89

Four chicken fillet strips, breaded and golden-fried. Served with hot vegetable of the day and choice of potato or rice pilaf. Honey mustard dressing on the side.

Chicken-Fried Steak 5.79

A southern specialty. Topped with rich country gravy. Served with hot vegetable of the day and choice of potato or rice pilaf.

Stir-Fry Chicken with Vegetables 5.39

Tender chunks of chicken breast, stir-fried with fresh vegetables. Served with rice pilaf and teriyaki sauce.

Spaghetti with Meatballs 5.79

A traditional favorite smothered with our tangy tomato sauce and a generous helping of meatballs.

Spaghetti 4.89

Topped with our tangy tomato sauce.

Grilled Catfish 6.45

Two tender fillets of farm-raised catfish, delicately seasoned with herbs. Served with hot vegetable of the day, tartar sauce and choice of potato or rice pilaf.

Shrimp Dinner 6.85

A dozen large shrimp, lightly breaded and golden-fried. Served with a zesty cocktail sauce, hot vegetable of the day and choice of potato or rice pilaf.

Grilled Breast of Chicken 5.99

A boneless, skinless breast of chicken, seasoned with lemon pepper and dill, then grilled. Served with hot vegetable of the day and choice of potato or rice pilaf.

Grilled Trout 6.35

A tender fillet of trout, delicately seasoned with lemon pepper and dill. Served with hot vegetable of the day, tartar sauce and choice of potato or rice pilaf.

Cod Dinner 5.99

Two fillets of tender cod, lightly battered and golden-fried. Served with hot vegetable of the day, choice of potato or rice pilaf and a side of tartar sauce.

Grilled Halibut 6.85

A tender, grilled halibut steak. Served with hot vegetable of the day, tartar sauce and choice of potato or rice pilaf.

LD63

FIGURE 9-1. *(Continued)*

Double-Dip Sundae 1.95

Two scoops of ice cream, covered with your favorite topping. Choose from rich chocolate, blueberry or strawberry. Crowned with whipped cream and nuts.

Hot Fudge Sundae 1.95

Two big scoops of vanilla ice cream smothered in rich hot fudge and topped with whipped cream and nuts.

Key Lime Pie 1.85

Coconut Cream Pie 1.85

Chocolate Cream Pie 1.85

Cherry Pie 1.75
A la mode, add .... .75

Apple Pie 1.75
A la mode, add.... .75

Cherry Cream Cheese Pie 1.85

FIGURE 9-1. (*Continued*)

Chocolate Cake 1.75

Calling all chocolate lovers! Luscious layers of dark chocolate cake, covered with rich chocolate icing.

Ice Cream Shakes 1.99

Here's a friend from the soda fountain days. We'll even give you an extra helping in the malt can. Try chocolate, vanilla or strawberry.

Denny's Banana Split 2.79

Rich chocolate, strawberry and vanilla ice cream smothered in hot fudge, strawberry and blueberry toppings. Crowned with whipped cream and nuts.

Denny's Mug O'Coffee .80

Our famous private blend. Regular or decaffeinated.

Finishing Touches

A la mode, add .75 Whipped topping, add .25

Pie prices and selection may vary by location. Please ask your server for details.

Hot Fudge Cake Sundae 2.55

Triple-layer chocolate cake topped with a scoop of vanilla ice cream, hot fudge, whipped cream and nuts.

Ice Cream by the Scoop

Chocolate, vanilla or strawberry.
Single........................ .90
Double 1.20

Blueberry Cream Cheese Pie 1.85

LD63

FIGURE 9-1. *(Continued)*

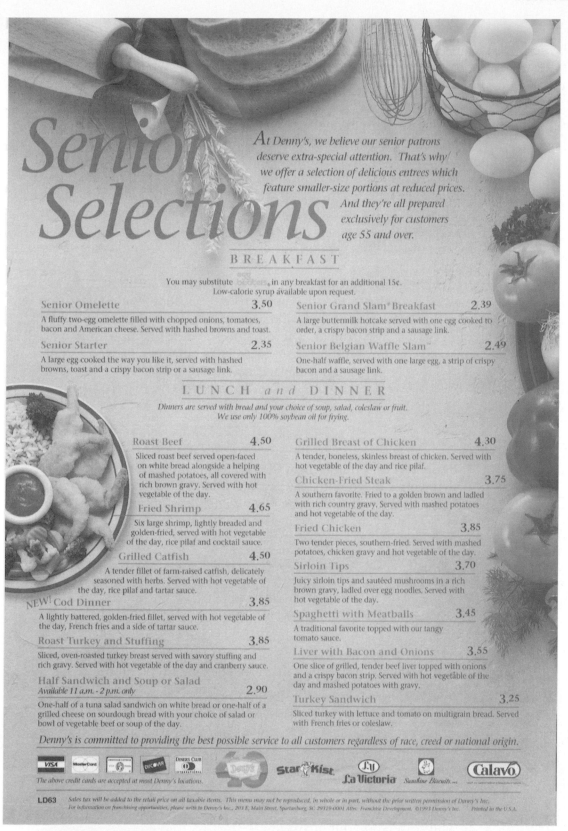

Senior Selections

At Denny's, we believe our senior patrons deserve extra-special attention. That's why we offer a selection of delicious entrees which feature smaller-size portions at reduced prices. And they're all prepared exclusively for customers age 55 and over.

BREAKFAST

You may substitute _____ in any breakfast for an additional 15¢.
Low-calorie syrup available upon request.

Senior Omelette 3.50

A fluffy two-egg omelette filled with chopped onions, tomatoes, bacon and American cheese. Served with hashed browns and toast.

Senior Starter 2.35

A large egg cooked the way you like it, served with hashed browns, toast and a crispy bacon strip or a sausage link.

Senior Grand Slam® Breakfast 2.39

A large buttermilk hotcake served with one egg cooked to order, a crispy bacon strip and a sausage link.

Senior Belgian Waffle Slam 2.49

One-half waffle, served with one large egg, a strip of crispy bacon and a sausage link.

LUNCH *and* DINNER

Dinners are served with bread and your choice of soup, salad, coleslaw or fruit. We use only 100% soybean oil for frying.

Roast Beef 4.50

Sliced roast beef served open-faced on white bread alongside a helping of mashed potatoes, all covered with rich brown gravy. Served with hot vegetable of the day.

Fried Shrimp 4.65

Six large shrimp, lightly breaded and golden-fried, served with hot vegetable of the day, rice pilaf and cocktail sauce.

Grilled Catfish 4.50

A tender fillet of farm-raised catfish, delicately seasoned with herbs. Served with hot vegetable of the day, rice pilaf and tartar sauce.

NEW! **Cod Dinner** 3.85

A lightly battered, golden-fried fillet, served with hot vegetable of the day, French fries and a side of tartar sauce.

Roast Turkey and Stuffing 3.85

Sliced, oven-roasted turkey breast served with savory stuffing and rich gravy. Served with hot vegetable of the day and cranberry sauce.

Half Sandwich and Soup or Salad 2.90
Available 11 a.m. - 2 p.m. only

One-half of a tuna salad sandwich on white bread or one-half of a grilled cheese on sourdough bread with your choice of salad or bowl of vegetable beef or soup of the day.

Grilled Breast of Chicken 4.30

A tender, boneless, skinless breast of chicken. Served with hot vegetable of the day and rice pilaf.

Chicken-Fried Steak 3.75

A southern favorite. Fried to a golden brown and ladled with rich country gravy. Served with mashed potatoes and hot vegetable of the day.

Fried Chicken 3.85

Two tender pieces, southern-fried. Served with mashed potatoes, chicken gravy and hot vegetable of the day.

Sirloin Tips 3.70

Juicy sirloin tips and sautéed mushrooms in a rich brown gravy, ladled over egg noodles. Served with hot vegetable of the day.

Spaghetti with Meatballs 3.45

A traditional favorite topped with our tangy tomato sauce.

Liver with Bacon and Onions 3.55

One slice of grilled, tender beef liver topped with onions and a crispy bacon strip. Served with hot vegetable of the day and mashed potatoes with gravy.

Turkey Sandwich 3.25

Sliced turkey with lettuce and tomato on multigrain bread. Served with French fries or coleslaw.

Denny's is committed to providing the best possible service to all customers regardless of race, creed or national origin.

FIGURE 9-1. *(Continued)*

coffee shop menu or they may impose a service charge and sometimes both. This does not sit well with the guest and as a result, some operations simply write it off as a guest service to entice the room rental which has a very high markup.

Due to the fact that the product must travel a long distance from the kitchen to the room, only those items that have good holding qualities should be listed on the room service menu. They also should have the ability to be transported easily. If the equipment is not available to properly hold the temperature, then foods which are highly susceptible to contamination and food-borne illness should be avoided. By all means, do not simply place the coffee shop menu in the guest's room and have this suffice as your room service menu. The room service menu should be a limited version of the hotel's restaurant menus and list only those items that fit the above criteria.

In most properties, room service menus, in addition to meals, also list items for parties and small receptions that would take place in the guest's room or suite. Larger functions would be handled by the catering department. These listings should include chips and dip, mixed nuts, crudites, fruit and cheese platters, as well as bottled liquor, mixes, beer, wine, and soda.

CONCLUSION

Throughout this chapter, emphasis has been on balance and variety. If you can gain the patronage of a customer with quality, he/she will eventually look for variety in your menu. Without that, you may lose sales. Try new ideas: Ride the trends. Use your imagination. Give your customers something to look forward to. It's just that simple!

QUESTIONS

1. Differentiate between fast food items and short order items and explain their importance in coffee shop menu planning.
2. Discuss how you would improve a coffee shop menu that was dull and unimaginative. Be specific.
3. Develop a breakfast menu for a coffee shop located in a truck stop on a major interstate.
4. Develop a lunch and dinner menu for a coffee shop in a luxury hotel.
5. Is a three-in-one menu or separate menus preferable for a coffee shop? Defend your answer.

FIGURE 9-2. A room service menu that includes institutional copy marketing the hotel's other restaurants and bars. (*Courtesy of the Doubletree Hotel, Overland Park, Kansas*)

Breakfast

Breakfast is Served

Monday through Friday from 6:30 a.m. to 11:00 a.m.

and Saturday and Sunday from 7:00 a.m. to 11:00 a.m.

Freshly Squeezed Orange Juice or Grapefruit Juice 3.25

Fruit and Vegetable Juices 2.50

Half Grapefruit 2.50

Fresh Seasonal Berries or Melon 3.50

Bakeries & Cereals

Basket of Fresh Baked Muffins 3.25

Wolferman's English Muffin 2.75

Danish Pastry 2.75

Hot and Cold Cereals with Fresh Fruit 2.95

Bagel with Cream Cheese 3.25

The Executive Express

Your Choice of Juice, Freshly Baked Muffin and Croissant.

Served with Whipped Butter, Preserves and Jams, Coffee, Tea

or Decaffeinated Coffee   5.95

The Natural

Low in Cholesterol and Saturated Fats, Naturally!

Birchermeusli 4.75

    Oatmeal and cereal with fruits, berries and nuts

Whole Grain Pancakes 5.75

    Fresh Fruit or Lite Maple Syrup

Veggie Frittata 6.50

    Egg Beaters, Scrambled in Margarine, Crisp Vegetables, and

    Lowfat Cheese

A suggested gratuity of 15% and applicable tax will be included.

Touch Extension 36 to Order   8/92

FIGURE 9-2. *(Continued)*

Eggs & Omelettes

Served with Breakfast Potatoes and Fresh Bakeries

Skillet Eggs 6.75

Two Eggs Any Style, with Ham, Bacon or Link Sausage

Classic Eggs Benedict 7.50

Toasted Muffin, Canadian Bacon, Poached Eggs, Hollandaise

Three Egg Omelette 7.00

Your Choice of Three Items: Ham, Bacon, Pepper

Mushrooms, Cheddar, Jack or Swiss Cheese

K.C. Steak and Eggs 9.95

Cakes & Waffles

Includes Choice of Bacon, Sausage or Ham Served with

Whipped Butter and Warm Syrup.

Golden Stack 5.75

Short Stack 4.50

Belgian Waffle 6.75

Any of the Above Topped with Fresh Berries   Add .50

Thick Sliced Cinnamon French Toast 6.50

On The Side

Hash Brown Potatoes 2.25

Link Sausage 3.00

Rasher of Bacon 3.00

Side of Ham 3.00

Canadian Bacon 3.25

One Egg .... 1.75   *Two Eggs* 2.50

A suggested gratuity of 15% and applicable tax will be included.

Touch Extension 36 to Order   8/92

FIGURE 9-2. *(Continued)*

Beverages

Coffee, Decaffeinated Coffee

Small Pot (3 Cups) 3.75

Large Pot (6 Cups) 5.50

Specialty Teas 1.00

Assorted Flavors

Hot Chocolate, Milk 1.00

A suggested gratuity of 15% and applicable tax will be included.

Touch Extension 36 to Order   8/92

FIGURE 9-2. *(Continued)*

All Day Dining

All Day Dining Available from 11:30 a.m. to 11:00 p.m. Daily.

Starters

K.C. Strip Steak Soup (Our Signature) .... Cup 2.95   Bowl 3.75

Baked French Onion .... Bowl 3.75

Chef's Kettle (Different Each Day) .... Cup 2.75   Bowl 3.50

Shrimp & Sauces 7.95
   Jumbo Shrimp with Cocktail and Remoulade Sauce

House Salad 2.95

Salads

Hot and Cold Chicken Salad 8.50
   Grilled Chicken Breast, Oriental Greens, Crisp
   Rice Noodles, Sweet Hoisin Sauce

Chef's Salad 8.50
   Crispy Greens with Julienne Meats and Cheeses, Tomato and Egg

Painter's Pallette 6.95
   Seasonal Fruit, Berries with Yogurt Dipping Sauce
   Freshly Baked Grain Muffin

Specialties

K.C. Steak Sandwich 9.25
   Served Open Face Topped with Dofino Cheese and Crispy Onions

Shrimp Scampy 9.25
   Sauteed with Butter, Garlic, Lemon over Cappilini Noodles

A suggested gratuity of 15% and applicable tax will be included.

Touch Extension 36 to Order   8/92

FIGURE 9-2. (Continued)

Sandwiches & Burgers

Served with French Fries

Doubletree Steak Burger 7.25

　One Half Pound Ground Chuck, Cheddar, Jack or Swiss Cheese

Boulevard Chicken Sandwich 7.50

　Grilled Breast on a Seven Grain Bun, Dofino Cheese,

　Avocado and Cilantro Mayonnaise

Jumbo Chicken Salad Croissant 6.75

Overland Park Club 7.50

　Toasted Triple Decker of Ham, Turkey, Bacon, Lettuce,

　Tomato and Swiss Cheese

Reuben Tradition 6.95

　Corned Beef, Swiss Cheese and Sauerkraut

　with Thousand Island Dressing

A suggested gratuity of 15% and applicable tax will be included.

Touch Extension 36 to Order　　　　　　　　　　　　　　8/92

FIGURE 9-2. *(Continued)*

After 5 P.M.

Available 5 p.m. to 11:00 p.m. Daily.

Appetizers & Salads

Louisiana Crab Cakes 7.25

   Basil Buerre Blanc

Santa Fe Spinach and Artichoke Dip 6.25

   Blue and Gold Corn Chips

Traditional Caesar Salad 4.75

   Parmesan Garlic Croutons

Small Garden Salad 2.95

Entrees

Includes Vegetable, Potato, House Salad, Rolls and Butter

K.C. Strip Steak 19.95

   14 oz. Broiled or Blackened

Perfect Prime Rib .... 10 oz.   16.95   14 oz.   18.95

   Slowly Roasted to Perfection

Roast Long Island Duckling 19.95

   Crisp Duckling in Classic Citrus Sauce

Chicken Breast Cordon Bleu 17.50

   Freshly Prepared, Herb Butter Sauce

Salmon Fillet 19.95

   Broiled with Lemon Butter

Ozark Mountain Trout 17.95

   Panned Fried, Almondine

Desserts

Peppermint Ribbon Ice Cream Pie (Our Specialty) 3.95

Triple Chocolate Death 3.95

N.Y. Deli Cheesecake (Fresh Strawberries Optional) 3.95

Dark Chocolate Terrine (Incredibly Rich) 3.95

A suggested gratuity of 15% and applicable tax will be included.

Touch Extension 36 to Order   8/92

FIGURE 9-2. *(Continued)*

Wines

In Addition to Our Wide Selection of Domestic and Imported Wines,

We are proud to Offer the Following House Selections

By the Bottle or by the Glass.

	Chardonnay	White Zinfandel	Cabernet Sauvignon
		Select	Premium
Glass		4.00	4.50
Bottle		20.00	22.00

Premium Wine By The Bottle

Cabernet Sauvignon	Chardonnay	White Zinfandel
Charles Krug 28.00	Château St. Jean 25.00	De Loach 21.00
Sequoia Grove 32.00	Kendall Jackson 32.00	Robert Mondavi 21.00
Jordan 43.00	Robert Mondavi 34.00	**Champagnes**
Beaulieu Vinyards George De La Tour Private Reserve 64.00	Jordan 39.00	Mumms Cordon Rouge 52.00
Opus 1 95.00	Far Niente 45.00	Moët and Chandon 48.00
		Dom Perignon 130.00

A suggested gratuity of 15% and applicable tax will be included.

Touch Extension 36 to Order   8/92

FIGURE 9-2. *(Continued)*

Hospitality Suggestions

Available from 11:00 a.m. Daily.

Please allow 45 minutes to 1 hour for preparation.

Dip the Chip Buffet (minimum 4 people) .... per person 4.75

Deluxe Mixed Nuts, Tortilla and Potato Chips with Freshly

Made Salsa and Bleu Cheese Dip

Deli Platter Sampler (serves 4) 22.50

Generous Slices of Ham, Roast Beef, Turkey, Salami, Cheddar and

Swiss Cheese with Appropriate Condiments and Breads

Cheese and Fruit Assortment (serves 4) 20.50

A Selection of Domestic Cheeses with Fresh Fruit and French Bread

Crudite Tray (serves 4) 17.50

Garden Fresh Vegetables with a Bleu Cheese Dip

Buffalo Chicken Wings .... per dozen 12.00

Hot and Spicy with Bleu Cheese Dip

"Iced and Spiced" Shrimp 22.50

One pound of Peel and Eat Shrimp, Cocktail Sauce and Lemon

(25-30 shrimp)

Bottled Beer

Domestic 3.00

Imported 3.25

Bar Setups 12.50

Fruit, Olives, Napkins, Ice and 1 Dozen Glasses

Ice

Bucket 3.00

Tub 10.00

A Wide Selection of Wines and Spirits are Available

Ask Your Operator for Premium Liquors Available

by the Bottle Complete with Bar Set-ups.

A suggested gratuity of 15% and applicable tax will be included.

Touch Extension 36 to Order   8/92

FIGURE 9-2. *(Continued)*

Enjoy genuine American cuisine at its best. Be it Breakfast, Lunch or
Dinner, you will find the atmosphere memorable and the food delightful.
Daily, enjoy Perfect Prime Rib, the house specialty or your choice from a
wide variety of Steaks, Seafood, or Rotisserie-Roasted Chicken or Duck
items. For the morning diner, Hearty Mid-Western Breakfast is Served
Daily with a-la-carte or buffet service as you please. Our guaranteed five
minute breakfast will help the busy traveler start the day.

Also Enjoy Our Traditional Sunday Brunch.

Butterfly Club

For after-hours relaxation or into-the-evening entertainment, the
Butterfly Club is the place to be. Weekday afternoons, our inviting bar
offers a complimentary buffet of appetizers, with a different international
theme each day of the week.

Evening has a distinctive sound at the Butterfly Club. It sings with live
performances of mellow musical favorites each Wednesday through
Saturday. Elegance resounds with our delightful selection of special
desserts, cordials, fine single-malt scotches, wines by the glass and savory
specialty coffees.

FIGURE 9-2.   *(Continued)*

Theme-Ethnic Menus

OBJECTIVES
- To differentiate the characteristics of theme and ethnic restaurants and menus.
- To understand how descriptive terminology is important to the success of the menu.
- To comprehend the fact that the design of the menu cover is critical to tying the theme to the restaurant.

IMPORTANT TERMS

Theme restaurant	Ethnic restaurant
Price range	Course sequence
Descriptive terminology	

INTRODUCTION

While other styles of restaurants are easy to define, theme restaurants, as well as ethnic restaurants, are difficult to classify due to their diversity. Some themes are nothing more then glorified fast food outlets with waiter/waitress service. For the most part, however, the skill levels of the staff are greater than fast food and, in many cases, surpass those of coffee shop personnel. Classification notwithstanding, there is a common thread between these operations when it comes to discussing menus.

GENERAL CHARACTERISTICS OF THEME RESTAURANTS

Theme restaurants are loosely categorized as those operations that are built around a certain characteristic or idea. This idea, called a *theme,* is followed throughout the operation. The building structure, decor, menu design, food items listed, and uniform all tie into and augment the theme. All operations that classify themselves as theme restaurants have waiter and/or waitress service. The skill level of service in these restaurants is slightly higher than one would find in a coffee shop. Cocktail service is common, requiring a more skilled server. This same slightly higher skill level would hold true for the production staff. In chain-operated theme restaurants, many (if not all) of the menu offerings are either produced in a commissary or prepared from frozen pre-portioned stock. It is imperative that the menu planner of a chain determine in advance if a menu item is easily adaptable to uniformity. Two reasons for this prevail: one, the aforementioned skill level and two, a chain's overriding need to have all of their restaurants identical. On the other hand, an independent theme restaurant would, for the most part, prepare their menu items from recipes and thus need kitchen employees with a higher degree of skill. However, care should be exercised by the menu writer not to exceed the staff's skill level.

Selling prices range from moderate to moderately high. This tells us two things. One, the average check will be higher than in a coffee shop and two, there will be a slower table turnover. Both of these points are important to the menu writer. The higher check average indicates a wider range of ingredients from which to choose in the makeup of menu items. The slower table turnover indicates a more leisurely meal by the customer which in turn affords more time in the kitchen for more time-consuming methods of preparation.

The vast majority of theme restaurants are trendy-type operations. A recent trend is hanging plants with various forms of memorabilia attached to brick or stuccoed walls. Currently, art deco is a

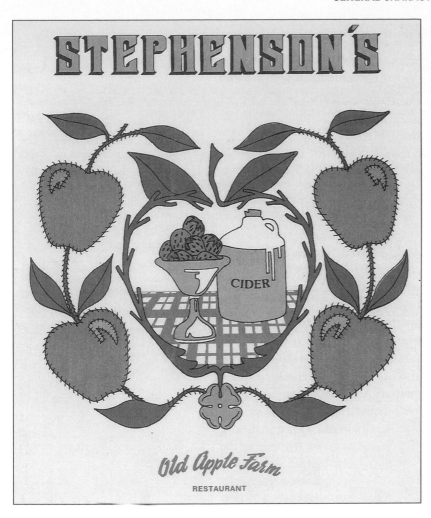

FIGURE 10-1. This restaurant carries the apple farm theme throughout its operation including building, decor, uniforms, and menu. (*Courtesy of Stephenson's Old Apple Farm Restaurant, Kansas City, Missouri*)

popular motif with its design accents, period lighting, and emphasis on color coordination, including mauve, grey, and taupe. By the time this is read, these trends could well have changed to some other innovation concocted by industry leaders.

GENERAL CHARACTERISTICS OF ETHNIC RESTAURANTS

Ethnic restaurants are an offshoot of theme restaurants. However, they are less trendy because they are based on a long-standing tradition—for example, French, Italian, Cajun, or Greek. Their theme features dishes of a particular culture, race, or country. A relative newcomer to the ethnic restaurant scene is the eclectic North American restaurant. Quite often regional in nature, it uses native fresh ingredients as well as local techniques to produce a product that is purely North American. Seafood from the Pacific Northwest and East Coast; beef from the Midwest; and fresh fruits, vegetables, and

A Little About The Apple Farm Restaurant

In 1870, when Highway 40 (Kansas City, Mo) was a mud road, the Stephenson fruit and vegetable farm had its beginning. From a little, one-room stone building, our grandparents sold homegrown produce to folks traveling between Lee's Summit and Independence. Old Timers say the little building was regarded as the half-way point between these two towns.

In 1935, Norman, our older brother, joined father in the orchard business. Since then, the orchard acreage has spread from Lee's Summit to locations in Blue Springs, Grain Valley and Sibley. From these orchards come our fresh apples, peaches, berries and the sweet cider which we serve all year long. Fresh produce from these orchards can also be bought, in season, at Norman's stand next to the restaurant.

Like most early Missouri settlers, our grandparents smoked meats, made apple butter, canned their own fruits and vegetables. And so, on April 16, 1946, when we opened our restaurant in the original stone building, it seemed natural to call it The Apple Farm. We had 10 booths then and served 38 people the first day.

Then, as now, we served old-fashioned hickory smoked meats, home-made apple butter, preserves and relishes, all prepared in our own kitchens in the unique manner that our grandparents had taught us.

Gradually, during seven remodelings, the original stone building has been engulfed. It remains, however, as part of the restaurant's superstructure.

In 1977, due to popular demand we decided to open two new restaurants, since our original restaurant had been expanded to it's capacity. One of the new restaurants is located 8 miles south of the Kansas City International Airport, in Platte Woods, Missouri. The other new restaurant is located in Jane, Missouri, on Highway 71, near Bella Vista, Arkansas.

Again, in 1985, we opened our newest restaurant, The Red Mule Inn. A casual neighborhood style pub and grill just across old U.S. 40 Highway from the Old Apple Farm.

We join the young men and women who are serving you in a warm welcome.

Les + Loyd

The Twins

Stephenson's
APPLE FARM RESTAURANT
40 HIGHWAY AND LEES SUMMIT ROAD · KANSAS CITY · MISSOURI

FIGURE 10-1. *(Continued)*

spices from Canada, the United States, and Mexico make this one of the newer exciting ethnic restaurant offerings.

Ethnic restaurants have waiter or waitress service. Those that have self-service would fall into the fast food category as far as menu planning is concerned and will be covered in a later chapter. The skill level of the service staff as well as the production staff of a full-service ethnic restaurant would be the same or higher than that found in a theme restaurant. Any one of the national chains of Mexican restaurants that have proliferated across the country involve an American style of service with no large degree of skill necessary. The production is mainly commissaried or frozen pre-portioned.

At the other end of the spectrum, for example, a nouvelle cuisine French restaurant, the skill level would be extremely high. Service would be formal French which requires much additional service training. In addition, the production area would require an executive and several sous chefs who would be highly trained. In a middle ground is an Oriental restaurant with American-style

Our Famous Apple Fritters

Bowl of 4 . . . . 1.50

Famous here at the Old Apple Farm for years.

Sweet Endings

Hot Apple Pie with Brandy Sauce 2.25
Made from scratch with fresh apples.

Hot Apple Dumpling with Whipped Cream . . 2.75
We think this is one of America's finest apple desserts. Since we grow several thousand bushels of apples each year, naturally we take great pride in the apple desserts we turn out—it's all in there—nothing is spared.

Apple Parfait 2.50
This is apple juice, sugar, butter and spices cooked together with a smidgen of brandy into a delicate delightful fruit sauce and then poured generously over our french vanilla ice cream.

Pecan Nut Ice Cream 1.95
Premium ice cream, especially made for us.

Pecan Nut Pie 2.25
A rich caramel custard filling topped with pure heavy whipped cream and garnished with gobs of Hickory Nuts.

Frozen Lemon Dessert 2.50
A very fine whip cream ice box dessert flavored with fresh lemons and served with lemon sauce.

Coconut Cheesecake 2.50

Gold Brick Chocolate Sundae . . . 2.50

Beautiful Private Banquets

Dinner from 12.50   Luncheons from 8.00

(plus taxes & service)

We cater off premise.

15% gratuity will be added to all groups of 8 people or more. If you request separate checks, please allow additional time.

Major Credit Cards Accepted. No personal Checks Please.

Apple Farm Dinners
From our Hickory & Apple Wood Smoker

Chicken (1/2) 12.95
The House Specialty. So tender it will fall off the bone.

Brisket of Beef Au Jus 13.95
Cooked long and slow in our oven. Very tender, served with our famous horseradish sauce.

Ribs (1/2 slab) 13.95
Pork Ribs served with Apple Farm B-B-Q Sauce.

Ham Steak 13.95
Center Cut, bone-in, served with wine & honey sauce.

Pork Chops (2) Center-cut. . . 14.95
Some guests eat these every time they come here.

Half N Half 14.95
Choice of any two: Chicken, Brisket, Ham or Pork Chop.

Baked Chicken 'n' Butter & Cream (1/2) . . 12.95
This is real old-fashioned baked chicken with lots of butter and cream, tender and delicious. Our recipe is in Better Homes and Gardens Cook Book "Famous Foods from Famous Places"

Chicken Livers (sautéed) . . . 12.95
If you are a liver 'lover you'll love these.

Seafood

Broiled Red Snapper 14.95
Florida Red Snapper Filet broiled in a light wine and garlic butter.

Hickory Smoked Deep Sea Whitefish 13.95
Delicious moist white meat, lightly smoked in butter and lemon.

Jumbo Shrimp (Lightly breaded and French Fried) . . 17.95
They're large and they're good, served with our fine shrimp sauce.

Steaks

Broiled Filet Mignon Steak 17.95
Cut from choice loins — Served with a buttery mushroom sauce.

Broiled K.C. Strip Steak 17.95
Served with a buttery mushroom sauce.

Marinated K.C. Strip Sirloin Steak . . 17.95
We marinate this in a special wine and garlic oil which adds a special delicious flavor to the steak. Served with a buttery mushroom sauce.

The Apple Farmer's Dinner (For the hearty appetite) . . 21.95
*Brisket of Beef — Ribs — Ham — Chicken
Apple Butter — Farm Relish — Apple Farm Fritter*

Served with all Dinners: Potato — Casserole Dish — Garnish —Hot Breads and Apple Butter

*Salads: Tossed Green, Frozen Fruit or Marshmallow
Blue Cheese Dressing .75*

Split Dinner for Adult $4.00 Additional. Includes Salad, Potato and Hot Breads.

At the Beginning

Sauted Chicken Livers 3.75
For the liver lover.

Hickory Smoked Chicken Gizzards . . 3.75
Delicious — tender as livers.
May be ordered as a dinner 12.95

Fresh Sweet Apple Cider 1.25
from our Mill and Farm.

Our Famous French Onion Soup en Tureen . . 2.95
the Chef's own creation — delicious.

Escargots 4.95
In a mild garlic and wine butter sauce.

Stuffed Mushrooms 4.95
With blue cheese and onions, flavored with a touch of wine and garlic.

A Taste of the Farm

Arrive after 6:00 p.m. Sunday
Arrive by 6:00 p.m. Monday through Friday
Arrive after 9:00 p.m. Saturday
Entrees from 6.95

Sunday Chicken Dinner

11:30 a.m. to 9:00 p.m. (includes Chef's Dessert)

(except Holidays)   8.95

Brunch On Sunday

10 a.m to 2 p.m.

A marvelous treat for all the family!

Adults $10.95, Children 6 through 10 $5.95
under 6 FREE

Coffee, Tea and Milk .85   Pepsi Cola & 7-up .85

FIGURE 10-1. *(Continued)*

The Cider Barrel

We have been making and freezing Apple Cider here for over 40 years. Our large cider mill is located at one of our orchards and from it comes many thousand gallons of cider each year. We supply much of the greater Kansas City trade with our apple cider in season, through the grocery stores. We think the finest apple cider in the world today is the cider you tasted in the barrel in our lobby. It is made with tree-ripened Missouri apples, grown in our own orchards. Our grandfather started growing apples in Jackson County back in 1890. In 1900 there were more apple trees in the state of Missouri than are presently growing in the state of Washington. Late in the fall, we take the right combination of select, tree-ripened Missouri apples and press them into that wonderful old Missouri beverage, sweet, pure, apple cider, then we put it into the freezer for your year-long enjoyment here at the restaurant.

Try our new restaurant north of the river in Platte Woods (8 miles south of the Kansas City International Airport). When in Bella Vista, Arkansas, visit Stephenson's Cider Mill Restaurant on Highway 71. Also, for a casual meal, stop by our Red Mule Inn across 40 Highway from the Old Apple Farm. There you can loosen your tie and relax.

FIGURE 10-1.   *(Continued)*

service which would not require an extraordinary amount of training. The production staff, however, would require several highly trained individuals with specialized skills. Because of the several degrees of training in the various types of ethnic restaurants, the menu writer must create menus that live up to the difficulty expected by the customer, yet stay within the bounds of the skill level of the staff.

The price range of full-service ethnic restaurants varies greatly from the moderate range all the way to the upper end of the high range. Mexican, Italian, and Oriental are but a few of the ethnic restaurants normally falling into the moderate range. Northern Italian, French, and North American eclectic almost always feature moderate to relatively high prices. As stated earlier, the higher the price range, the higher the check average, and the slower the table turnover. In the case of a French restaurant, the table turnover could be as low as 1.5 to 2 times a night. Therefore, the check average would have to be high in order for the restaurant to achieve a profit. The menu writer must recognize that to get a high check average, the customer must perceive a value relationship between the meal and the price paid. Therefore, the menu must be written using unusual, rare, or expensive ingredients prepared and served with a high degree of skill level. As one can see, the scope of theme and ethnic restaurants is great, but the principles of menu planning and writing for them have a fairly common bond.

COURSE SEQUENCE

The courses offered in theme and ethnic restaurants and the sequence of those courses are fairly standard in conjunction with other type menus. The major difference is in the number of courses offered. Theme restaurants tend to have a more limited offering than do ethnic operations. Both types will normally list hot and cold appetizers, salads, entrees, vegetables, starches, desserts, and beverages. Theme restaurants quite often offer sandwiches and side dishes in addition to the above while ethnic restaurants do not. However, these restaurants might opt to add a cheese and fruit course. There are, of course, exceptions to the rule.

The majority of theme and ethnic restaurants use the a la carte menu as opposed to the table d'hote menu. In all menus written for this style of restaurant, it is imperative to stay within the theme or ethnic origins of the establishment. Only a few, if any, generic dishes should be added to satisfy those in a party whose tastes do not coincide with the particular theme or ethnic origin of the restaurant. Certainly, balance is critical between courses and within courses of theme and ethnic menus. No matter the nationality of an ethnic menu, balance should always be sought even though certain dishes may be omitted due to ethnic or religious beliefs.

DESCRIPTIVE TERMINOLOGY

In no other type of menu is descriptive terminology as critical as it is in theme and ethnic menus. It is, however, for different reasons that terminology becomes critical. In the case of theme restaurants, the menu is the focal point of the theme. It is the instrument that ties together the decor, the uniforms, the food, and the general ambience of the restaurant. Two criteria are required to accomplish this: the menu design, which will be discussed later, and the descriptive terminology.

When writing a menu for a theme restaurant, first consider the theme itself. Think of words which best describe that theme and list them. Take this list and then work these key words into your descriptive terminology. For example, if we were to write a menu for a seafood house, a list could be developed using such words as seafaring, nautical, fisherman, catch, net, freshwater, saltwater, cold, icy, and so on. These words could then be used to describe the various menu listings. In addition to having the descriptive listings tie

FIGURE 10-2. An excellent example of a North American eclectic menu. (*Courtesy of Fedora Cafe and Bar, Kansas City, Missouri and Tyson's Corner, Virginia*)

APERITIFS

The word derives from the Latin *aperio*, meaning "to open" and that is the purpose of an aperitif, to open a meal.

CAMPARI
PERNOD
APEROL
LILLET Red or White
SWEET VERMOUTH Martini & Rossi
or Cinzano
DRY VERMOUTH Martini & Rossi
or Cinzano

SINGLE MALT SCOTCHES

Auchentoshan   10 yr. old
The Glenlivet   12 yr. old
The Glenfiddich   12 yr. old
Glenmorangie   10 yr., 18 yr. old
Dalmore   12 yr. old
Macallan   12 yr., 18 yr., 25 yr. old
Cragganmore   12 yr. old
Sheep Dip   8 yr. old
        Ask about our many other selections

IMPORTED VODKAS

Absolut
Absolut Citron
Absolut Peppar
Finlandia
Stolichnaya Cristall
Tanqueray Sterling
Wyborowa

BOURBONS

Blanton's Single Barrel
Booker Noe
Jim Beam   7 yr. old
Makers Mark
Wild Turkey "Rare Breed"
Baker's 107
Knob Creek
Basil Hayden's

SPECIALTY DRINKS

FEDORA MARTINI Our Grand Martini with your choice of Gin or Vodka
BURNT MARTINI Vodka with a swirl of Scotch
RASPBERRY MARTINI Vodka with a swirl of Chambord
FEDORA MANHATTAN Bourbon and Sweet Vermouth
FRENCH CONNECTION Grand Marnier & Courvoisier married
HARRY'S OLD FASHIONED Simply a Classic!
THE IRISH RASPBERRY Chambord and Bailey's Irish Cream

BEERS AND ALES

Amstel Light – Holland
Bass Ale Draft – England
Beck's Light & Dark – Germany
Boulevard Pale Ale Draft – Kansas City
Boulevard Wheat – Kansas City
Budweiser – U.S.A.
Bully Porter – Kansas City
Guiness Stout Draft – Ireland
Heineken – Holland
Miller Lite – U.S.A.
Steinlager – New Zealand
Warsteiner – Germany

WATERS AND SODAS

Evian – Large or Individual
Perrier – Large or Individual
San Pellegrino
LaCroix – Sparkling, Berry, Lemon, Orange
Chapelle – Peach, Plum, & Pear

CAFE, CAPPUCCINO AND AFTER DINNER DRINKS

WHITE COFFEE Truffles White Chocolate Liqueur and our Three Bean coffee topped with whipped cream and white chocolate shavings
CAPPUCCINO FEDORA Laced with Amaretto and Frangelica
CAPPUCCINO Regular & Decaffeinated
ESPRESSO Regular & Decaffeinated
ST. MORITZ Chambord topped with heavy cream
SEMI FREDDO CAFE White chocolate ice cream and Espresso topped with whipped cream

FIGURE 10-2. *(Continued)*

FEDORA CLASSICS

FIRST COURSES

Hot Artichoke Dip with Crisp Garlic-herb Toast.   5.35
House-cured Salmon: Cucumber Salad and Mascarpone Mousse.   6.95
Golden Fried Onion Crisps served with Malt Vinegar.   2.95
Carpaccio of Beef: Enoki Mushrooms & Parmesan-Garlic Sauce.   5.95

LARGE SALADS

Baby Field Greens & Sliced Tomatoes, Provolone, Genoa Salami
& Fresh Basil with Balsamic Vinaigrette.   7.50
Grilled Romaine "Caesar Salad" with shaved Parmesan & Pan Roasted Croutons.   7.95
Savoy Spinach Leaves, Spiced Pecans, sliced Strawberries, Sweet Red Onions,
& Poppyseed Dressing.   7.25
Salad of Grilled Duck, Spiced Pecans, Enoki Mushrooms & fresh Raspberries
with Raspberry Hoisin Dressing.   8.50

SIDE SALADS

Salad Fedora: House blended Seasonal Greens with Creme Herb Dressing or Balsamic Vinaigrette.   2.75
Greek Salad, Romaine, Spiced Beets, Feta Cheese, Sweet Red Onions, Olives and Oregano Vinaigrette.   2.95
Savoy Spinach Leaves, Spiced Pecans, sliced Strawberries, Sweet Red Onions,
& Poppyseed Dressing.   3.25

SANDWICHES

Fresh Baked Croissant: Stuffed with Virginia Ham & Vermont Cheddar
served with Honey Dijon Sauce.   7.25
Oven Roasted Chicken Club, thinly sliced, with Lettuce, Tomato, Bacon and Garlic Mayonnaise
on Crusted French Bread.   6.95
210 Burger, half pound, char-grilled Chuck Steak burger on a toasted roll.   6.75

MAIN COURSES

Farm House Chicken with Pearl Onions, Mushrooms & Smoked Bacon braised in
a Cabernet Sauvignon Sauce.   10.25
Penne with Roasted Garlic, Plum Tomato Sauce & Fresh Basil.   8.25
Spit-Roasted Baby Chicken, marinated and basted with Lemon, Garlic & Fresh Herbs.   9.95
Spit-Roasted Indiana "Pekin" Duck, with Raspberry Hoisin Sauce.   13.95
Sauteed Calves Liver, Crisp Bacon, Carmelized Onions with Balsamic Vinegar Glaze.   8.95
Fettuccine Alfredo Cream with Three Cheeses & a topping of Prosciutto Ham.   8.95
Blackened Filet Mignon coated with Fedora Cafe's 'Private Blend' of Spices & pan seared.   13.95

PIZZA

Thin Crust, 24" Oval   8.95
Italian Sausage & Roasted Red Pepper: Plum Tomato Sauce & Three Cheese Blend.
Chicken & Pesto: Sweet Basil Sauce, Char-grilled Chicken, Roma Tomatoes & Romano Cheese.
White Pizza: Roasted Garlic, Italian Herbs, Butter & Three Cheese blend.
Pizza Margherita: Tomatoes, Fresh Basil, Garlic, Mozzarella & Romano Cheese.

Calzone with freshly-made Italian Sausage, Four Cheeses, Fire Roasted Red
Peppers, Fried Garlic & Fresh Basil.   8.95

SIDE DISHES

Pomme Frites Fedora Cafe   1.95
Paneed Potato Cakes   2.25
Sauteed Savoy Spinach   2.25
Escalloped Vermont Cheddar Potatoes   2.50

FIGURE 10-2. (Continued)

FRESH SPECIALTIES FOR TODAY

Fedora Cafe strives to offer you the finest FRESH Meats, Fish, Vegetables and Fruits available. We are dependent upon the Weather, Seasons and Air Express Connections. If we are forced, by one or several of these elements to eliminate a selection from our menu, please accept our apologies.

SOUP OF THE DAY
Tomato-Cabbage with Smoked Ham
cup 2.50   bowl 3.50

PASTA
Fusilli with Pancetta
Garden Peas, Mushrooms, Three Cheeses & Cream 8.95

Seafood Linguine with Romano Cream
-or- a Spicy Red Sauce   10.95

PIZZA
Italian Sausage, Roasted Peppers & Gorgonzola Cheese   8.95

FRESH FISH
Chilean Swordfish Wood Grilled and Herb Marinated -or-
Pan Blackened with Cajun Spices
18.50

Atlantic Baby Halibut
Poached in Saffron Fennel Broth
17.95
may we suggest: Buena Vista Sauvignon Blanc glass 4.50

ENTREES
Wood Grilled Boneless Breast of Duckling
with a Fresh Fig & Orange Sauce
with Moroccan Couscous
18.95
may we suggest: Joseph Drouhin La Foret Rouge Pinot Noir   glass 5.25

VEGETABLES
Green Beans   2.25
Seasonal Fresh Vegetable Medley   1.95
Asparagus   3.50

DESSERTS & BERRIES
Rainier Cherry Almond Tart   3.75
Peaches & Cream Chocolate Gateau   3.50
California Strawberries   2.95
California Raspberries   3.95
Great Lakes Blueberries   3.50

Your Host: Bill Essmann
Your Chef: Dan Palmer

In consideration of other dining guests, cigar and pipe smoking in the lounge only please.

FEDORA'S NEW PLATES

Penne with Grilled Chicken,
Toasted Almonds, Orange Zest, Garlic, Oregano and Asparagus in a Chicken Broth.   8.50

Belgium Endive & Chilled Shrimp Platter:
sliced Avocado and Pink Raifort Sauce.   9.50

Pecan Crusted Breast of Chicken
with escalloped Vermont Cheddar Potatoes.   11.95

Roasted Native Lamb Chops
with Rosemary Garlic Jus & Eggplant Torte.   17.95

Heartland Grille
Medallions of Filet Mignon & Pork and Lamb Chop served with East Texas Onion Pudding.   16.95

"U.S.D.A." Prime T-Bone Steak
Char-grilled, served with Roasted Shallot Sauce.   17.95

SWEETS

Profiteroles, Miniature Cream Puffs filled with Unsweetened Whipped Cream & coated with Fedora's Hot Fudge Sauce.   2.50

Tartufo, White Chocolate Ice Cream coated with chunked Ambrosia White Chocolate with Hot Fudge Sauce.   3.50

Truffle Cake, Flourless, fallen Chocolate Cake made with Dark Sweet Chocolate.   3.25

Six Nut Caramel Tart baked in Shortbread Crust, with Butter Pecan Ice Cream.   2.95

Country Cobbler Mixed Berries topped with a Sweet Buttermilk Crust.   2.75

Creme Brulee with crisp broiled Sugar Crust.   2.25
With Fresh fruit   p.a.

Semi-Freddo Cafe:
White Chocolate Ice Cream floating in Freshly Brewed Espresso with Whipped Cream   3.25

BEVERAGES

Freshly Brewed:
Fedora Three Blend Coffee   1.25
Decaffeinated Coffee   1.25

Iced Tea or Iced Coffee   1.25

Paradise Tropical Iced Tea   1.25

Coke, Diet Coke & Sprite   1.25

© HRG, INC. 10/92D

FIGURE 10-2.   *(Continued)*

into the theme, the institutional copy should also be used for this purpose with the net effect being a perfect menu coordinating the restaurant's theme.

Ethnic restaurants' use of descriptive terminology takes on a different, although important, role. Here it is used to translate. Many ethnic menus are written in the language peculiar to their region. *Never* write a menu in a foreign language without an English translation beneath the foreign terminology. Some restaurants, particularly French, refuse to do this, perhaps to create some sort of snob appeal. The only thing it accomplishes is to make a majority of their patrons uncomfortable. Avoid surprises. Let your customers know exactly what they are getting.

MENU DESIGN

The physical design of the theme restaurant menu is as critical as the artwork. This, as well as the descriptive terminology, ties the theme together for the customer. A clever menu writer with a good imagination can do wonders with an ordinary theme menu. Many theme restaurants are known almost as much for their unusual menus as they are for their food and service. This creates and excellent advertising device as well as an excellent word of mouth campaign.

CONCLUSION

Theme and ethnic menus are among the most interesting and fun to write. Knowledge of the subject or country is important so that the menu will contain unusual items expressing that particular idea or culture. Menu design, as well as descriptive terminology, is imperative to incorporate the theme or country with the decor and general ambience of the restaurant. Knowledge of the interrelationship between staff skill levels, check average, and table turnover is necessary to achieve a profit and give the customer a good price value relationship. When you have mastered the strategies described in this chapter, you will find that it's just that simple.

QUESTIONS

1. Develop a menu for a theme restaurant. Explain how the building architecture and decor will carry out this theme.
2. Explain the differences and similarities of theme and ethnic restaurants.

3. Explain the importance of descriptive terminology on theme and ethnic restaurant menus. Give examples to reinforce your explanation.

4. Discuss the different levels of skill, training, and menu price ranges of the various types of ethnic restaurants. Give examples of each in your discussion.

5. Develop a North American eclectic menu for your area using locally grown foods and cooking techniques.

CHAPTER ELEVEN

Banquet/Show Menus

OBJECTIVES
- To understand the functions of the sales department.
- To know how banquets are packaged for selling.
- To understand the importance of the function sheet.
- To comprehend the six principles of banquet menu planning.
- To differentiate between banquet menus and show menus.

IMPORTANT TERMS

Function sheet	Fixed menu
Long-range pricing	Over/under guarantees

INTRODUCTION

Banquet and show menus have certain peculiarities which are exclusive to them and differentiate them from other types of menus. While there are some minor differences between banquet menus and show menus, the basic principles which apply to one also apply to the other, thus the two types are included in one chapter.

BANQUET MENUS

In order to fully comprehend the problems of writing menus for banquets, the organizational structure of the establishment must first be understood. Banquets are handled daily all over the world in establishments ranging from small restaurants serving 15 people at a civic luncheon to large hotels serving 1,500 people at a formal dinner. Even in institutional operations, banquets are big business. Occasionally, even civic centers get into the act serving banquets of several thousand convention delegates. Regardless of size, the same principles apply. Only the logistics change. Proper planning is the key to any successful event.

The organizational structure varies with the size of the establishment. In a small restaurant one person would book the event and supervise the set up, decoration, preparation, service, and the billing. In a large hotel, these functions would be separated among various individuals responsible for their own particular area. In operations ranging in scope from the small restaurant to the large hotel these responsibilities would be divided according to the size of the establishment. To clearly delineate each area's function, we will approach the execution of a banquet from the point of view of a large hotel.

The first step in the banquet sequence is the booking of the event. This is handled by the sales department, which in addition to planning banquets, is responsible for selling meeting rooms as well as guest rooms to large groups. The persons handling the function need to, among other things, be expert menu planners. It is at this stage that the actual menu is decided upon. The sales person takes in account the type of group, their theme, the dollars they wish to spend, the number to attend, and their desires as to food groups and type of service they wish. These needs are then matched to the facilities the hotel has to offer and the staff skill level. These criteria will be discussed in detail later in this chapter, but for now suffice it to say that these functions happen in the sales department.

Once the details are decided upon between the sales department and client, a function sheet or banquet event order is prepared and sent at the appropriate time to the purchasing department, kitchen, banquet service department, and accounting department.

MEETING AND BANQUET FACILITIES

With more than 14,000 square feet of functional meeting space, Doubletree is the ideal choice for meetings of up to 1,000 and banquets of up to 640. The facilities include a variety of meeting rooms, executive conference suites and a tiered lecture theater. Our Convention Service Department will provide complete planning of your housing and meeting arrangements, audiovisual equipment needs and exceptional catering services. We even offer our Meeting Planners Guarantee: If anything doesn't meet your written specifications, you don't pay for it. We do.

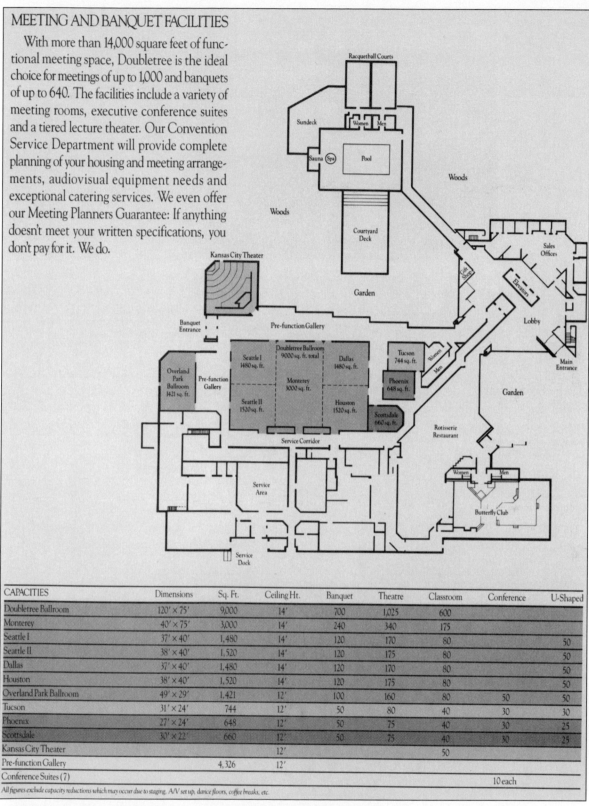

CAPACITIES	Dimensions	Sq. Ft.	Ceiling Ht.	Banquet	Theatre	Classroom	Conference	U-Shaped
Doubletree Ballroom	120' × 75'	9,000	14'	700	1,025	600		
Monterey	40' × 75'	3,000	14'	240	340	175		
Seattle I	37' × 40'	1,480	14'	120	170	80		50
Seattle II	38' × 40'	1,520	14'	120	175	80		50
Dallas	37' × 40'	1,480	14'	120	170	80		50
Houston	38' × 40'	1,520	14'	120	175	80		50
Overland Park Ballroom	49' × 29'	1,421	12'	100	160	80	50	50
Tucson	31' × 24'	744	12'	50	80	40	30	30
Phoenix	27' × 24'	648	12'	50	75	40	30	25
Scottsdale	30' × 22'	660	12'	50	75	40	30	25
Kansas City Theater			12'			50		
Pre-function Gallery		4,326	12'					
Conference Suites (7)							10 each	

All figures exclude capacity reductions which may occur due to staging, A/V set up, dance floors, coffee breaks, etc.

FIGURE 11-1. An advertisement marketing the features of the meeting and banquet facilities of a large hotel. (*Courtesy of the Doubletree Hotel, Overland Park, Kansas*)

DOUBLETREE HOTEL · AT CORPORATE WOODS

10100 College Blvd., Overland Park, KS 66210 ◆ 913-451-6100 ◆ FAX: 913-451-3873

Doubletree Hotels 800-222-TREE ◆ APOLLO ◆ SABRE ◆ DATAS II ◆ PARS ◆ SystemOne

LOCATION

Situated in a wooded, park-like setting, at I-435 and U.S. 69, the Doubletree is right in the heart of the bustling College Boulevard business corridor and less than 20 minutes from Kansas City.

ACCOMMODATIONS

The beautiful, 18-story Doubletree offers 357 executive-tailored guest rooms, including 17 luxurious suites. Non-smoking floors and accessible rooms for individuals with disabilities are also available.

SURROUNDING ATTRACTIONS

At the Doubletree, you're within minutes of dozens of shopping, dining and night life options. Plus, the popular Country Club Plaza, Worlds Of Fun Amusement Park and Kansas City's professional sports events are all just a short drive away.

RECREATION

You'll have plenty of ways to stay in shape or simply relax. You can take a dip in our large, indoor pool. Kick back in the sauna or whirlpool. Or get in a game of racquetball. There are also miles of wooded jogging trails leading directly from the hotel.

DINING/ENTERTAINMENT

At the Rotisserie Restaurant, you'll enjoy classic dining amidst an elegant setting. For live entertainment and a conversational atmosphere, the sophisticated Butterfly Club is the place to be. Plus, Doubletree is surrounded by a variety of other dining choices, all within walking distance.

SERVICE FACILITIES

Laundry and valet services. Instant check in and check out, business services and room service. And, of course, our homemade chocolate chip cookies on your first night.

DOUBLETREE
HOTEL · AT CORPORATE WOODS

1-800-222-TREE

We're waiting to welcome you at over 85 Doubletree Hotels and Canadian Pacific Hotels & Resorts in North America.

FIGURE 11-1. *(Continued)*

This function sheet includes such information as the name of the group, number to be served, the menu, special set up requirements, billing procedure, and other information that is different from normal procedure. The various departments use this data in such areas as purchasing and staffing.

BANQUET MENU PLANNING

The principles of menu planning remain virtually the same for small restaurant banquets or large hotel functions. These principles are:

1. Fixed menu
2. Demographics
3. Theme
4. Staff skill level
5. Pricing
6. Meeting length

FIXED MENU

In banquets, the entire menu is fixed. In other words, it is selected by one person in the preliminary planning stage and there is no selection made on the part of the banquet guest. Not only is the selection fixed, but the sequence of courses is fixed. Because the menu is set, all items selected for service at a banquet must be popular with the patrons attending that function.

Another factor to consider when selecting courses is that service is simplified if the first course can be preset prior to service. This would normally be an appetizer. Therefore, a cold appetizer would be preferable to a hot one. The wishes of the client should be considered, however, over the ease of service. If they prefer a hot appetizer over a cold one—so be it. Serve it to them.

The sequence of dishes served at banquets has traditionally followed the light-heavy-light sequence. This format was believed to have been developed at the Brown Palace Hotel in Denver, Colorado. This sequence refers to the fat content of each dish. Thus, one would plan a menu starting with a dish that contained little or no fat, then build to a dish that had a high fat content and then schedule dishes that reduced correspondingly in fat. While this format is still used in more traditional banquets, the majority of banquets today follow the appetizer, salad, entree, vegetable, starch, dessert, beverage format with little or no regard to fat content in any particular course.

ORGANIZATION

CONTACT

MAILING ADDRESS

PHONE | HOME
FAX # | BUS.

IN-HOUSE CONTACT (IF DIFFERENT THAN ABOVE)

READER BOARD POSTING (IF DIFFERENT THAN ABOVE)

MEETING ROOM SET-UP

DOUBLETREE
HOTEL · AT CORPORATE WOODS

BANQUET EVENT ORDER

DAY	MONTH	DATE	YEAR

FUNCTION

MENU

EVENT	ROOM	NO. PERSONS	TIME

ROOM RENTAL

AUDIO-VISUAL REQUIREMENTS

METHOD OF PAYMENT

BF #:_____ ☐ CASH

_____ ☐ CHECK

CC #:_____ ☐ CREDIT CARD

_____ ☐ DIRECT BILL

ADV DEP REQD:_____

Doubletree Hotel agrees to provide the above as quoted and to make every effort to assure a successful group activity.

By _____ Date _____

I accept the above arrangements and understand the Attendance Guarantee is required by _____ . I understand the attendance guarantee represents the minimum billing and if not received, the above expected figure will be the guarantee.

Accepted By _____ Date _____

CUSTOMER

FIGURE 11-2. A banquet event order used to communicate a function to all of the hotel's departments, along with an invoice for billing the event. (*Courtesy of the Doubletree Hotel, Overland Park, Kansas*)

PRINTED BY THE STANDARD REGISTER COMPANY, U.S.A. ZIPSET - ®

DOUBLETREE

185066

GROUP
FUNCTION

ROOM	DAY	DATE

BILLING ADDRESS

COVERS	DESCRIPTION	AMOUNT

EQUIP. RENTAL

ROOM RENTAL

BAR		
	FOOD	
	SUB TOTAL	
	BAR	
	SERVICE CHARGE	
SIGNATURE X	TAX	

TOTAL ▶

FIGURE 11-2. *(Continued)*

DEMOGRAPHICS

Since the menu is fixed, it is important that all dishes selected be popular with the attendees of the banquet. The demographics of the group, therefore, become important. Certain selections might be eliminated due to religious or ethnic considerations. Still, other groups, due to economics or education, would prefer certain food selections over others. Age is another factor to be taken into consideration. We certainly wouldn't propose the same menu to teenagers that we would to a group of elderly ladies having a high tea.

THEME

Quite often a group holding a special function will request a theme. This could be a religious or ethnic group celebrating an event, a corporate sales meeting, a club-sponsored fund raiser, or any other of many reasons that bring people together to feast and enjoy each other's company. When this is the case, the banquet should carry out the theme of the group and/or event. This is done in two ways. First, the general decor of the room, as well as table decorations, should carry out the theme. Second, the menu should also reflect the theme. Therefore, the person responsible for writing the menu should have a vivid imagination and the ability to select foods which will tie together the theme with the menu. Banquets are festive affairs and with unrestrictive planning, the menu writer through decor and menu selection can add greatly to the fun and camaraderie of the event. Not only is the selection important, but printed menus placed at each guest's place with descriptive terminology carrying out the theme will aid in tying the event together. All too often, unfortunately, I have attended banquets with boring roast beef, green beans amandine, etc., etc., etc., served, when with minimal foresight so much fun could have been had planning the proper menu.

SKILL LEVEL

Along with selecting foods that are popular, fit the demographics of the group involved, and support the theme, one other fact should not be overlooked—the skill level of the staff. One could very easily get overzealous when planning the menu, but if it cannot be carried out to perfection, it should be scrapped and a new menu prepared. Remember to consider both the production and service staff. Not every kitchen can properly prepare a consomme, a chicken kiev, or a veal cordon bleu. Quite often, convenience foods can extend a kitchen's skill level, but caution should be exercised in terms of quality and cost. Always check out a product—convenience or staff prepared—prior to committing to a client that it can be served.

The abilities of the service staff also need to be considered in the planning of an event. The majority of banquets are served either buffet style or American style. This normally poses no great problem for

FIGURE 11-3. A complete set of food and beverage banquet menus, along with the hotel's policies regarding events. Notice the variety of themes that can be used with the "set menus," as well as their policy of developing menus other than the printed ones. (*Courtesy of the Doubletree Hotel, Overland Park, Kansas*)

BETTER THAN COFFEE BREAKS

BETTER THAN COFFEE BREAKS

JOHNSON COUNTY FAIR
Apple Cider, Lemonade, Honey Roasted Peanuts,
Hot Soft Pretzels, Doubletree Chocolate Chip Cookies,
Whole Fresh Fruit and Soft Drinks

COUNTRY STORE
Doubletree Chocolate Chip Cookies,
Assorted Dime Store Candies, Lemonade,
Assorted Soft Drinks

POST TIME/DAY AT THE RACES
Hot Soft Pretzels, Mini Pizzas, Nachos and Cheese, Peanuts,
Popcorn, Non-Alcoholic Beer, and Assorted Soft Drinks

VIP CONFERENCE SETTING
Mineral Waters at Each Setting Along with
Jars of Hard Candies, Pads and Pencils.
(Available for All Set-ups Except Theatre Style)

HIGH TEA
Finger Sandwiches, Crumpets,
Butter, Preserves, Petit Fours,
Chocolate Dipped Strawberries and Specialty Teas

HEALTH FOOD BREAK
Seasonal Fresh Whole Fruits, Fruit Yogurt,
Granola Bars and Assorted Fruit Juices

HOT SUMMER DAY
All Your Favorite Frozen Ice Cream Treats to Include:
Ice Cream Bars, Fudgesicles and Popsicles,
Lemonade, Frozen Candy Bars, Assorted Soft Drinks

SODA FOUNTAIN
Make Your Own Sundae with Vanilla Ice Cream,
Three Sauces, Chopped Nuts, Whipped Cream, Cherries,
Floats and Chocolate Ice Cream Shakes

MOM'S COOKIE JAR
Assorted Freshly Baked Cookies, (3 Kinds)
Brownies, Milk and Assorted Soft Drinks

DOUBLETREE
HOTEL · KANSAS CITY

FIGURE 11-3. (Continued)

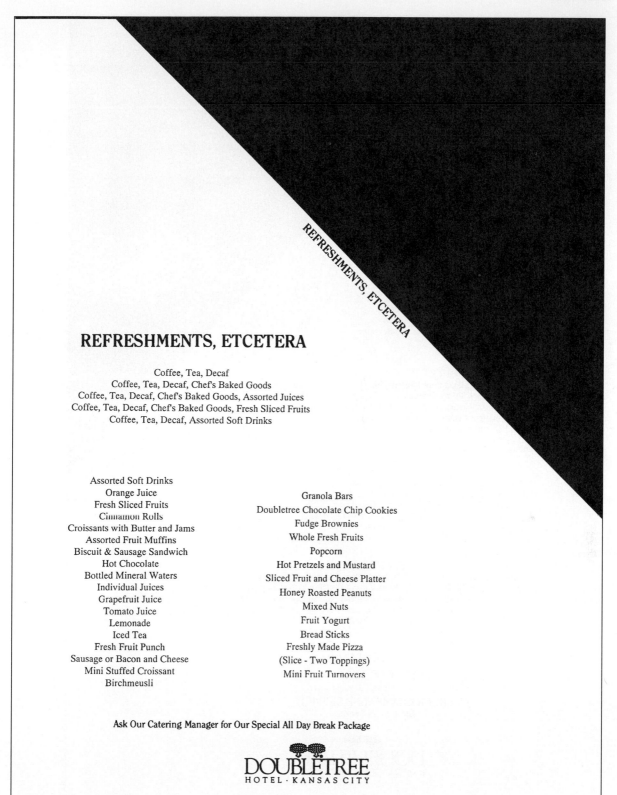

REFRESHMENTS, ETCETERA

REFRESHMENTS, ETCETERA

Coffee, Tea, Decaf
Coffee, Tea, Decaf, Chef's Baked Goods
Coffee, Tea, Decaf, Chef's Baked Goods, Assorted Juices
Coffee, Tea, Decaf, Chef's Baked Goods, Fresh Sliced Fruits
Coffee, Tea, Decaf, Assorted Soft Drinks

Assorted Soft Drinks
Orange Juice
Fresh Sliced Fruits
Cinnamon Rolls
Croissants with Butter and Jams
Assorted Fruit Muffins
Biscuit & Sausage Sandwich
Hot Chocolate
Bottled Mineral Waters
Individual Juices
Grapefruit Juice
Tomato Juice
Lemonade
Iced Tea
Fresh Fruit Punch
Sausage or Bacon and Cheese
Mini Stuffed Croissant
Birchmeusli

Granola Bars
Doubletree Chocolate Chip Cookies
Fudge Brownies
Whole Fresh Fruits
Popcorn
Hot Pretzels and Mustard
Sliced Fruit and Cheese Platter
Honey Roasted Peanuts
Mixed Nuts
Fruit Yogurt
Bread Sticks
Freshly Made Pizza
(Slice - Two Toppings)
Mini Fruit Turnovers

Ask Our Catering Manager for Our Special All Day Break Package

DOUBLETREE
HOTEL · KANSAS CITY

FIGURE 11-3. *(Continued)*

BREAKFAST BUFFETS

$35.00 Service Charge will be Added
for Less than the Minimum Amount

BUFFET I
Assorted Chilled Juices, Fresh Sliced Fruit Platter,
Fluffy Scrambled Eggs, Assorted Cold Cereals, Crisp Bacon,
Sausage Links, Breakfast Potatoes, Chef's Baked Goods,
Country Gravy and Buttermilk Biscuits, Butter, Jellies and Beverages
(minimum of 35 people)

BUFFET II
Assorted Chilled Juices, Fresh Sliced Fruit Platter, Chilled Grapefruit Halves,
Cheese Blintz with Fruit Toppings, Fluffy Scrambled Eggs, Cinnamon French Toast,
Crisp Bacon, Sausage Links, Breakfast Potatoes, Assorted Breakfast Breads,
Syrup, Whipped Butter, Jellies and Beverages
(minimum of 35 people)

BUFFET III
(Healthy Choice)
Vanilla Yogurt with Three Fruit Toppings and Granola, Sliced Fresh Fruits
and Seasonal Berries, Whole Grain Cereal with Skim Milk, Fruit and Bran Muffins,
Baked Buffet Eggs (Egg Beaters), Baked Ham Slices (95% Fat Free),
Assorted Chilled Juices and Beverages
(minimum of 50 people)

BUFFET IV
Assorted Chilled Juices, Eggs Benedict, Fresh Sliced Fruits with Berries,
Pigs in a Blanket with Blueberry Syrup, Medallions of Beef Tenderloin, Lyonnaise Potatoes,
Mini Croissants and Flavored Cream Cheeses, Bagels, Assorted Breakfast Breads,
Whipped Butter, Jellies, and Beverages
(minimum of 50 people)

OMELETTE STATION
Add 3.95 per person

2-HOUR CHAMPAGNE SERVICE
Add 4.00 per person

FIGURE 11-3. *(Continued)*

BREAKFAST

ALL AMERICAN
Fluffy Scrambled Eggs, Choice of: Crisp Bacon,
Ham, Sausage Links, or Canadian Bacon,
Served with Breakfast Potatoes with Fresh Fruit Garnish

COUNTRY BREAKFAST
Fluffy Scrambled Eggs, Buttermilk
Biscuits with Country Gravy, Choice of:
Smoked Ham, Bacon or Sausage Links,
with Fresh Fruit Garnish

BAKED OMELETTE
With Your Choice of Fillings: Ham and Cheese,
Mushroom and Cheese, or Denver Mix,
Breakfast Potatoes with Fresh Fruit Garnish
(maximum of 50 people)

BELGIAN WAFFLE
With Powdered Sugar, Fruit Topping and Syrup,
Choice of: Crisp Bacon, Smoked Ham, Sausage Links, or Canadian Bacon,
Served with Whipped Butter with Fresh Fruit Garnish
(maximum of 50 people)

MID WESTERN
2 - 2oz. Medallions of Beef Tenderloin,
Fluffy Scrambled Eggs, Lyonnaise Potatoes
with Fresh Fruit Garnish

PIGS IN A BLANKET
Three Sausage Links Wrapped in Buttermilk Pancakes,
Served with Syrup and Whipped Butter,
with Fresh Fruit Garnish

CROISSANT SANDWICH
Open Faced Croissant with Fluffy Scrambled Eggs, Topped with Cheese and
Canadian Bacon or Sausage Patty, with Fresh Fruit Garnish

SOUTH OF THE BORDER
Breakfast Burrito (Scrambled Eggs, Potatoes,
and Spicy Sausage), Topped with Salsa and
Monterey Jack Cheese, with Fresh Fruit Garnish

EGGS BENEDICT
Canadian Bacon, Hollandaise Sauce, Served with
Breakfast Potatoes with Fresh Fruit Garnish
(maximum or 75 people)

FRESH FRUIT BREAKFAST PLATE
Sliced Melon, Fresh Berries, Nut Bread or Muffin,
Cream Cheese, Whipped Butter, Assorted Jellies and Yogurt Sauce (for Dipping)

All Breakfasts Include: Orange Juice, Beverage, Chef's Baked Goods

DELUXE CONTINENTAL
Coffee, Tea, Decaf, Assorted Juices, Fresh Sliced Fruit,
Chef's Baked Goods, Bagels and Cream Cheese

DOUBLETREE
HOTEL · KANSAS CITY

FIGURE 11-3. *(Continued)*

BRUNCH BUFFETS

$35.00 Service Charge for Less than 50 People

BRUNCH BUFFET I

Fresh Sliced Fruit Platter
Assorted Juices
Pasta Salad
Marinated Vegetable Salad
Garden Green Salad
with Choice of Dressings

(Choice of Two)
Sauteed Sole Florentine
Garden Fresh Quiche
Beef Stroganoff
with Fresh Egg Pasta
Chicken Veronique
Seafood Newburg

Fluffy Scrambled Eggs
Crisp Bacon and Sausage Links
Breakfast Potatoes
Mini Croissants
Butter and Jams
Beverage Choices

BRUNCH BUFFET II

Assorted Juices
Fresh Sliced Fruit Platter
Assorted Cheeses
Two Seasonal Chilled Salads
Bagels with Smoked Salmon
and Cream Cheese
Chef's Omelette Station with
Assorted Condiments

(Choice of Three)
Garden Fresh Quiche
Beef Tips Chasseur
Chicken Veloute in Pastry Shell
Grilled Porkloin
Salmon Bernaise
Cashew Chicken

Roast Beef
(Carved to Order add $2.00 per person)

Fluffy Scrambled Eggs
Seasonal Vegetables
Crisp Bacon and Sausage Links
Breakfast Potatoes
Chef's Baked Goods
Beverage Choices

2-Hour Champagne Service

Our Catering Manager is ready to help you create that special theme brunch buffet:
South of the Border, French Bistro, All American Hero, and Swiss Alps . . .to name a few.
Make your program a memorable one with unlimited opportunities.

DOUBLETREE
HOTEL · KANSAS CITY

FIGURE 11-3. *(Continued)*

LUNCHEON BUFFETS

$35.00 Service Charge
for Less than 50 People

SALAD BUFFET
Soup du Jour, Assorted Crudite with Herbal Dip,
Tossed Salad with Choice of Dressings,
Bacon Bits, Croutons, Cheddar Cheese,
Toasted Almond Pineapple Chicken Salad,
Tuna Salad, Sliced Fruit with Domestic Cheese Tray,
Assorted Crackers and Bread Sticks, Mini Croissants,
Chocolate Mousse and Strawberries Romanoff

ITALIAN BUFFET
Tossed Salad with Choice of Dressings,
Bacon Bits, Croutons, Cheddar Cheese,
Marinated Tortellini Salad, Antipasto Tray,
Lasagne with Italian Sausage, Linguini with
Marinara and Alfredo Sauces, Chicken Parmesan,
Garlic Toast, Vegetable Medley
Spumoni Ice Cream and Canolli

MARKET PLACE DELI BUFFET
Tossed Salad with Choice of Dressings, Bacon Bits, Croutons,
Cheddar Cheese, Marinated Artichoke Salad, Pasta Salad, Cole Slaw,
Relish Tray, (Sliced Onion, Tomato, Dill Pickle Spears, Olives)
Choice of Four Meats: Ham, Turkey, Beef, Pastrami or Corned Beef
Cheddar and Swiss Cheeses, Assorted Breads and Condiments
Doubletree Chocolate Chip Cookies, Fruit Pies, Double Fudge Brownies
Soup du Jour - Add 1.00 per person

COUNTRY PICNIC BUFFET
Tossed Salad with Choice of Dressings, Bacon Bits,
Croutons, Cheddar Cheese, Southern Fried Chicken,
Country Fried Pork Chops, Mashed Potatoes and Gravy,
Farmers Style Green Beans, Crudite with Herbal Dip,
Biscuits with Honey and Whipped Butter,
Fruit Cobbler, Pecan Pie and Cinnamon Rolls

ORIENTAL BUFFET
Oriental Chicken Salad, Mandarin Fruit Salad,
Marinated Vegetable Salad, Egg Drop Soup,
Chinese Egg Rolls with Sweet and Sour, and
Hot Mustard Sauce, Beef with Broccoli and Oyster Sauce,
Sweet and Sour Tempura Pork, Fried Rice,
Stir Fried Vegetables, Chinese Almond and Fortune Cookies

LUNCHEON BUFFET
Tossed Salad with Choice of Dressings, Bacon Bits, Croutons, Cheddar Cheese,
Spinach Salad with Hot Bacon Dressing, Artichoke Salad, Tortellini Salad, Waldorf Salad
Choice of Two: Fried Chicken (KC Spiced), Top Sirloin with Mushroom Sauce,
Marinated Grilled Chicken Breast, Beef Stroganoff or Stuffed Sole with Lobster Sauce
Rice and Potato, Vegetable du Jour, Rolls and Butter
Doubletree Chocolate Chip Cookies, Cheesecake, Chocolate Mousse and Carrot Cake

SOUTH OF THE BORDER BUFFET
Build Your Own Taco: Shredded Lettuce,
and Cheeses, Diced Onions, Olives, Tomatoes,
amd Scallions, Tortilla Chips, Corn and
Flour Tortillas, Mexican Style Ground Beef,
Guacamole, Chicken Enchiladas, Spanish Rice,
Pinto Beans, Ice Cream with Kahlua,
Sopapillas in Cinnamon Sugar with Honey

KANSAS B-B-Q
Tossed Salad with Choice of Dressing,
Bacon Bits, Croutons, Cheddar Cheese, Hamburgers,
Hot Dogs, Bar-B-Que Chicken, Buns and
Condiments, Relish Platter, Potato Salad,
Cole Slaw, Sliced Fruit Tray, Doubletree
Chocolate Chip Cookies, Double Fudge Brownies
($35.00 grill fee)

DOUBLETREE
HOTEL · KANSAS CITY

FIGURE 11-3. *(Continued)*

LIGHT LUNCHEONS

LIGHT LUNCHEONS
(*Naturally Lower in Sodium and Cholesterol)

COBB SALAD*
Tossed Salad with Chicken Breast, Bleu Cheese Bits, Crumbled Bacon,
Tomato and Cucumber Slices, Olives, and Chopped Eggs,
Served with Choice of Two Dressings

SAMI'S THAI BEEF SALAD
Marinated Beef and Vegetables in a
Shallot Dressing, Served over Assorted Greens
with Appropriate Garnishes

MARINATED GRILLED CHICKEN BREAST*
Served over Pasta with Broccoli,
Tomato, Black Olives in a
Peppercorn and Parmesan Dressing

CHEF'S SALAD*
Crisp Salad Greens, Julienne of Turkey Breast and
Ham, Swiss and American Cheeses, Quartered Eggs, Tomatoes,
and Fresh Vegetable Garnish with Choice of Two Dressings

BOX LUNCH
Two Pieces of Fried Chicken and 1/2 Hoagie
Sandwich, Doubletree Chocolate Chip Cookie,
Fresh Whole Fruit and Potato Chips,
Accompanied by a Cold Soft Drink

ARHAM SANDWICH
Lavosh Bread Rolled with Ham,
Turkey, Cheddar, Swiss, and
Herbed Cream Cheese, Served with
Pasta Salad and Egg Garnish

INDIVIDUAL DELI PLATTER
Roast Beef, Smoked Ham, Sliced Turkey, Swiss and American Cheeses,
Potato Salad, Pasta Salad, Bermuda Onion and Tomato Garnish,
Served with Appropriate Condiments and Assorted Breads

CROISSANT SANDWICH
Large Croissant Filled with Your Choice of
Chicken Salad, Tuna Salad, Club Sandwich
or Vegetarian, or Choose any Two with Mini Croissants

BROILED SALMON*
Served with Your Choice of Two Sauces
Bearnaise or Chinese Mustard Glaze,
Stir Fry Vegetables and Grilled New Potatoes

GRILLED CHICKEN BREAST CAESAR SALAD*
Classic Salad Topped with Broiled Chicken Breast,
and Appropriate Garnishes

DESSERTS
Fruit Sorbet with Cookie, Brownie a la Mode,
Apple or Peach Cobbler, Cheesecake with Strawberry Sauce, Carrot Cake

All Light Luncheons Include: Rolls, Butter and Beverage

DOUBLETREE
HOTEL · KANSAS CITY

FIGURE 11-3. *(Continued)*

LUNCHEONS

STARTERS
Fresh Fruit Cup, Fresh Seasonal Greens
with Choice of Dressing,
Soup du Jour or Marinated Artichoke Salad

SPECIALTY STARTERS
Spinach Salad with Hot Bacon Dressing,
Butter Lettuce with Raspberry Vinaigrette,
Seafood Pasta Salad or Kansas City Steak Soup
(Priced Individually)

SOUTHERN FRIED CHICKEN BREAST
Southern Fried Chicken Breast with Georgia Cured Ham,
Whipped Potatoes and Country Gravy, Garden Vegetables

LONDON BROIL
Marinated Grilled Flank Steak,
Served Over French Bread Crouton,
Potato du Jour, and Garden Vegetables

STUFFED PORK CHOP CORDON BLEU
Stuffed with Ham and Swiss Cheese,
Served with Potato du Jour
and Garden Vegetables

MARINATED GRILLED CHICKEN BREAST
(Healthy Choice)
Marinated with Fresh Herbs and Olive Oil,
Served with Wild Rice and Garden Vegetables

CHICKEN PARMESAN
Boneless Breast of Chicken, Breaded and Lightly
Sauteed with Provolone Cheese and Marinara Sauce,
Served over Fresh Egg Pasta and Garden Vegetables

OPEN FACE STEAK SANDWICH
6oz. K.C. Strip on Sourdough Bread,
Served with Your Choice of Potato,
and Garden Vegetables

BEEF, CHICKEN OR PORK FAJITA
Served with Soft Flour Tortilla, Shredded Lettuce, Diced Tomato,
Sour Cream, Guacamole, Spanish Rice and Your Choice of Meat.
(Choice of Two - $1.25 Extra)

PRIME RIB SANDWICH
6oz. Prime Rib, Served on French Bread Crouton,
Potato du Jour, and Garden Vegetables

BOSTON BAKED COD
Lightly Breaded Cod Filet with
Potato du Jour and Garden Vegetables

SEAFOOD LINGUINI
Tender Linguini Noodles with Crabmeat and Shrimp Tossed with
Alfredo Sauce and Topped with Parmesan Cheese, Served with Garlic Toast

All Luncheons Include: Rolls, Butter and Beverage

DESSERT SELECTION

DOUBLETREE
HOTEL · KANSAS CITY

FIGURE 11-3. *(Continued)*

SPECIALTY DINNER BUFFETS

SPECIALTY DINNER BUFFETS

$35.00 Service Charge for Less than 50 People

STEAK FRY

Tossed Seasonal Greens - Choice of Dressings,
Crudite with Herbal Dip, Deviled Eggs, Sliced Watermelon.
Choice of Two: 12oz. KC Strip, 16oz. T-Bone Steak, 8oz. Tenderloin.
Marinated Chicken Breast, 10oz. Pork Chop or Marinated Tuna Steak.

Grilled Ears of Corn, Baked Potatoes, Ranch Beans,
Rolls and Butter, Beverage, Hot Fruit Cobbler a la Mode,
Pecan Pie, Fudge Brownies
($35.00 Grill Fee)

ITALIAN BUFFET

Antipasto Tray, Seasonal Greens with Italian Dressing, Tortellini Salad.
Baked Lasagna, Chicken Parmesan, Fettucini with 2 Sauces - Alfredo and Marinara.
Garlic Toast, Zucchini with Red Pepper, Beverage,
Cannolli, and Amaretto Cake

CHUCK WAGON BUFFET

Potato Salad, Cole Slaw, Relish and Crudite Tray, Sliced Watermelon.
Fried Chicken, Sliced Brisket, BBQ Spare Ribs,
Steak Fries, Corn on the Cob, Farmers Green Beans,
Rolls and Butter, Beverage,
Fruit Cobbler, Strawberry Shortcake, Pecan Pie
($35.00 Grill Fee)

DOUBLETREE
HOTEL · KANSAS CITY

FIGURE 11-3. _(Continued)_

DINNER BUFFETS
$35.00 Service Charge for Less than the Minimum Amounts

DINNER BUFFETS

BUFFET I
Seasonal Greens - Choice of Three Dressings,
Marinated Vegetable Salad, Tri-Color Cheese Tortellini Salad
CHOICE OF TWO:
Braised Tenderloin Beef Tips in Red Wine Sauce, Seafood Newburg,
Chicken Parmesan, Braised Pork Chops, Roast Sliced Sirloin Bordelaise,
Baked Cod with Fresh Herbs and Lemon Butter, Roast Baron of Beef
(with Carver - Add 2.00 per person)
CHOICE OF TWO:
Oven Roasted Potatoes, Wide Egg Noodles, Wild Rice,
Cappelini, Lemon Herb Rice, Anna Potatoes

Vegetable du Jour, Rolls and Butter, Beverage Choices

Cheesecake with Fruit Sauce, Chocolate Layer Cake, Strawberry Mousse
(minimum 50 people)

BUFFET II
Seasonal Greens - Choice of Three Dressings,
Spinach Salad with Hot Bacon Dressing, Marinated Artichoke Hearts with Hearts of Palm,
Relish and Crudite Tray with Herbal Dip, Fresh Sliced Fruit Tray
CHOICE OF THREE:
Stuffed Pork Loin with Apples and Almonds, Steak Dijon, Baked Salmon Bearnaise,
Stuffed Sole with Lobster Sauce, Sirloin Pepper Steak in Brandy Sauce,
Chicken Piccata, Chicken Breast Hunters Style, Roast Baron of Beef
(with Carver - Add 2.00 per person)
CHOICE OF TWO:
Pommes Berni, Potatoes Anna, Wild Rice, Herb and
Lemon Rice, Cappelini, Wide Egg Noodles

Vegetable du Jour, Rolls and Butter, Beverage Choices

Petit Fours, Pecan Pie, Mini Eclairs, Pound Cake with Raspberry Sauce and Whipped Cream
(minimum 50 people)

BUFFET III
Romaine, Spinach and Bibb Lettuce with Raspberry Vinaigrette Dressing,
Marinated Artichoke Hearts and Hearts of Palm, Fresh Fruit in Port Wine,
Seafood Salad - Shrimp, Scallops and Crab Vinaigrette, Sami's Thai Chicken Salad
CHOICE OF THREE:
Veal Oscar Mousseline, Sliced Stuffed Beef Tenderloin with Glace de Viande,
Ballantine of Chicken Breast with Morel Sauce, Roast Long Island Duckling with Lingonberry Sauce,
Shrimp and Scallop Kebobs Served over Angel Hair Alfredo,
Marinated Grilled Tuna Steak Beurre Orange, Whole Roast Entrecote Dijonaise, Baron of Beef
(with Carver - add 2.00 per person)
CHOICE OF TWO:
Pommes Berni, Potatoes Anna, Wild Rice, Lemon and Herb Rice, Au Gratin Potatoes, Cappelini
CHOICE OF TWO:
Asparagus with Hollandaise, Broccoli and Cauliflower with Cheese Sauce, Snow Peas
with Water Chestnuts and White Wine Stir Fry, Broiled Tomato with Herbs and Parmesan Cheese

Rolls and Butter, Beverage Choices

Creme Brulee, Cream Puff Swans, Chocolate Layer Torte
Strawberries Romanoff, Petit Fours
(minimum 50 people)

DOUBLETREE
HOTEL · KANSAS CITY

FIGURE 11-3. *(Continued)*

DINNER ACCOMPANIMENTS

STARTERS

Spinach Salad with Hot Bacon Dressing
Fresh Seasonal Greens with Choice of Dressings
Soup du Jour (Tureen)
Spinach, Watercress and Romaine with Choice of Dressing
Caesar Style Salad (prepared tableside Add $1.00 per person)
Antipasto Salad

SPECIALTY STARTERS
Shrimp and Crab Claw Cocktail
Seafood Louie in Avocado
Lobster or Shrimp Bisque with Caviar and Sour Cream
Coquille St. Jacques
Smoked Salmon with Traditional Garnishes
Kansas City Steak Soup (House Specialty)
Marinated Artichoke Salad with Garlic Crouton
Bibb Lettuce, Toasted Pecans, Bleu Cheese Croutons with Raspberry Vinaigrette
Three Cheeses and Apples with Cracker Assortment
(Priced Individually)

DESSERTS
Chocolate Sundae, Pecan Pie, Brownie a la Mode,
Cheesecake with Fruit Sauce, Chocolate Torte, Carrot Cake,
Fruit Sorbet with Cookie, Creme Brulee, German Chocolate Cake

SPECIALTY DESSERTS
Bananas Foster, Strawberries Romanoff, Ginger Flan,
Poached Pear in Chocolate Cup, Cherries Jubliee,
Chocolate Cup with Fresh Berries, Cream Puff Swans
(Priced Individually)

DOUBLETREE
HOTEL · KANSAS CITY

FIGURE 11-3. *(Continued)*

DINNER

DINNER

ROCK CORNISH GAME HEN
Boneless, Served with Blended Wild Rice, Broiled Tomato

KANSAS CITY STRIP STEAK
10oz. or 14oz. Maitre d'Butter and Onion Straws

MEDALLIONS OF BEEF & CHICKEN
Sauteed with Shallots and Finished with Cream

TOURNEDOS OF BEEF
Sauteed Tenderloin Medallions of Beef Served
with Bearnaise and Topped with Fluted Mushroom Cap

VEAL OR CHICKEN OSCAR
Your Choice, with Crabmeat and
Asparagus Spears, Topped with Bearnaise

STUFFED SOLE WITH CRAB & SHRIMP
Topped with Lobster Sauce

VEAL MARSALA
Tender Veal Medallions Sauteed and
Served over Fresh Egg Pasta

GRILLED VEAL CHOP
Served with Glace de Viande,
Wild Mushroom and Proscuitto Ham

CHICKEN PICATTA
Two Breasts, Egg Dipped and Rolled in Parmesan Cheese, Sauteed with Capers
and Lemon Butter Wine Sauce, Served over Angel Hair Pasta

FILET OF BEEF DIJONAISE
8oz. Beef Tenderloin Broiled to Perfection
Served with Champagne Dijon Sauce

GRILLED SALMON
Buerre Blanc Sauce
Garnished with Diced Cucumbers

ROAST PRIME RIB OF BEEF
10oz. Cut, Seasoned and Roasted in Natural Juices
Served with au Jus and Horseradish Sauce

BREAST OF CHICKEN CHAMPAGNE
Topped with Champagne Sauce and Morels
or Burgundy Sauce and Fresh Herbs
with Proscuitto Ham

DOUBLETREE MIXED GRILL
Lamb Chop with Mint Juniper Sauce, Quarter Roast
Long Island Duckling with Port Glaze,
and 4oz. Medallion of Beef Burgundy

FILET MIGNON
Your Choice of 8oz. or 10oz. Served with Sauce Bearnaise
and Fluted Mushroom Cap

DOUBLETREE
HOTEL · KANSAS CITY

FIGURE 11-3. *(Continued)*

HORS D'OEUVRES

SPECIALTY PLATTERS

KILO OF BRIE EN CROUTE
Baked In a Savory Pastry with Almonds
Served with Assorted Crackers and Tart Apples

ISLAND FRUIT FONDUE
Pineapple Palm Tree Display with Seasonal Fresh
Sliced Fruits and Hot Fudge Fondue for Dipping

FRUIT, VEGETABLE AND CHEESE DISPLAY
A Selection of Seasonal Fresh Sliced Fruits, Vegetables and Cheeses
with Whole Fruit and Vegetable Montage, Displayed with Breads and Crackers

EAST SIDE DELI PLATTER
A Wide Selection of Deli Delights to Include:
Cold Cuts, Cheeses, Assorted Breads, Relishes,
Condiments Whole Kosher Dills
and Deviled Eggs

SEASONAL FRESH FRUIT PLATTER
Melons, Pineapples, and Berries,
Served with Choice of Dipping Sauces:
Honey Lime, or Sour Cream
and Brown Sugar

ASSORTED CRUDITE WITH HERBAL DIP
Selected Fresh Vegetables with Creamy Herb Dip

DOMESTIC CHEESE PLATTER
Finest Domestic Cheeses Displayed with
Grapes, Berries and Assorted Crackers

IMPORTED CHEESE PLATTER
Finest Imported Cheeses Displayed with
Grapes, Berries and Assorted Crackers

SMOKED SALMON WITH TRADITIONAL GARNISHES
To Include Capers, Red Onion, Boiled Eggs,
Cream Cheese, Mini Bagels and Assorted Crackers

DOUBLETREE
HOTEL · KANSAS CITY

FIGURE 11-3. *(Continued)*

HORS D'OEUVRES

SPECIALTY PLATTERS

KILO OF BRIE EN CROUTE
Baked In a Savory Pastry with Almonds
Served with Assorted Crackers and Tart Apples

ISLAND FRUIT FONDUE
Pineapple Palm Tree Display with Seasonal Fresh
Sliced Fruits and Hot Fudge Fondue for Dipping

FRUIT, VEGETABLE AND CHEESE DISPLAY
A Selection of Seasonal Fresh Sliced Fruits, Vegetables and Cheeses
with Whole Fruit and Vegetable Montage, Displayed with Breads and Crackers

EAST SIDE DELI PLATTER
A Wide Selection of Deli Delights to Include:
Cold Cuts, Cheeses, Assorted Breads, Relishes,
Condiments Whole Kosher Dills
and Deviled Eggs

SEASONAL FRESH FRUIT PLATTER
Melons, Pineapples, and Berries,
Served with Choice of Dipping Sauces:
Honey Lime, or Sour Cream
and Brown Sugar

ASSORTED CRUDITE WITH HERBAL DIP
Selected Fresh Vegetables with Creamy Herb Dip

DOMESTIC CHEESE PLATTER
Finest Domestic Cheeses Displayed with
Grapes, Berries and Assorted Crackers

IMPORTED CHEESE PLATTER
Finest Imported Cheeses Displayed with
Grapes, Berries and Assorted Crackers

SMOKED SALMON WITH TRADITIONAL GARNISHES
To Include Capers, Red Onion, Boiled Eggs,
Cream Cheese, Mini Bagels and Assorted Crackers

DOUBLETREE
HOTEL · KANSAS CITY

FIGURE 11-3. *(Continued)*

CARVED TO PERFECTION

CARVED TO PERFECTION

WHOLE ROAST BREAST OF TURKEY
Traditional or Hickory Smoked

GLAZED BONE-IN HAM

BAR-B-Q ROAST BEEF BRISKET

ROAST STEAMSHIP ROUND OF BEEF

WHOLE ROASTED PEPPERED TENDERLOIN OF BEEF

WHOLE ROAST ENTRECOTE DIJONNAISE (Striploin)

**WHOLE ROAST LEG OF LAMB WITH
GARLIC AND FRESH ROSEMARY**

All of the Above are Served with Rolls and Appropriate Condiments

$35.00 Carver Fee (2-hours)

LIGHT SNACKS

Mixed Nuts	French Onion Dip
Smoked Almonds	Ranch Style Dip
Potato Chips	Bleu Cheese Dip
Tortilla Chips	Salsa Dip
Butter Mints	Guacamole
Honey Roasted Peanuts	Chili Con Queso
	Herbal Dip

DOUBLETREE
HOTEL · KANSAS CITY

FIGURE 11-3. *(Continued)*

BEVERAGE MENU

We proudly display and pour the following as our Select and Premium Brands on both Hosted and Cash Bar functions

	SELECT	PREMIUM
Scotch	Grants	Cutty Sark
Bourbon	Jim Beam (White)	Weller's Reserve
Vodka	Smirnoff	Stolichnaya
Gin	Seagrams	Beefeaters
Rum	Bacardi (Silver)	Barcardi
Tequila	Jose Cuervo White	Jose Cuervo (Gold)
Wine	Sebastiani	Your Catering Manager will assist with wine selections from our Premium Wine List.
Champagne	Available upon request	
Cordials	Available upon request	

NOTE: In addition to the brands listed above, the Doubletree Hotel will be happy to quote pricing on any liquor, beer or wine your hospitality requires. Simply ask your Catering Sales Manager.

BOTTLE SALES ARE AVAILABLE FOR HOSPITALITY ROOMS ONLY.

HOST SPONSORED CONVENIENCE PLAN

Our completely stocked bar with Bartender charges included will offer unlimited consumption of beverages, based on a per person rate for the length of time that the bar is open. Your cost will be based upon the guaranteed attendance or the actual attendance, if higher. We offer our Select and Premium Brands - mixed drinks, beer, and wine.

PER PERSON	SELECT	PREMIUM
One Hour	7.95	8.95
Two Hours	13.00	15.00
Each Additional Hour	3.00	3.25

HOST SPONSORED CONSUMPTION PLAN

Our Bartender will offer your guests Select or Premium brand liquors. The bar will be stocked completely, including all mixes, bar fruits, and soft drinks. Charges are based upon measured quantities of liquor consumed at a 1¼oz. serving of liquor per drink.

SELECT	PREMIUM
3.25 Mixed	3.75 Mixed
2.75 Beer	2.75 Domestic Beer
3.25 Imported Beer	3.25 Imported Beer
3.25 Wine	Wine - (Select from our List)
3.00 Wine Coolers	3.00 Wine Coolers
Soft Drinks - Complimentary	Soft Drinks - Complimentary

DOUBLETREE
HOTEL · KANSAS CITY

FIGURE 11-3. *(Continued)*

BEVERAGES

WINE LIST

Our Catering Sales Manager has available a wide variety of Domestic and Imported Wines. Doubletree Hotels is proud to offer a selection of Sebastiani as our Select Wines.

CASH BAR

The Doubletree Hotel will have a Cashier sell drink tickets to your guests, who may exchange the tickets for beverages served by our Bartenders.

	SELECT	PREMIUM
Cocktails	3.50	4.00
Wine	3.50	4.00
Wine Coolers	3.50	4.00
Beer	3.00	3.00
Mineral Water	2.00	2.00
Imported Beer	3.25	3.25
Soft Drinks	1.75	1.75

LABOR CHARGES

A $15.00 per hour charge (with a minimum of 3 hours) will be charged for the bartender. Unless otherwise requested, the hotel will schedule one (1) bartender for every 100 people at a hosted or cash bar.

A $10.00 per hour charge (with a minimum of 3 hours) will be charged for a cashier on a cash bar. Unless otherwise requested, the hotel will schedule one cashier for every 200 people at a cash bar.

The hotel agrees to waive the cost of the bartender and cashier fees at the rate of one per each $450.00 in bar sales.

The Doubletree Hotel of Overland Park is the only licensed authority to sell and serve alcoholic beverages for consumption on the premises. Therefore, liquor is not permitted to be brought into the hotel.

All alcoholic beverages served under our licenses will require that beverages be dispensed by Hotel servers and bartenders.

In accordance with Kansas State Law, the Doubletree Hotel will request proper identification of any person of questionable age and refuse service if the person is under age or cannot produce proper ID. Service will also be refused to any person who, in the Hotel's judgement, appears to be intoxicated.

With the exception of cash bars, all prices are subject to a 10% Excise tax.

DOUBLETREE
HOTEL · KANSAS CITY

FIGURE 11-3. *(Continued)*

WINE LIST

Our Catering Sales Manager has available a wide variety of Domestic and Imported Wines. Doubletree Hotels is proud to offer a selection of Sebastiani as our Select Wines.

CASH BAR

The Doubletree Hotel will have a Cashier sell drink tickets to your guests, who may exchange the tickets for beverages served by our Bartenders.

	SELECT	PREMIUM
Cocktails	3.50	4.00
Wine	3.50	4.00
Wine Coolers	3.50	4.00
Beer	3.00	3.00
Mineral Water	2.00	2.00
Imported Beer	3.25	3.25
Soft Drinks	1.75	1.75

LABOR CHARGES

A $15.00 per hour charge (with a minimum of 3 hours) will be charged for the bartender. Unless otherwise requested, the hotel will schedule one (1) bartender for every 100 people at a hosted or cash bar.

A $10.00 per hour charge (with a minimum of 3 hours) will be charged for a cashier on a cash bar. Unless otherwise requested, the hotel will schedule one cashier for every 200 people at a cash bar.

The hotel agrees to waive the cost of the bartender and cashier fees at the rate of one per each $450.00 in bar sales.

The Doubletree Hotel of Overland Park is the only licensed authority to sell and serve alcoholic beverages for consumption on the premises. Therefore, liquor is not permitted to be brought into the hotel.

All alcoholic beverages served under our licenses will require that beverages be dispensed by Hotel servers and bartenders.

In accordance with Kansas State Law, the Doubletree Hotel will request proper identification of any person of questionable age and refuse service if the person is under age or cannot produce proper ID. Service will also be refused to any person who, in the Hotel's judgement, appears to be intoxicated.

With the exception of cash bars, all prices are subject to a 10% Excise tax.

FIGURE 11-3.   *(Continued)*

PRICE LIST

PRICE LIST

BETTER THAN COFFEE BREAKS
Johnson Country Fair 5.95
Country Store 5.75
Post Time 6.25
VIP Conference Setting 3.50
High Tea..7.50
Health Food Break 5.50
Hot Summer Day 4.50
Soda Fountain 5.95
Mom's Cookie Jar 5.75

REFRESHMENTS, ETCETERA
Coffee Service (Gallon) 27.00
Coffee/Tea/Decaf 1.95
Coffee/Tea/Decaf/Chef's Baked Goods 3.25
Coffee/Tea Decaf/Chef's Baked Goods/
   Assorted Juices..........................5.50
Coffee/Tea/Decaf/Assorted Soft Drinks 2.75
Assorted Soft Drinks (each) 1.75
Orange Juice 1.95
Fresh Sliced Fruits 1.95
Chef Baked Goods (dozen) 15.00
Cinnamon Rolls (dozen) 18.00
Croissants with Whipped Butter and Jam (each) 2.50
Assorted Fruit Muffins (each) 1.50
Biscuit and Patty Sausage Sandwich (each) 2.75
Hot Chocolate 1.75
Bottled Mineral Water (each) 1.95
Individual Bottled Juices.....................1.95
Grapefruit Juice 1.75
Tomato Juice 1.75
Lemonade 1.75
Iced Tea 1.75
Fresh Fruit Punch 1.75
Stuffed Croissant (each) 2.25
Birchmeusli 4.95
Granola Bars (each) 1.75
Doubletree Chocolate Chip Cookies (dozen) 12.00
Fudge Brownies (each) 1.75
Whole Fruit (each) 1.75
Popcorn 1.50
Hot Pretzels and Mustard (each) 2.00
Fruit and Cheese Platter 1.75
Vegetable and Dip Platter 1.50
Honey Roasted Peanuts......................2.00
Mixed Nuts.....................................2.50
Fruit Yogurt (each) 2.50
Assorted Hard Candy 1.50
Breadsticks 1.00
Fresh Pizza (Slice-2 Toppings) 3.00
Mini-Fruit Turnovers (each) 1.75

BREAKFAST
All American 8.25
Country Breakfast 8.50
Baked Omelette...............................10.50
Belgian Waffles 9.25
Mid-Western 14.25
Pigs In A Blanket 8.00
Croissant Sandwich 9.75
South of the Border 8.50
Eggs Benedict 12.25
Fresh Fruit Plate...............................9.75
Deluxe Continental Breakfast: Coffee/Tea
   Decaf/Assorted Juices/Sliced Fruit/Chef's
   Baked Goods/Bagels and Cream Cheese 6.95

BREAKFAST AND BRUNCH BUFFETS
Buffet I 11.50
Buffet II 12.50
Healthy Buffet III 11.00
Buffet IV 19.75
Omelette Station (per person) 3.95
Brunch I 23.50
Brunch II 28.50

LUNCHEON BUFFETS
Salad Lunch Buffet 14.25
Italian Buffet 16.95
Market Place Deli Buffet 13.25
Picnic Buffet 15.50
Oriental Buffet 16.75
Luncheon Buffet 16.25
South of the Border Buffet 14.95
Kansas BBQ 16.50

LIGHT LUNCHEONS
Cobb Salad 9.95
Sami's Thai Beef Salad 10.50
Marinated Chicken with Pasta 9.50
Chef's Salad 9.95
Box Lunch 9.50
Arham Sandwich 9.95
Individual Deli Platter 11.25
Croissant Sandwich 11.00
Broiled Salmon 16.75
Grilled Chicken Caesar 10.75

LUNCHEON
Southern Fried Chicken Breast 12.25
London Broil 13.50
Stuffed Pork Chop 13.25
Grilled Chicken Breast 11.75
Chicken Parmesan 12.00
Open Face Steak Sandwich 15.00
Fajitas 11.50
Prime Rib Sandwich 15.00
Boston Baked Cod 11.75
Seafood Linguini 14.25

Please Add 18% Service Charge and 6.5% Sales Tax to All Food and Beverage Items.

DOUBLETREE
HOTEL · KANSAS CITY

FIGURE 11-3. *(Continued)*

(SPECIALTY DESSERTS AND STARTERS
PRICED INDIVIDUALLY)

DINNER BUFFETS
Dinner Buffet I 22.95
Dinner Buffet II 25.95
Dinner Buffet III 31.95
Steak Fry 28.00
Italian Buffet 21.95
Chuck Wagon 21.95

HORS D'OEUVRES AND HOSPITALITY
Mixed Nuts...16.00
Smoked Almonds 18.95
Potato Chips 7.50
Tortilla Chips 7.50
Butter Mints 9.50
Honey Roasted Peanuts......................................9.50
French Onion Dip 10.00
Ranch Style Dip 10.00
Bleu Cheese Dip 14.00
Salsa Dip 12.00
Guacamole 14.00
Chili Con Queso 14.00
Herbal Dip 12.00

DINNERS
Rock Cornish Game Hen 19.75
Kansas City Strip Steak
    10 oz. 24.50
    14 oz. 28.50
Medallions of Beef and Chicken 21.75
Chicken Oscar 18.75
Veal Oscar 25.50
Tournedos of Beef 22.50
Stuffed Sole 22.50
Veal Marsala 23.75
Grilled Veal Chop 28.50
Chicken Picatta 18.25
Filet Dijon 23.50
Grilled Salmon 22.25
Roast Prime Rib of Beef au Jus 22.75
Chicken Champagne with Morels 18.25
Doubletree Mixed Grill 25.50
Filet Mignon - 8 oz. 23.50
    10 oz. 26.75

SPECIALITY PLATTERS
Kilo of Brie En Croute 50.00
Fruit Fondue Tree (100 People) 275.00
Fruit, Vegetable, Cheese Display
    (Serves 75 People, per person)...........................4.00
East Side Deli Platter (per person).........................7.25
Seasonal Fresh Fruit Platter 175.00
Assortment of Crudites and Herbal Dip.............125.00
Domestic Cheese Platter 200.00
Imported Cheese Platter 250.00
Smoked Salmon 200.00

CARVED TO PERFECTION
Whole Roasted Turkey Breast 120.00
Glazed Bone-In Ham 195.00
Steamship Round of Beef 475.00
Entrecote Dijonnaise 175.00
Brisket of Beef 125.00
Whole Peppered Tenderloin 175.00
Leg of Lamb 150.00

CARVER FEE $35.00 for Two Hours

COLD SELECTIONS (Priced per 50 pieces)
Cold Shrimp on Ice 135.00
Crab Claws 135.00
Clams on the Half Shell 80.00
Oysters on the Half Shell 85.00
Marinated Mussels 75.00
Marinated Green Lip Mussels (in Season)............85.00
Finger Sandwiches 80.00
Mini Club Sandwiches 80.00
Arham Sandwiches 85.00
Smoked Salmon Mousse in Cucumber 80.00
Medallions of Lobster 200.00
Steak Tartar 90.00
Cream Cheese Endive or Artichoke Petal 75.00
Assorted Canapes 75.00

HOT SELECTIONS (Priced per 50 pieces)
Chicken Satees 75.00
Beef Satees 80.00
Chicken Drummettes 75.00
Chicken or Beef Kebobs 80.00
Petite Quiche Lorraine 70.00
Breaded Mushrooms 65.00
Crab Rangoon 85.00
Clams Casino 90.00
Oysters Rockefeller 90.00
Italian Stuffed Mushroom Caps 75.00
Seafood Stuffed Mushroom Caps 85.00
Spinakopita 70.00
Potstickers 70.00
Chinese Egg Rolls 70.00
Seafood Quiche 80.00
Breaded Cauliflower 70.00
Breaded Mozzarella 70.00
Meatballs with Three Sauces 65.00

ICE CARVINGS - $150.00 and up

Please Add 18% Service Charge and 6.5% Sales Tax to All Food and Beverage Items.

DOUBLETREE
HOTEL · KANSAS CITY

FIGURE 11-3. *(Continued)*

BANQUET POLICIES

Our menus feature a selection of our most popular items. These are merely suggestions. We would be delighted to arrange banquet menus to suit your particular requirements. We also offer well known regional, national and international dishes, as well as theme parties complete with appropriate decorations, entertainment and costumed service personnel. In order to assure you and your guests a well organized function, we encourage you to read the following policies and discuss any clarification desired with our Catering Sales Manager.

PRICES: All menu prices are subject to change without prior notice.

The quotation herein is subject to proportionate increases to meet increased cost of foods, beverages and other costs of operation existing at the time of performance of our undertaking by reason of increases in present commodity prices, labor cost, taxes or currency values. Patron expressly grants the right to the Hotel to raise the prices herein quoted or to make reasonable substitutions on the menu and agrees to pay such increased prices and to accept such substitutions.

MENU SELECTIONS: Menu selections are requested a minumum of three (3) weeks prior to event.

FOOD: All food items must be supplied and prepared by the Hotel. Menu selections, room requirements and all other arrangements must be received three (3) weeks prior to the function. Banquet service is based on a set number of guests per food server. Should additional or special service be required, we will be happy to do so at an additional charge. Food may not be removed from hotel at end of function.

GUARANTEES: Food function attendance must be definitely specified by 3:00 p.m. two (2) working days prior to the event. This number will be considered the minimum guarantee, not subject to reduction, and charges will be made accordingly. The Hotel cannot be responsible for service to more than 5% over the guarantee. The guarantee is the minimum number of guests that will be charged for. A Service charge of $35 will be charged for meal functions with less than our minimum amount of guests in attendance.

**Saturday, Sunday, and Monday guarantees must be received by 3:00 p.m. the preceding Thursday.

BEVERAGES: The Doubletree Hotel, as a licensee, is responsible for the administration, sale, and service of alcoholic beverages — liquor, beer, and wine — in accordance with the Kansas Liquor Laws. It is our policy, therefore, that all liquor, beer and wine must be supplied by the Hotel.

ROOM AND RENTAL: Function rooms are assigned according to the anticipated guaranteed number of guests. If there are fluctuations in the number of attendees, the Hotel reserves the right to reassign the room reserved. Changes in room arrangements within twenty-four (24) hours of the function may result in additional labor charges if the assigned room has already been set up. The Hotel reserves the right to charge a service fee for any extraordinary room requirements. An additional labor charge will be added for functions held on our decks. The Doubletree reserves the right to cancel any banquet or meeting sixty (60) days prior to the scheduled function.

OUTSIDE FOOD AND BEVERAGE: No food and beverage of any kind will be permitted to be brought into any public hotel area by the Patron or any of the Patron's guests or invitees. All food, liquor, wine and beer must be supplied by the Doubletree Hotel.

BARTENDER: An additional service charge of $25.00 will be assessed per bar, should beverage sales not exceed $200.00 per bar.

SIGNAGE: No signs or displays are permitted in public areas without prior hotel approval, we will be happy to assist in printing directional or informational signs.

FIGURE 11-3. *(Continued)*

CONTROL: If patron chooses to utilize tickets , add decorations or flowers, specify room diagrams, etc., for a function, please inform catering manager 2 weeks before scheduled function.

MUSIC AND
ENTERTAINMENT: The Catering Department will be pleased to arrange music and/or entertainment for any patron's functions. Should patron choose to make the arrangements, a copy of the signed contract should be provided to the Catering Office in advance of the function.

Should the volume from musical groups, entertainment or public address systems create disturbances, the Hotel reserves the right to request of the Patron and/or entertainers to lessen volume and, if necessary, to perform without amplification. It is advisable that all entertainment programs be reviewed with the Catering Office prior to contracting said entertainment.

SERVICE CHARGE: All food and beverage prices are subject to 18% Hotel Service Charge and all applicable state and local taxes in accordance with Agency 92 Article 19 of the Kansas Retailer Sales Regulations.

AUDIO VISUAL: All audio visual equipment is contracted from Hoover audio visual company at modest prices. Enclosed is a complete audio visual list as well as price list. Please check with the Catering Department for arrangements, availability and confirmation of costs.

SECURITY
AND LIABILITY: The Hotel cannot assume any responsibility for the damage or loss of any merchandise or articles left in the Hotel prior to, during, or following an event. In the instance that valuable items are to be left in any banquet area it is recommended that a security patrol be retained at the group's expense. The Doubletree Hotel reserves the right to inspect and control all private functions through the service of a private security company. The hourly fee of said security will be passed on to the group. Liability for damages to the premises will be charged accordingly.

BILLING: Payment shall be made prior to the function unless credit has been established to the satisfaction of the Hotel. Once credit is approved, the balance of the account is due and payable thirty (30) days after the date of the function. A service charge of 1½% per month is added to any unpaid balance over thirty (30) days old. A Credit Application may be obtained through the Catering Department. Once your firm's application has been approved, all catering charges along with any Master Account charges may be direct billed. All requests for direct billing should be authorized by the Hotel's Accounting Office at least thirty (30) days prior to scheduled events. If deposit is required it becomes non-refundable thirty (30) days prior to the event.

GROUP
SHIPMENTS: Any freight or shipping charges incurred as a result of materials, i.e., literature, audio visual equipment, etc., being shipped to the Doubletree Hotel remain the sole responsibility of the Conference, Association or Group, etc. The Catering Sales Manager should be informed prior to shipping. Return of materials, equipment are not the responsibility of the hotel, however, arrangements can be made. Parcels may not be received more than two days prior to event.

CANCELLATION
POLICY: Should a meal function be cancelled less than sixty (60) days prior to your group's arrival, the Doubletree Hotel will require that client pay the estimated banquet room rental for reserving the room on a definite basis. Should a meal function be cancelled less than 7 days prior to function, Doubletree Hotel would require that client pay 50% of estimated revenue based on menu function arrangements.

CATERING MANAGER: _____ DATE: _____

ACCEPTED BY: _____ DATE: _____

DOUBLETREE
HOTEL · KANSAS CITY

FIGURE 11-3. *(Continued)*

most restaurants and hotels. Some banquets, however, particularly the more traditional, will use Russian style service. Perfection is a key criteria in these functions both in preparation and service.

Specialized training and experience is necessary to properly serve a traditional banquet with Russian service. I attended an elegant event recently at a luxury hotel noted for its cuisine and service. During the cocktail hour preceding the banquet, canapes were served by waiters decked out in tuxedos and white gloves. One guest inquired as to the makeup of these canapes beautifully arranged on a silver tray. "Hell, if I know," was the waiter's reply. While amusing at the time, I thought of all the hard work, skill, and years of training the person responsible had put into the making of those canapes. What a shame it had to be ruined by a waiter who was probably an on-call, unskilled, part-time, moonlighting employee. What a blow to the reputation of that prestigious hotel. Make sure the employees can measure up to the function and menu planned. If they can't, don't book it.

PRICING

To determine what price to charge for a banquet, refer to the chapters on costing and pricing. Those principles apply to banquets as well as to other types of food service operations. There are, however, four additional factors that need to be taken into consideration when discussing banquets. They are long-range pricing, tax, gratuities, and guarantees. Many times banquets are planned and booked several months in advance. To quote a selling price based on today's costs for a function six months away will often leave the operator with little or no profit. To circumvent this problem it is necessary to project what the costs will be when the function is held.

Careful study by the person responsible for determining the selling price should be undertaken to ascertain how the commodity futures market is behaving. To estimate what the costs will be in the period the function is planned requires some speculation, of course. Once these estimated costs are determined, a selling price can then be quoted to the client. Since we are dealing with estimates on what is likely to happen in the future, these figures will not always be accurate. They will, however, help to avoid a loss and will greatly increase the odds for a proper profit margin. Some hotels opt to avoid this problem by setting menus with the client but will not quote a price until 30 days prior to the event. While this makes it easy for the hotel or catering company, it may jeopardize the client who must have registration materials printed months in advance. We must remember who is the buyer and who is the seller.

When quoting a price for a banquet, tax and gratuities are always included. This way the client knows exactly what the function will cost. If additional banquet costs are to be incurred, they also should be discussed early. These include set up charges, bar charges, and audio visual fees, among others. Gratuities, or tips, are normally added to the bill at the rate of 15 percent. Some luxury properties will charge 20 percent while other smaller properties may go as low as 10 percent. Tax is also added at the percent which is applicable for that particular governing unit. A few fortunate areas have no sales tax. Others are taxed by the state, county, and municipality in which they are located. Still others may have a tourism or convention tax imposed on top of sales taxes. A word of caution regarding the amount to be taxed: A few states impose sales tax on labor, while the service is charged for separately. In this case, a gratuity might not be taxed, whereas a service charge could be taxed. In other words, watch the semantics. In any event, check the law regarding sales tax in your area.

Occasionally, a client will want a price quote that is inclusive (i.e., there is $20 to spend per person for everything). To figure a quote of this nature, add together the tax and gratuity percents and add 1 (100 percent) to this figure. Divide the client's desired spending amount by this number. For example:

5%	sales tax	
+20%	gratuity	
=25%	total plus 100% = 1.25	$1.25\overline{)\$20} = \$16$

Therefore, if a bride and her mother come to you with a budget of $20 per person, you could quote a meal selling for $16. When the tax and gratuity are added, the total cost would come to the budgeted $20.

The guarantee has little to do with pricing other than it is used to figure the total bill. However, since it is usually discussed with the client at the time of price, it will be included here. Guarantees normally work one of three ways. Over-under, over only, and no variance. In all methods, the client must, at some point, guarantee that a certain number of guests will attend the banquet. This time will vary anywhere from one week to 24 hours prior to the event. The variance in time is dependent upon a particular operation's purchasing policies and delivery availability.

In the *over-under method*, a percentage is determined by management in which they will allow a client to vary from the guarantee. Normally this is 5 percent. In companies with very liberal policies it could be as high as 10 percent. For example, if a client booked a banquet with a guarantee of 500 people and the hotel had a 5 percent over-under policy, the variance of people attending (and paying) could range from 475 to 525. The 475 is the minimum that would be billed and the 525 is the maximum that would be produced. If only 450 people showed up, the client would be billed for 475.

In the *over only method*, the guarantee is the minimum with the overage coming from a predetermined percentage, usually 5 percent but in some cases 10 percent. In the foregoing example, 500 would be the minimum billed the client, with the production maximum set at 525 (using the 5 percent figure).

The *no variance method* is exactly as the name implies: there is no leeway. Five hundred are billed and five hundred are prepared. Regardless of which method is used, it is imperative that an operation protect itself against no shows. Certain variable costs, particularly food and labor, are inherent in preparing for a banquet. If lower sales are recorded than anticipated, it will result in a loss.

MEETING LENGTH

Although the length of the banquet and possible subsequent meeting has little to do with the planning of the menu, it is quite important to the planning of the function itself. Often banquets are scheduled one right after the other in the same room. In this case, it is necessary to know the length of time needed to serve the meal, hold the meeting, clean the room, and reset it for the next function. All too often in order to gain the optimum income by booking as many banquets as possible, inadequate time is allowed between functions. This results in upset, highly stressed customers and does nothing to enhance the goodwill of the organization.

SHOW MENUS

Show menus are used in operations that serve dinner followed by a theatre presentation or a Las Vegas type revue. Some dinner theatres serve a buffet prior to the performance. For those operations, the principles offered in the chapter on buffets will suffice. Other establishments opt for waiter service prior to the show. For those, the principles given in this chapter are the same for show menus as they are for banquets with one exception, there is a choice of foods given to the customer.

In developing show menus of this nature, two facts should be kept in mind. First, the menu should be limited and second, it should be quick to serve. Limited means no more than five entrees. The accompanying items would also be limited in number. Speed is essential because all meals must be served and the dishes cleared prior to the entertainment. Therefore, it would be prudent to list only fast food items on the menu. In other words, items that can be prepared prior to service and simply dished up upon request. Avoid short order or foods that need to be cooked to order. Menu prices on show menus are always higher than normal because the price of the entertainment is included in the selling price of the meal. Some operations charge one price regardless of the entree selected, while others have a separate price for each entree. Regardless of which method is used, the price of entertainment is included.

CONCLUSION

For a successful banquet to happen, the menu must be right. Plan it with foods that are popular with the group involved. Take into consideration the theme of the event. Make sure the client understands all costs and the guarantee. Don't overshoot the skills of your staff and don't overbook the room. If you follow these principles, you're on your way to catering a successful event. It's just that simple.

QUESTIONS

1. Explain in your own words the six principles of banquet menu planning.
2. Using all skills learned in this chapter, write a banquet menu for your local high school football team which has just won the state championship.
3. Assuming you have a 5 percent sales tax on the price of a banquet, a 15 percent gratuity charge, and a 5 percent over-under policy. Explain to your client the cost per person of a banquet selling for $20 as well as the total cost of that banquet assuming a guaranty of 1,000 people. Include in your explanation the over-under policy.
4. Develop a menu for the Bell Road Barn Players dinner theatre rendition of *South Pacific*.

CHAPTER TWELVE

Buffets

OBJECTIVES
- To appreciate the advantages that a buffet offers over a traditional menu.
- How visual appeal takes the place of descriptive terminology.
- The importance of line movement and table placement.
- How to set up buffet tables to control costs.
- To understand the different types of buffets.

IMPORTANT TERMS

Visual appeal	Garnishment
Supporting displays	Zoning
Table placement	Arranging to profit

INTRODUCTION

There is no other type of menu planning that will let a person show off artistic skills better than a buffet. Buffets can turn an ordinary menu or occasion into a festive party.

A buffet offers several advantages to restaurant and food service operations. First and foremost, food can be presented to the customer in dramatic fashion. I have witnessed many culinary art displays which have taken hours to prepare, have been carefully balanced, and have been correct down to the smallest detail. I have also attended buffets that were prepared by persons who are unskilled in the art of *garde manger,* but who nonetheless put on an attractive display of foods. With basic cooking skills and following a few fundamental concepts, anyone with a slight degree of artistic ability can prepare an attractive buffet.

Another advantage of buffets is that they can result in tremendous labor savings in any operation. Consider the dining room, where fewer service personnel will be needed due to the fact that the customers are essentially waiting on themselves except for beverage service. In the production area, there is no short order cooking, only mass production of multiple units of several items which will increase productivity considerably. Thus, in both the front and back of the house, tighter scheduling will result in lower labor costs.

A third advantage of buffets is that with proper menu planning techniques, food costs can be lower than with a conventional menu. In-season foods along with leftovers can be incorporated into the menu with little difficulty. Since the majority of buffets served do not require a printed menu, the food service manager is wide open as to what foods can be used.

The planning of a buffet menu presents a somewhat different approach than conventional menus to the person responsible for such activities. First and foremost is the fact that the menu is presented to the customer visually rather than in printed form. Instead of selecting which items to consume by reading, the patron selects the food by viewing the actual food itself. Because of this, certain principles must be followed to ensure the salability of the buffet and, most important, to ensure profitability.

VISUAL APPEAL

The visual appeal of any buffet serves the same purpose as descriptive terminology on the printed menu—to sell. If the products look good and the overall merchandising effect is artistically done, the buffet will be welcomed by the customer. The old adage "It looks good, therefore, it will taste good" couldn't be more true. To properly merchandise a buffet, three elements are required: fresh food, attractive garnishing, and creative supporting display material.

FRESH FOOD

Nothing can destroy the effect of a buffet quicker than food that does not appear fresh. Wilted or brownish lettuce in a salad bowl, dried sauce with a skin on an entree item, or stale, dried-out bakery items are all miscues that you have probably witnessed on buffet lines. They distract from the salability of the buffet. The cause of the stale look is twofold: too much food placed on the table and improper temperature.

The menu planner must decide not only what times to serve, but how much of each item to place on the table at any one time. Various foods deteriorate over different time periods. Oftentimes stale-looking food was probably fresh at the beginning of the meal period, but deteriorated after several hours of sitting on the table. Small batch preparation and timely table placement will overcome this problem.

Temperature is another factor that needs to be taken into considera-tion in maintaining a fresh look. This is especially critical in operations where buffets are not an everyday occurrence and where temporary setups are used. Cold foods need to be well chilled, not only from an appearance standpoint but also to avoid contamination. Never set foods which are intended to be chilled on a non-refrigerated table. Merely setting them on a bed of ice will not get the job done either. They must be set in dishes which are immersed in ice to a level equal to the top of the food line. If not, the food that is above the ice takes on the temperature of the room and will begin its deterioration and contamination process.

Safety and appearance must not compromise service. Service personnel must keep a watchful eye on the availability of food. To have an entree run out is a disaster. Imagine 10 to 20 guests standing around, empty plates in hand, griping about the service.

GARNISHMENT

Garnishing on a buffet goes beyond simply adding a lot of colorful food to a plate to enhance its presentation. While this is certainly important and must be used, buffet garnishment also includes decorative pieces. Whole hams, turkeys, and fish are often used to enhance a table. One or two of these pieces, properly placed and displayed, will add to the overall color and excitement of the buffet presentation. Accompanying items such as sauces and relishes can also be cleverly used as a garnish. Cranberry relish in baskets

FIGURE 12-1. Platter arrangement and edible visual display material make for an attractive display. (*Courtesy of the Greater Kansas City Chef's Association*)

FIGURE 12-1. (*Continued*)

carved out of oranges makes a colorful display surrounding a platter of cold turkey. Various types of greens such as romaine, leaf lettuce, spinach, and savory cole should be used to underline cold presentations.

FIGURE 12-1. *(Continued)*

SUPPORTING DISPLAY MATERIAL

Supporting display material is a miscellaneous category and includes all *non-edible* display pieces that are used to enhance the buffet. First and foremost among these is ice carvings. Over the years these have become a traditional part of buffets. Often used as a center piece, they are one of the binding factors that tie the theme of the party and the buffet together. In addition to being used as display pieces, ice carvings can also become serving dishes, typically to serve shrimp from a bowl carved out of ice.

Other non-edible display devices include flowers, ferns, greens, and leaves. These can be used to add color to the table. An important fact to remember is that these should not be used on the platters of food, nor should they touch the platters. Only edible food should be on the platters. All non-edible goods are for table color enhancement only.

A final factor of supporting display material is height. A long, flat surfaced, one-level table is boring. Give the buffet dimension by building up certain areas. By using wooden boxes or bulk milk cartons covered with linen, the table can take on the added dimension of height. High and low stainless steel or silver serving dishes can also be used for height variance. But remember to achieve a balanced look when using height. The linen used to cover the boxes should be the same as the linen used on the table. White is the traditional color because it gives a clean appearance and enhances the food. However, other colors can be used to tie in with the decor of the room. Make sure that the color selected does not detract from the food served.

FIGURE 12-2. Examples of supporting display material. Top left, blown sugar. Right, tallow. Bottom Left, pastillage. Bottom right, chocolate. (*Photographs courtesy of the Greater Kansas City Chef's Association*)

FIGURE 12-3. Fresh-looking food, supporting display material, various heights, and clever use of linens combine to make up a buffet table with great eye appeal. (*Photographed at the French Embassy, Washington, D.C. Courtesy of Marriott Management Services*)

FIGURE 12-3. (*Continued*)

LINE MOVEMENT AND ZONING

The speed at which the line moves is critical to the success of any buffet. Nothing puts the damper on a gala event quicker than having to stand in a slow moving line. To avoid this problem, the buffet table or tables should be zoned. A zone is a section that serves 50 people. Each zone should be identical and contain the same selection and assortment as every other zone. Thus, if you are serving 200 guests, there would be four zones. In extremely large buffets, zones can be set for 100 guests. For service of 1,000 people it would be

FIGURE 12-3. (*Continued*)

easier to set up 10 large zones rather than 20 smaller ones. Zoning is most predominant in banquet buffets where a large number of patrons are arriving at about the same time. In restaurants where the guests are arriving over a longer period, the number of zones would be determined by the number of seats in the restaurant and the estimated grouping, in terms of number, of the arrivals.

TABLE SHAPES AND PLACEMENT

Buffets do not require a long rectangular table. They can take on any shape, with size determined by the number of zones necessary. When deciding where to place tables, the location of the kitchen should be taken into consideration in order to adequately service the buffet. An L-shaped table works well when the placement is in the corner of a room. A circle or U-shape is desirable for the center of a room. When the table is to be placed along a wall, the familiar rectangle works best. For large banquets, where multiple zones are

FIGURE 12-4. Two examples of zoning arrangements on a large grand buffet. (*Photographs courtesy of the Greater Kansas City Chef's Association*)

FIGURE 12-4. (*Continued*)

used, consider spreading the tables throughout the room for maximum effectiveness as well as speed of service. Traffic patterns are crucial. Diners must not bump into each other.

WRITING THE MENU

Several factors need to be taken into consideration when deciding what food items should be placed on a buffet table. The first of course, is profit. Other factors, while not as important as profit but still warranting consideration, are the demographics of the

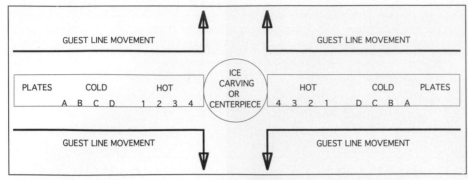

FIGURE 12-5. A basic example of identical zoning for a multiple-line buffet.

customers, the theme of the group or restaurant, and the general ambience of the selected foods.

PROFIT

In considering profit on a buffet, the menu planner has a much more difficult task at hand than merely marking up an item for the menu. In a normal menu markup, the portion is predetermined. If all goes well, the exact cost as well as the exact profit is known. With buffets, the portions are left up to the customer. How much of which items will they select? The only answer to this dilemma is that it must be dealt with in generalities. In other words, the food cost and subsequent profit must be looked at in total rather than for each specific item. (See Chapter 3 for a discussion on salad bar costs—the same principle applies for buffets.)

Action can be taken, however, by the person responsible for buffet planning to control costs. Once the selling price is established, items can be selected in a cost range to adhere to that price. Take chicken, for example. A buffet in a low price range would have chicken and dumplings, while a moderate range would call for baked or fried chicken. A higher priced buffet would probably opt for chicken duxelle or kiev (not because of food cost but rather the labor cost). The same format can be followed for all menu items. Crab claws and shrimp would be eliminated from a low cost buffet but included on a high cost offering.

Another action that can be taken to control costs is plate size. The scientific axiom that "nature abhors a void" is definitely true here. Given an empty space on a plate, a customer will fill it. A large plate will rapidly become filled on a buffet line because the customer is hungry when going through the selection process. This large plate may be filled to a point where the customer will not be able to consume it all. Thus wasted cost occurs. Conversely, with a smaller plate, while the customer is finishing his/her first plate and returning for seconds, the digestion process is taking place. The customer becomes filled, thus selecting a lesser amount on the return trip.

Another factor to consider in controlling cost is the arrangement of particular items on the table. Buffets should be merchandised to profit. That is, the lower cost items should be placed first and succeeding items placed in direct proportion to their cost. This should be done for each food category. Color and texture distribution also need to be taken into account when arranging the table but not to the exclusion of cost. Some clever manipulation and well conceived planning needs to be taken into account to properly achieve this goal.

When writing a buffet menu, one of the key considerations, outside of profit, should be the demographics of the customers involved. Age, income, sex, occupation, and ethnic origins all need to be taken into account when deciding what items are to be placed on the menu. For example, a group of secretaries at a banquet luncheon buffet would require a lighter menu than a group of blue collar workers at a dinner buffet.

In addition to demographics, theme is another consideration that must be accounted for in planning buffets. When booking banquet buffets, the theme of the group must be taken into consideration by choosing products that reinforce that theme. In addition to the menu, supporting display material should also carry out the theme of that function. In restaurants where buffets are an everyday occurrence, the theme and decor of the *establishment* should be reflected in the buffet items. If the restaurant is generic in nature, then the buffet is open to a wide assortment of menu choices. Even in this situation, however, it is a wise idea to change items from time to time to arouse the customer's curiosity. People love theme parties. Feature a Friday seafood buffet, a Western buffet, or try the American Culinary Federation's current theme—American Bounty. The ideas are endless.

One final consideration on buffet menus. Make sure that the items selected complement each other as far as taste and flavor are concerned. On the other hand, contrast should be exploited in the areas of texture, shape, and size. Contrast is particularly important in cooking methods and color. A well-planned buffet with many vivid, contrasting colors will whet the appetite of even the most discerning diner.

HORS D'OEUVRE BUFFETS

A different style of buffet, the hors d'oeuvre buffet, is used primarily for cocktail parties, although in some cases it is used for appetizer service prior to a banquet. Consequently, the menu for an hors d'oeuvre buffet should be drawn up entirely of "finger food," that is, food items that do not require utensils. Also, the buffet tables should be scattered throughout the room. In other words, several tables rather than one with a line effect should be used. This arrangement encourages people to move about and socialize rather than standing in line, filling a plate and sitting down. Each table should be categorized differently. For example, one table could have fruit and cheeses, another canapes, one or more with hot hors d'oeuvres, and still another could have seafood, and so on. The other factors regarding buffets remain the same.

FORMAL BUFFET

In more formal buffet presentations, one common rule is eliminated, the arranging of foods to cost. In formal buffets, items are arranged to taste rather than cost. Also remember that arrangement always follows the normal category selection—that is, appetizers, salads, cold platters, hot foods, and desserts.

Another criterion of formal buffets is that they are more exacting and artistic. They tend to follow closely the standards and guidelines for culinary arts expositions and competitions as written by the American Culinary Federation. There will be more classical items and dishes than would be found in a regular buffet. A higher degree of art form is also found in formal buffets including such things as tallow carvings, salt sculptures, and pulled sugar. Formal buffets should only be attempted by chefs with several years of training and culinary expertise.

CONCLUSION

Buffets are an exciting alternative to regular menu service. Make sure they are visually appealing. Color contrasts, different heights, ice carvings, flowers, and unusual table arrangements will all help to make a buffet a successful event. Proper food selection for your client with a variety of tastes, textures, and color will make it gastronomically appealing. Tie the foods, colors, and decorations together to match the theme of the event. All of these criteria create a buffet that is an exciting and successful party. It's just that simple.

QUESTIONS

1. Explain what is meant by merchandising to profit on a buffet.
2. Write a menu for and diagram on an hors d'oeuvre buffet serving 300 guests for the Western States Cattle Breeders Association.

3. Discuss why buffets are essentially more profitable than a la carte menu service.

4. Explain the importance of visual appeal of buffets. Tell what you can do and should avoid in creating good visual appeal.

5. Give several examples of supporting display material on a buffet with an Oriental theme.

6. Discuss the factors which would make a buffet profitable including how the cost of the buffet should be determined.

CHAPTER THIRTEEN

Cafeterias

OBJECTIVES
- To differentiate between the various cafeteria designs.
- To understand the difference between the two categories of cafeterias.
- To comprehend the principles of writing cafeterias' menus
- To appreciate the concepts of arrangement of food on a cafeteria line.

IMPORTANT TERMS

Straight line cafeteria	Bypass system
Sawtooth	Free flow cafeteria
Institutional cafeterias	Commercial cafeterias
Cycle menus	Line diagrams
Food merchandising	

INTRODUCTION

Cafeterias can be placed into two categories: commercial-for-profit restaurants and not-for-profit, in-house operations. Commercial cafeterias have their strongest customer base across the southern part of the United States and are growing in popularity in the Midwest. While there are a few independent operators, the majority of these operations are owned by large chains. Popular with senior citizens and, to some extent, families, they owe their success to a wide variety of freshly prepared food with an emphasis on nutritional offerings such as fruits, salads, and a selection of vegetables. Of course, the fresh baked breads, cakes, pies, and pastries don't hurt sales either. They give the customer something that is missing in the majority of fast food and theme restaurants, which is the opportunity to select a nutritionally well-balanced meal.

Not-for-profit, in-house cafeterias are a huge part of today's food service industry. They can be found almost anywhere: in schools, colleges, nursing homes, hospitals, manufacturing plants, office buildings, correctional facilities, and others. While many of these facilities run their own operations, the majority are contracted out to firms who specialize in running this type of food service operation. Commonly thought of as captive audience feeding, nothing could be farther from the truth. Except for a few instances (e.g., correctional facilities, hospitals, or some nursing homes), the majority of customers in these places can exercise a choice to either eat in, bring a sack lunch, or leave the premises to eat out at a local restaurant. It is, therefore, a highly competitive business and the menu is of paramount importance in the success of the operation.

Menu writing for cafeterias follows most of the principles previously discussed; however, there are a few peculiarities and these will be discussed in this chapter.

CAFETERIA STYLES

Cafeterias come in many different styles, but most follow four basic designs:

1. straight line
2. bypass line
3. sawtooth
4. free flow.

The *straight line* is designed exactly as the name implies—a straight line. Of all the styles, it is the slowest moving as two things determine speed in a cafeteria line. First, the speed at which the cash is taken and second, the fact that the line moves as fast as the slowest person. In this design the customer is reluctant to pass a slower moving patron. The straight line cafeteria is, however, the most common design found in commercial cafeterias because it takes up the least amount of square footage and, more important, the average customer feels most comfortable with the design. In the following designs, customers are encouraged to pass others and blockages in the line are avoided. Many people at first feel uncomfortable about butting in.

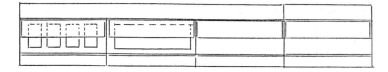

FIGURE 13-1. Example of straight line style.

The *bypass line* is a variation of the straight line system with the first section serving primarily salads and cold sandwiches, the second section serving hot foods, and the third section serving desserts and beverages. The second section is indented, thus making it easier for customers to jump the line if they do not wish to order hot foods. This system is particularly popular with those operations that offer grill service as it allows the line to continue moving while customers are waiting for their grilled items.

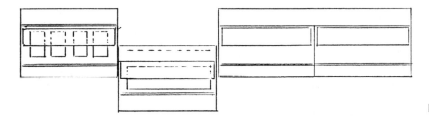

FIGURE 13-2. Example of bypass line.

The *sawtooth* is also a variation of the straight line system with each section being set at a diagonal to the previous section. With this method, the customer can go directly to the area or areas of their choosing.

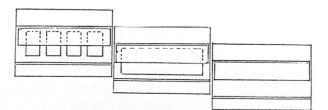

FIGURE 13-3. Example of sawtooth line.

The *free flow system* is designed so that the patrons can go directly to the area or areas serving those items that they desire.

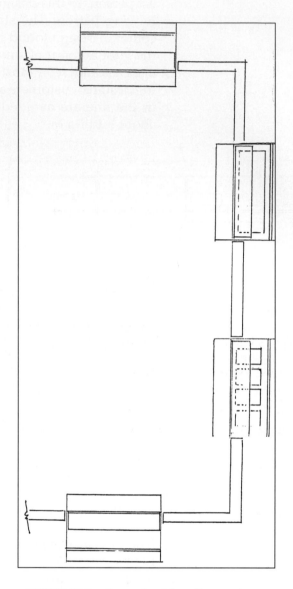

FIGURE 13-4. Example of free flow system.

While there are many different layouts for the free flow system, one of the most popular is the shopping center concept which is shaped like a giant U. Free flow systems are very common in employee cafeterias and other situations where there is repeat business. Due to the fact that they are confusing to the uninitiated, they have not had much success commercially. Once the system is figured out by the customer, it offers fast service with a minimum of waiting.

DEMOGRAPHICS

In order to discuss cafeteria demographics, it is necessary to look at the two categories—non-profit and profit. The demographics of non-profit cafeterias are as diverse as the operations themselves. There is considerable difference in the menus for a college dormitory cafeteria and an in-plant cafeteria for General Motors. In order to properly develop a menu, the menu writer must first ascertain the needs of the group in that particular institution. Many contract feeders ignore this fact and send menus from the home office to the client cafeterias. These menus, generic in nature, cannot meet the specific needs of each institution and, consequently, result in dissatisfied patrons. As stated in an earlier chapter, customers' wants and needs must be carried out in menu selections.

The astute contract companies, as well as the firms that operate their own food service, leave the menu planning up to the unit manager. This works well in that the local manager is in tune with the client base and can fit menus to the demographic diversity of that particular group.

Commercial cafeterias, on the other hand, fit a rather tight demographic spectrum. Predominantly located in the South and Midwest, cafeterias are rather evenly split between downtown and suburban locations which can be either free standing or located in shopping malls. Commercial cafeterias are popular with those people over 40-years old. Since a large portion of this group constitutes senior citizens, the idea of no tipping and selecting a few items from a wide choice are particularly inviting. Small portions with low prices charged for quality, nutritional food also enhance the cafeteria's image with this group.

Several cafeteria chains are attempting to change their demographic base. As one chain executive put it, "Every time we read the obituaries we find that we've lost some customers." One Midwest chain in particular has instituted an advertising campaign comparing their cafeterias to fast food chains in an effort to lure the younger set. In it they compare value, price, speed of service, and nutrition. The effect of this campaign has had success in that their family business has increased dramatically.

CAFETERIA MENUS

When writing menus for cafeterias, there are several principles previously discussed that need to be either modified or emphasized. The primary reason for this is that the customer is making their selection based upon actually viewing the food rather than reading about it on a printed menu. Therefore, the principles of variety in regard to color, texture, cooking methods, and food items become paramount as the line must be appealing in order to sell.

When selecting menu listings, how they will look is as important as how well they complement each other. Variety is the key. First, consider color. It would be unwise, for example, to put green beans lyonnaise, peas and pearl onions, spinach with bacon bits, and buttered broccoli spears on the menu. While these vegetables could very well be an excellent complement to the entrees selected, they will not merchandise well as they are all the same color. Even though some of them are garnished with color, the overall effect on the line is green. Because items selected must complement each other as well as give a good spectrum of color, the spinach might be replaced with beets and the broccoli with carrots.

Variety in textures should also be sought. How boring the line would look if all of the textures in each category were the same. Consider the salad section. There should be *variety* in texture. Include roughage (tossed garden salad), smooth (gelatin salads), smooth and crunchy (cole slaw), contrasts in fruit (such as fresh versus cooked or stewed). With imaginative selection in regard to texture, it is quite easy to work in color at the same time.

Various styles of cooking methods also need to be considered. Variety in this area in terms of simmered, braised, roasted, sauteed, fried, deep fried, and baked foods should be included on the menu. Remember, customers are selecting food based on sight not by printed menu. Consider how dull your hot food line would look and taste if all entrees were deep fried. Not only that, what would the color spectrum be?

FIGURE 13-5. One way of injecting variety into a cafeteria menu is to use various theme promotions. (*Courtesy of Marriott Management Services*)

Food variety is the final opportunity for dining interest. Each area on the cafeteria line should have the widest variety of foods possible. For example, the salad section would include fruits, vegetables, starches, dairy, and miscellaneous items such as gelatins. Entrees could include beef, veal, pork, lamb, poultry, variety meats, cheese, and eggs. All of these groups may not be possible or even desirable. Maybe lamb is a slow seller; if so, eliminate it. Remember, regardless of size or demographics, variety must be built into the menu plan.

Not only must the above varietal areas be considered, but production must be taken into account. Since the customer is choosing by sight, it is imperative that all foods on the line *look* fresh at all times. It is a known fact that some foods have excellent holding qualities while others deteriorate rapidly. Foods that withstand a longer time frame on the line can be produced in larger batches, while foods that lose color and quality quickly should be produced in smaller batches. In writing the menu, care must be exercised so that there is not an overabundance of small batch cookery.

One other criterion is the plating of the final product. This should be, ideally, rapid with one motion. More than one motion will slow the customer line movement, with several motions bringing it to a complete stop. Fast lines mean high profits. For example, fried chicken quartered is one motion, from the steam table to the plate. If it's served with cream gravy, then it's two motions. Either way it's fast. On the other hand, a sandwich prepared from scratch requires several motions by the server and the entire line stops while it is being constructed.

Most successful cafeteria chains prefer to emphasize foods cooked fresh from raw ingredients as opposed to using convenience foods. Indeed, some chains that introduced some frozen entrees or pre-made salads backed off of this approach when customers complained and sales dropped. Some institutional cafeterias, on the other hand, are leaning more and more on convenience foods to keep labor costs down. Sometimes this is not as cost effective as it first appears. Could it be that convenience foods, not properly used, are one of the contributing factors to dissatisfaction with captive audience feeding?

One final word on writing menus for cafeterias. The most successful method is to set the menus up on a cycle. The length of the cycle depends on the type of cafeteria. Institutional and in-plant feeders would require a longer cycle due to the repeat customers. Plan a 4- to 5-week cycle. On the other hand, commercial cafeterias, due to transient customers, could get away with a cycle of 2 to 3 weeks. In either case, the longer the cycle the better, to ensure the greatest variety possible.

Once the menu is written, the job is not complete. The menu writer must next diagram the line indicating where each and every

FIGURE 13-6. The shopping center approach in a cafeteria layout enables the operator to set up several stations, thus injecting variety into the menu. Here an ethnic theme is used. (*Photographed at American University, Washington, D.C. Courtesy of Marriott Management Services*)

FIGURE 13-6. (*Continued*)

FIGURE 13-6. (*Continued*)

menu item is to be located. Failure to do this will result in a haphazard arrangement. All of the work to incorporate color, texture, cooking methods, and variety into the menu will be for naught if the person setting the line does not fully understand the proper location of each and every item.

FOOD ARRANGEMENT

The proper way to set up a cafeteria line is to follow the normal meal sequence. Start with appetizers, then salads and entrees. Entrees should be in the order of solids (roasts), semi-solids (Salisbury steaks, croquettes), and extenders (casseroles). After entrees come vegetables, starches, breads, desserts, and beverages. There could be a few exceptions to the above order. Many cafeterias do not serve appetizers. Why is a mystery. Appetizers are excellent add-ons and many lend themselves to cafeteria service. A few, of many examples, include shrimp cocktail, fruit compotes, or relish plates. Some cafeterias opt to offer desserts twice. Once at the start of the line and later in their natural order. The philosophy behind this is that a customer will purchase a dessert with a relatively empty tray at the start of the line. Conversely, with the dessert at the end of the line and a full tray, the customer may decide that they have spent enough and will bypass desserts. Other customers, however, will choose a dessert at the end of the line to round out their meal. Other than these two exceptions, the order of foods should be as indicated previously.

Once the menu is written and the line sequence set, do not forget to merchandise the food. Garnishes should be indicated for items that require them. Make sure you include garnishes as part of the overall menu plan so they are not overlooked or ignored. One would think that with all of the prior planning to ensure a colorful, fresh-looking line, garnishing would be unnecessary. This fact could not be farther from the truth. Again, in cafeterias more than any other type of operation, people eat with their eyes. Garnishing is imperative. A well-merchandised line will sell and sales is the name of the game.

CONCLUSION

Write the menu for the customer, taking into account demographics. Build the menu around this theme and take into account color, texture, cooking methods, and variety of available foods for a well-rounded menu. Specify exactly how the line is to be set and merchandised. Doing this properly will result in a successful cafeteria operation. It's just that simple.

QUESTIONS

1. Discuss the various styles and shapes of cafeteria lines and explain the advantages and disadvantages of each.
2. Explain the difference between institutional and commercial cafeteria demographics.
3. What is the basic difference between an a la carte menu and a cafeteria menu?
4. Discuss menu cycles and tell what length of cycle should be used for which type of cafeteria. Give examples.
5. Diagram a buffet table and a cafeteria line using the same menu.

CHAPTER FOURTEEN

Cycle Menus and Nutrition

OBJECTIVES
- To understand how to use various time frames for cycle menus.
- To differentiate how cycle menus fit into different types of food service.
- To know the importance of nutrition in menu writing.
- To understand the basic four food groups.
- To comprehend how to put together a comprehensive cycle menu.

IMPORTANT TERMS

Cycle menus	The basic four food pyramid
Type A lunch	Cycle menu planning procedures
Calories	

INTRODUCTION

Cycle menus are used in many food service operations and present their own particular sets of standards or rules. Commercial restaurants in almost all categories use them for their daily specials, to augment their regular printed menu. In non-profit food services (i.e., schools, colleges, hospitals, nursing homes, in-plant feeders, and so on) they are used almost exclusively.

Cycle menus are written for a specific period of time and are then repeated, intact, over and over until a new menu is written.

The length of time for a cycle menu will vary, depending on the nature of the operation and its clientele. For example, in a hospital food service where the patient stay is short term, normally four to five days, the cycle would be short. In this instance, a one- or two-week cycle would suffice for patient service. Thus, a menu would be written for breakfast, lunch, and dinner for each day of the week for a one- or two-week period. At the end of this period, the cycle would then be repeated.

For a college dorm, where the length of stay is substantially longer (a semester or academic year) the cycle would likewise be longer. In this case, a cycle would be written for four or five weeks and then repeated. Using this method, the menu will have a greater variety for the clients than the two-week cycle. Quite often, after a four- or five-week cycle menu has been in use for a period of three months, the menu is scrapped and a new cycle is written. Often this is done four times a year corresponding with the four seasons. Not only is variety ensured, but seasonal goods such as fresh fruits and vegetables can be used as well as seasonal themes.

COMMERCIAL USE

In commercial operations, cycle menus may be used in two ways. First, as a clip-on of daily specials and second, as a production list for items listed on the menu as du jour (of the day). In setting up a cycle for daily specials, several factors need to be considered. They are price, balance, and use of leftovers.

PRICE

Price is important as the customer perceives a daily special as a value that is greater than the value received on the printed menu. Therefore, care should be exercised by the menu planner to choose those items that will reinforce this perception. Specials which have a lower ingredient cost than those listings on the printed menu will achieve this goal. For example, a restaurant which serves luncheons in the $4 to $5 range would probably have ingredient costs of between $1.20 and $2. By developing a cyclical menu of daily specials with an ingredient cost of around a dollar, they could sell these in the $3.50 range and still maintain their projected food cost standard as well as giving the customer a greater perceived value.

BALANCE

As previously discussed, balance of foods should be considered when several specials are listed. Balance must exist between such categories as meat, poultry, seafood, and non-meat entrees. Also, a good balance should exist between cooking methods—broiling, roasting, frying, and casserole items.

LEFTOVERS

One of the primary reasons behind daily specials is the use of leftovers. Therefore, the cycle menu should not be so tight as to preclude this important function. Many cycle menus have a listing daily or periodically known as Chef's Choice, which is nothing more than a $5 word for leftovers. Frequently, restaurants will develop a one-week cycle for their specials. The purpose of this is so that their regular customers will know in advance what will be served on a given day. Monday's listings will be the same every Monday and so on throughout the week. While this takes away the element of variety, it can develop a restaurant's reputation for certain products. Bender's Tavern in Kansas City has a waiting line on Wednesdays for their ham hocks and beans. You can probably find several restaurants in your area who follow this type of cyclical menu planning successfully.

Quite often a restaurant will opt not to have a list of daily specials but rather will inject variety into the printed menu by use of the French term "du jour." Listings such as soups, vegetables, potatoes, and sometimes house specialties, such as quiche, all have du jour listed after them. In this case, it is wise to set up a cycle menu to cover these items. In this way, purchasing and production can be adequately covered and the service personnel will know exactly what is to be served day by day. Without a cycle menu there is too much repetition. Pretty soon, the soup du jour is vegetable or French onion day after day. Employees become lazy in this area and tend to avoid anything new or different. Suddenly the menu is in a rut.

CAPTIVE AUDIENCE

The makeup of cycle menus becomes extremely important in food service operations where the patrons are the same day after day. Although selection and popularity of items are to be carefully considered, in no other type or style of menu is nutrition and variety as important as it is in captive audience cycle menus.

NUTRITION

Everyone knows, or should know, the value of nutrition to a person's health and well-being. However, for reasons unknown, many people in the past have chosen to ignore nutrition when selecting their food. There appears to be a dramatic switch away from this behavior as more and more people are jogging, exercising, and participating in sports. With an increasing awareness of physical fitness comes a welcome improvement in the diet. Today, people are selecting more natural foods with healthier methods of preparation. Fried foods and junk foods are definitely on the decline. This is not to preclude, however, that you should strike these items from the menu; they still sell.

Your responsibility as a food service manager varies greatly in regard to the nutritional well-being of your customer. A restaurant manager would have the lowest degree of responsibility in this area. That is not to say that they would have no responsibility at all. Consideration has to be given to those customers who are classified as "regulars." They depend on you to receive a balanced meal. Consideration also needs to be given to those people who eat out regularly but possibly frequent your restaurant only once in a while. You have a responsibility to offer them a nutritionally satisfying meal as do the other restaurants that they might frequent. Too often our industry has come under attack from nutritionists who complain that people who eat out regularly cannot get a well-balanced meal. A restaurant manager, or a student who is a future manager, can put a stop to this drivel by providing your customers with choices that would provide for their nutritional requirements. Many restaurants already do this and quite wisely so, as the customer who desires, even demands, a balanced diet will frequent them, resulting in increased sales for that establishment.

A word of caution is in order here, do not go off of the deep end and turn your establishment into a health food store (unless that is your stated purpose of being). Many of your customers still like fried foods, excess starches, and calorie-laden desserts. Your responsibility is to provide a choice. The customer who is nutritionally concerned should be able to so choose. For the customer who desires to choose "non-nutritional" food, the selection should also be there. You cannot, nor is it your job to, force nutrition on your customers. You may not be able to change behaviors, but you can accommodate them.

For those people who are involved in semi-captive audience food service operations, the nutritional responsibility increases. Food service in plants, offices, schools, and so forth needs to be more aware of balanced diets as their patrons depend on them for one or more of their daily meals. Quite often in these operations, the services of a dietitian are engaged to assure that the meals follow accepted nutritional standards. In the primary and secondary school system, the Type A lunch program, which will be discussed later in the chapter, is followed to assure school children of receiving a balanced noon meal. Whether or not professional help is given in the form of a consulting or staff dietitian or mandated by law, the food service manager of this type operation needs to be aware of and educated in areas of nutrition. The health of a large number of people is dependent on the menu selected.

In captive audience food service operations, the situation changes dramatically. Here the food service manager has a direct responsibility to the patrons for every meal being nutritionally balanced. In hospitals, nursing homes, institutions, prisons, and so forth, the patron has no choice in the matter. They must eat in that food service and eat what is put in front of them . . . or not eat. In these operations, help is almost always at hand for the food service manager. A registered dietitian (RD), who is a member of the American Dietetic Association, is usually on the staff to handle the nutritional problems. In many such operations the food service manager and RD are one and the same. Many years of training, both academically and on the job, are necessary to become a Registered Dietitian. In addition to normal or regular diets, quite often special diets need to be handled to accommodate people with specific restrictions. No matter what area of food service you are involved in or intend to become involved in, nutrition will always play a role—sometimes less, sometimes more. The more your patrons depend on you to meet their nutritional needs, the more you must know.

THE BASIC FOUR

The *basic four* was developed by the United States Department of Agriculture to act as a guideline in food selection for an average healthy person. In 1992, it was modified to resemble a pyramid to more accurately reflect the amounts of each food group a person should consume. An adult following this program will ingest 1,200 calories per day, more or less, depending on their selection of foods within each group. For those persons who require additional

Food Guide Pyramid

A Guide to Daily Food Choices

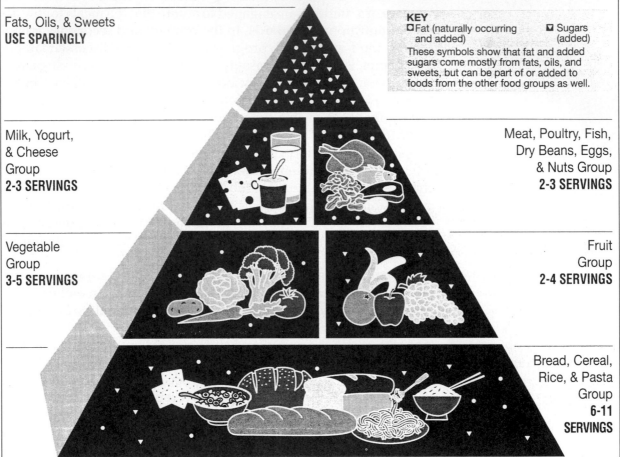

Fats, Oils, & Sweets
USE SPARINGLY

KEY
□ Fat (naturally occurring and added)   ■ Sugars (added)
These symbols show that fat and added sugars come mostly from fats, oils, and sweets, but can be part of or added to foods from the other food groups as well.

Milk, Yogurt, & Cheese Group
2-3 SERVINGS

Meat, Poultry, Fish, Dry Beans, Eggs, & Nuts Group
2-3 SERVINGS

Vegetable Group
3-5 SERVINGS

Fruit Group
2-4 SERVINGS

Bread, Cereal, Rice, & Pasta Group
6-11 SERVINGS

SOURCE: U.S. Department of Agriculture/U.S. Department of Health and Human Services

Use the Food Guide Pyramid to help you eat better every day. . .the Dietary Guidelines way. Start with plenty of Breads, Cereals, Rice, and Pasta; Vegetables; and Fruits. Add two to three servings from the Milk group and two to three servings from the Meat group.

Each of these food groups provides some, but not all, of the nutrients you need. No one food group is more important than another — for good health you need them all. Go easy on fats, oils, and sweets, the foods in the small tip of the Pyramid.

To order a copy of "The Food Guide Pyramid" booklet, send a $1.00 check or money order made out to the Superintendent of Documents to: Consumer Information Center, Department 159-Y, Pueblo, Colorado 81009.

U.S. Department of Agriculture, Human Nutrition Information Service, August 1992, Leaflet No. 572

FIGURE 14-1. The food guide pyramid showing the four food groups and the number of servings you should have per day from each group. (*Courtesy of the United States Department of Agriculture, Washington, D.C.*)

How to Use The Daily Food Guide

What counts as one serving?

Breads, Cereals, Rice, and Pasta
1 slice of bread
1/2 cup of cooked rice or pasta
1/2 cup of cooked cereal
1 ounce of ready-to-eat cereal

Vegetables
1/2 cup of chopped raw or
  cooked vegetables
1 cup of leafy raw vegetables

Fruits
1 piece of fruit or melon wedge
3/4 cup of juice
1/2 cup of canned fruit
1/4 cup of dried fruit

Milk, Yogurt, and Cheese
1 cup of milk or yogurt
1-1/2 to 2 ounces of cheese

Meat, Poultry, Fish, Dry Beans, Eggs, and Nuts
2-1/2 to 3 ounces of cooked lean
  meat, poultry, or fish
Count 1/2 cup of cooked beans,
  or 1 egg, or 2 tablespoons of
  peanut butter as 1 ounce of lean
  meat (about 1/3 serving)

Fats, Oils, and Sweets.
LIMIT CALORIES FROM THESE
especially if you need to lose weight

> The amount you eat may be more than one serving. For example, a dinner portion of spaghetti would count as two or three servings of pasta.

How many servings do you need each day?

	Women & some older adults	Children, teen girls, active women, most men	Teen boys & active men
Calorie level*	about 1,600	about 2,200	about 2,800
Bread group	6	9	11
Vegetable group	3	4	5
Fruit group	2	3	4
Milk group	**2-3	**2-3	**2-3
Meat group	2, for a total of 5 ounces	2, for a total of 6 ounces	3 for a total of 7 ounces

*These are the calorie levels if you choose lowfat, lean foods from the 5 major food groups and use foods from the fats, oils, and sweets group sparingly.

**Women who are pregnant or breastfeeding, teen-agers, and young adults to age 24 need 3 servings.

A Closer Look at Fat and Added Sugars

The small tip of the Pyramid shows fats, oils, and sweets. These are foods such as salad dressings, cream, butter, margarine, sugars, soft drinks, candies, and sweet desserts. Alcoholic beverages are also part of this group. These foods provide calories but few vitamins and minerals. Most people should go easy on foods from this group.

Some fat or sugar symbols are shown in the other food groups. That's to remind you that some foods in these groups can also be high in fat and added sugars, such as cheese or ice cream from the milk group, or french fries from the vegetable group. When choosing foods for a healthful diet, consider the fat and added sugars in your choices from all the food groups, not just fats, oils, and sweets from the Pyramid tip.

FIGURE 14-1.   *(Continued)*

calories, increased servings can be obtained from either the basic four or from an additional group which lists other foods not included in the basic four. Children and others who require less than 1,200 calories would, conversely, reduce their intake via smaller portions within each group while at the same time striking a balance between the groups.

It is extremely important that every food service manager recognize and understand the basic four. There should not be a menu printed anywhere, whether in a public restaurant or private institution, that does not have selections which include these groups. This should not be a difficult task. The plan is sufficiently broad so that the menu writer is not handicapped by narrowing menu selections.

TYPE A LUNCH

For those food service managers concerned with feeding primary and secondary school age children, the Type A lunch becomes the model for menu planning. Enacted in 1946 by Congress, the National School Lunch Act provides cash assistance for schools who choose to participate in this program. It also provides for the school to receive surplus food commodities as well as consultation regarding food purchasing, equipment, and management of the school lunchroom. In order to receive this assistance, the school must operate on a non-profit basis, provide free or reduced price lunches to children of poverty level families, not discriminate in any way, and serve a nutritious Type A lunch.

The makeup of the Type A lunch is as follows:

1. Fluid milk, 1/2 pint, served as a beverage.
2. Protein-rich food, such as 2 oz. cooked or canned lean meat, fish, poultry; 2 oz. cheese; 1 egg, 1/2 cup cooked dry beans or peas; 4 tablespoons peanut butter; or an equivalent of any combination of these in a main dish.
3. Vegetables and fruits, at least 3/4 cup, consisting of two or more servings. One serving of full-strength juice may be counted as not more than 1/4 cup of the requirement.
4. Whole-grain or enriched bread (1 slice), or muffins, cornbread, biscuits, rolls made of enriched or whole grain flour.
5. Butter or fortified margarine, 1 teaspoon, as a spread, as a seasoning, or in food preparation.

Note. It is also necessary to provide a Vitamin C rich food daily as well as a Vitamin A rich food at least twice a week.

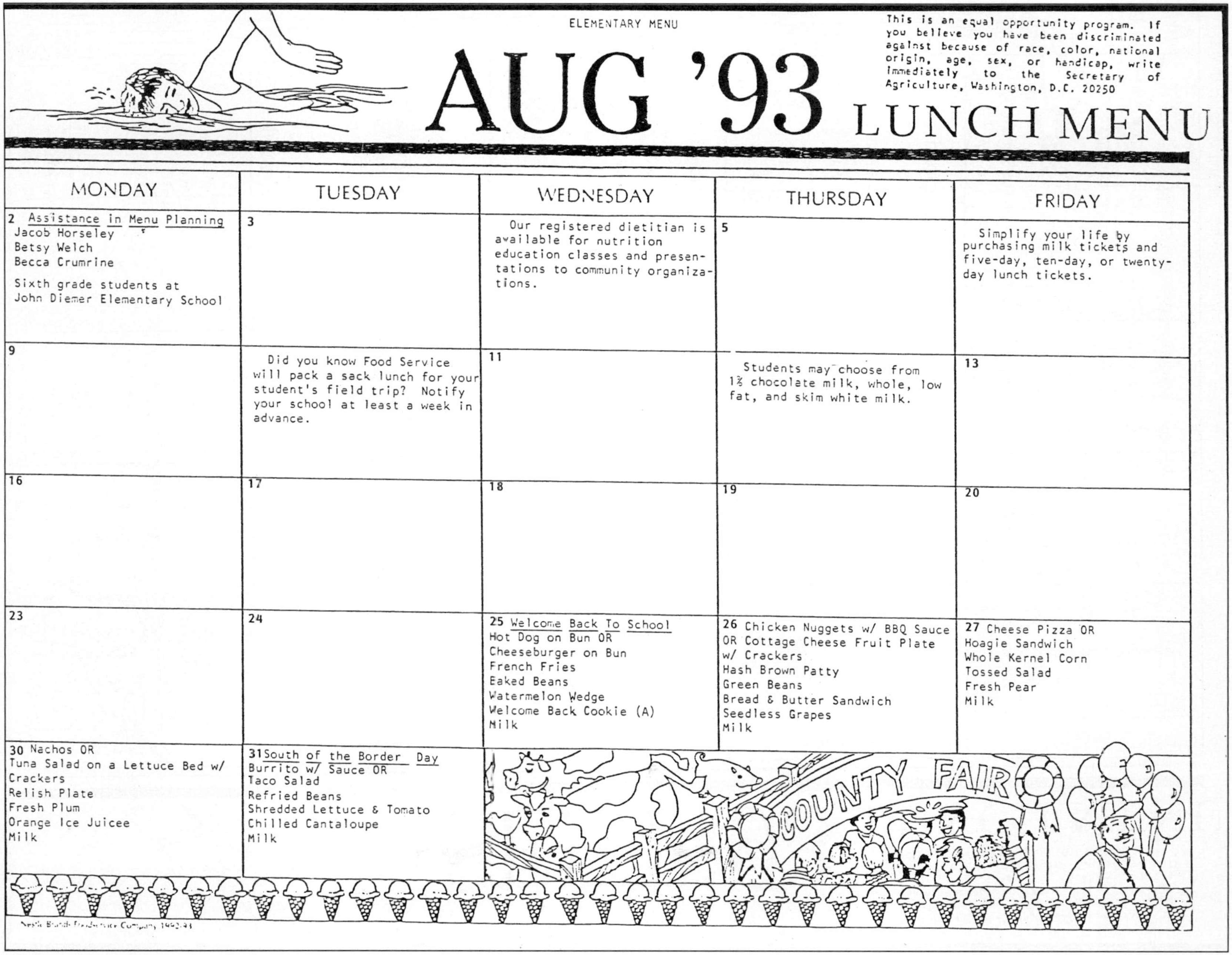

ELEMENTARY MENU

AUG '93 LUNCH MENU

MONDAY	TUESDAY	WEDNESDAY	THURSDAY	FRIDAY
2 Assistance in Menu Planning Jacob Horseley Betsy Welch Becca Crumrine Sixth grade students at John Diemer Elementary School	3	Our registered dietitian is available for nutrition education classes and presentations to community organizations.	5	Simplify your life by purchasing milk tickets and five-day, ten-day, or twenty-day lunch tickets.
9	Did you know Food Service will pack a sack lunch for your student's field trip? Notify your school at least a week in advance.	11	Students may choose from 1% chocolate milk, whole, low fat, and skim white milk.	13
16	17	18	19	20
23	24	25 Welcome Back To School Hot Dog on Bun OR Cheeseburger on Bun French Fries Baked Beans Watermelon Wedge Welcome Back Cookie (A) Milk	26 Chicken Nuggets w/ BBQ Sauce OR Cottage Cheese Fruit Plate w/ Crackers Hash Brown Patty Green Beans Bread & Butter Sandwich Seedless Grapes Milk	27 Cheese Pizza OR Hoagie Sandwich Whole Kernel Corn Tossed Salad Fresh Pear Milk
30 Nachos OR Tuna Salad on a Lettuce Bed w/ Crackers Relish Plate Fresh Plum Orange Ice Juicee Milk	31 South of the Border Day Burrito w/ Sauce OR Taco Salad Refried Beans Shredded Lettuce & Tomato Chilled Cantaloupe Milk			

COUNTY FAIR

FIGURE 14-2. An example of an elementary school lunch menu. (*Courtesy of the Shawnee Mission School District, Shawnee Mission, Kansas*)

ELEMENTARY MENU

SEPT '93 LUNCH MENU

This is an equal opportunity program. If you believe you have been discriminated against because of race, color, national origin, age, sex, or handicap, write immediately to the Secretary of Agriculture, Washington, D.C. 20250

MONDAY	TUESDAY	WEDNESDAY	THURSDAY	FRIDAY
6		1 Chicken Nuggets w/ Finger Roll OR Ham & Cheese on White & Wheat Mashed Potatoes and Gravy Mixed Vegetables Fresh Peach Milk	2 Fiestada Pizza OR Peanut Butter & Jelly Sandwich Whole Kernel Corn Tossed Salad Fresh Fruit Cup Milk	3 Chicken Patty on Bun w/ Lettuce Leaf OR Hot Dog on Bun Tater Tots Raw Broccoli & Cauliflower w/ Dip Chilled Watermelon Chocolate Brownie Milk
LABOR DAY	7 Sausage Pizza OR Mini Chef's Salad w/ Crackers Whole Kernel Corn Tossed Salad Seedless Grapes Lime Sherbet Milk	8 Breakfast For Lunch Pancakes w/ Sausage Patty OR Deli Turkey on Wheat Bun Hash Brown Patty Chilled Grape Juice Fresh Fruit Cup Milk	9 Tacos w/ Soft Shells OR Deli Cold Plate w/ Crackers & Roll Tater Tots Lettuce & Tomato Cup Fresh Fruit Milk	10 Chicken Drumstick OR Beef Fritter Mashed Potatoes w/ Gravy Relish Plate Hot Roll Chilled Cantaloupe Milk
13 Chicken Nuggets w/ Wheat Roll OR Fish Wedge on Bun Tater Sticks Fresh Plum Grape Ice Juicee Milk	14 Potato Bar w/ Assorted Toppings w/ Banana Bread OR BBQ Ribbette on Homemade Bun w/ Hash Brown Patty Broccoli w/ Cheese Watermelon Wedge Milk	15 Pepperoni Pizza OR Cheese and Fruit Plate w/ Wheat Roll Whole Kernel Corn Raw Cauliflower & Cherry Tomato w/ Dip Fresh Fruit Cup Milk	16 Spaghetti w/ Meat Sauce & French Bread OR Corn Dog Mixed Vegetables Tossed Salad Seedless Grapes Chocolate Cake w/ Icing Milk	17 Nachos OR Mini Chef's Salad w/ Crackers Tri Tater Lettuce Salad Cinnamon Bun Cantaloupe Wedge Milk
20 Hot Dog on Bun OR Chicken & Noodles w/ Finger Roll Potato Coins Fresh Fruit Cherry Ice Juicee Milk	21 Tacos w/ Sauce OR Toasted Cheese Sandwich Whole Kernel Corn Lettuce & Tomato Cup Fresh Nectarine Chocolate Chip Cookie Milk	22 Cheese Pizza OR Deli Turkey on Wheat Bun Mixed Vegetables Tossed Salad Fresh Fruit Cup Milk	23 SPORTS DAY Beef Patty on Royals Charbroil Bun OR Chiefs Macaroni & Cheese Blades French Fries Wildcat Lettuce Leaf, Tomato Slice, Dill Pickles The Attack Watermelon Wedge Jayhawk Milk	24 Chicken Nuggets w/ Sauce OR Beef Fritter Mashed Potatoes & Gravy Green Beans Cinnamon Roll Seedless Grapes Milk
27 Chicken Parmesan w/ Spaghetti & French Bread OR BBQ Ribbette on Bun Steamed Peas Fresh Pear Orange Freezie Milk	28 Pizza OR Fish Munchies w/Cornbread Whole Kernel Corn Relish Plate Chilled Cantaloupe Milk	29 Lasagne w/ Bread Stick OR State Fair Corn Dog Green Beans Tossed Salad Seedless Grapes Peanut Butter Cookie Milk	30 Chicken Nuggets w/ Roll OR Ham & Cheese Roll-Up Tater Tots Seasoned Spinach Celery Sticks Fresh Fruit Milk	

MAGNESIUM NITRON

FIGURE 14-2. (Continued)

FIGURE 14-3. Nutrition education as well as an appealing display of nutritional food is important in elementary school feeding. (*Photographs courtesy of Marriott Management Services*)

FIGURE 14-3. (*Continued*)

SPECIAL DIETS

Throughout a food service manager's career, special diets for customers will appear from time to time. This occurs frequently in captive audience operations and occasionally in commercial restaurants where a loyal following may frequently dine. In hospitals, nursing homes, and institutions, staff dietitians are available to execute special diet requests. In operations where requests of this nature are not the norm, the food service manager could be at a quandary as to how to plan a menu as well as to prepare it for such a customer.

A special diet is normally prescribed by a physician much in the same manner that medicine is prescribed. It is, therefore, imperative that the food service manager who accepts this responsibility follow the directions exactly. Failure to do so could result in serious consequences to the customer. When confronted with this situation, it would be wise to obtain the services of a consulting dietitian who can not only assist with planning the menu for your customer, but also instruct the production staff in the proper preparation of the meals.

Some of the more common types of special diets are:

Low sodium (salt)	Soft diet
Sodium free	Low calorie
Low fat	Caffeine free
Fat free	

CALORIES

Many restaurants list low calorie plates to satisfy those customers who are losing weight, wish to maintain a lower calorie intake, or think they are on a diet only to order a rich dessert. Nonetheless, care must be exercised in planning such menus. Many times I have observed "low calorie plates" which were anything but low calorie.

Two criteria should be followed when planning low calorie plates. One, the plate should be nutritionally balanced following the "basic four" pyramid and second, the calories for each item as well as the total calories for the plate should be listed. You should also be able to back up and prove these claims if challenged. Diabetics and other people with medical problems depend on accurate statements. Portion control in the kitchen must be exact to avoid an over or under-statement on the menu. (Indeed, portion control on EVERY item coming out of the kitchen should be exact to ensure profit.)

VARIETY

Due to the fact that a person may receive many, if not all, of their meals in an institutional-type food service, variety also becomes an important factor. The single largest complaint heard in employee cafeterias, dormitories, and schools is that the food is terrible. Terrible usually means boring, the same, lack of variety.

Another reason is that the food does not taste the same as it does at home. Let's face it, some problems we can solve and some we cannot. Short of hiring every college student's mother to work in the dorm kitchen and prepare food for her child, the industry cannot make it taste like Mom's. One solution, however, could be to have a contest in which a student submits one of Mom's recipes and these recipes are then featured throughout the semester with an acknowledgment to the student. Another solution would be through student surveys to find out what the markets' desires are and then fulfill them. Take the case of a hospital patient. First, they're sick and don't feel like eating anyway and second, odds are they are on a restricted diet. Of course the food doesn't taste like home. One thing that can be done, however, is to assure the patron of variety. There is no reason whatsoever that a person should be bored. Variety can easily be achieved by avoiding repetition of items within the cycle and by not repeating the cycles too often.

To avoid monotony, offer a variety of food items, cooking methods, temperature, consistency, and texture.

SELECTION AND POPULARITY

These two factors go hand in hand. When at all possible, a cycle menu should have a selection of items in each category, the more selection the better. The opposite, of course, is true for production purposes. Therefore, a balance should be sought, with two or three offerings in each category. Because of this limited selection, at least one item in each category should be popular. If, due to circumstances, there is no selection on the menu, then all offerings must be popular with the clientele involved. If, for example, a non-selective menu of pan fried liver and onions, buttered brussels sprouts, and harvard beets were served, there would be few takers. This meal is fine nutritionally, colorwise, texturewise, and otherwise, except the items are all low on the popularity poll. If only a few people are going to eat it, what good is it?

MENU PLANNING PROCEDURES

Planning a cycle menu is quite easy if you are organized. A menu planning worksheet with the seven days of the week across the top and the three meals down the left side will help make the job quite effortless. Next, surround yourself with several good cookbooks and/or reference sheets to help spark your imagination. Then follow these simple steps:

1. Plan your main dinner entree by compiling a list and grouping them by category (beef, fish, fowl, meatless) and texture (solid, casserole, sauce); decide on frequency of popular and less popular items.

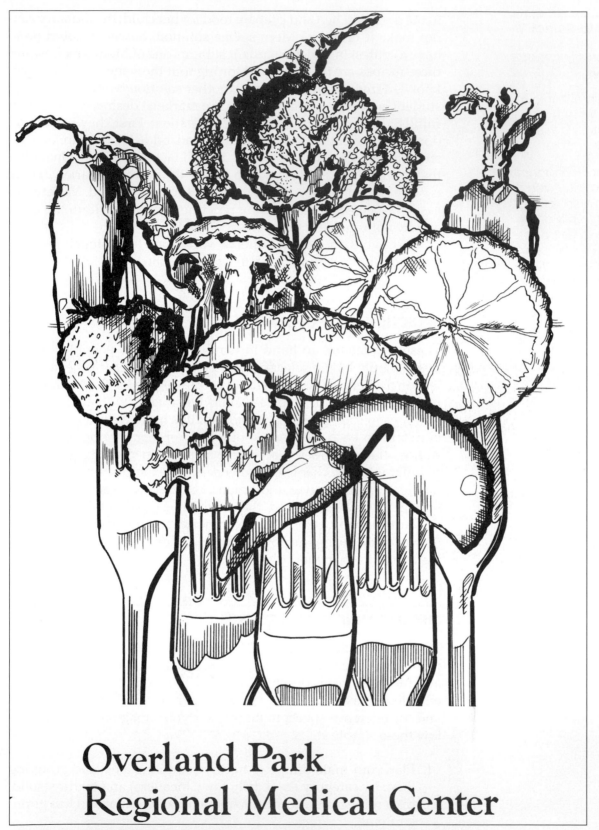

Overland Park Regional Medical Center

FIGURE 14-4. An example of a seven-day cycle hospital food service menu. Notice how the built-in variety is achieved with proper planning. (*Courtesy Overland Park Regional Medical Center, Overland Park, Kansas*)

How to Select Your Menu

The ordering procedure should be as follows:

Each menu item has a number next to it. Write the number of your selection in the boxes of the daily Marking Sheet.

Example: Spaghetti & Meat Sauce on Monday would be ordered by putting "2" in the entree box on the Luncheon Marking Sheet. Similarly, "1" in the dessert box would result in Fresh Fruit being served as a part of the noon meal. Be sure to circle each item from the bread, beverage, and condiment section you wish to receive.

Complete your Marking Sheet soon after receiving it. If you have to leave the room, please leave your finished Marking Sheet on the bed side table. If for some reason you cannot complete your Marking Sheet by pick up time, the Food Service Department will make a selection for you.

If you have a question, please ask for a Food Service representative.

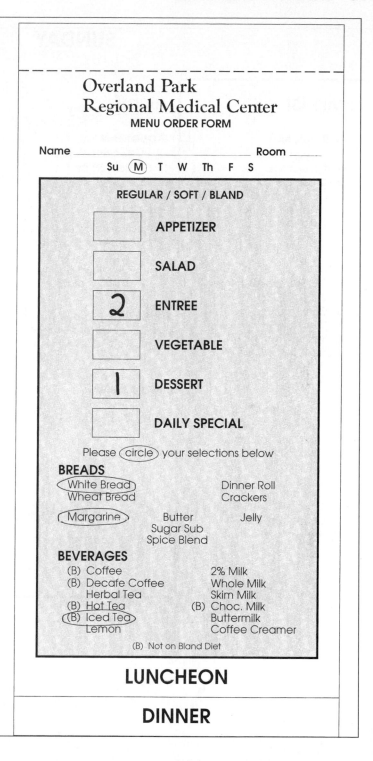

FIGURE 14-4. (Continued)

SUNDAY

Regular, Soft, Bland

BREAKFAST

Fruits & Juices
1. Orange Juice
2. Apple Juice
3. Grape Juice
4. Grapefruit Juice
5. Prune Juice
6. Banana Half
*B 7. Fresh Fruit in Season

Cereals
1. Old Fashioned Oatmeal
2. Cream of Rice
3. Corn Flakes
4. Rice Krispies
5. Special K
* 6. Shredded Wheat
*B 7. Raisin Bran
*B 8. All Bran

Breakfast Entrees
1. Scrambled Eggs
2. Low Chol. Scrambled Eggs
3. Breakfast Pastry
4. Fruited Yogurt
5. Bacon
6. Grilled Ham
B 7. Sausage
8. Cheese Omelet
9. Belgian Waffle

LUNCH

Appetizers
1. Tomato Bisque
2. Beef Broth
3. Apple Juice

Salads
*B 1. Marinated Cucumbers
2. Tossed Salad Greens
* 3. Tomato Slices
4. Garnished Cottage Cheese
5. Gelatin Salad

Entrees
1. Broiled Red Snapper
2. Roast Beef with Au Jus
3. Turkey on Croissant

Vegetables
1. Whipped Potatoes
2. Green Beans
3. Whole Baby Carrots

DINNER

Appetizers
1. Cream of Asparagus Soup
2. Chicken Broth
3. Grape Juice

Salads
1. Melon Salad
2. Tossed Salad Greens
* 3. Tomato Slices
4. Garnished Cottage Cheese
5. Gelatin Salad

Entrees
1. Chicken Kiev
2. Breaded Pork Chop

Vegetables
*B 1. Wild Rice
2. Parsiled Rice
3. Peas
4. Sliced Beets

Desserts

*B 1. Fresh Fruit in Season
2. Sherbet
B 3. Chocolate Chip Cookies
4. Custard

5. Ice Cream
6. Chilled Canned Fruit
* 7. Blueberry Pie
B 8. Apple Spice Cake

* Not on Soft Diet
B Not on Bland Diet

FIGURE 14-4. *(Continued)*

MONDAY

BREAKFAST

Fruits & Juices
1. Orange Juice
2. Apple Juice
3. Grape Juice
4. Grapefruit Juice
5. Prune Juice
6. Banana Half
*B 7. Fresh Fruit in Season

Cereals
1. Old Fashioned Oatmeal
2. Cream of Rice
3. Corn Flakes
4. Rice Krispies
5. Special K
* 6. Shredded Wheat
*B 7. Raisin Bran
*B 8. All Bran

Breakfast Entrees
1. Scrambled Eggs
2. Low Chol. Scrambled Eggs
3. Breakfast Pastry
4. Fruited Yogurt
5. Bacon
6. Grilled Ham
B 7. Sausage
8. Cheese Omelet
9. Belgian Waffle
10. French Toast

LUNCH

Appetizers
1. Cream of Mushroom Soup
2. Chicken Broth
3. Grapefruit Juice

Salads
1. Citrus Sections
2. Tossed Salad Greens
* 3. Tomato Slices
4. Garnished Cottage Cheese
5. Gelatin Salad

Entrees
1. Breaded Veal with Sauce
B 2. Spaghetti & Meatsauce

Vegetables
1. Oven Brown Potatoes
* 2. Broccoli Spears
3. Summer Squash
4. Wax Beans and Pimento

DINNER

Appetizers
1. Minestrone Soup
2. Beef Broth
3. Cranberry Juice

Salads
*B 1. Stuffed Celery
2. Tossed Salad Greens
* 3. Tomato Slices
4. Garnished Cottage Cheese
5. Gelatin Salad

Entrees
1. Baked Walleye Pike
2. Beef Burgundy

Vegetables
1. Seasoned Noodles
* 2. Mixed Vegetables
3. Spinach
4. Carrot Coins

Desserts

*B 1. Fresh Fruit in Season
2. Sherbet
B 3. Chocolate Chip Cookies
4. Custard

5. Ice Cream
6. Chilled Canned Fruit
7. Peach Pie
8. Cheese Cake

Daily Specials

1. Hamburger on Bun
2. Cheeseburger on Bun
3. Grilled Cheese Sandwich
4. Sliced Turkey Sandwich

*B 5. Chef Salad
6. Cottage Cheese Fruit Plate
7. Quiche
8. Tuna Salad on Croissant

* Not on Soft Diet
B Not on Bland Diet

FIGURE 14-4. (*Continued*)

TUESDAY

BREAKFAST

Fruits & Juices
1. Orange Juice
2. Apple Juice
3. Grape Juice
4. Grapefruit Juice
5. Prune Juice
6. Banana Half
*B 7. Fresh Fruit in Season

Cereals
1. Old Fashioned Oatmeal
2. Cream of Rice
3. Corn Flakes
4. Rice Krispies
5. Special K
* 6. Shredded Wheat
*B 7. Raisin Bran
*B 8. All Bran

Breakfast Entrees
1. Scrambled Eggs
2. Low Chol. Scrambled Eggs
3. Breakfast Pastry
4. Fruited Yogurt
5. Bacon
6. Grilled Ham
B 7. Sausage
8. Cheese Omelet
9. Belgian Waffle
10. French Toast

LUNCH

Appetizers
1. Chicken Noodle Soup
2. Beef Broth
3. Pineapple Juice

Salads
*B 1. Marinated Vegetables
2. Tossed Salad Greens
* 3. Tomato Slices
4. Garnished Cottage Cheese
5. Gelatin Salad

Entrees
1. Baked Scrod with Lemon
2. Roast Pork with Apple Slices

Vegetables
1. Scalloped Potatoes
*B 2. Whole Kernel Corn
3. Rosebud Beets
4. Early June Peas

DINNER

Appetizers
1. Cream of Tomato Soup
2. Chicken Broth
3. Lemonade

Salads
1. Jellied Cranberry Salad
2. Tossed Salad Greens
* 3. Tomato Slices
4. Garnished Cottage Cheese
5. Gelatin Salad

Entrees
1. Meat Loaf
B 2. Turkey and Dressing
3. Roast Turkey

Vegetables
1. Whipped Potatoes
* 2. Cauliflower
3. Italian Green Beans
4. Asparagus Spears

Desserts

*B 1. Fresh Fruit in Season
2. Sherbet
B 3. Chocolate Chip Cookies
4. Custard

5. Ice Cream
6. Chilled Canned Fruit
7. Cherry Pie
B 8. Boston Cream Pie

Daily Specials

1. Hamburger on Bun
2. Cheeseburger on Bun
3. Grilled Cheese Sandwich
4. Sliced Turkey Sandwich

*B 5. Chef Salad
6. Cottage Cheese Fruit Plate
B 7. Quiche
8. Tuna Salad on Croissant

* Not on Soft Diet
B Not on Bland Diet

FIGURE 14-4. (Continued)

WEDNESDAY

BREAKFAST

Fruits & Juices
1. Orange Juice
2. Apple Juice
3. Grape Juice
4. Grapefruit Juice
5. Prune Juice
6. Banana Half

*B 7. Fresh Fruit in Season

Cereals
1. Old Fashioned Oatmeal
2. Cream of Rice
3. Corn Flakes
4. Rice Krispies
5. Special K

* 6. Shredded Wheat

*B 7. Raisin Bran

*B 8. All Bran

Breakfast Entrees
1. Scrambled Eggs
2. Low Chol. Scrambled Eggs
3. Breakfast Pastry
4. Fruited Yogurt
5. Bacon
6. Grilled Ham

B 7. Sausage
8. Cheese Omelet
9. Belgian Waffle
10. French Toast

LUNCH

Appetizers
1. Beef Vegetable Soup
2. Chicken Broth
3. Apple Juice

Salads
1. Shrimp Salad
2. Tossed Salad Greens

* 3. Tomato Slices
4. Garnished Cottage Cheese
5. Gelatin Salad

Entrees
*B 1. Southern Fried Chicken
2. Baked Chicken
3. Salisbury Steak

Vegetables
1. Whipped Potatoes
2. Broiled Tomato
3. Spinach

DINNER

Appetizers
1. Cream of Potato Soup
2. Beef Broth
3. V-8 Juice

Salads
*B 1. Mandarin Orange Romaine
2. Tossed Salad Greens

* 3. Tomato Slices
4. Garnished Cottage Cheese
5. Gelatin Salad

Entrees
1. Orange Roughy
2. K.C. Strip

Vegetables
1. Baked Potato
2. Glazed Carrots
3. Wax Beans with Pimento

Desserts

*B 1. Fresh Fruit in Season
2. Sherbet

B 3. Chocolate Chip Cookies
4. Vanilla Pudding

5. Ice Cream
6. Chilled Canned Fruit

B 7. Chocolate Cream Pie
8. Banana Cake

Daily Specials

1. Hamburger on Bun
2. Cheeseburger on Bun
3. Grilled Cheese Sandwich
4. Sliced Turkey Sandwich

*B 5. Chef Salad
6. Cottage Cheese Fruit Plate

B 7. Quiche
8. Tuna Salad on Croissant

* Not on Soft Diet

B Not on Bland Diet

FIGURE 14-4.   (*Continued*)

THURSDAY

BREAKFAST

Fruits & Juices
1. Orange Juice
2. Apple Juice
3. Grape Juice
4. Grapefruit Juice
5. Prune Juice
6. Banana Half
*B 7. Fresh Fruit in Season

Cereals
1. Old Fashioned Oatmeal
2. Cream of Rice
3. Corn Flakes
4. Rice Krispies
5. Special K
* 6. Shredded Wheat
*B 7. Raisin Bran
*B 8. All Bran

Breakfast Entrees
1. Scrambled Eggs
2. Low Chol. Scrambled Eggs
3. Breakfast Pastry
4. Fruited Yogurt
5. Bacon
6. Grilled Ham
B 7. Sausage
8. Cheese Omelet
9. Belgian Waffle
10. French Toast

LUNCH

Appetizers
1. Cream of Chicken Soup
2. Beef Broth
3. Fruit Punch

Salads
*B 1. Pasta Salad
2. Tossed Salad Greens
* 3. Tomato Slices
4. Garnished Cottage Cheese
5. Gelatin Salad

Entrees
1. Baked Filet of Sole
2. Hot Roast Beef Sandwich

Vegetables
1. Whipped Potatoes
2. Julienne Beets
* 3. Broccoli Spears
4. Green Beans with Mushrooms

DINNER

Appetizers
1. Beef Noodle Soup
2. Chicken Broth
3. Grape Juice

Salads
*B 1. Spinach Salad
2. Tossed Salad Greens
* 3. Tomato Slices
4. Garnished Cottage Cheese
5. Gelatin Salad

Entrees
1. Swedish Meatballs
2. Cornish Game Hen

Vegetables
1. Rice Pilaf
2. Summer Squash
3. Asparagus Spears

Desserts
*B 1. Fresh Fruit in Season
2. Sherbet
B 3. Chocolate Chip Cookies
4. Custard

5. Ice Cream
6. Chilled Canned Fruit
7. Apple Pie
* 8. Carrot Cake

Daily Specials
1. Hamburger on Bun
2. Cheeseburger on Bun
3. Grilled Cheese Sandwich
4. Sliced Turkey Sandwich

*B 5. Chef Salad
6. Cottage Cheese Fruit Plate
B 7. Quiche
8. Tuna Salad on Croissant

* Not on Soft Diet
B Not on Bland Diet

FIGURE 14-4. (Continued)

FRIDAY

BREAKFAST

Fruits & Juices
1. Orange Juice
2. Apple Juice
3. Grape Juice
4. Grapefruit Juice
5. Prune Juice
6. Banana Half
*B 7. Fresh Fruit in Season

Cereals
1. Old Fashioned Oatmeal
2. Cream of Rice
3. Corn Flakes
4. Rice Krispies
5. Special K
* 6. Shredded Wheat
*B 7. Raisin Bran
*B 8. All Bran

Breakfast Entrees
1. Scrambled Eggs
2. Low Chol. Scrambled Eggs
3. Breakfast Pastry
4. Fruited Yogurt
5. Bacon
6. Grilled Ham
B 7. Sausage
8. Cheese Omelet
9. Belgian Waffle
10. French Toast

LUNCH

Appetizers
1. Split Pea Soup
2. Chicken Broth
3. Cranberry Juice

Salads
1. Pineapple Orange Salad
2. Tossed Salad Greens
* 3. Tomato Slices
4. Garnished Cottage Cheese
5. Gelatin Salad

Entrees
1. Swiss Steak
2. Macaroni & Cheese

Vegetables
1. Parslied Potatoes
2. Spinach
3. Sliced Carrots

DINNER

Appetizers
1. Vegetable Soup
2. Beef Broth
3. Grapefruit Juice

Salads
*B 1. Marinated Artichoke Hearts
2. Tossed Salad Greens
* 3. Tomato Slices
4. Garnished Cottage Cheese
5. Gelatin Salad

Entrees
1. Halibut Steak
2. Beef Stroganoff

Vegetables
1. Seasoned Noodles
2. Early June Peas
3. Wax Beans

Desserts
*B 1. Fresh Fruit in Season
2. Sherbet
B 3. Chocolate Chip Cookies
4. Tapioca Pudding
5. Ice Cream
6. Chilled Canned Fruit
7. Banana Cream Pie
B 8. Eclair

Daily Specials
1. Hamburger on Bun
2. Cheeseburger on Bun
3. Grilled Cheese Sandwich
4. Sliced Turkey Sandwich
*B 5. Chef Salad
6. Cottage Cheese Fruit Plate
B 7. Quiche
8. Tuna Salad on Croissant

*- Not on Soft Diet
B Not on Bland Diet

FIGURE 14-4. (Continued)

SATURDAY

BREAKFAST

Fruits & Juices
1. Orange Juice
2. Apple Juice
3. Grape Juice
4. Grapefruit Juice
5. Prune Juice
6. Banana Half
*B 7. Fresh Fruit in Season

Cereals
1. Old Fashioned Oatmeal
2. Cream of Rice
3. Corn Flakes
4. Rice Krispies
5. Special K
 * 6. Shredded Wheat
*B 7. Raisin Bran
*B 8. All Bran

Breakfast Entrees
1. Scrambled Eggs
2. Low Chol. Scrambled Eggs
3. Breakfast Pastry
4. Fruited Yogurt
5. Bacon
6. Grilled Ham
B 7. Sausage
8. Cheese Omelet
9. Belgian Waffle

LUNCH

Appetizers
1. Cream of Potato Soup
2. Chicken Broth
3. Lemonade

Salads
*B 1. Coleslaw
2. Tossed Salad Greens
 * 3. Tomato Slices
4. Garnished Cottage Cheese
5. Gelatin Salad

Entrees
1. Roast Veal Normandie
B 2. Lasagna
*B 3. Filet of Fish Sandwich
4. Baked Filet of Cod

Vegetables
*B 1. O'Brien Potatoes
2. Whipped Potatoes
3. Asparagus Spears
4. Vegetable Medley

DINNER

Appetizers
1. French Onion Soup
2. Beef Broth
3. Pineapple Juice

Salads
*B 1. Bean Salad
2. Tossed Salad Greens
 * 3. Tomato Slices
4. Garnished Cottage Cheese
5. Gelatin Salad

Entrees
1. Filet Mignon
2. Chicken and Noodles
3. Ham Sandwich on a Bun

Vegetables
1. Baked Potato
2. Sauteed Mushrooms
3. Broiled Tomato
*B 4. Corn on the Cob

Desserts

*B 1. Fresh Fruit in Season
2. Sherbet
B 3. Chocolate Chip Cookies
4. Custard

5. Ice Cream
6. Chilled Canned Fruit
 * 7. Strawberry-Rhubard Pie
B 8. Devils Food Cake

* Not on Soft Diet
B Not on Bland Diet

FIGURE 14-4. *(Continued)*

2. List the entree on your menu planning worksheet using popular items only.

3. Complete steps 1 and 2 for lunch and breakfast.

4. Add second and third entrees. These entrees should complement the main entree and can be from the less popular list.

5. Plan the vegetables, starches, and soup for lunch and dinner.

6. Plan your salads. Salads should offer variety in type, color and consistency.

7. Plan desserts—same as salads.

8. List breads, condiments and beverages.

9. List hot/cold cereals, breakfast fruits and juices.

10. Review menu for color, frequency of items served, texture, and consistency. Make adjustments as necessary.

CONCLUSION

When writing cycle menus, make them interesting. Good variety, popular items, and nutritionally balanced menus properly prepared and served will go a long way toward making clients happy. It's just that simple.

QUESTIONS

1. What cycle length would you recommend for the following type of food service?
   a). Hospital
   b). College dorm
   c). In-plant food service
   d). Commercial restaurant

2. What three factors should be taken into account for clip-on specials and why are they important?

3. Discuss the difference when writing menus for a captive audience as opposed to a commercial restaurant.

4. Discuss the role of nutrition in menu planning for:
   a). Commercial restaurants
   b). Semi-captive food service
   c). Captive food service

5. Explain and give examples of the "basic four food pyramid."

6. Write a one week menu for a:
   a). Type A lunch for a grade school
   b). College dormitory

Menu Analysis

OBJECTIVES	• To learn how to analyze a menu from both the profitability and aesthetic aspects.
	• To understand menu engineering and menu scoring methods of menu analysis.

IMPORTANT TERMS	Stars	Plow horses
	Puzzles	Dogs
	Menu engineering	Menu scoring
	Aesthetic analysis	

INTRODUCTION

Throughout the textbook, we have delved into all of the various components of a successful menu. This chapter will help you evaluate menus. When analyzing a menu, two criteria must be met in declaring it a success. One, it must be profitable, and two, it must be aesthetically pleasing to our customer. In examining menu profitability, there are many formulas available. Two of the most popular are presented in this chapter and another product mix is presented in Chapter 16. The reason that they are popular is not only that they are useful, but they force the manager to take a strong look at the menu and its profitability.

STARS, PLOW HORSES, PUZZLES, AND DOGS

This method, developed by Donald Smith, Westin Distinguished Professor at Washington State University, breaks menu items into four classifications:

1. stars,
2. plow horses,
3. puzzles, and
4. dogs.

To use this method, the contribution margin of each item is determined. To figure the contribution margin (CM), take the total food cost (FC) and subtract this from the selling price (SP). Thus, the formula looks like this:

$$SP - FC = CM$$

Remember, food cost is total. That is the time cost plus garnish cost plus any accompaniments served with that item such as salad, potatoes, rolls, butter, and so on.

FIGURE 15-1. Contribution margin in dollars vs. food cost in percent.

	Steak Dinner	Fish Sandwich	Coffee
Selling price	$15.00	$4.00	$0.75
Cost	$7.50	$1.00	$0.15
Food cost %	50%	25%	20%
Cont. Margin $	$7.50	$3.00	$0.60

In the above example, coffee has the lowest food cost but is also contributing the least amount in terms of real dollars to the profit picture.

Notice in the illustration that the relationship between food cost percent and contribution margin in dollars is often quite different from each other. In other words, an item which has a high contribution margin in dollars does not necessarily have a low food cost in percent. Too often, managers are led to believe that low food cost percents are the primary objective. Not so. As one cynical wag put it, you don't take percents to the bank, you take money.

USING MENU ENGINEERING

Let's see how menu engineering works in actual practice. Johny's Grill is a table specialty restaurant with 10 items on its dinner menu. Figure 15-2 shows how menu engineering was used to analyze Johny's menu for a 30-day period.

1. First, the operator lists all menu entrees in column A. Only entree items are listed. Do not list appetizers, desserts or other side items. Do not list alcoholic beverage sales on this list. The ratio of food to beverage sales is a key to successful merchandising in most restaurants. The analysis of beverage sales, however, should be done separately. While we separate purchases for the purpose of our menu analysis, the successful operator is always concerned with the guests' total expenditure. Daily specials must also be analyzed separately. By listing purchases of daily specials separately, their impact on the menu is more easily identified. If the operator's suggestive selling program is effective, daily specials should become popular with relatively high contribution margins.

2. The total number of purchases for each item is listed in column B, menu mix. All purchases are listed on a per person basis.

3. Each item's sales is divided by the total number of purchases—3,000 in this case—to determine that item's menu mix percentage, column C.

4. In column D, each item's menu mix percentage is categorized as either high or low. Any menu item that is lower than 70 percent of the menu mix average percentage is considered low. Any item that is 70 percent or above average is considered high. On a 10-item menu, for example, each item would theoretically get 10 percent of the mix. On a 20-item menu the average would be 5 percent. For Johny's ten item-menu, we multiply 10 percent times 70 percent to get the desired menu mix percentage rate of .07, or 7 percent. Any item 7 percent or higher is considered high. Any item less than 7 percent is low.

5. Each item's published menu selling cost is listed in column E.

6. Each item's standard food cost is listed in column F. An item's standard portion cost is composed of standard recipe costs, gar-

nish cost, and supplemental food cost. Not all items, however, will have all three cost components.

7. The contribution margin for each item is listed in column G. Contribution margins are determined by subtracting the item's standard food cost (column F) from its selling cost (column E).

8. In column H we determine the total menu revenues by multiplying the number of purchases of each item (column B) by its selling cost (column E).

9. In column I we determine the total menu food cost by multiplying each item's standard food cost (column F) by the number of items purchased (column B).

10. The total menu contribution margin is listed in column J. This is determined by multiplying each item's contribution margin (column G) times the item's total number of purchases (column B).

11. In column K we list the contribution margin percentage for each item. This is determined by dividing each item's contribution margin by the total menu contribution margin which is the total of column J. $10,538.

12. Each item's contribution margin is categorized as either high or low in column L, depending upon whether or not the item exceeds the menu's average contribution margin. The menu's average contribution margin is determined by dividing the total contribution margin ($10,538) column J, by the total number of items sold, 3,000. The average contribution margin for Johny's Grill is $3.51.

13. We use all the data we have gathered to classify each item into categories in column M. Each menu item is classified as either a star, plow horse, puzzle, or dog level in standard marketing theory terms.

14. In column N we list the decisions made on each item. Should the item be retained, repositioned, replaced or repriced?

THE FOUR KEY MENU CATEGORIES

When accurate information has been gathered and analyzed for each menu item as we have done in Figure 15-2, the items are then categorized for decision making. All menu items can be grouped into four categories: stars, plow horses, puzzles, and dogs.

Stars. Menu items high in both popularity and contribution margin. Stars are the most popular items on your menu. They may be your signature items.

Plow Horses. Menu items high in popularity but low in contribution margin. Plow horses are demand generators. They may be the lead item on your menu or your signature item. They are often significant to the restaurant's popularity with price-conscious buyers.

Puzzles. Menu items low in popularity but high in contribution margin. In other words, puzzles yield a high profit per item sold, but they are hard to sell.

Dogs. Menu items low in popularity and low in contribution margin. These are your losers. They are unpopular, and they generate little profit.

HOW TO USE THE CATEGORIES

Once you have grouped your menu into the four key categories, you are ready to make decisions. Each category must be analyzed and evaluated separately.

Stars. You must maintain rigid specifications for quality, quantity, and presentation of all star items. Locate them in a highly visible position on the menu. Test them occasionally for price rigidity. Are guests willing to pay more for these items, and still buy them in significant quantity? The super stars of your menu—highest priced stars—may be less price sensitive than any other items on the menu. If so, these items may be able to carry a larger portion of any increase in cost of goods and labor.

Plow Horses. These items are often an important reason for a restaurant's popularity. Increase their prices carefully. If plow horses are highly price sensitive, attempt to pass only the cost of goods increase on to the menu price. Or, consider placing the increase on to a super star item. Test for a negative effect on demand (rigidity). Make any price increase in stages (from $4.55 to $4.75 then $4.95). If it is necessary to increase prices, pass through only the additional cost. Do not add more. Relocate nonsignature and low contribution margin plow horses to a lower profile position on the menu. Attempt to shift demand to more profitable items by merchandising and menu positioning. If the item is an image maker or signature item, hold its current price as long as possible in periods of high price sensitivity.

    Determine the direct labor cost of each plow horse to establish its labor and skill intensiveness. If the item requires high skills or is labor intensive, consider a price increase or substitution. Also, consider reducing the item's standard portion without making the difference noticeable. Merchandise the plow horse by packaging it with side items to increase its contribution margin. Another option is to use the item to create a "better value alternative." For example, prime rib can be sold by the inch, and steaks can be sold by the ounce. This offers guests an opportunity to spend more and get more value.

Puzzles. Take them off the menu, particularly if a puzzle is low in popularity, requires costly or additional inventory, has poor shelf life, requires skilled or labor intensive preparation, and is of inconsistent quality. Another option is to reposition the puzzle and feature it in a more popular location on the menu. You can try adding value to the item through table d'hote packaging. Rename it. A puzzle's popularity can be affected by what it is called especially if the name can be made to sound familiar.

Decrease the puzzle's price. The item may have a contribution margin that is too high and is facing price resistance. Care must be taken, however, not to lower the contribution margin to a point where the puzzle draws menu share from a star. Increase the menu's price and test for rigidity. A puzzle that has relatively high popularity may be rigid.

Limit the number of puzzles you allow on your menu. Puzzles can create difficulties in quality consistency, slow production down, and cause inventory and cost problems. You must accurately evaluate the effect puzzle items have on your image. Do they enhance your image?

Dogs. Eliminate all dog items if possible. Food service operators are often intimidated by influential guests to carry a dog item on the menu. The way to solve this problem is to carry the item in inventory (assuming it has a shelf life) but not on the menu. The special guest is offered the opportunity to have the item made to order upon request. Charge extra for this service. Raise the dog's price to puzzle status. Some items in the dog category may have market potential. These tend to be the more popular dogs, and may be converted to puzzles.

Whenever possible, replace dogs with more popular items. You may have too many items. It is not unusual to discover a number of highly unpopular menu items with little, if any, relation to other more popular and profitable items held in inventory. Do not be afraid to terminate dogs, especially when demand is not satisfactory.

Using the above explanations, let's analyze and attempt to improve our menu. Menu planning is both a science and an art. We have just completed the scientific part. The numbers tell us an accurate story of what actually happened. The changes we make are the art part of the equation. This is not as exact as the numbers. There are many options available and we will not all agree on these

FIGURE 15-2.   Stars, plow horses, puzzles, & dogs

A Entrees	B Purch.	C Mix %	D Mix Cat.	E Selling Price	F Food Cost	G Cont. Margin	H Total Rev.
ITEM 1	170	06%	LOW	$5.95	$2.10	$3.85	$1012
ITEM 2	450	15%	HIGH	$6.25	$2.60	$3.65	$2813
ITEM 3	350	12%	HIGH	$4.50	$1.25	$3.25	$1575
ITEM 4	380	13%	HIGH	$4.95	$1.55	$3.40	$1881
ITEM 5	80	03%	LOW	$6.10	$3.00	$3.10	$ 488
ITEM 6	410	14%	HIGH	$5.50	$1.80	$3.70	$2255
ITEM 7	290	10%	HIGH	$5.85	$2.45	$3.40	$1697
ITEM 8	320	11%	HIGH	$4.85	$1.60	$3.25	$1552
ITEM 9	440	15%	HIGH	$5.25	$1.50	$3.75	$2310
ITEM 10	110	04%	LOW	$4.95	$1.60	$3.35	$ 545
TOTALS	3000						

A Entrees	I Total food Cost	J Total Cont. Mgn.	K Cont. Margin %	L Cont. Mgn.	M Class. Cat.	N Decision
ITEM 1	$ 357	$ 655	06%	HIGH	PUZZLE	LOWER S.P. TO $5.75
ITEM 2	$1170	$ 1643	16%	HIGH	STAR	LEAVE IT ALONE
ITEM 3	$ 438	$ 1138	11%	LOW	PLOW HORSE	RAISE S.P. TO $4.75
ITEM 4	$ 589	$ 1292	12%	LOW	PLOW HORSE	LEAVE IT ALONE
ITEM 5	$ 240	$ 248	02%	LOW	DOG	ELIMINATE IT
ITEM 6	$ 738	$ 1517	14%	HIGH	STAR	LEAVE IT ALONE
ITEM 7	$ 711	$ 986	09%	LOW	PLOW HORSE	REDUCE PORTION
ITEM 8	$ 512	$ 1040	10%	LOW	PLOW HORSE	RAISE TO $5.25
ITEM 9	$ 660	$ 1650	16%	HIGH	STAR	LEAVE IT ALONE
ITEM 10	$ 176	$ 369	04%	LOW	DOG	ELIMINATE IT
TOTALS		$10538		AVE.C.M. $3.51		

options. However, the decisions made will have a direct impact on the success of our menu.

Item #1. A puzzle. High contribution margin, but very low unit sales. Lowering the selling price to $5.75 could increase unit sales.

Item #2. A star. Leave it alone.

Item #3. A plow horse. Lowest selling price on menu as well as lowest contribution margin which in turn is the best price value relationship. By carefully increasing the selling price to $4.75, the item is the still lowest priced but the contribution margin increases.

Item #4. A plow horse. Probably signature item of the restaurant based on high number sold. An increase in selling price would break the $5 barrier. A decrease in portion size or change in formula could ruin sales. Leave it alone.

Item #5. A dog. Eliminate it and replace with a new and exciting menu item.

Item #6. A star. Leave it alone.

Item #7. A plow horse. By reducing the portion of this item and its cost to $2.20, the contribution margin would increase. Assuming a minimal drop in sales, this item would become a star.

Item #8. A plow horse. Let's try breaking the price barrier by packaging it with a side item and selling it for $5.25. Cost would increase to $1.85.

Item #9. A star. Leave it alone.

Item #10. A dog. Eliminate it and replace it with a trendy new item.

MENU SCORING

Another method of evaluating menu profitability is menu scoring. This method was developed by Michael Hurst, Professor of Florida International University. It was devised to ascertain if menu changes (i.e., additions, deletions, and price adjustments) actually improved the profitability of the menu by comparisons of a menu score. To determine a menu's score simply follow these steps.

A) Determine the items that contribute a major portion of sales income and select those to be evaluated. Unless the income from sandwiches, salads, beverages or others is significant, do not include these.

B) Calculate the food cost for each item to be evaluated (Column D).

C) Prepare a menu count for the period of the items to be evaluated (Column B).

D) Calculate the menu score as follows by obtaining:
   1. Total item sales dollars (Column F) [number of items sold (Column B) × their selling price]. Column C
   2. Total item food cost dollars (Column G) number of items sold (Column B) × item food cost (Column D).
   3. Total the sales dollars for all items to be evaluated (Column F), total the food cost dollars for all items to be evaluated (Column G), and total the number of items sold of those to be evaluated in the period (Column B).
   4. Figure the composite food cost by dividing total cost (Column G) by total sales (Column F).
   5. Dollar meal average—total sales dollars (Column F) divided by total number of items sold (Column B).
   6. Gross profit percentage of items evaluated during the period. Sales in percent (100%)—(Column F) less food cost in percent

(Step 4), equals gross profit percent for items evaluated during the period.

7. Average gross profit dollars per meal—dollar meal average (Step 5) times gross profit percentage (Step 6).
8. Percentage of menu being tested—total number of items sold (Column B) divided by total number of customers served by the operation during this period.
9. Menu score—gross profit average (Step 7) times percentage of customers eating items evaluated (Step 8).

The higher the score, the more profitable the menu. One menu score by itself is useless as scores need to be compared against each other to determine if the menu is increasing in profitability.[1]

FIGURE 15-3. Menu scoring exercise.

A Item	B # Sold	C Item Sell Price	D Item Food Cost	E FC %	F Total Sales	G Total Cost	
Totals							

STEP 4.
<u>TOTAL COST</u> = COMP. FOOD COST
TOTAL SALES

STEP 5.
<u>TOTAL SALES</u> = DOLLAR MEAL AVERAGE
ITEMS SOLD

STEP 6.
SALES %
<u>– FOOD COST %</u>
GROSS PROFIT

STEP 7.
AVERAGE SALE
<u>× GROSS PROFIT %</u>
GROSS PROFIT %

STEP 8.
<u>TOTAL MEALS TESTED</u> = % OF MENU BEING TESTED
TOTAL MEALS SOLD

STEP 9.
GROSS PROFIT $
<u>× % MENU UNDER TEST</u>
MENU SCORE

WHICH METHOD TO USE

Whichever method is used, they both accomplish basically the same thing. They force management to look at their menu in terms of profitability. Profitability can only mean one thing to the restaurateur—success.

Reprinted with permission from *Management By Menu, Second Edition*, by Lendal H. Kotschevar. Copyright © 1987 by the Educational Foundation of the National Restaurant Association, Chicago, Il.

ANALYZING AESTHETICS

In addition to being profitable for the owner, the menu must be pleasing to the customer. In order to analyze the aesthetics we need to look at the art work, design, layout, type, copy, merchandising, marketing, mechanical considerations, and creativity. A menu aesthetics checklist, Figure 15-4, takes all of these areas into consideration and numerically rates each of them. Thus a person can rate their own menu in terms of style and salability.

CONCLUSION

Menu analysis is important. If we have done our work correctly, we will have a good score. Analysis should be done both objectively and subjectively, using either the Smith or Hurst methods to ascertain the profitability of the menu—subjectively, scoring the menu for aesthetics. If the analysis shows a poor menu, we need to regroup and make improvements. If, on the other hand, it shows that a good menu has been produced, we have taken the first step toward running a successful operation. It's just that simple!

FIGURE 15-4. Menu aesthetics checklist.

Cover
___ Reflects the theme of the restaurant
___ Has imaginative and creative artwork
___ Has unusual shape or design
___ Is constructed of durable stock
___ Gives address, phone, and other pertinent information
___ Is clean

Inside
___ Categories are listed in proper sequence
___ Headings are used to separate categories and are in bold type
___ Listings are worded utilizing descriptive terminology
___ Truth in menu is followed
___ Prime space is properly used for high gross item and is boxed in
___ Type is easily read and is 12 points minimum
___ Wine and cocktails, if applicable, are suggested in the appropriate locations
___ Clip-ons, if used, are printed on the same quality of paper and in the same style of type
___ Clip-ons do not cover regular item listings
___ Psychological pricing is utilized
___ There are no add-on charges (i.e., sour cream or bleu cheese extra)
___ Negative terminology is not used
___ Artwork is used to tie in with the cover and the theme of the restaurant
___ Institutional copy is used to enhance the theme
___ Marketing for banquets, catering, carry outs, and/or delivery is present

QUESTIONS

1. Using the following data, develop a star, plow horse, puzzle, and dog chart as well as a menu scoring chart (using four out of the six entrees).

Entree	Purchases	Selling Price	Cost
Item I	$150	$9.95	$4.70
Item II	300	7.25	2.90
Item III	250	8.75	3.50
Item IV	500	6.95	2.45
Item V	50	7.50	3.60
Item VI	400	8.95	2.70

2. Complete a star, plow horse, puzzle, and dog marketing grid for the above problem.

3. Improve the above menu using the concepts learned in this chapter. Defend all of your changes.

4. Redo the star, plow horse, puzzle, and dog chart as well as your menu scoring chart to see if the changes have improved your menu.

CHAPTER SIXTEEN

Profitability and the Menu

OBJECTIVES
- To illustrate how profitability is tied to a menu.
- To comprehend how product mix can define an operation's problem areas.
- To understand how a menu interrelates with each department in a food service.

IMPORTANT TERMS

Standard costs	Product mix
Inventory turnover	Quality control
Portion control	

INTRODUCTION

As we stated at the start of the text, everything starts with the menu and most important, profit starts with the menu. Exactly how the menu relates to profitability is sometimes a confusing issue. To clarify this, a logical walkthrough of a typical operation will be taken. Start with the menu itself, then move on to purchasing, receiving, storage, production, and service, to observe how the menu interrelates to each of these areas and also how in some cases it interrelates to established controls.

THE MENU

Before we can begin our discussion of profitability in relation to the menu, we must first understand standard costs. Standard costs are ideal costs. In other words, they are what the costs should be. Standard costs are determined by management and are used as a measurement against actual costs. Once standard cost percents are determined, then the menu selling prices can be figured. As studied in the chapter on menu pricing, the selling price needs to cover all costs not just food costs. How well an operation meets its objective in relation to standard costs is shown on the income statement. When variable and semi-variable costs, such as food and labor, are out of line, many things could have gone wrong to cause this to happen. The first logical step in tracing this problem is the menu.

Food cost in particular can be checked by developing a product mix which is done by following these logical steps:

1. Up date cost cards by verifying that all costs are current. If they are not, then change them to reflect current costs.
2. Divide the current cost of the item by the menu selling price to determine a percentage.
3. Count the number of items sold for the period under study.
4. Multiply the number of items sold by the selling price to get total sales for each item.
5. Multiply total sales of each item by the standard food cost percent developed in B to get total food cost in dollars for the time.
6. Total the sales column and the food cost column.
7. Divide the total of the food cost column by the total of the sales column to get a composite food cost percentage.

The composite food cost percentage from the product mix should then be compared to the standard food cost for the restaurant. If there is a variance between the composite and the standard, and this variance equals the difference between the standard and the actual on the income statement, then the problem of a high food cost lies in the menu pricing structure. For example, if a standard food cost of 35 percent has been decided on by management and the income statement shows an actual food cost of 40 percent and a subsequent analysis of the product mix also shows 40 percent, the menu pricing structure needs to be increased 2 percent overall or the composite food cost (product mix) needs to be lowered 2%.

FIGURE 16-1.

Item	No. Items Sold	Price	Sales	Food Cost %	Food Cost $
Prime Rib	350	$8.50	$2,975	38%	$1,130
Red Snapper	190	6.95	1,320	34%	449
Chicken Kiev	340	6.75	2,295	30%	689
K.C. Strip	225	8.50	1,913	42%	803
Rack of Lamb	40	7.95	318	40%	127
			$8,821		$3,198

36.3% food cost

$8,821/$3,198

The first inclination of most managers in this case is to increase prices. While this would certainly be a solution to the problem, it may not be the wisest choice. Care must be taken when increasing prices not to exceed the price value relationship perceived by the customers. However, in some instances, this would be the only viable choice.

Other alternatives would be to eliminate high cost-slow selling items (dogs in our discussion in the previous chapter) and replace them with low cost items that have high sales potential. Another consideration would be the evaluation of portions. However, as in the case of increasing prices, care must be exercised not to exceed the price value relationship by cutting portions to the extent of causing customers discontent.

When comparing the product mix with the actual food cost, if the variance is greater than the standard, the problem is partially with the menu and partially with other factors. For example, if the actual food cost percent on our income statement was 40 percent and the product mix showed a food cost of 38 percent and our standard food cost was 35 percent, we could conclude that 2 percent of the variance was in menu pricing and 3 percent was a problem other than pricing.

If, on the other hand, the food cost percent on the product mix and the standard were equal and the actual had a variance, then the entire problem relates to other areas. In the above example, if the product mix and standard were both 35 percent and the actual were

40 percent, then none of our problems would be pricing related. To investigate where these problems could be, start with purchasing.

PURCHASING

There are three considerations to be studied in the relationship of the menu to purchasing. The first of these is price fluctuation of goods purchased. The menu should be carefully scrutinized to see if it contains listings that drastically change from season to season. Fresh produce is a prime example. While listings of this nature cannot be completely avoided, they should be kept to a minimum. Ideally, the menu would contain only listings that have a relatively stable price throughout the year, thus giving a constant cost/price structure. In cases where this is not possible, then a worst case scenario should be used. In other words, when listing an item which has a price fluctuation, use the highest projected purchase price when figuring its cost.

Another area to be checked is the quality level of goods purchased. This level should be compatible to the quality stated on the menu. To do otherwise would be in violation of the Truth in Menu agreement. Furthermore, the quality level stated on the menu and subsequently purchased should be compatible in its selling price with the demographics of the customer. For example, if the menu stated USDA prime steaks and this is what was purchased, is the customer willing to pay for this level of quality? Would more steaks be sold if the menu listing were changed to USDA choice at a lower selling price? This would have to be ascertained for each individual restaurant depending on the circumstances of its customers. The point is that an overzealous menu writer can sometimes put the operation in a bind when purchasing costs and subsequently menu selling prices are not compatible with what the customer is willing to pay.

The third area to be investigated is inventory turnover. The menu should be selling a sufficient number of any particular item to warrant its being purchased. Here we return to our discussion of dogs. They should be removed from the menu to avoid purchasing unused goods which do nothing more than spoil, drive up the food cost, and tie up cash flow.

STORAGE

Closely related to the purchasing of goods is the storage of goods. Two issues need to be considered here: First, the aforementioned purchasing of unnecessary items which take up storage space; and, second, the storage of goods in the proper amount to conduct business. To elaborate further on this subject, foods need to be divided into two categories: perishable and non-perishable. Perishable goods are those items which have a very short shelf life, such as fresh meats, fresh produce, dairy products, and bakery items. Perishables should be inventoried and ordered frequently, depending on the product, daily or at the most every three days. Non-perishables, on the other hand, have a longer shelf life. Staples such as canned goods, dehydrated items, flours, and mixes, fall into this category. Non-perishables are normally ordered weekly.

Two things can happen at this stage, both bad. One, there is an inadequate supply of goods to meet consumer demand; and, two, there is an overabundance of goods, thus tying up cash flow. To avoid this, an accurate account of customers and their selections is necessary.

PRODUCTION

The relationship between the menu and production controls lies primarily in two areas, one, quantity and two, quality. With quantity control, the prime fact is producing only the amounts necessary to meet demand. To properly achieve this, the aforementioned formula for determining the amount of goods to purchase can also be utilized to specify the number of each item on the menu to prepare for any given meal period. The objective of quantity control is to eliminate leftovers. While the goal of absolutely no leftovers is practically impossible to achieve, the closer the operation comes to achieving this, the better its food cost will be. When confronted with a leftover problem, management oftentimes struggles with various options trying to figure out a way to disguise them into salable items. Often the selling price gets reduced, resulting in a higher food cost percentage. Worse yet is not even using leftovers, which will leave the operator with a cost that will never be recovered. As stated by many wise restaurateurs, the best way to handle leftovers is to not have them in the first place.

Quality control in the kitchen is also an important aspect of controlling food cost. Starting with the menu, the customer perceives a certain item tasting the way the menu describes it. This item is, in turn, listed that way because the standardized recipe indicates the outcome. That item is further costed out based on the amounts of particular ingredients called for in the standardized recipe. The selling price is determined by the financial needs of the restaurant and is based on the recipe cost. All of this, as you have discovered, is an exacting science. When quality control is lacking and the standardized recipes are not followed, the whole scheme falls into disarray. The item is "overprepared," using more expensive ingredients or more of one particular ingredient resulting in a higher cost than was originally intended. Worse yet, costs are cut by eliminating or using low quality ingredients resulting in dissatisfied customers and, consequently, lost sales.

PLATING

The final consideration for using the menu as a cost control device is in the plating function. Here again, two things can go wrong: overportioning or underportioning. On the menu listing portions are sometimes explicit, like a "12 oz. sirloin steak." Many times a portion is implied such as a "heaping serving of spaghetti." To cut a portion below what the menu states or implies would be in violation of Truth in Menu and would also result in an irate customer. To overportion would result in a cost for that item over and above your original intention. Portion control is an exacting science and must be followed without exception to please both the customer and the income statement.

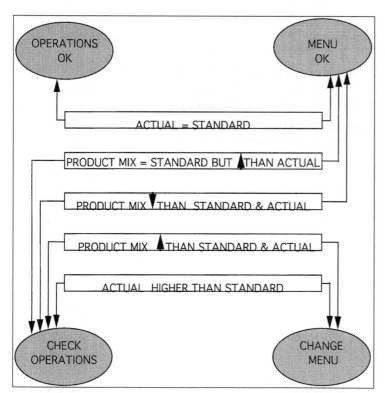

FIGURE 16-4. *Actual vs. product mix. U.S. Standard*

CONCLUSION

While the total discussion of controls in a food service operation is beyond the scope of this text, those controls that pertain to the menu have been illustrated. The menu, in essence, ties the entire operation together and without using it as a control, the manager loses one of the most effective tools available to keep food costs in line. The entire operation starts with the menu. Product description and portions help the customer decide what to order. This same menu tells the operator which items to purchase and how much, how to prepare items, and what size portions to serve. By planning and writing the menu properly and by following the plan set forth on the menu, two things will happen, both good. The restaurant will have satisfied customers and the operation will most likely be profitable. It's just that simple!

QUESTIONS

1. If you had a standard food cost of 38 percent, a product mix of 38 percent, and an actual food cost of 42 percent, tell what you would do to correct the problem.

2. If you had a standard cost of 38 percent, a product mix of 42 percent, and an actual food cost of 42 percent, tell what you would do to correct the problem.

3. Complete a product mix using the data below.

4. Complete a menu item by percent chart using the data below.

5. Assuming you project a total of 600 covers sold, tell how many of each item you should prepare.

Entree	Number Sold	Sell Price	Food Cost %
Item I	20	10.95	40%
Item II	100	8.75	30%
Item III	50	12.00	32%
Item IV	150	9.50	38%

Index